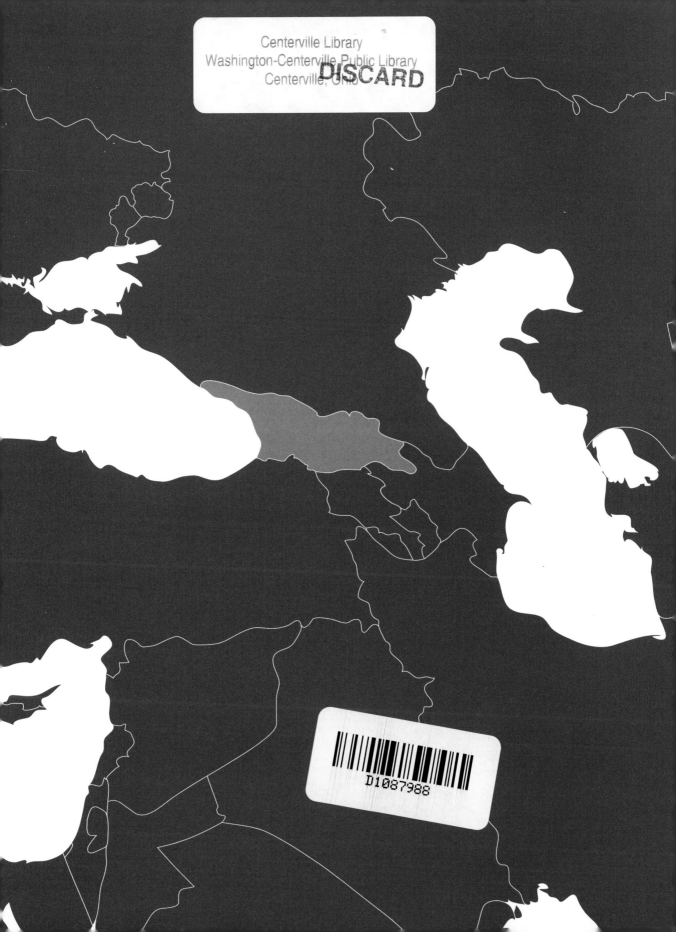

TASTING GEORGIA: THE CHAPTERS

1 Tbilisi p. 58
2 The Centre: Shida Kartli, Kvemo Kartli and Mtskheta p. 88
3 East to Kakheti p. 120
4 South-west to Samtskhe-Javakheti p. 194
5 West to Imereti p. 232
6 The Black Sea Coast: Guria and Adjara p. 278
7 West to Samegrelo p. 318
8 North-west to Svaneti: Zemo and Kvemo Svaneti p. 352
9 West and North to Racha-Lechkhumi p. 378
10 North to Kazbegi and Upper Mtskheta-Mtianeti p. 406

Tasting Georgia

A FOOD AND WINE JOURNEY
IN THE CAUCASUS

WITH 70 RECIPES

Tasting Georgia

A food and wine journey
in the Caucasus

Written and
photographed by

CARLA CAPALBO

Interlink Books

WITH THANKS TO LIVING ROOTS
AND JOHN H. WURDEMAN V

CONTENTS

ACKNOWLEDGEMENTS p. 15

PREFACE p. 17

GEORGIA: A SHORT HISTORY p. 20

AN INTRODUCTION TO GEORGIAN WINE p. 23
   How to make wine in *qvevri* p. 23
   The history of wine in Georgia p. 25
   The *Tamada*'s Tale p. 29

AN INTRODUCTION TO GEORGIAN FOOD p. 30
   About the *supra* p. 30

RELIGION, SONG AND DANCE AND THE GEORGIAN FEAST
   BY JOHN H. WURDEMAN V p. 34

THE ELEMENTS OF GEORGIAN CUISINE: INGREDIENTS p. 36

HOW TO COOK GEORGIAN FOOD p. 46
   About the recipes pp. 46-47
   How the Georgians Cook p. 48
   KHACHAPURI AND FILLED BREADS p. 49
      The Master Recipes pp. 51-53
   KHINKALI p. 54
      The Master Recipe p. 55

I TBILISI p. 58
   Tbilisi: a brief history p. 62   Where to Eat, Drink, Shop and
   Stay p. 63   Three women chefs p. 72

   Mulberry and goat cheese salad p. 74   *Stuffed tomatoes* p. 76
   Beef and chickpea stew p. 78   *Stuffed vine leaves* p. 80
   Chicken with pomegranate juice p. 82   *Pumpkin with walnuts* p. 84
   Mussels chakapuli p. 86

2 THE CENTRE: MTSKHETA AND THE KARTLIS p. 88

Mtskheta p. 91   Jighaura p. 95   Saguramo p. 95   Chardakhi p. 96
Mukhrani p. 106   Gori p. 107   Patara Ateni p. 107   Didi
Ateni p. 108   Ateni Sioni p. 109   Uplistsikhe p. 109   Garikula p. 112
Kiketi p. 113   Tamarisi p. 116   Marneuli p. 116
Shavnabada p. 116   Bolnisi p. 119   Dmanisi p. 119

*Walnut paste p. 100   Aubergine/eggplant rolls p. 102
Aubergine/eggplant family style p. 104*

3 EAST TO KAKHETI p. 120

Kakheti and its wines p. 123   Kakheti food and history p. 125
Tusheti p. 126   Zemo Alvani p. 129   Alaverdi p. 133
Laliskuri p. 136   Artana p. 142   Ikalto p. 145   Vardisubani p. 145
Shuamta p. 147   Telavi p. 151   Shalauri p. 152   Kisiskhevi p. 154
Gremi p. 155   Sabue p. 155   Nekresi p. 157   Lagodekhi p. 157
Bakurtsikhe p. 158   Sighnaghi p. 159   Bodbe p. 179
Mirzaani p. 179   Khornabuji p. 180   Bodbiskhevi p. 180   Kvemo
Magharo p. 181   Manavi p. 184   Davit-Gareja p. 193

*Tushetian pancakes p. 138   Tushetian potato and cheese
khinkali p. 140   Lamb chakapuli p. 148   aubergine/eggplant
ajapsandali p. 170   Herbed oyster mushrooms p. 172
Wilted purslane salad p. 174   Stewed sour cherries p. 176
Tarragon and egg pie p. 186   Green beans with eggs p. 188
Chilled yogurt soup p. 190*

4 SOUTH-WEST TO SAMTSKHE-JAVAKHETI p 194

Phoka p. 197   Vardzia p. 200   Chachkari p. 206   Khizabavra
Valley p. 208   Khertvisi p. 211   Nijgori p. 212   Khizabavra p. 226
Saro p. 228   Akhaltsikhe p. 228   Borjomi p. 231   Akhaldaba p. 231
Bakuriani p. 231

*Beef and tomato stew p. 202   Grilled meatballs p. 204   Meskhetian
khachapuri p. 218   Small potato khinkali dumplings p. 220   Noodle
and yogurt soup p. 222   Stewed fruits and onions p. 224*

5 WEST TO IMERETI p 232

Food and Wine p. 235   Maqatubani p. 239   Kldeeti p. 248
Zestaponi p. 249   Kvaliti p. 249   Terjola p. 258

Nakhshirghele p. 262   Dimi p. 272   Baghdati p. 272   Kutaisi p. 273
Natural and Archælogical sites in Imereti p. 275   Kumistavi p. 275
Sataplia p. 275   Tskaltubo p. 275   Zeda Gordi p. 275
Okatse p. 275   Chiatura p. 275   Sormoni p. 276   Gelati p. 276
Vani p. 276   Persati p. 276

Duck with blackberry sauce p. 244   *Leeks with walnut paste* p. 246
Leafy greens with walnut paste p. 256   *Green beans with walnut
paste* p. 256   Lobio: *beans with walnuts and spices* p. 266   Tkemali:
sour plum sauce p. 268   *Beets with sour plum sauce* p. 268   Bazhe:
spiced walnut paste p. 270   *Beets with spiced walnut paste* p. 270

6 THE BLACK SEA COAST: GURIA AND ADJARA p. 278
About Guria p. 282   Ozurgeti p. 283   Bakhmaro p. 283
Ureki p. 283   Shekvetili p. 283   Kolkheti p. 283   Sakvavistke p. 283
Dablatsikhe p. 283   Dvabzu p. 294   The Gurian house p. 295
About Adjara p. 298   Tsikhisdziri p. 298   Kobuleti p. 298
Batumi p. 310   Goderdzi p. 311   About the Black Sea p. 312
Eating in Batumi p. 313   Gonio-Apsaros p. 314   Sarpi p. 314
Kvashta p. 314   Acharistskali p. 315

Gurian Christmas khachapuri p. 288   'Backcombed' aubergines /
eggplant p. 290   *Hazelnut paste* p. 292   Chirbuli: *eggs with onions
and tomatoes* p. 300   Kharcho: *chicken and walnut stew* p. 302
Achma: *baked layered pasta* p. 304   *Fish baked with walnuts* p. 308
Adjarian khachapuri p. 316

7 WEST TO SAMEGRELO p. 318
Megrelian food p. 322   The Megrelian house p. 322
To see in Samegrelo p. 324   Mukhuri p. 324   Martvili p. 324
Didi Chkoni p. 325   Salkhino p. 325   Tsachkhuri p. 327
Targameuli p. 328   Nosiri p. 340   Senaki p. 340   Poti p. 340
Anaklia p. 340   Zugdidi p. 341

Spicy green and red pepper ajika p. 334   *Megrelian* khachapuri p. 336
Cold chicken satsivi *with spiced walnut sauce* p. 338   *Spicy
ribs* p. 344   Tchvishtari: *cheesy cornbread* p. 346   Elarji: *cornmeal
with cheese* p. 348   *Chicken with* bazhe *nut sauce* p. 350

8 NORTH-WEST TO SVANETI p. 352
   On Svanetian food p. 355   Svaneti: a short history p. 356
   Becho Valley p. 360   Ushkhvanari p. 360   Ushba p. 370
   Mestia p. 371   Ski slopes and glaciers p. 372   Hatsvali p. 372
   Tetnuldi p. 372   Ushguli p. 373   Chvibiani p. 374

   Kubdari: *spiced meat bread* p. 364   *Cooked and raw salad* p. 366
   Braised meatballs p. 368   *Mushrooms and red peppers* p. 376

9 WEST AND NORTH TO RACHA-LECHKHUMI p. 378
   Khvanchkara p. 382   Grape varieties of the region p. 382
   Ambrolauri p. 382, 386   Nikortsminda p. 384   Patara Chorjo p. 387
   Dzirageuli p. 394   Oni p. 400

   Cooked ajika p. 392   *Beet-green bread* p. 396   *Beans stewed with
   herbs* p. 398   Lobiani: *bean-filled bread* p. 402   *Grilled chicken with
   garlic sauce* p. 404

10 NORTH TO KAZBEGI AND UPPER MTSKHETA MTIANETI p. 406
   Food p. 410   Tsitelsopeli p. 410   Ananuri p. 410
   Khevsureti p. 411   Shatili p. 411   Mutso p. 411   Gudauri p. 414
   Stepantsminda p. 414   Kazbegi p. 414   Gergeti p. 420
   Arsha p. 421

   Meat-filled khinkali *dumplings* p. 416   *Cheese and potato
   bread* p. 418

BIBLIOGRAPHY AND TRAVEL INFORMATION p. 423

RECIPE INDEX AND MEAL PLANNER p. 426

INDEX p. 429

*Opposite:
A pastoralist
near Gudauri
watches his
flock*

ACKNOWLEDGEMENTS

A book like this is a collaborative project, so my first thank you goes to the many Georgian women and men who generously welcomed me into their homes, kitchens, vineyards and cellars to share food, wine and friendship. *Didi madloba!*

The team at Living Roots, directed by John Wurdeman and Ia Tabagari, have been constant supporters, offering contacts, experience and practical help: Shota Lagazidze, my wonderful travelling companion and interpreter through the months of research; Mariam Iosebidze, who tirelessly answered my questions; and Tamara Natenadze, who assisted them and helped with the Georgian translations. Mari Lukhumaidze provided a home away from home in Tbilisi. Thanks, I couldn't have done this without you, dear friends!

I am very grateful to The Georgian National Tourism Administration for their support and involvement, especially Giorgi Chogovadze and Masho Bojgua. At the Georgian National Wine Agency, Tamta Kvelaidze helpfully answered many wine questions.

Outside of Georgia, special thanks go to: Caroline Brooke Johnson for her editing skills and help as we did the layout; my publisher, Alexander Fyjis-Walker for his continuing collaboration, and Anaïs Métais for her editorial assistance; Bahi Para for his support with the photos and so much more; Andrei Palamarchuk, for believing in my photographs; beekeeper Andrea Paternoster for his knowledge about beeswax; Ketevan Kalandadze for answering urgent Georgian questions; Isabelle Lousada for helping me through the hard bits; Adam Sodowick for support with communications; Nancy Norman Lassalle for her enthusiasm about the project; and Luigina and Giulio Aiello for keeping an eye on my house. Olympus produced my amazing OMD EM1 camera; I never leave home without it.

When writing my Collio book, Josko Gravner and his late son, Miha, sparked my curiosity about the origins of *qvevri*. Through Slow Food I met Ramaz Nikoladze and Soliko Tsaishvili. Eric Narioo and Doug Wregg introduced me to John Wurdeman. John's invitation to Georgia and his enthusiasm, energy and belief in Georgia's culture and potential helped turn a wild idea into this book. Thanks go to his wife, Ketevan, their children, Lazare and Gvantsa, and to everyone at Pheasant's Tears for their boundless hospitality, including Gia and Tamriko Rokashvili.

My interest in Georgia began long before my first visit: as a child, when my mother danced in his New York City Ballet, I met the Georgian choreographer, George Balanchine. She visited Georgia before I did and returned saying: "You're going to love Georgia, the food and wine are delicious and there are cows in all the roads." This book is a way of thanking her for her inspiring commitment to culture, and for putting up with me as I wrote it. She was right. I do love Georgia.

Opposite: Checking the walnuts before pounding them

PREFACE

Traditions are interesting when they're alive
Luarsab Togonidze

Like many wine lovers, I first visited Georgia to understand more about its ancient winemaking culture. I soon discovered that Georgia's unique food and hospitality are as exciting as its wine. The warmth and generosity of Georgia's people captivated me, as did its physical beauty. After decades living in remote parts of Italy, Georgia feels both different and familiar to me. Despite having its own language and history, Georgia is an agricultural country and the small family farms, with their mixed crops, animals and vineyards, remind me of a way of life that has all but disappeared in many places. I wanted to see more, and to write about what I found.

Since then, I've travelled for weeks at a time through most of Georgia, collecting stories, recipes and wines and taking photographs. Locating the people I wanted to visit wasn't always easy so I initially decided to write a food and wine travel book, similar in structure to my Italian regional books, with maps and descriptions of the people and places I encountered in order to help my readers find them too. I usually started in Tbilisi and structured the book as trips to be taken from the capital; that's why I've sometimes combined more than one region in a single chapter.

Georgia's food is still largely unknown and very few cookbooks exist, unlike, say, for Italian cuisine. I find Georgian food so colourful, vibrant and delicious that I couldn't resist including recipes for many of my favourite dishes. They vary as much as their cooks' landscapes and cultural histories so I've left them in situ throughout the book. For a complete recipe index, see p. 426.

I love the Georgian way of eating, with multiple dishes arranged on the table at once. It's both an ancient and a modern way to eat, dominated by fresh vegetable cookery with aromatic herbs, nuts and delicate spices that make the flavours distinctive. Meats are usually stewed or grilled; breads are stuffed with cheeses and greens. If the cooking techniques are mainly simple, complexity is attained by combining diverse dishes. At home, my friends love the recipes I've been cooking. I hope this book inspires many others to enjoy them too, and to visit Georgia to discover for themselves the generosity of the Georgian table.

*Opposite:
Vegetable
shop, Tbilisi*

*Overleaf:
Early morning in the
Mtkvari
River Valley
near Vardzia,
Samtskhe-
Javakheti,
southern
Georgia
(see p. 200)*

GEORGIA: A SHORT HISTORY

Georgia's history is extraordinarily complex. This small country – roughly the size of Scotland or West Virginia, or a quarter of Italy – has been fought over for millennia. Georgia has been desired – and possessed – for its strategic position between the Greater and Lesser Caucasus Mountains and the Black Sea, at the crossroads between Asia, Europe, Russia and the Middle East, as well as for its remarkable natural beauty. Its almost Mediterranean climate allows for the success of many crops that can't as easily be grown further north or south. These include the grapes that are cultivated on the lower mountain slopes and in the fertile valleys in many parts of the country.

From its earliest origins, Georgia claims a blood line leading back to Noah via his son Thargamos' great-grandson, Karthlos. The Georgians' name for their own country, Sakartvelo, derives from this descendency.

In ancient times the area was divided between the kingdoms of Colchis (Kolkheti) in the west and Iberia in the east. Georgia was first unified as one kingdom in the 9th to 10th centuries by King Bagrat III of the Bagrationi dynasty. This unification allowed for what is now called Georgia's Golden Age, as the country flourished under King David IV the Builder and his daughter, Queen Tamar (often referred to as 'King' Tamar); they remain two of the country's most iconic rulers.

The Mongol invasion in the 13th century began a fracturing that resulted in medieval Georgia being divided into small rival kingdoms and principalities even as they battled Ottoman and Persian invaders.

Georgia was annexed by the Russian Empire in 1801 after seeking its help to defend against Persian and Ottoman attack. (In 1864 serfdom began to be phased out in Georgia, some three years after Russia abolished it.) After a large-scale peasant revolt in 1905, the Marxist Social Democratic Party became the dominant political movement in Georgia. Ioseb Besarionis dze Jughashvili (Joseph Stalin), a Georgian Bolshevik, became a leader of the revolutionary movement in Georgia and went on the control the Soviet Union, with all-too familiar consequences.

Georgia was briefly independent as a Democratic Republic between 1918 and 1921 before the Red Army invaded, forcibly incorporating it into the Transcaucasian Socialist Federative Soviet Republic from 1922. In 1936 Georgia became the Georgian Soviet Socialist Republic until the dissolution of the Soviet Union. From 1972 to 1985 Eduard Shevardnadze held the post of First Secretary. He initially fought corruption and helped reinstate the constitutional status of the Georgian language.

More recently, Georgia has been independent since 1991 when Zviad Gamsakhurdia was briefly elected first President of Georgia. By 1992 Shevardnadze was again at the helm, but became embroiled in separatist unrest that culminated in two regions – Abkhazia and so-called South Ossetia (the Georgians prefer to call it Tskhinvali after its main town) – declaring autonomy from Georgia with Russia's backing. This effectively means that two large regions inside the country are off-limits for the Georgians, offering Russia a valuable foothold there.

In 2003 the Rose Revolution (which had the advantage of being bloodless) forced Shevardnadze to resign. In 2004 Mikheil Saakashvili formed a new government and was able to prevent the loss of a third region, Adjara, but the conflict with Abkhazia and South Ossetia led to the 2008 Russo-Georgian War. Saakashvili was voted out in 2012 and was replaced by Giorgi Margvelashvili in 2013, when Bidzina Ivanishvili's Georgian Dream coalition took power. They also won the election in October 2016.

Today Georgia is doing its best to remain an independent democracy. As a tolerant Orthodox Christian country, it is the most pro-European nation in the region. Georgia is currently increasing its international profile in very positive ways, with food and wine tourism an important part of that process.

Alaverdi Monastery in Kakheti has survived successive attacks since the 11th century

AN INTRODUCTION TO GEORGIAN WINE

This book focuses on the ancient and distinctive Georgian tradition of making wine in the large terracotta vessels called *qvevri* (also spelled *kvevri*) or *churi/tchuri* in western Georgia, recognised as Intangible Cutural Heritage by UNESCO. The so-called natural winemakers who are bottling wines made in this way – now more than 50 – form only a tiny percentage of Georgia's enormous wine output. Compared to the millions of bottles produced in steel tanks or wooden barrels by the large-scale commercial wineries who make up the bulk of Georgia's export market – much of which goes to Russia and the Eastern Bloc countries – these *qvevri* winemakers only produce tens of thousands of bottles between them. (Many more make wines this way for their families, but don't bottle or sell them.)

Yet their importance cannot be overstated. Not only are they the keepers of a historic winemaking tradition, but it is these wines that are attracting the interest of wine enthusiasts everywhere. The *qvevri* winemakers have become cultural ambassadors for Georgia: their wines have made their way on to the wine lists of many top international restaurants, and their unique method is driving wine tourism to Georgia from all over the world.

In my travels through Georgia I visited only *qvevri* winemakers and have chosen to focus most of the book's wine writing on them. Many other wine companies exist and can be found through the sites on p. 425. Some offer other facilities such as restaurants or hotels, and I've included those whenever possible.

HOW TO MAKE WINE IN *QVEVRI*

After the handmade terracotta coil pots have been fired and impregnated with beeswax inside to create a micro-coating around the clay's pores (see p. 240 for more on the *qvevri*-making process), they're usually given an external wire armature to protect them from the pressure created during fermentation and small earth tremors, and an external coating of powdered lime with cement or sand for strength and as a disinfectant. The *qvevri* are buried up to their necks in sand and gravel to facilitate the passage of air and absorb any shocks from the ground. A Georgian cellar contains buried *qvevri* of varying sizes to accommodate different volumes of wine.

At harvest time the grapes are crushed – either by foot or now more usually using a hand or mechanical crusher – and pumped or allowed to fall by gravity into a clean *qvevri*. Depending on the region or winemaker's style, stems may or may not be included. The winemakers who grow their vines without herbicides and pesticides rely on wild or spontaneous yeasts

*Opposite:
Gela Pata-
lashvili, of
Pheasant's
Tears winery,
helps to bury
a* qvevri *in
the ground
(see p. 167)*

that live in the grape skins to trigger the first, or alcoholic, fermentation. No 'selected' or factory-produced yeasts or other chemical 'correctors' are used. Sometimes a small amount of sulphite paper is burned inside the *qvevri* to disinfect them before they're filled, and tiny amounts of sulphites may be added at bottling time, although most village producers avoid their use.

During fermentation, the cap is punched back down into the must using a long pole with sticks running crosswise through its end. The secondary, or malolactic, fermentation follows the first as the wine's tart, malic acids (as in apples) are converted to softer-tasting, lactic acid (as in milk).

When the fermentation has run its course, the solids drop naturally into the *qvevri*'s pointed bottom. Red wines may be removed from their solids soon after this, while white wines are usually given the short or extended skin contact that characterizes the so-called orange wines. When the fermentation is complete, the *qvevri*'s top is sealed, though a tiny amount of oxygen still enters through the clay pores. The wine may be separated from the skins very quickly, or remain on them for several months, extracting tannins, phenols, flavour and anthocyanins from them as it goes. If long-macerated Kakhetian wines tend to be robust in their colour and tannins, west-Georgian wines are often very fresh, paler in hue and lower in alcohol thanks to spending much less, if any, time on the skins.

The kiln has to be kept stoked for one week when firing qvevri *(see p. 240)*

"*Qvevri* means 'that which is buried'," says John Wurdeman of Pheasant's Tears winery. "Once it's in the ground, the clay vessel is able to harness seasonal temperature shifts to help form the wine. Autumn's warmth spurs spontaneous fermentation, while winter's chill helps the wine stabilize." The Georgians use descriptive imagery to describe the *qvevri*'s role in making the wine. "A wine may stay on the skins for varying lengths of time but it needs to spend at least nine months with its 'mother': whatever remains of the skins and stems after maceration.

"This allows the wine to stabilize after which it can be 'put on its feet' and stand alone in a fresh *qvevri* away from the lees. The grapey residues – what's left of the stems, skins and seeds – are then distilled into *chacha*, the popular high-proof spirit."

Georgian wines were usually drunk within their production year but some winemakers are now allowing them to age longer in *qvevri* with excellent results. At the end of the cycle, the emptied *qvevri* is scrubbed with lime using a cherry-bark tool and flushed out with clean water before being filled again with the new season's crushed grapes. *Qvevri* can last for decades if not centuries if they are well cared for.

Upside-down qvevri

THE HISTORY OF WINE IN GEORGIA

Giorgi 'Kvevri' Barisashvili is a prominent wine historian and œnologist who teaches traditional and natural winemaking at the Ilia State University. Giorgi lives in the historic centre of Mtskheta, a few steps from its magnificent cathedral (see p. 94). He talked to me about the country's wine history.

"During Soviet times, when *qvevri* wines were not respected or allowed, we lost much of our acquired wisdom about *qvevri*," he says. "Bad habits were formed because quantity mattered more than quality. Happily there's now a renewed interest in making *qvevri* wines that's respectful of the soil and grapes." Despite the Prohibition-like rulings coming from Russia that later spread to the rest of the Soviet Union, many families and old people in the villages continued to make wine in *qvevri*.

Detail of grapes and vine carving on Mtskheta Cathedral

"People often quote the number 8,000 years to quantify how long Georgia has been making wine but it's impossible to know exactly when its origins were. I'd say they go back at least that far as we have found artefacts that prove it. But for me, the most important aspect of this assertion is that we know that our winemaking tradition has been unbroken for all that time. It's been kept alive here by people who, each year for thousands of years, have harvested their grapes and made wines in *qvevri*."

Kakhetian Rkatsiteli with long skin maceration

This continuum also holds for the *qvevri* makers. If a family like the master potter's, Zaliko Bozhadze (see p. 239), lost its know-how by skipping a generation, there would be no way for his grandchildren to maintain it. "This kind of knowledge must be passed from father to son, and we think that's happened for at least 8,000 years in Georgia."

The wild grape, *Vitis sylvestris*, whose natural growing pattern is to climb high into the tops of trees to reach the sun and bear fruit, was domesticated in Georgia. "It happened in stages," he continues. "Vines have been trained onto tree supports for over 5,000 years in systems called variously *shashobili* and *maghlari*. From the late Bronze Age, in the first millennium BC, a new technique was developed of low training on posts, called *dablari*. We're sure that if our ancestors had wanted the vines just for the fruit, they would have left them in the forest where they didn't need special care. At some stage picked grapes must have begun to ferment into wine and that's when the vines began to be domesticated and planted among fruit trees in the orchards. *Babilo* means a vine growing on a tree support and it refers to the spiralling action the plant naturally makes, like the tower of Babylon. Only a sedentary – not a nomadic – culture could do this as it required time and stability."

Rkatsiteli grapes

In ancient times – from around 400 BC to 300 AD – some *qvevri* were cut in half from top to bottom and used as sarcophagi for burying people. "They've been found in several excavations in Georgia. The deceased was buried in this egg-shaped container with wine jugs and vessels, as if to send him back symbolically to where he had come from."

"While we don't know exactly when humans began to make wine, the earliest relics we've found here are indeed from 8,000 years ago: grape seeds, tannins and tartaric wine residues in clay pieces from a *qvevri*. But we've found vine fossils from 1 million years ago (now in the Batumi Museum, p. 310) and we think the vine originated during the Chalk Age, between 145 and 66 million years ago."

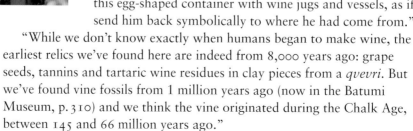

There were the two main starting places for the culture and proliferation of wine varieties in Georgia: in the east, the valley of the Alazani River which flows from Tusheti to Azerbaijan and, in the west, throughout the regions that formed part of the ancient kingdom of Colchis (or Kolkheti), stretching all the way down to parts of modern Turkey." Over time, more than 525 distinct varieties were cultivated in Georgia, named for their villages or the people who had discovered or bred them. "Unfortunately, our country has also been characterized by wars: when our enemies came, they destroyed the vineyards as well as the villages, and many varieties just disappeared."

I ask Giorgi about a legend I've heard, of Georgian fighters in olden days going to battle with vine cuttings tucked under their chain mail, suggesting that if they died in battle vines would grow from their burial places.

"As poetic as this story is, I believe it's the other way around," Giorgi says. "Old men in the villages have told me that when a man went into battle he would place a vine cutting from his vineyard under his armour because he never knew if his village and vineyard would still be there when he came back. It was one way to save one of their most precious possessions."

Similarly, a Georgian's *marani*, or cellar, is of huge importance. "Even in high mountain areas where no vines can grow, each family had a cellar and would buy grapes in the valleys and crush them in their own *marani* to make wine. When two Georgian men meet each other, the first greeting is, 'How are you?' The second is, 'How is your vineyard?'"

Amiran Vepkhvadze scoops fresh must from a qvevri in his cellar in Imereti

THE *TAMADA'S* TALE

Luarsab Togonidze is a restaurateur, singer, ethnographer and expert on Georgian traditional artefacts, attire and customs. He's also an acclaimed *tamada*, or toastmaster. When we meet, he's wearing a black *chokha*, the handsome, calf-length wool coat that's been a symbol of Georgian identity since the Middle Ages. He's holding a silver *azarpesha*, the long-handled drinking vessel the *tamada* may use to share wine with other guests at the dinner table.

The tamada: *Luarsab Togonidze is an experienced toastmaster*

"My family has been involved in the hospitality business for several generations," he says. "My great-grandfather had two restaurants in Tbilisi but during the dangerous Soviet times the family left the city for our clan's homelands in Racha." Luarsab's father later took over running the country's most popular restaurant, Salobie (see p. 94), and Luarsab is himself a partner in two Tbilisi restaurants, Azarpesha and Polyphonia (see pp. 68 and 70).

"The Georgian *supra*, or feast, is punctuated by toasts given by the meal's informally appointed *tamada*," he says. "It's the *tamada*'s role to act as the master of ceremonies and be a wonderful host. Good toasts were an essential part of our life and my grandfather invited me to give my first toast when I was seven. All the family's generations were there: they listened attentively and it made me feel part of the community."

Toasts may be given for many subjects. God, peace, family and guests are constants, but a skilled *tamada* will fashion toasts to suit the company and its mood. Some regions prescribe their order (Guria, for instance, always begins with a toast to peace).

"We're also attentive to how much wine we drink," Luarsab says. "My grandfather warned that alcohol is a tool but can also become a weapon, and to be aware of how much people in the room are drinking." Despite the rules governing how the toasting is to be carried out – other diners can't make toasts without the *tamada*'s approval – a good *tamada* makes everyone seated at the table feel special. I'm always impressed too by how Georgian toasts are able to move from the personal to the universal. Here's part of a toast Luarsab gave to music, an integral part of the Georgian *supra*.

Opposite: Tool of the toastmaster's trade: the silver azarpesha *containing an orange wine*

"My dear friends, let's drink for the people who created these songs. Art and culture don't have boundaries. They flow like rays of sunlight that warm without expectations. I want to drink to those talented people – many no longer with us – who live on in these songs. So this toast is for all composers, many of whose names we don't know. Their vision, their sense of beauty and their love are alive in all their music, and in us."

AN INTRODUCTION TO GEORGIAN FOOD

FALLING IN LOVE WITH GEORGIAN FOOD

The first time I was invited to a Georgian *supra*, or feast, in Tbilisi, I was amazed by the abundance, variety and colours of the dishes that were served. Here was food that seemed exotic yet familiar, rich in fresh vegetables and salads, subtly spiced but vibrantly flavoured with more nuts and fresh herbs in one meal than we use in a month. And it was absolutely delicious.

It may have ancient roots, but this cuisine always feels modern to me, and it fits right into the way I love to eat, with plenty of dishes to choose from and an emphasis on exciting tastes and combinations. Georgian food is perfect for today's more casual lifestyle as it celebrates the pleasure of sharing food with friends around a table without a rigid course-by-course structure. It has the added bonus of being easy to prepare, with very few exceptions. I've put together many Georgian meals as I've cooked my way through the recipes in this book, and all my friends have fallen in love with this wonderful food and its culture.

ABOUT THE *SUPRA*

The Georgians have a unique way of eating that's a direct reflection of their legendary – and seemingly boundless – sense of hospitality. The place to best experience this is at a *supra*, or Georgian feast, where food, wine and music come together as the quintessential expression of Georgian culture.

At a *supra*, the table is laden with food before anyone sits down. The centre of a long table hosting, say, twenty people will be set with at least seven or eight cold dishes – from stuffed aubergines/eggplants and vegetable medleys to fermented blossoms and cheeses flavoured with mint – each of which will have been divided into four or five plates and positioned along the table so guests won't have to reach far to get them. Diners are given small plates and serve themselves from the dishes close to them. Even tables laid for just four or five people are treated this way.

Once everyone is seated and has started eating, other dishes – including hot stews, stuffed breads, dumplings and barbecued meats – begin to arrive and are placed beside (and sometimes even on top of) the first set of foods. If a serving plate is emptied, the dish is not removed but replenished by the attentive hosts. The diner's plate is changed once or twice during the meal: they're encouraged to make a fresh start on the food without the remains of the first round. This abundance holds true at all levels of society, including in simple, rural households where water may still be pumped by hand

Small supra:
lunch in
Adjara

from a well in the garden. When it comes to hosting and feeding guests, the Georgian table is always generous.

The pace at a *supra* meal is leisurely: the idea is to spend the time convivially, enjoying friendship, lively conversation and music with great food and wine. (The singers and dancers are often seated at the table too, and burst into song as the spirit moves them, several times during the meal.)

The *supra* is hosted and given structure by a *tamada*, or toastmaster (see p. 29 for more on this) whose role it is to pace the drinking even as he (or, occasionally, she) brings the group together in his toasts. After each toast, the diners raise their glasses and reply: '*Gaumarjos!*' (May victory be with you!)

The *supra*, in its current form and with the *tamada* as host, seems to have come into being in the 19th century, in part as a reaction to the Russian – and then Soviet – domination of Georgia. "We shared a common religion with the Russians, but our dining culture was a powerful way to reinforce and celebrate our pride in being Georgian," says Luarsab Togonidze, the respected Tbilisi *tamada*. "Like our language and its unique alphabet, it helped to differentiate us from them."

"In earlier times, Georgia had a feudal system with aristocrats, a farming class, traders and merchants, and each had their own styles of eating," says John Wurdeman. "Despite those different classes, Georgians believed it was important to partake of food together and that the guest was sacred. Indeed, there's a popular story of a nobleman inviting a visiting foreign dignitary's coachman to join them at his table, much to the chagrin of the elitist dignitary."

Florian Mühlfried, an anthropologist who has written about Georgia's social customs, takes it one step further. He explains that for the Georgians, eating and drinking wine together has always been an important social activity, even in times of hardship and shortages.

Wiggle room: Georgian food adapts beautifully to the modern table

"Many Georgians believe that wine originated in Georgia and that […] it has long played a key role in Georgian identity. They regard wine as a metaphor for Georgian blood and those who share wine at a *supra* as virtual kinsmen," he writes. Suffice it to say that, as a guest at a *supra* in modern-day Georgia, one is embraced in an exciting and welcoming cultural experience that has few parallels.

Like wine, food is influenced by the terroir in which it's been produced. Georgia may not be a very large country – it's close to the size of Ireland or West Virginia – but it contains diverse geographical zones, including subtropical lowlands, near-desert areas and highlands. In the upper Caucasus, for example, potatoes grow more readily than wheat, and this has helped shape that local cuisine.

Georgia's food culture has also been influenced through time by the myriad nations that have bordered or dominated it. The Persians and Ottomans, in particular, left their mark on cooking styles, flavours and ingredients. The recipes in this book exemplify this delicious diversity. They also show that, while each area may have adapted its cooking to the foods and ideas they encountered, a core gastronomic identity exists in Georgia that no amount of foreign influence has been able to undermine.

That may explain one aspect of Georgian culinary culture that has struck me. The repertoire of foods that a visitor to Georgia is likely to encounter is sometimes fairly limited, as each restaurant or even home cook will often prepare many of the same dishes in much the same way. And, when it comes to traditional recipes, most Georgians are extremely conservative in their attitude to change or variation.

As someone who has been brought up cooking the food of many countries, and very open to experimentation and fusion in food, I quickly realized that this was not the case in Georgia. After eating *khachapuri* a number of times – the addictive cheese-filled bread that features on every Georgian table – I started imagining how good it could also be with the addition of fresh herbs, or sautéed onions. But the reaction to this suggestion from some of my Georgian friends was cool, to say the least. For them, *khachapuri* can only ever be filled purely with cheese . A Georgian chef friend, Meriko Gubeladze, who cooks on Georgian TV, regularly receives outraged letters from her viewers whenever she makes even small changes to any of the country's most familiar recipes. It's understandable, as these foods are part of the country's national identity. But for those of us cooking outside of Georgia, there's also room to wiggle!

RELIGION, SONG AND DANCE AND THE GEORGIAN FEAST

JOHN H. WURDEMAN V

What we give to others remains ours for eternity,
what we keep for ourselves we have already lost.
Shota Rustaveli

Georgia's layered history and multi-ethnic influences are seen in its architecture, music, wine and feasting traditions. Invaded by the much larger and stronger powers that surrounded it, Georgia has nonetheless maintained its Eastern Orthodox religion, unique script and distinct languages long after those conquering empires have vanished. And Georgia still boasts thousands of polyphonic songs and a robust way of feasting that incorporates food, wine, poetry, song and dance.

Top:
Didgori
polyphonic
singing group

Below:
Traditional
Georgian
instruments:
bagpipes and
tambourine

The sacred role of wine dates back to pagan times when it was believed the vine ascended towards the sun as its roots penetrated the earth. In Georgia today the vine and its wine remain highly symbolic in church ornamentation and in the texts of chants. Devout Georgians still fast for large periods of the year. Most Wednesdays and Fridays are fasting days, and there are long fasts before Christmas and Easter, and on special feast days. Fasting in the Orthodox tradition can be more or less strict but it generally suggests a vegan diet, with fish occasionally allowed. That's why Georgian cuisine includes many healthy and delicious vegan dishes.

Known since ancient times for their generous hospitality – as the 12th-century poet, Rustaveli, illustrates above in his epic, *The Knight in the Panther's Skin* – Georgians delight in dazzling and honouring their guests. The drawn-out *supra* feast is punctuated by the *tamada*'s toasts and interlaced with rich polyphonic songs. Here a mixture of improvisation within strict parameters reminds me of the tension between rules and their breaking in baroque or flamenco music.

Wine flows steadily but guests and hosts are expected to keep their cool and be able to comment on life's most sacred aspects, including love, the family, religion and nature. Toasts are preset or created by the *tamada* and are often followed by poetry. A good *tamada* speaks well and inspires others to follow suit on these themes.

Georgia's famed polyphonic songs are what first attract many foreigners to Georgia, myself included. From 1999 until 2006, my wife, Ketevan, and I collected and recorded traditional music and dances from all over the country. Georgian polyphony can be compared in texture to Corsican and some Sardinian music. It is sung in three parts, and is believed to have had this structure since antiquity. The music is sung in an untempered scale and can produce seemingly dissonant, hair-raising harmonies that sound like echoes from the ancient past. Pre-Christian scribes travelling with Greek armies and Byzantine emperors told of Georgia's rare harmonic music, both folk and ecclesiastical. Its complexity and beauty was unlike anything they'd heard before.

Dancing at a supra

As with wine and food, the spirit of the songs changes regionally: light and playful near the sea, austere and mystical in the highlands, and reflective and philosophical in the eastern valleys. Songs from western Georgia have slightly more angular, abrupt chord changes and dynamic movement, while the eastern are highly ornamental and melismatic. Few cultures have maintained a musical tradition as rooted to feasting. The singers are usually also diners at the *supra* and suddenly break into song during the meal.

Georgian dances are inseparable from the songs. They're accompanied by assorted instruments, including traditional drums (*doli*), bagpipes (*chiboni*) and lutes (*panduri*) . The dancers get up from the table and explode into dance, filling the room with electricity.

Men's dance moves are often expressive of their region's landscape and history, with warrior-like movements that may include swords and daggers. Men court and protect female dancers. Her role is modest as she respectfully evades her suitor or acts as a peacekeeper between two warring men. There's little gender equality here: both can be quite fiery but they remain fundamentally different and reflect the traditionally different roles of the sexes. As with the songs, certain rhythms, moves and patterns are meant to be adhered to, yet within this framework there's room for personal interpretation.

The years since Georgia gained its independence from the Soviet Union in 1991 have been full of turmoil, but also of rebirth. Georgians have begun to rediscover their nationality and to rebuild their noble traditions, expanding once again their myriad native grapes and cheeses. Modern restaurants are exploring forgotten recipes and creating new ones as the homogeneity of the Soviet period rapidly disappears in favour of an expanded Georgian repertoire. We can expect exciting times as Georgia continues to rebuild the multi-cultural diversity it boasted for so long.

THE ELEMENTS OF GEORGIAN CUISINE: INGREDIENTS

This is an alphabetical compendium of some of the principal foods in the Georgian repertoire and larder that you'll find in this book.

AJIKA, whose name is derived from the Abkhazian word for salt, is a concentrated, capsicum-based paste and comes in many forms: cooked and raw, red and green, dry and wet. It's always spicy and fiery from the chillies that are its star ingredient and is used most in the regions near the Black Sea. It can be very concentrated, and is used in marinades or as a condiment. See recipes on pp. 335 and 392.

BEANS (*lobio*) Dried and fresh beans are a Georgian staple. *Lobio*, whether they're stewed dry beans, or boiled green beans (often served with walnut sauce, as in *pkhali*), appear on every *supra* table. Kidney beans are common, but many thinner-skinned varieties ranging from pale beige to near-black can be found in late summer at the markets. There are speckled beans like tiny bird's eggs too. See recipes on pp. 266 and 399.

BREAD (*puri*) In Georgia, bread is made from diverse grains and comes in many shapes and sizes. The most delicious are baked in the *toné*, a terracotta cylinder produced by the master potters who make the *qvevri* for wine. The cylinder is placed on the ground, often with an insulating plaster or basket-work surround. Hot embers from burning vine prunings or other woods are placed inside, on the ground, and heat the clay walls. When the walls are piping hot, the moist dough sticks to the sides of the oven and bakes the bread. The most spectacular are long, curved traditional baton loaves called *puri*, *shotis puri* or *tonis puri* and more rounded loaves with one or two 'handles' called *shoti*. Their varied thicknesses ensure that parts of the loaves are crisp and others soft. *Lavashi* is the thin, pancake-like bread used to wrap around kebabs. Two bakers I've featured are on pp. 65 and 66.

BUTTER (*karaki*) Butter is ubiquitous in Georgia as almost everyone has access to a cow. It's one of the main fats in cooking, either whole or clarified (*erbo*), and is a key element in many dishes (it's rubbed onto baked *khachapuri* to soften and enrich the dough). In the highlands, simple breads may be filled with a roux of butter and flour (*kada*).

CHACHA is distilled from the grape skins, stems and seeds left over after the winemaking process. Akin to *grappa* and *marc*, it's usually drunk in shots in Georgia, during meals or even at breakfast (as a hangover cure).

CHEESE (*khveli*) There are dozens of Georgian cheese varieties produced from the milk of cows, sheep, water buffalo and goats. Many are made domestically in limited areas but here are some of the most readily available:

Guda, a pungent sheep's cheese from the Tushetian mountains cured inside a sheep skin.

Imeruli, from Imereti, is a white cow's milk cheese that's found throughout Georgia and is usually the basis for *khachapuri* with *sulguni*. It has a pleasantly sour flavour and a squeaky, springy texture.

Sulguni, a pulled-curd, brined cheese from Samegrelo, is often baked in *khachapuri* and is compared to cow's-milk mozzarella. When sliced paper thin, it's wrapped around mint-seasoned curds (*nadughi*) and in *gebzhalia*; or it can be boiled and kneaded with mint for *gadazelili khveli*. *Sulguni* is also popular smoked, and can be found in russet-coloured rounds at the markets.

Tenili, a string-like cheese listed in Slow Food's Ark of Taste, is made from high-fat sheep or cow's milk in Meskheti, the southern part of Georgia. It requires great manual skill to produce.

Chechili, another pulled-curd cheese popular also in Armenia. It's often sold braided, and is sometimes smoked.

The toné *oven at Pheasant's Tears, p. 166*

CHILLI, CHILI or CHILE (*tsitseli*) Hot peppers are a vital ingredient in Georgian cooking, and are more prevalent in the western side of the country.

Churchkhela *hanging in the market*

CHURCHKHELA are the closest the Georgians come to candies. They look like hanging sausages but are made of nuts and reduced grape must or fruit juice. Walnuts, hazelnuts or other nuts are beaded onto strings and dipped in the boiled must or juice thickened with flour. No sugar is added. They are hung to dry and served sliced into rings or chunks for a healthy, chewy snack. *Churchkhela* are now rarely homemade but are sold throughout Georgia.

COMPOTES These are sweet, concentrated fruit syrups diluted with water at the table (like British squash) and are often served alongside wine as a drinking option. When homemade from local fruits such as cherries, they can be delicious. See p. 156.

CORNMEAL Corn (*maize*) is a staple in western Georgia, particulary in Samegrelo. Ground, dried cornmeal (like *polenta*) is used in porridge (*ghomi*), porridge with cheese (*elarji*), cornbread (*mchadi*) and cheesy corn-bread (*tchvishtari*). *Ghomi* means millet and suggests that millet was used as a staple in western Georgia before the arrival of New World corn. (Wheat was the staple in eastern Georgia.) See pp. 347 and 348.

Cornelian cherries, *often used for compotes*

EGGS (*kvertskhi*) Chickens run free throughout Georgia and almost every family has its own, so eggs are a key source of protein in rural areas.

FERMENTATION Before refrigeration, fermentation was an effective way to preserve vegetables and provide the tangy, sour flavours the Georgians love as counterpoints to their rich, fatty cheese and meat dishes. Georgian families ferment all sorts of plants, from green tomatoes and cucumbers to chillies, whole heads of garlic and the blossoms of the bladdernut (see *jonjoli*) and acacia trees. No meal would be complete without an assortment of fermented vegetables, and they are always served with *lobio*, stewed dried beans.

FISH (*tevzi*) Freshwater fish from lakes and rivers are found throughout Georgia, while catch from the Black Sea is more popular in western Georgia. Dried and smoked fish are also eaten.

FRUIT (*khili*) Most Georgians have access to a family orchard or to the country's wild fruit trees. In season, roadside vendors hawk fruits, including yellow cherries, plums, pears, peaches and wild berries. Other fruits used for cooking include pomegranate, blackberries, barberries, mulberries and plums of every colour and size (see *tkemali*). The tart and fragrant Cornelian cherry (*Cornus mas*; *shindi* in Georgian) is used in sauces and to accent salads and vegetable dishes. Blackberries are fermented and boiled for sauces (see p. 244). Mulberries are dried and used in stews with beef.

Fruit is often served instead of prepared desserts at Georgian meals, as in *churchkhela* and *tklapi* (pp. 38 and 43-44).

Home-grown yellow cherries

GARLIC (*niori*) is used fearlessly in Georgian cooking, with some dishes calling for a whole head of garlic. It's always a component of nut pastes and is popular fermented too. Use as much as you like in these recipes.

GRAINS AND PULSES/LEGUMES Georgia's agricultural biodiversity dates from ancient times. Today's cuisine still features many types of grain and legumes, including lentils (*ospi*), fava beans (*sirzi*), chickpeas (*mukhuro*), and grass pea (*Lathyrus sativus*, *lispira* in Georgian). These plants provide important proteins during Lenten and fasting periods. *Tsiteli doli* is a native wheat variety that can be digested by many with gluten intolerances.

GOZINAKI One of the few traditional Georgian desserts, this is made for the Christmas holidays from honey and walnuts.

HERBS The abundant use of fresh, aromatic herbs is a distinctive aspect of Georgian cuisine. The most popular include:

Basil (*mtsvane rehani*, *rehani*). Found in both the green and opal/red varieties, basil is used in raw and cooked dishes, and in salads.

Herbs at the greengrocer's stall

Bay leaf (*dapnis potoli*) is often used in stews and marinades.

Celery leaf (*niakhuri potoli*) adds a distinctive note to green *ajika* and other dishes with vibrant, green flavours.

Coriander/cilantro (*kindzi*) is the most widely used, in all stages of its growth, from flowers and seed pods to leaves and stems.

Cumin (*kvliavi*) is not as commonly used. In Svaneti it appears in *kubdari*, the meat-filled breads.

Dill (*kama*) is popular throughout the country, in stews and salads; it shines in yogurt soups.

Mint (*pitnis*) leaves are often used with coriander to brighten walnut pastes and cheese dishes.

Edible marigold

Parsley (*okhrakhushi*): the flat-leaf variety is common in Georgia and is used in combination with other herbs in many dishes.

Summer savory (*kondari*): this herb is often used dried, as an alternative to mild wild thyme. In season, it's also used fresh.

Tarragon (*tarkhuna*) is the most distinctive fresh herb in Georgian cooking, and features in many dishes, including *chakapuli* stews (see pp. 87 and 148). It stars too in tarragon lemonade, the emerald-green soda pop that goes so well with salty Georgian food.

Thyme (*ombalo*) grows wild and in gardens, in many varieties.

JONJOLI Found at almost every Georgian meal, *jonjoli* are the fermented buds of *Staphylea colchica*, the Caucasian or Colchis bladdernut tree or bush. The plant grows readily in Georgia, in the wild and in gardens, and its unopened buds – resembling pale lilac clusters – are picked, salted and packed into jars. Like other fermented vegetables, delicately sour *jonjoli* are favourite accompaniments for stewed beans, *lobio*. (See photos on p. 183). Acacia blossoms can be used as a substitute.

Grilled khachapuri

KHACHAPURI AND FILLED BREADS *Khachapuri*, the cheese-filled bread, is Georgia's best-loved dish and appears at almost every meal. Other regional breads contain meat, potato and beet-green fillings. *Khachapuri* may be baked, cooked in a pan and sometimes roasted on a grill or barbecue. See pp. 49-53 for more on *khachapuri*, as well as the Master Recipes. See list on pp. 426-27.

KHINKALI These popular dumplings – including soup dumplings – are found throughout Georgia with fillings ranging from meat to cheese and potato. They're usually eaten without a sauce, sprinkled with black pepper. See pp. 54-57, 141, 221 and 417.

MARIGOLD (*saphran*) The bright orange-yellow powdered spice that the Georgians call 'saffron' is ground from the petals of the orange French marigold (*Tagetes patula*). The dried petals are also used in cooking. The marigold has an earthy, lightly spiced flavour, and adds colour and warmth to raw and cooked dishes. The fresh leaves are also edible and sometimes used.

MATSONI is a fermented milk product similar to yogurt. It is creamy and has a mild, sour or tart flavour. It's used as one of the dough starters for *khachapuri* and other filled breads, and also appears in many recipes. Look for similarly live, unsweetened, probiotic yogurt or *kefir*.

MEATS Most of Georgia's farm animals – including cows, sheep, and goats – are allowed to graze freely, and many live to a good age before being butchered. This can make some meat tougher than we're used to but it gives it great flavour and the animals live much more dignified and independent lives.

The Georgians traditionally boil their meats for stews or soups but some people brown the meat first, as I have done in these recipes.

Kebabs and grilled, skewered meats (*mtsvadi*) are favourites in eastern Georgia, and are often cooked over vine prunings. The chunks of succulent meat are served simply with slices of raw onion on them, accompanied by *ajika* or other sauces. Chicken and quail are also popular meats. Game can be found in

Butcher at Bodbiskhevi market, Kakheti

the autumn and winter months, especially in mountainous regions. Goat is prevalent in the southern areas near Turkey and is popular during Muslim holidays.

MUSHROOMS (*soko*) Wild mushrooms are found in large quantities throughout Georgia and feature in many recipes. Although dozens of varieties can be found, the most sought-after are Cæsar and oyster mushrooms (see p. 236).

NUTS Walnuts (*nigvzi*) are the most important stars in Georgian gastronomy and help make its cookery so unique. They feature in the spiced and herbed walnuts pastes at the heart of many vegetable and meat dishes. After being pounded in a mortar and pestle, walnuts can be squeezed by hand and a few drops of precious oil extracted to sprinkle on top of stews or other dishes.

Walnut trees grow throughout the country and the nuts are sold in many grades in the markets. Walnuts are most prevalent in the cuisine of western Georgia, where hazelnuts/filberts (*tkhilis*) sometimes replace them (particularly in Guria). Almonds are used but to a much lesser extent.

Always buy walnuts in halves as broken pieces oxidize more quickly and can become rancid and bitter. Nuts need careful storing: buy them in small batches and refrigerate in airtight containers to make them last longer. Always taste your nuts before cooking with them: they should be sweet and cleanly nutty. If they are old or rancid they'll spoil any dish you put them into so are best avoided.

Nuts don't benefit from extended cooking. The Georgians add theirs to hot dishes just a few minutes before the dish is ready to be served.

OILS (*zeti*) In Georgia, where the olive is not a native plant, the primary oil for cooking is sunflower. In Kakheti, the sunflower oils are full of character; they're unrefined and may be toasted. Lighter oils, such as grapeseed, are also used. Look for good quality rather than refined, industrial oils. Extra virgin olive oil has such a distinct flavour that it would change the balance of many Georgian dishes, so use neutral but organically produced cold-pressed oils.

PASTES Nut-based pastes – especially walnut and, on the west coast of Georgia, hazelnut – are key elements of Georgian cuisine and are used to give character and punch to vegetable and meat dishes. They originate in the mortar and pestle, though most can also be made in a processor. See p. 427 for the pastes in this book.

Ground pomegranate

PLUM see *tkemali*

POMEGRANATE (*brotseuli*) This late-ripening fruit – cultivated and wild – is used raw, juiced, dry and ground. It's also boiled into a sour, tangy syrup, *narsharab*.

SALADS No summer Georgian meal is complete without a fresh cucumber and tomato salad, often arranged with fresh herbs (especially red basil), spring onions/scallions and chillies. It's usually served as a fresh palate-cleanser without oil when part of a *supra*. Some Russian-influenced salads include mayonnaise.

SALT (*marili*) is an important preservative for the many fermented foods in Georgia. It's used in all aspects of cookery. The most distinctive, spiced salt mix is Svanetian Salt, *svanuri marili*: see p. 370.

SAUCES Georgian meals often feature small bowls of sauces to accompany the myriad dishes at a *supra*. These vary from sour plum (*tkemali*, see p. 269) to nut sauces (see pp. 101, 270, 339 and 350) and include fiery *ajika* (see pp. 335 and 392), pomegranate and walnut (see p. 101) and blackberry sauce (see p. 244). A spicy tomato sauce like a loose ketchup often comes with grilled meats or kebabs. Also see PASTES.

SPICES Georgian food is delicately spiced using a combination of several spices. The key spices are: dried chilli (*tsitseli*); crushed or ground coriander seed (*kindzis tesli*); dried and ground blue fenugreek (*utskho suneli*); marigold petals (see entry above) and black pepper (*pilpili*). Note: since ground coriander seed is often stale, I prefer to crush whole seeds with a pestle.

Other spices include ground barberries (*kotsakhuri*); caraway seed (*kvliavi*); cinnamon (*darichini*); cloves (*mikhaki*); ginger root (*janjapil*); nutmeg (*muskat*); ground dried pomegranate and sumac (*tutubo*).

Khmeli suneli (dried spices) is a spice mix bought in markets or made at home to personal taste. It usually contains coriander seed, fenugreek, chilli and ground marigold petals but varies by region.

TKEMALI (plum) sour sauces. Unripe green plums are boiled for *tkemali*, the sour plum sauce with added spices and herbs that is one of the Georgian table's most iconic condiments (see p. 269). Most cooks in Georgia make their own, and it's easy to make and store when plums are in season.

Assorted tklapi *fruit leathers*

TKLAPI is fruit 'leather', made from fruits that have been boiled, puréed and spread thin on a flat surface. *Tklapi* is eaten for dessert or snacks, or can be softened in hot water to add sourness to stews and sauces.

TOMATO (*pomidori*) The Georgian tomato has a uniquely rosy colour, more madder than vermilion. In season, when it's sun-ripened, it has great flavour and features in many salads and dishes. If the only tomatoes you can find are hot-housed and tasteless, substitute imported plum tomatoes in the cooked dishes.

VEGETABLES are a key feature of Georgian cuisine, and are important for the many fasting periods in which meat and sometimes dairy foods are not eaten. No *supra* table would be complete without them. Aubergine/eggplant is popular, often paired with walnut pastes (see p. 102). Root vegetables, including carrots, beetroot/beets, leeks, onions and potatoes are also always available. The Georgians eat many greens – beans, spinach, beet greens, cabbage, nettles and foraged leaves – in *pkhali* (or *mkhali*), cooked with walnut pastes or in salads. There may not be as much variety in the vegetable selection in Georgia but the vegetables are usually local and seasonal.

VINEGAR (*dzmari*) is usually made from wine in Georgia and is often used sparingly. Many so-called pickles are made without it, see entry on FERMENTATION above.

WILD GREENS The Georgians love foraging for edible wild greens, including greenbriar (*Smilax*; *ekala* in Georgian), leeks, nettles, purslane, sorrel and sheep's sorrel and violet leaves. Marijuana is found in mountainous areas and was once a popular ingredient there.

WINE (*ghvino*) Here are a few of the most common Georgian words connected to wine: *azarpesha* (wine drinking cup); *qvevri, kvevri, churi* and *tchuri* are all words for the clay vessels the wine is made in; *marani* (cellar); *tamada* (toastmaster); *tolumbashi* (toastmaster's assistant).

YOGURT see *MATSONI*

Opposite: The distinctive Georgian tomato

HOW TO COOK GEORGIAN FOOD

ABOUT THE RECIPES

The recipes in this book have been written for people who may never have tasted Georgian food as well as for those who already love it. So I've given very detailed and measured ingredient suggestions (including for garlic and herbs) throughout. This is not really the way Georgians who are familiar with these recipes cook. They rely on instinct and experience, adding a handful of herbs or a sprinkling of spices where they know they'll work. Try the 'measured' way first and then feel free to add more spices or herbs or chilli according to your preference. (Some Georgian cooks use very large quantities of garlic. I've toned that down in some recipes, but use as much as you like!)

The recipes have been gathered from the many Georgian women and men who generously prepared them for me in their homes and restaurants. As well as cooking in Georgia, I've tested them at home in London with local ingredients and a mixture of Georgian and UK-sourced spices. (Most of the key ingredients – from ground fenugreek to coriander seeds and sour plum sauce – can now thankfully be found in speciality shops or online.)

The biggest difference is in the flavour and types of cheese available outside Georgia. After all, few of us have a family cow to provide us with milk every morning from which to fashion our own. I've suggested the substitutes I like best for *khachapuri* and the other cheese-filled breads, but experiment with your own favourites too.

As this book originates in the UK, I've used British spellings and ingredient names throughout, but have also given the US name whenever possible. The measurements are given in metric, Imperial and US systems, including the US cup (approximately 240ml/8fl oz), but I always start by weighing my dry ingredients and I strongly urge home cooks to do the same by investing in modern electronic flat scales. They're inexpensive, very easy to use and more accurate than the cup system. (For example, the weight of flour or walnut halves is much more precise than their volume in cups.)

The spoon measurements are the UK/US standard:

1 tablespoon (tbsp) = approximately 15 millilitres (ml)
1 teaspoon (tsp) = approximately 5ml

Note: Georgian is a unique language with a distinct alphabet (*Mkhedruli*), one of only about 46 alphabets in existence worldwide today. The Georgian words in this book are common transliterations, and I've chosen not to change them for plurals when using them in English sentences.

PORTION SIZES

The Georgian meal is always a combination of four, five, six or more dishes served at the same time. Each dish is intended to be one part of that bigger whole, as are my recipes. A stew, for instance, is not seen as an all-in-one main course but as one of a meal's components, where it stretches to more people. So it's hard to say exactly how many people each recipe will feed but I've included indications whenever possible. If you cook the recipes as stand-alone dishes, use the lower number in my serving estimates.

A NOTE ABOUT DESSERTS

I've rarely been served a Georgian dessert at any of my meals there so I decided not to include them in this book. The usual ending to a meal in Georgia is either fresh fruit and nuts, *churchkhela* or fruit leather (see pp. 38 and 43-44). While a few confectioneries do exist at New Year – like *gozinaki*, nuts cooked in honey – I've preferred to focus on the much wider repertoire of savoury dishes.

THE GEORGIAN MENU

The key to preparing a meal like a Georgian is to serve multiple dishes at once and to eat from smaller plates, so the diner's plate is never overfilled. Instead, diners are encouraged to take a taste of each dish and go back for more as they like.

Georgians think of single dishes as part of a more complex whole, and they always aim to create a balance between contrasting textures and flavours, raw and cooked foods, spiced and herbed dishes. They also offer sour, bitter and piquant notes (from chillies) as accents in sauces, pastes and fermented ingredients.

For reference, I've included menus throughout the book from meals I ate in Georgia, highlighting their main dishes. These were always accompanied by bread, *khachapuri* or other filled breads, plates of cheeses, fermented vegetables (like pickles), sour plum and other sauces and *ajika*. Soups, when they come, are usually served in individual bowls. The obligatory dish on every *supra* table from spring to autumn is some version of cucumber and tomato salad, often heaped with whole bunches of washed fresh herbs, and almost never dressed with oil or vinegar. These fresh ingredients are intended as palate cleansers, and remain light and refreshing. This salad is often beautifully arranged.

The meal sequence almost always begins with cold dishes, followed by hot, and then passes to *khachapuri*, *khinkali*, fried potatoes, barbecued meats and other foods that are cooked after the meal has begun.

HOW THE GEORGIANS COOK

The most important pieces of equipment in the Georgian kitchen are the mortar and the pestle. Whether of wood, stone or both (often the mortar is wooden and the pestle is a stone, an heirloom passed down from mothers to daughters), they are still used throughout Georgia for crushing and grinding spices, herbs and nuts. While they can be replaced by the modern food processor, the crushing action of the pestle does encourage the essential oils of nuts and herbs to be released from their ingredients, and makes Georgian pastes more deeply flavoured.

Shallow clay baking dishes, *ketsi,* are popularly used for making cornbread and other foods. They are often filled and stacked during cooking in the oven or in a fireplace near wood embers.

Many rural households cook in wood-burning ovens that also have a hot plate on top of the stove that's useful for starting to cook the underside of the country's many filled breads.

Meats are often cooked over impromptu fires made of vine prunings or wood. Their embers also heat the clay ovens known as *toné,* for baking bread (see pp. 36 and 37).

Traditional mortar and stone pestle

The key to reproducing the flavours of Georgian food is to use good-quality, fresh ingredients (preferably organically grown), and to flavour them with fresh – not tired – spices and aromatic herbs.

KHACHAPURI AND FILLED BREADS

Khachapuri is undoubtedly the most iconic Georgian recipe. The flat, cheese-filled breads come in many versions and are served at almost every meal. They also easily make the transition from the formal dinner table to snack or casual food. Many small bakeries in Tbilisi and around the country feature the filled breads that make delicious, inexpensive and satisfying meal options. At a *supra*, *khachapuri* is served hot and arrives with the other hot dishes after the meal has begun.

Several regions have their own *khachapuri*, varying from the Imeretian (cheese inside) to other styles with added cheese on top or potato or hard-boiled eggs inside. For a full list of *khachapuri* and filled bread recipes in this book, see p. 426.

HOW THE GEORGIANS FORM THEIR FILLED BREADS

The Georgians have developed a unique way of shaping *khachapuri* and other filled breads. They pat or roll their rather soft dough into a disc, heap the filling on top in a substantial ball, and then draw the dough up and around the filling to enclose it completely, pinching the dough together at the seams. The ball is then turned over – hiding the seams on the underside – patted once more into a disc shape, and sometimes rolled out to make the bread thinner. A small air hole is poked in the centre of the top, and the bread is baked, with or without an egg wash. (Alternatively, some people cook their breads in a dry skillet on the stove, without the added air hole.) Often the bread is started on a wood-burning stove or in a pan, and then finished in the oven.

This process sounds straightforward. I've watched countless times as dextrous Georgian cooks form their filled breads perfectly this way, making it look so easy. But it takes skill and experience to seal the dough without making it uneven, which can lead to breads that are much thicker or irregular on the underside and sometimes too thin on top.

I prefer the simpler, foolproof method described on p. 52. It's similar to theirs in all but shape, as it produces square breads instead of round.

The traditional way to form khachapuri

ABOUT IMERETIAN KHACHAPURI

This is the most popular version of *khachapuri*, and despite originating in Imereti region, it's found throughout Georgia. This bread is filled with a mixture of cheeses and is then oven-baked or cooked in a dry pan on the stove. Use this as your master recipe, following the individual recipes in the book for other fillings.

Cooking khachapuri *in a skillet*

A note about the cheese: in Georgia, *khachapuri* is made primarily using home-made fresh or aged cow's milk cheeses. Even the cheeses sold in Georgian markets are mostly produced in small quantities, in non-industrial dairies. The filling should be soft, creamy, oozy and have a pleasant sour tang. For that stringiness, some *sulguni* – a pulled-curd cheese similar to mozzarella made in Samegrelo – is usually added (see more about Georgian cheeses on p. 37).

Since these cheeses are practically impossible to find outside Georgia, I've tried many combinations of cheeses – including the feta that many people recommend as a substitute – and have come up with a combination I find gives that sour quality while remaining true to the cow's-milk tradition. I was also surprised to discover that pizza mozzarella from the supermarket worked better than the artisan mozzarella I prefer for salads. Try my version and then experiment with your own!

ABOUT THE DOUGHS

Every cook in Georgia has their own preferred method of making dough for *khachapuri* and other filled breads. They vary from slow-rising yeast doughs to doughs made more quickly that rely on acidic live yogurt (*matsoni*), baking soda (bicarbonate of soda) and even Georgian sparkling mineral water to activate the dough. The idea is to make a light, airy dough.

I'm opting for two doughs: a yeast dough as well as a dough that uses yogurt and baking soda. They're both good but they produce different textures and styles for the breads. The yeast dough is the classic and makes a better bread crust, but the yogurt dough takes an hour less time so it's useful when guests drop by unexpectedly and you want to whip up a quick *khachapuri*.

As I travelled through the regions watching home cooks producing these breads, I found that most Georgians keep their *khachapuri* doughs simple: the cheese fillings are so rich that there's no need to add lots of butter or milk to the dough. They all rub the top of the baked bread with butter as soon as it comes out of the oven. This softens the bread – stopping it from cracking or becoming leathery – adds a sheen, and enriches it.

THE MASTER DOUGH RECIPE (YEAST)

It's almost as easy to make two breads as to make one, and they can be re-heated if any are left over, so here are the recipes for 1 or 2 breads.

PREPARATION **120 minutes (including rising time)**
BAKE **25–30 minutes**

FOR **2 BREADS, 8** SERVINGS EACH

400g / 14oz / 3¼ cups strong /
   bread flour
1 tsp sugar
1 tsp quick-acting/instant yeast
1 tsp salt
290ml / 10fl oz / 1¼ cups
   warm water
1 tbsp sunflower oil

FOR **1** BREAD, **8** SERVINGS

225g / 8oz / 1⅘ cups strong /
   bread flour
1 tsp sugar
¾ tsp quick-acting yeast
¾ tsp salt
150ml / 5fl oz / ½ cup plus 2 tbsp
   warm water
1 tbsp sunflower oil

HOW TO MAKE THE DOUGH

You can make these doughs the traditional way – by hand, mixing the warm water into the dry ingredients and kneading on a floured board for 5–7 minutes – or proceed as follows:

Put the flour, sugar, yeast and salt in the bowl of a food processor and process briefly. Pour in the warm water and process again. The dough will come together and form a ball. Continue processing for 2 minutes.

Turn the dough out onto a lightly floured surface. Dust your hands with flour and knead the dough for another 2 minutes. It should be slightly sticky and not too firm. Spread the oil around the bottom and sides of a large bowl. Place the dough ball in the bowl, turning it once to pick up some of the oil. Cover the bowl with a clean tea cloth and place it in a warm place for 90–115 minutes. (If you're not using the oven for anything else, turn it on low for 5 minutes before you knead the dough. Then put the bowl with the dough into the turned-off oven to rise.)

When the dough has risen, punch it down, turn it out onto a lightly floured board and knead it for just a minute to form a smooth ball. Divide the dough into equal halves if you are making two breads.

Preheat the oven to 170°C / 325°F / Gas 3. Place a flat, heavy iron baking sheet in the centre of the oven. Fill and form the bread while the oven heats up.

THE CHEESE FILLING

I like using a combination of four cheeses, in equal parts: For each Imeretian *khachapuri* I use 60g/2oz each of grated cheddar, Emmental or other Swiss cheese, mozzarella (firm is best) and cottage cheese, but you can experiment and use your own favourites.

TO FILL 1 KHACHAPURI

225g/8oz mixed cheeses, at room temperature
freshly grated black pepper
1 egg, beaten

Mix the four cheeses in a small bowl. Season with pepper. If you like, also add half of the beaten egg, keeping the rest to paint on the top of the bread.

HOW TO FORM AND BAKE THE FILLED BREADS MY WAY

On a lightly floured sheet of baking parchment, roll and pat the dough into a square about 30cm/12in wide. Straighten the edges by cutting away any bulges. Shape your filling evenly into another square, like a diamond in the centre of the dough square (see top photo).

One at a time, fold each corner of dough in towards the centre, pinching the seams firmly as you go to seal the bread, like making an envelope. Turn the bread carefully over onto another sheet of baking paper. Pat or roll it out gently to stretch the bread a little more. If you're going to bake the bread in the oven, make a small air hole in the centre and paint the top with a little beaten egg.

Slide a flat baking tray under the bread's baking parchment, open the oven and slide the bread – on its paper – onto the preheated baking tray already in the oven. This will ensure the underside of the bread is crisp and well cooked. Make sure the heat source for your oven is coming only from below or you will inadvertently grill your bread and toughen its dough.

Bake for 25–30 minutes, or until the top is pale golden and the dough is cooked. The bread may rise but don't worry, it will settle again after baking.

Remove the bread from the oven and immediately rub a tablespoonful of butter all over the top of the bread. This keeps the dough soft and pliable. Cut into squares or wedges and serve hot.

Steps in making khachapuri *my way*

To reheat a filled bread, sprinkle or rub a little water over the top of the bread and place it in a preheated oven at 180°C/350°F/Gas 4 for about 10 minutes, or until the filling is heated through.

THE SKILLET METHOD

If you prefer to cook the bread in a skillet on the stove, don't make the air hole or paint the top with the egg. This method works best with the yeast dough.

Use a heavy skillet or non-stick frying pan a little bigger than the bread (if the pan is too thin, the bread will burn). Make sure your filled bread has no extra flour on it or this too will burn. Heat the pan, without oil, over medium to low heat and slide the bread into it. Cook slowly for about 10–12 minutes, checking occasionally to make sure the underside is not burning. When the dough has set on the first side and it's a light gold, turn the bread over and continue cooking 8–10 minutes more.

Slide the bread onto a plate and rub about 1 tablespoonful of butter onto the top of the dough. Serve hot.

THE MASTER DOUGH RECIPE (YOGURT AND BAKING SODA)

This dough is easy to make and seems happiest when mixed by hand (rather than in the processor) and baked in the oven. Make sure your yogurt is at room temperature.

FOR ONE BREAD, **8 servings**
PREPARATION **60 minutes**
COOK **25–30 minutes**

170g / 6oz / 1½ cups strong / bread flour
½ tsp salt
¾ tsp baking soda (bicarbonate of soda)
170g / 6oz / ¾ cup plain live yogurt, at room temperature
1 tbsp sunflower oil
flour, for kneading

In a medium mixing bowl, combine the flour with the salt and baking soda. Stir in the yogurt and half of the oil. Mix well using your hands.

Lightly flour a work surface. Turn the dough out onto it and knead, adding more flour if necessary, until it's smooth and has stopped sticking to the surface (don't add too much flour as it should be quite a soft dough). Use the remaining oil to lightly oil a clean, medium mixing bowl. Put the dough ball into it, turning it over so the top is oiled too. Cover the bowl with a clean tea cloth and leave it in a warm place for about 45 minutes. Then follow the instructions for forming and filling the bread (see opposite).

KHINKALI

Khinkali are Georgian dumplings. They're one of Georgia's most popular foods and are said to have arrived with the Mongol invasions, though perhaps not in their present form. No *supra* would be complete without a platter of steaming *khinkali* being served towards the end of the meal. They make a warming complement to the feast's complex flavours and each diner usually eats just a few of them, depending on the size. Despite being available throughout the country, *khinkali* are still associated with the high mountain areas where they originated. In Kazbegi, they're likely to be filled with spiced meat and their broth (see p. 417), while in Tusheti they're mostly stuffed with cheese, potato or a mixture of both (see p. 141). Smaller versions are made in Samtskhe-Javakheti (see p. 220).

Khinkali are designed to be eaten by hand. In the case of meat-filled *khinkali* – or 'soup dumplings' – you hold each dumpling aloft by its 'stem' (like a mushroom or an open umbrella) as you take a small bite from the side of the cushiony top and suck out the hot broth before chewing your way into the filling. The thick stem is then often discarded.

A platter of steaming khinkali

Khinkali are not served with a sauce but are usually simply sprinkled with ground black pepper. In some areas, onions caramelized in butter are spooned over them, especially the small, potato-filled variety.

The doughs vary between basic flour-and-water mixtures to those with added egg or oil, which can make the larger *khinkali* easier to work. In the high Caucasus, *khinkali* were made using available ingredients, often only flour and potatoes. This is subsistence food: earthy, hearty and filling. If you serve them alone, there's no reason not to make a sauce to accompany them.

Khinkali *after the broth has been sucked out*

THE MASTER KHINKALI RECIPE

This is the master recipe for *khinkali* dough with egg (for the plain flour and water variety, see p. 221), with instructions about how to form and cook the dumplings. They're not difficult to prepare, but may require a little practice to make them look as evenly and beautifully pleated as the Georgians do. Georgians use a wooden cutter like a large egg cup to cut out the dough, but you can use a glass or round cookie cutter.

MAKES **24–30 dumplings**
PREPARATION **60 minutes**
COOK **10 minutes**

260g / 9oz / 2 cups plain/all-purpose flour
1 egg, at room temperature
120ml / 4fl oz / ½ cup water
½ tsp salt
2 bay leaves

Mix the first four ingredients together by hand or in a food processor until they form a ball (add a little more flour or water, if necessary, to make the dough hold together). Turn it out onto a floured surface and knead for 4–5 minutes, or until the dough is smooth and elastic. Place the dough in a lightly oiled bowl and cover with a clean tea cloth while you prepare the filling.

HOW TO FORM KHINKALI

Make the dumplings in small batches so the dough doesn't dry out. Divide the dough roughly into thirds. Sprinkle a flat surface lightly with flour. Make a ball with one third and roll it out to a thickness of about 6mm / ¼in. (Keep the remaining dough covered while you work.) You can vary the size of the dumplings by rolling out thicker dough for larger *khinkali* that will hold more filling.

Using a thin glass or circular cookie cutter 6.5cm / 2½in in diameter, cut as many circles as will fit. (Peel off the excess dough, make it into a ball and put it back with the remaining dough.)

Roll each circle out into a larger circle of about 10cm-4in in diameter for medium-size dumplings. Place a spoonful of filling into the centre of a rolled-out circle and begin pleating the dough edge, gathering the top like a cloth pouch to trap the filling in the centre. When you have pleated all the way around, pinch the top edges together firmly – you can even give them a little twist – to make sure the *khinkali* is well sealed. (If you don't want the stems, lightly press the top-knot down into the dumpling with your finger.) Set the finished *khinkali* on a piece of lightly floured parchment paper and continue with the remaining dough. You'll see after you've made the first one how much filling to use.

Bring a large pan of salted water with two bay leaves in it to the boil. Lower the *khinkali* into the water and stir carefully with a wooden spoon without piercing the dumplings to make sure they don't stick to the bottom of the pan. Boil for 8–10 minutes (or until the meat has cooked through, in that variety). Serve hot, sprinkled with freshly ground black pepper.

In the photographs, the cook is closing a cheese *khinkali*, but they can also be made with other fillings.

Opposite: Darejani Itchirauli cuts the dough circles before rolling them out and filling them

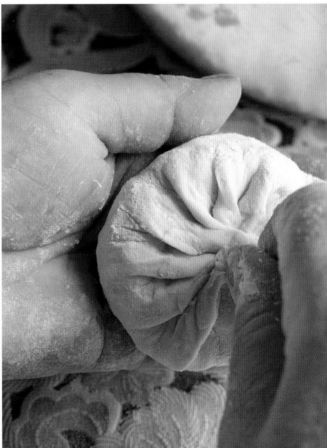

1. TBILISI

Whenever I arrive in Tbilisi I'm reminded of Alexandre Dumas's colourful descriptions of the city as it was in the 1850s. I love imagining the hilly lanes near the Persian baths crowded with camels, and the costumed people from distant countries leading mules packed with silks and spices into the caravanserais.

The spice traders and their camels may be long gone but some of that exoticism endures in Tbilisi's older districts of wooden houses with fret-worked balconies and shady tree-lined streets. They offer an exciting contrast to the modern structures by international architects that now punctuate the city on both sides of the Kura, or Mtkvari, River.

View from the 2010 Bridge of Peace, designed by Michele De Lucchi

Tbilisi is rich in culture, with a monumental opera house, grand avenues, theatres and museums. Its varied and often elegant architecture from many periods attests to the city's continued importance and artistic life. It may be slightly crumbling in parts but that's part of the charm.

John Steinbeck too wrote of Tbilisi – or Tiflis as it used to be known – and of its well-dressed citizens and their culture of hospitality, great foods and wines. That hasn't changed. Tbilisi offers countless gastronomic attractions, from markets and traditional restaurants to *khachapuri* bakeries and natural wine bars. The country's recent stability has generated a new crop of cafés and restaurants where the emphasis is on light food and relaxed, hip environments – often with women chefs at the helm.

Tbilisi has long been an important wine hub. Much of what is now the city was planted to vineyards before urban development engulfed them in the late 20th century. Dumas went to a banquet – or *supra* – where the wine consumption was of five to six bottles per person and describes a 'bewildering variety of drinking vessels of all shapes and sizes' crafted for that purpose. Anyone who's had the pleasure of attending a *supra* among Georgian friends will know the dishes are abundant and the wine flows freely. If you're visiting Georgia in search of traditional wines produced in *qvevri* – the large clay vessels that are buried in the ground – the best are now available in the city.

As in all my favourite cities, Tbilisi's streetlife is compelling. I love wandering through the Dry Bridge Flea Market and browsing Rustaveli Avenue's outdoor booksellers with food vendors selling paper-wrapped snacks of sunflower seeds, nuts and the unripe green plums that are a national favourite. Vegetable and other food stalls spill out into the narrower streets that lead away from that central axis to older residential neighbourhoods with their distinctive wooden houses, many of which are now being restored. Some are reached up steep, winding streets that reveal breathtaking views of the city. It's a safe and appealing city to explore on foot.

Previous pages: Abanotubani, the historic sulphur bath district in Tbilisi

Opposite: Metekhi bridge and church, with the equestrian statue of King Vakhtang Gorgasali

TBILISI: A BRIEF HISTORY

The city's historical and cultural features are amply documented in other travel guide books (my favourite is Bradt's) but a brief history will supply some background.

The origins of the city date back to the 4th millennium BC, but the official legend attributes its founding to King Vakhtang 'the Wolf Head' of Iberia in the late 5th century AD. While the king was out hunting in thick forests with his falcon, a pheasant was wounded and fell into a steaming

Marjanishvili Square

hot spring. The king was so taken by the healing powers of the waters and the beauty of the area he decided to build a city there. Tbilisi – 'place of warmth' – was born.

The city's favourable climate and strategic position on east–west trade routes between Asia and Europe attracted a multi-ethnic population. Tbilisi still enjoys a reputation for religious and ethnic tolerance. As with so much of Georgia, that desirability was the cause of fighting between foreign powers with interests in the region, including the Romans, Arab Caliphate, Persians and Byzantines. Tbilisi was under Muslim rule for four centuries until King David the Builder liberated it in 1122. Despite his much smaller army, David defeated the Seljuk Turks, established peace and reunited the Georgian state. During Queen Tamar's reign (1178–1213) – in what is known as the Georgian Golden Age – Shota Rustaveli composed his epic poem, *The Knight in the Panther's Skin*. It was first printed in Tbilisi in 1712, and the city's main avenue now bears the poet's name.

Stability did not last long: the city was razed to the ground and rebuilt several times in the centuries that ensued. By the time Alexandre Dumas visited, Tbilisi was once more cosmopolitan and thriving. Since then it has suffered and survived more wars – and the difficulties of the Soviet and post-Soviet periods – but it remains an attractive, intriguing cross between Mediterranean, Middle Eastern and Eastern European influences.

WHERE TO EAT, DRINK, SHOP AND STAY

MARKET AND FOOD SHOPS

There are several food markets around the city. The largest, Dezerterebi Bazar, near the main train station and Station Square Metro, spreads through the streets and a converted train shed in that area. Samgori Bazar, near the Samgori Metro station, also occupies several streets and squares behind the main road. Smaller local markets exist in other neighbourhoods, with a group of food stalls and flower sellers in the streets beneath 9 April Park, below Kashveti Church, on Rustaveli Avenue. The popular Dry Bridge Flea Market, off Gamsakhurdia Bank, operates daily and is a good place to try out your bargaining skills. If you're looking for paintings, Vernissaj is the weekend open-air art market in the park below the flea market.

Aristæus – The Georgian Basket This is my favourite one-stop store for food presents to bring home. The shop specializes in Georgian cheeses, preserves, sauces, pastes like *ajika*, honeys, fruit sweets (*churchkhela*), and many more delicacies. You can stop in for a cheese tasting and glass of wine too. Leselidze, 33; tel: +995 32 2920037

Top to bottom: Fruit and vegetable stall; display at the Dry Bridge Flea Market; honey at Aristæus – The Georgian Basket

Badagi These elegant shops specialize in Georgian fruit sweets (*churchkhela*) and are a step up from the street-sold version, with apple, pear, plum and grape flavours available. There's even Rkatsiteli for the wine-crazy. The shop sells *tklapi* too – flat fruit 'leather' circles that can be added to cooked foods or torn into strips and eaten as a healthy snack. For *churchkhela*, the fruit juice is boiled for 30 minutes and then left to stand for 12 hours. The juice is thickened with flour and the nuts on strings are dipped into it. They are dried for several days and improve after a few weeks' ageing. www.badagi.ge

Kvelis Sakhli – The Cheese House Ana Mikadze and her son run this cheese shop, one of three in Tbilisi. They specialize in unusual Georgian cheeses and their accompaniments. Kazbegi Avenue, 20; tel: +995 32 2394059

Sunflower Health Food Store You would hardly expect to find one of Georgia's best organic produce shops tucked behind McD's on Rustaveli Avenue, but this farm shop sells fresh and preserved seasonal vegetables grown in Marneuli and Dmanisi, including microgreens, and herbs, vinegars, bread and jams. Dzmebi Kakabadzeebis, 3; tel: +995 32 2988013

Tea House Shota Bitadze has a remarkable collection of teas for sale in his small shop next door to Ghvino Underground. Most come from different Georgian regions – white, green and black – but others arrive from Japan and China. There are tisanes of rose hip, quince and herbs too. Galaktioni Tabidze Street, 15; tel: +995 59 3322512

Vinotheca Right next door to Aristæus (see above), this large wine shop carries both natural and other Georgian wines. Leselidze, 31

Sasha Jabidze www.vinotheca.ge

*Jean-Jacques
Jacob*

TWO OF MY FAVOURITE TBILISI BAKERIES

The Baker's Tale 1: Sasha Jabidze Alexandre 'Sasha' Jabidze has been baking bread for 63 years, 22 of which in a large underground space beneath Sioni Church, off Lezelidze. He was born in Imereti near Terjola, on the border with Racha, in 1938.

"At school some kids had books but I studied the history and culture of baking bread," he says, as he mixes the dough far below street level in central Tbilisi. He's wearing a once-colourful T-shirt and is covered with a light dusting of flour. "In the Black '90s, before I was given this space by the patriarch, I worked in a factory. But I preferred baking. In Soviet times each loaf had to weigh more than one kilo. Now it's 600 grams so we use less flour but the price has remained the same," he says with a shake of the head. "In those days the bread was circular, a *shoti* with two handles, whereas now it's a half-*shoti* with just one. Each area of Georgia has its own shape."

Did he come from a bread-making family? "No, when I was a child everyone baked at home so there was no work in the villages for bakers. That changed when people left for the city factories and had no time to grow grain or make bread." A steady stream of people heads down the deep stairs from the street to the bakery below, where hot breads, pastries and savoury doughs await. Sioni Street, 13/40

The Baker's Tale 2: Jean-Jacques Jacob You have to be an early bird to get the best (non-Georgian) bread in Tbilisi. On Saturday mornings many of the city's intellectuals and hipsters set out for a residential area where a small organic market is held. There, selling his breads beside his neighbour's vegetables, is Jean-Jacques Jacob, a Frenchman from Brittany who bakes sourdough loaves in Kakheti. He's on a mission.

"I was en route for Egypt to grow vegetables in the desert when I visited Georgia," he says, as he hands me a cookie made from honey and native wheat. "I'm gluten intolerant so I never could eat bread in France but Georgian bread didn't hurt me." He changed his plans and set up Momavlis Mitsa, or 'land of the future', an association of people working the land with respect.

"Nicolas Joly, a pioneer of the biodynamic wine movement, is my close friend. I saw there was room here for an organic movement of farmers and we're recruiting more now."

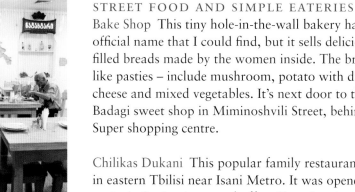

The wheat he uses, *Tsiteli doli* or Caucasian Red, is an endangered or heirloom species native to southern Georgia. "I wanted to grow and maintain it as almost no one was still working with it here." Jean-Jacques brought a stone mill from France and bakes the bread in a wood-burning oven. He sells to the market and to some of the top restaurants in Tbilisi, including Azarpesha and Ghvino Underground.

You'll find him in the courtyard halfway down Didim Mirtskhulava Street on Saturday mornings.

STREET FOOD AND SIMPLE EATERIES

Bake Shop This tiny hole-in-the-wall bakery has no official name that I could find, but it sells delicious filled breads made by the women inside. The breads – like pasties – include mushroom, potato with dill, cheese and mixed vegetables. It's next door to the Badagi sweet shop in Miminoshvili Street, behind the Super shopping centre.

Chilikas Dukani This popular family restaurant is in eastern Tbilisi near Isani Metro. It was opened in 1961, in Soviet times, and offers Georgian-Armenian food: assorted barbecued meats cooked to order on an outdoor grill, varied steaming *khinkali*,

Top: Bake Shop breads

Bottom: Chilikas Dukani

meats stewed in clay pots, salads and *khachapuri*. It's a mix of old Tbilisi style with some modern elements on the so-called Kakheti Highway.
www.chilikasdukani.ge

Lagidze Water This Tbilisi soda fountain is a Georgian favourite. Lagidze Water was first opened in 1887 on Rustaveli Avenue by the 'Lemonade King' but now has a modern branch inside the Sameba (Trinity) Cathedral complex. The idea of adding natural fruit syrups to sparkling water – think squash if you're British – caught the city's imagination. This is classy fast food, with *khachapuri* and other bakes to go with the drinks. Don't miss the electric green tarragon flavour (my favourite), or try lemon, grape, chocolate or cream. Avlabari Metro. www.facebook.com/LagidzeWater

Syrups at Lagidze Water

Machakhela Khachapuri Restaurant This casual eatery is a convenient, central place to sample and compare *khachapuri* and other filled breads – including bean-filled *lobiani*, egg-topped Adjarian *khachapuri*, vegetarian filled breads, and many others. Great quality fast food; there are several Tbilisi branches. Leselidze, 26; tel: +995 32 2102119

CAFES, WINE BARS AND BOOKS
Ghvino Underground Just a short walk from Freedom Square, Vino Underground, as it's usually called, should be the most important address on any natural-wine lover's to-do list. Opened in 2012 by eight *qvevri* wine bottlers from around the country, this was Georgia's first wine bar. Offering a showcase for the rapidly expanding natural wine movement in Georgia, Underground has helped introduce neophytes and afficionados to growers from around the country. It's always a pleasure to go there, whether to sample a new wine with artisan cheeses or a light meal, meet the producers and other enthusiasts, or plan a visit to a winemaking region of Georgia. Open till late. Galaktion Tabidze,15; www.vinounderground.ge

Ghvino Underground

G.Vino is a recent addition to the city's wine bar scene, and features Georgian 'tapas' with natural and conventional Georgian wines by the glass or bottle. Erekle II Street, 6; tel: +995 598932121

Prospero's Books, Caliban's Coffeehouse The place for Anglophiles in Tbilisi to hang out and meet. A book shop with café attached, Prospero's is in a quiet courtyard you duck into from bustling Rustaveli Avenue, a literary oasis away from the madding crowds. It carries a large assortment of books – and maps – about Georgia and the Caucasus, has free wifi, cool coffee and more. Rustaveli Avenue, 34; tel: +995 32 2923592

RESTAURANTS

Azarpesha Along with Ghvino Underground, Azarpesha has been at the forefront of the new enogastronomic scene (and food and wine tourism) in Tbilisi. Opened in 2013, this restaurant with a small wine bar features a 150-strong list of natural wines from Georgia, Europe and beyond. The delicious food is created by chef Ketevan Mindorashvili, in partnership with John Wurdeman of Pheasant's Tears (see p. 166) and Luarsab and Nino Togonidze, of Salobie restaurant (see p. 95). Many of the dishes are inspired by regional and traditional Georgian recipes with a creative twist given by the chef. If the mood is hip and relaxed, the roots are serious, as Luarsab's impressive collection of drinking vessels and early Georgian artefacts attests.

Azarpesha   Ingorovka Street, 2; tel: +995 598466663

Barbarestan Barbara Jorjadze was an early Georgian feminist and writer. Her cookbook – *Sruli Samzareolo* or *Full Cuisine* – was published in 1885 and was the first to be written by a woman. Barbarestan, opened in 2015, is a concept-driven restaurant based on her dishes, adapted for a modern kitchen. The room has been stylishly furnished and there's a wine cellar downstairs. Aghmashenebeli Avenue, 132; tel: +995 32 2943779

Culinarium Lermontov Street, 1/17; tel: +995 32 2430103. See p.73

The Dining Room Keti Bakradze has created a sophisticated, stylish restaurant serving non-Georgian food for the hip Tbilisi crowd. The eclectic menu ranges from Italian gnocchi and ravioli to salmon tartare and steak with truffle sauce. Paliashvili Street, 38; tel: +995 32 2250900

Kakhelebi is a restaurant on the road out of the centre towards eastern Georgia, not far from Tbilisi airport. It's my favourite place for traditional Kakhetian food, with an emphasis on well-sourced ingredients. Tushetian cheeses, highland teas and wild mushrooms appear on an extensive menu that always features roasted meats – including young water buffalo patties with barberries. Don't miss the puffy *khachapuri*, seasonal oyster mushroom soups and assorted vegetable dishes. The lofty rooms have windows too high to see out of but interesting early photos and artefacts engage the eyes. www.kakhelebi.ge

Kakhelebi's khachapuri

Kiwi Vegan Café, Tbilisi's first vegan restaurant, sees tofu and falafel featuring on the daily specials with green smoothies and other healthy options. Vertskhli Street, 41; tel: +995 32 2990456

Megruli Oda In Georgia, country restaurants often have gardens dotted with small cottages and covered tables where guests can dine in the greenery and be separate from other parties. You don't have to go far to have a similar experience: Megruli Oda ('the house from Samegrelo') is in Dighomi district, at the western end of the city, and offers all the Megrelian specialities in its pretty gardens: super cheesy *khachapuri*, walnut-enriched soups, vegetables spiced with walnuts and marigold, and rich cornbreads are always part of the fare here. Marshal Gelovani Avenue, (Vazha-Pshavela Metro); tel: +995 599183897

Megruli Oda

Mukha Tsakatukha is another recent café-restaurant where freshly baked breads, quiches, soups, salads and tartines are on the menu. Good atmosphere for casual, healthy food with some natural wines. Akhvlediani Street, 15; tel: +995 322920053

Polyphonia Recently opened, this relaxed restaurant features a rotating menu of traditional Georgian ethnic cuisines prepared by home cooks from differing regions. The idea is to showcase the food from the more remote regions and encourage the artisan cheese and food makers to continue their crafts. It's owned by the Azarpesha team, and is located in the space formerly occupied by the iconic Shavi Lomi, Amaghleba Street, 23.

Starters at Pur Pur

Pur Pur If you're in the mood for a break from Georgian food and want a colourful, relaxed place to hang out for a meal, Pur Pur is a good option. It's situated upstairs in a large 19th-century villa on the corner of Lado Gudiashvili Square (don't miss the unusual sculptural steel fencing around its borders). The menu is as eclectic as the décor, with Indian fabrics, bunches of wildflowers and assorted furniture creating an artsy city interior, a pretty setting for the European-style food (but, sadly, no natural wines). Open for lunch and dinner, with live music every evening. www.purpur.ge

Puris Sakhli (Bread House) This restaurant, located near the baths, specializes in classic Georgian cuisine with freshly baked breads; it's a favourite with Georgians who want to maintain the traditions of their delicious culinary culture. Gorgasali, 7; tel: +995 32 2303030

Shavi Lomi Meriko Gubeladze's flagship restaurant has moved to Qvlividze Street, 28; see p.73.

Shavi Lomi's symbol is Pirosmani's black lion

Tabla This handsome Georgian-themed restaurant is part of the ICR group and offers traditional Georgian dishes in a series of well-appointed dining rooms that can accommodate small parties and large groups with folk music if desired. Chavchavadze Avenue, 33; tel: +995 32 2602015

The Writer's House A handsome period villa whose shady garden becomes one of Tbilisi's favourite outdoor dining spots during summer. See p.73. Machabeli Street, 13; tel: +995 5950311112

HOTELS

This is a short list of hotels I like and have stayed in. There are of course many more! (See also p. 441.)

Rooms Hotel This stylish, luxury designer hotel in central Tbilisi has the coolest vibe, a huge garden, a restaurant and inspired breakfasts. There's also a sister hotel in the breathtaking mountains of Kazbegi at Stepantsminda (see pp. 420-21). www.roomshotels.com/tbilisi

Hotel Gomi 19, in the old part of city, has a panoramic terrace with some of the biggest, highest views in Tbilisi. The unpretentious hotel is incredibly welcoming thanks to its owner, Mari Lukhumaidze, who's the best hostess I know. It's my home away from home! hotelgomi19@gmail.com

Betsy's Hotel was the first place I stayed in Tbilisi and remains a favourite for relaxed, comfortable visits in a quiet neighbourhood above Rustaveli Avenue. www.betsyshotel.com

View from the terrace of Hotel Gomi

Vinotel On the left bank, near the river, Vinotel is a classically furnished hotel with several distinctive dining rooms and a large wine cellar that includes natural wines. www.vinotel.ge

THREE WOMEN CHEFS

KETO

Ketevan Mindorashvili is a multi-talented Kakhetian woman whose activities range from music and dance to cooking. Keto, as she is known, is the leader of the Georgian polyphonic music ensemble, Zedashe, and has helped collect, save and revive ancient chants, songs and dances from all over Georgia. At her studio in Sighnaghi above Pheasant's Tears Restaurant (she's married to John Wurdeman), extraordinary music is always to be heard as the group rehearses and trains young singers and dancers in the complex and stirring traditional music. She has toured the world with the ensemble.

When she's in Georgia, Keto also cooks. She's been the inspiration behind the food at two Tbilisi restaurants: Azarpesha, where she's trained a new generation of chefs in traditional and more innovative Georgian cuisine, and Polyphonia, where the focus is on the unique dishes of Georgia's diverse regions (see pp. 68 and 70). Her latest project is in her native Sighnaghi, where she will run her own restaurant in the newly constructed Pheasant's Tears cellar, below the town in the Alazani Valley (see p. 166).

Keto with a Zedashe musician

Keto's delicious food ranges from forgotten traditional Georgian dishes to more contemporary creative combinations of Georgian, Middle-Eastern and Mediterranean ingredients. For Keto's recipes, see pp. 74-81.

MERIKO

Meriko Gubeladze is one of Georgia's culinary stars. She has a flair for creating the kind of relaxed but chic restaurants that people adopt as an extension of their homes, and maintains that Georgian food is as much about lifestyle as it is about specific recipes. In her restaurants – from Shavi Lomi, to the vegetarian Kafe Leila and the Lisi Lake Restaurant – she sets her style: cosmopolitan and comfortable, with enjoyable food and wine to share with friends.

Meriko

The charismatic Meriko is well known to the Georgian public for her weekly TV show, *Skhva Shade*, on food and cooking. "I didn't train as a chef but picked it up from home and when I lived in New York and Mexico," she says. "My idea was to make delicious food from organic ingredients that were Georgian in spirit but not necessarily in form. I wanted to make lighter, modern versions of some of the classics but many Georgians are strongly tied to tradition and whenever I make changes to an iconic dish – like adding fresh herbs to a *lobiani* bean pie, for instance – I get letters of complaint from our viewers," she smiles. "Luckily there's lots of positive feedback too."

After five years, her flagship Shavi Lomi restaurant has moved to a larger space with a much bigger kitchen in an up-and-coming neighbourhood near an arts complex on the left bank (see p. 70). "I'm excited to finally have the space to experiment and develop new ideas," she says. For Meriko's recipes, see pp. 82-85.

TEKUNA

Professional chef Tekuna Gachechiladze is another of the women who has contributed to changing the image of contemporary Georgian food. A well-known figure on TV, Tekuna now runs two Tbilisi restaurants: Culinarium, a chef's table where she also gives private cooking lessons (in fluent English) and, in summer, the Writer's House (see pp. 69 and 70).

Tekuna

"Like other cuisines in countries that have known many occupiers, Georgian food is a fusion," she says. "Half-moon shaped dumplings were introduced here in the 13th century by the Mongols. Our pre-Christian, sun-worshipping ancestors living in the high Caucasus turned them into round, spiral-shaped *khinkali*."

Tekuna favours lightening classic Georgian dishes and making them more elegant. She's known for her dainty cornmeal and cheese *elarji* balls and signature mussel *chakapuli* (see pp. 86-87). www.culinarium.ge

Mulberry and goat cheese salad

TUTIS SALATI   თუთის სალათი

Keto makes this salad at Azarpesha Restaurant when mulberries – both white and black – are in season and Georgia's many mulberry trees are laden with the sweet fruit. The mulberry tree is a symbol of the former silk trade. Since mulberries may not be easy to come by, substitute them with blackberries. Use a mixture of fiery and bitter greens – such as rocket/arugula, watercress and mizuna – to contrast with the sweet berries and savoury cheese.

SERVES 4
PREPARATION 10 minutes

150g/5oz mixed salad leaves,
   washed and dried
150g/5oz/1¼ cups mulberries or
   blackberries
100g/3½oz soft goat's cheese
4 tbsp cold-pressed sunflower oil
1 tbsp white wine vinegar
¼ tsp salt
ground chilli or black pepper

Arrange the salad greens in a serving platter. Dot with dollops of the goat's cheese.

Mix the oil, vinegar and salt in a teacup. Drizzle over the salad and toss well. Sprinkle with the berries.

Dust the salad with ground chilli or freshly ground black pepper and serve.

Stuffed tomatoes

POMIDVRIS TOLMA   პომიდვრის ტოლმა

Keto stuffs these tomatoes with a delicious combination of mushrooms and herbs before baking. Use oyster mushrooms or a mix of domesticated and wild mushrooms – like chanterelles or porcini. Serve one per person at a *supra*.

SERVES 3–7
PREPARATION **30 minutes**
COOK **45 minutes**

7 firm, medium tomatoes
   (900g / 2lb)
3 tbsp sunflower oil
150g / 5 oz / 1 cup finely sliced white
   onion
¼ tsp ground fenugreek
¼ tsp coriander seeds, crushed
12g / ⅓oz / 3 garlic cloves, finely
   chopped
400g / 14oz mushrooms, cleaned
   and sliced
20g / ⅔oz / 1½ tbsp butter
1 tbsp flour
100ml / 3½ fl oz / scant ½ cup water
10g / ⅓oz / ¼ cup finely chopped
   coriander / cilantro
2 tbsp finely chopped parsley
2 tbsp finely chopped dill
½ tsp salt
black pepper
60g / 2 oz sliced or grated
   mozzarella

FOR THE SAUCE
8g / ¼oz / 2 garlic cloves, chopped
2 tbsp chopped opal or green basil
2 tbsp extra virgin olive oil

Slice the top fifth off the tomatoes. Carefully scoop their insides out, turning the seeds and cores into a bowl. Arrange the tomato shells in a shallow baking or pie dish.

In a medium frying pan, heat the oil. Stir in the onion, fenugreek and coriander seeds and cook slowly for 5 minutes. Add the garlic and continue to cook until the onions are pale gold, 7–8 minutes. Add the mushrooms and cook over medium-high heat, stirring occasionally, until the mushroom water starts to dry out and the mushrooms begin to sauté, about 15 minutes. Remove from the heat.

In a small saucepan, melt the butter. When it's frothing, add the flour, stirring constantly with a wooden spoon or whisk for 2 minutes. Add the water and cook for 2–3 minutes more, or until the mixture starts to thicken. Remove from the heat and stir into the mushrooms. Fold in the chopped herbs and season with salt and black pepper. Preheat the oven to 180°C / 350°F / Gas 4.

Using a hand blender, purée the tomato cores and seeds, basil and garlic together. Add the olive oil and blend again. Pour the mixture into a strainer, pushing the juices through with a spoon. Season with salt and pepper.

Fill each tomato to the top with the mushroom mixture. Top each tomato with a slice or sprinkling of cheese. Pour the tomato sauce into the dish around the tomatoes. Bake for 30–35 minutes, or until the tomatoes are cooked. Serve hot or warm.

Beef and chickpea stew

CHASHUSHULI   ჩაშუშული მეხუდოთი

"Ginger has always been known in Georgia thanks to the ancient Spice Routes," says Keto. "It gives an unusual and delicious twist to this stew." If you have time, soak 220g/8oz/1½ cups dried chickpeas overnight before boiling them until they are tender; otherwise, use canned. Use fresh or dried chilli: the stew should have a little kick from the chilli's heat.

SERVES **6 or 8–10 as part of a** *supra*
PREPARATION **20 minutes**
COOK **100–120 minutes**

5 tbsp sunflower oil
1kg/2lbs 3oz stewing beef, cubed
300g/10oz/2 cups chopped onion
**50g/1¾oz/½ cup finely chopped
    ginger root**
**20g/¾oz/6 garlic cloves, finely
    chopped**
240ml/8fl oz/1 cup white wine
**480g/3 cups cooked, drained
    chickpeas**
**480ml/16fl oz/2 cups beef broth
    or water**
fresh or dried chilli, to taste
1½ tsp salt
**15g/½oz/⅓ cup finely chopped
    parsley**
3 tbsp finely chopped mint
3 tbsp finely chopped dill
freshly ground black pepper

Heat 2 tablespoons of the oil in a heavy casserole and brown the beef, a little at a time, turning the pieces until they lose their raw colour.

Remove each batch of browned beef to a bowl while you brown the rest. This will take around 20 minutes.

Preheat the oven to 180°C/350°F/Gas 4.

When all the meat has been browned and is in the bowl, lower the heat, pour 3 more tablespoons of oil into the pan and add the onions, ginger and garlic.

Stir well to scrape up the meat cooking juices, cover the pan and cook slowly for 8–10 minutes, until the onions are soft. Don't let them burn.

Pour the wine into the onions, raise the heat and cook for 2 minutes.

Stir in the chickpeas and bring to the boil.

Stir in the meat and its juices. Pour in the hot broth or water (it should almost cover the meat). Add the chilli, salt and parsley and mix well.

Cover the casserole and place in the centre of the oven for 90–120 minutes or until the meat is tender.

Taste for seasoning. Stir in the mint and dill and allow to stand for 5 minutes before serving.

Stuffed vine leaves

TOLMA ტოლმა

This exotic recipe from eastern Georgia, rediscovered by Keto, calls for lamb and vine leaves, two symbols of her native Kakheti region. Vine leaves are stuffed with herbed lamb and rice and served with fresh tomato purée and yogurt sauce studded with dried fruits. If you can't find preserved vine leaves, use chard or cabbage leaves.

MAKES 12–14
PREPARATION 75 minutes
COOK 40 minutes

60g / 2oz / ⅓ cup white rice
14 preserved vine leaves
225g / 8oz ground lamb
4g / ⅛oz / 1 garlic clove, minced
¼ tsp ground cumin
20g / ⅔oz / ⅓ cup finely chopped
    coriander / cilantro
1 tbsp chopped dill
4 tbsp extra virgin olive oil
260g / 9 oz / 1 large tomato, peeled
240ml / 8fl oz / 1 cup plain yogurt
50g / 1¾oz / ⅓ cup finely sliced
    dried apricots
60g / 2 oz / ⅓ cup finely sliced
    prunes
⅛ tsp dried summer savory or
    thyme, or fresh thyme
salt and freshly ground black
    pepper

Boil your rice to the half-cooked point. It should still be chewy. Drain and allow to cool.

Separate the vine leaves in a large bowl and pour boiling water over them. Leave for 10 minutes.

In a medium bowl, mix the rice with the lamb, garlic, cumin, herbs and 2 tablespoons of the oil. Season with pepper and ½ teaspoon of salt. Place one vine leaf on a board in front of you, shiny side down. (If there is a hole, patch it with another piece of leaf.) Using about 3 tablespoonfuls of meat, make a cylinder about 6cm / 2½in long and place it on the pointed end of the vine leaf. Roll the leaf tightly around the meat, tucking in the ends to seal it. Set it on a plate and repeat with the remaining leaves. Steam the bundles for 15 minutes over boiling water.

Quarter the tomato and remove any tough green or white parts.

Place the tomato in the bowl of a hand-blender and process to a purée. In a small bowl, mix the yogurt with the dried fruits, thyme, black pepper, the remaining oil and ½ teaspoon of salt. Preheat the oven to 180°C / 350°F / Gas 4.

Pour the tomato purée into a 25cm / 10in, flat-sided baking dish in an even layer. Arrange the stuffed vine leaves in the dish.

Spread the central area with the yogurt sauce. Bake for 25 minutes. Remove from the oven and allow to stand for 5 minutes before serving from the dish.

Chicken with pomegranate juice

KATAMI BROTSEULIT   ქათამი ბროწეულით

"My mother used to make this without browning the chicken first, but I prefer the rich flavour you get from the chicken's browning juices," says Meriko. "Georgian pomegranates are both sweet and sour, and have good tannic structure and acidity, so if yours taste too sweet, add a firm squeeze of lemon to the dish to bring back its zest. The origins of this dish are Jewish, and it's very easy to make."

SERVES **6**
PREPARATION **15 minutes**
COOK **45 minutes**

**1kg / 2lb chicken pieces, with some
    skin left on**
flour for dredging
3 tbsp sunflower oil
**200g / 7 oz / 1½ cups chopped
    onion**
1 tsp coriander seeds, crushed
**½ tsp dried summer savory or mild
    thyme, or 1 tsp fresh**
2 bay leaves
240ml / 8fl oz / 1 cup water
**360ml / 12fl oz / 1½ cups fresh
    pomegranate juice**
the seeds of 1 pomegranate
**salt and freshly ground black
    pepper**

Dredge the chicken pieces lightly in flour, shaking off any excess. Heat the oil in a sauté pan large enough to fit all the chicken in one layer. Brown the chicken on all sides over medium heat, turning once or twice, about 12–15 minutes.

Stir in the onion and cook with the chicken for 5 minutes or until the onion starts to soften. Add the coriander seeds, herbs, water and half of the pomegranate juice, stirring well. Season with salt and pepper. Bring to the boil, lower heat and simmer for 30 minutes, turning the chicken occasionally, until the juice runs clear when a knife is inserted in the thickest part of the chicken.

Remove from the heat and stir in the remaining pomegranate juice. Check the seasoning. Sprinkle with the pomegranate seeds and a few leaves of fresh thyme before serving.

Pumpkin with walnuts

GOGRA NIGVZIT გოგრა ნიგვზით

Cornus mas, a flowering tree in the dogwood family, produces Cornelian cherries, beloved by the Georgians for their sour tang. They're often used in cooking and preserving and are displayed in shiny heaps in the markets in early autumn. You can substitute dried cranberries or sour cherries here, with steamed or baked pumpkin or squash. "This recipe is based on one from Barbara Jorjadze's cookbook, published in 1885," says Meriko. "Baked pumpkin will result in a dryer mixture."

SERVES **6–8**
PREPARATION **40 minutes**
COOK **20 minutes**

650g / 1lb 7 oz / 4 cups diced steamed or baked pumpkin or squash

75g / 2½oz / ¾ cup walnut halves

½ tsp coriander seeds, crushed

¼ tsp ground fenugreek

8g / ¼oz / 2 garlic cloves, chopped

¼ tsp salt

2 tbsp white wine vinegar

3–4 tbsp water

20g / ⅔oz / ¼ cup finely chopped spring onion / scallion, greens and whites

10g / ⅓oz / ¼ cup finely chopped fresh coriander / cilantro

30g / 1oz / ¼ cup sliced Cornelian cherries or dried cranberries

¼ tsp finely sliced green chilli (optional)

12 toasted walnut halves

Place the cool diced pumpkin or squash in a medium mixing bowl.

In the bowl of a food processor, or using a mortar and pestle, combine the walnuts, coriander seeds, fenugreek, garlic and salt. Process to a paste. Stir in the vinegar and process again.

Turn the mixture into a bowl and stir in the water to loosen the paste. Add the spring onions / scallions and fresh coriander / cilantro.

Stir the walnut mixture into the pumpkin and mix well. Add the cherries or cranberries and mix again.

Turn the pumpkin into a serving bowl and allow to rest for at least an hour at room temperature.

Decorate with the chilli and toasted walnuts before serving.

Mussels chakapuli

CHAKAPULI   ჩაქაფული

Chakapuli is usually made as a veal or lamb stew and is given its distinctive taste by tarragon and sour plum sauce. Here Tekuna has found a new way to showcase those aromatic flavours using mussels. Always look for fresh, live mussels and keep them refrigerated until you are ready to cook them. Wash them in lots of clean, cold water and remove any 'beards' and barnacles before cooking. Discard any mussels that don't open during cooking. Make your own *tkemali*, sour plum sauce (see p. 269), or use store-bought. If you don't have the sauce but do have sour-plum fruit leather, tear a hand-size strip into small pieces and soak it in a cupful of boiling water before adding it to the mussels.

SERVES **6–8**
PREPARATION **40 minutes**
COOK **15–20 minutes**

3 tbsp extra virgin olive oil

300g / 10 oz / 2 cups finely chopped white onion

16g / ½oz / 4 garlic cloves, finely chopped

240ml / 8fl oz / 1 cup white wine

2 kg / 4lbs 6oz fresh mussels, washed

240ml / 8fl oz / 1 cup *tkemali* (sour plum sauce)

50g / 1¾oz / 1½ cups fresh tarragon leaves, roughly chopped

50g / 1¾oz / 2 cups fresh coriander / cilantro leaves, finely chopped

50g / 1¾oz / ½ cup thinly sliced spring onions / scallions, green and white parts

green chilli, to taste (optional)

salt and freshly ground black pepper, to taste

Heat the oil in a saucepan large enough to comfortably hold all the mussels. Stir in the onion and garlic and cook, covered, for 7–8 minutes over medium heat, or until the onions have softened.

Raise the heat and add the wine. Bring it to the boil before adding the mussels.

Cover the pan and cook for 5–6 minutes.

Stir the mussels and cover again. Cook for 3–4 minutes more or until all the mussels have steamed open and are cooked and hot.

Stir in the sour plum sauce, herbs, spring onions/scallions and optional chilli. Mix well. Cook for a minute more before removing from the heat.

Season to taste and serve immediately.

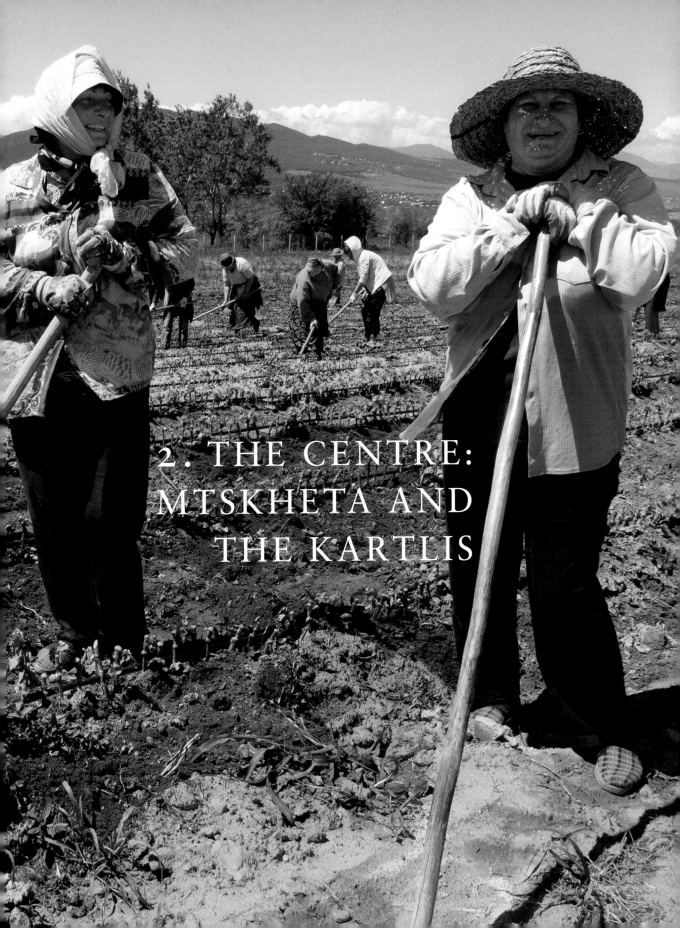

2. THE CENTRE: MTSKHETA AND THE KARTLIS

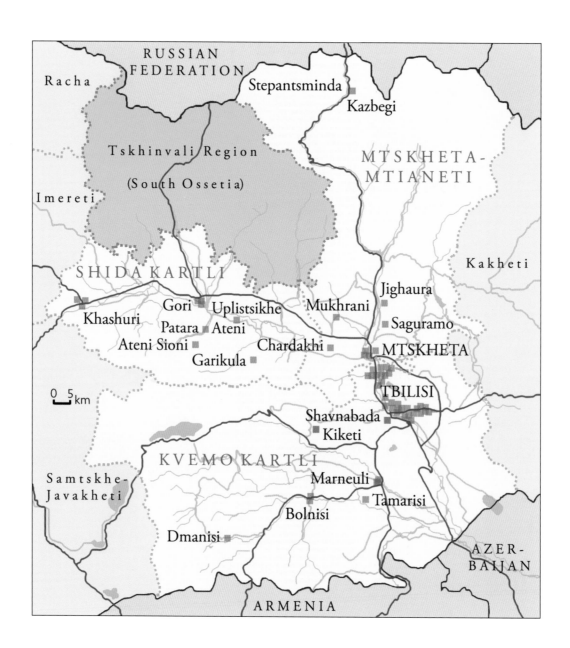

Ateni Sioni p. 109
Bolnisi p. 119
Chardakhi p. 96
Dmanisi p. 119
Didi Ateni p. 108
Garikula p. 112
Gori p. 107
Jighaura p. 95

Jvari p. 92
Kazbegi p. 406
Khashuri p. 106
Kiketi p. 113
Marneuli p. 116
Mtskheta p. 91
Mukhrani p. 106
Mukhatgverdi p. 95

Patara Ateni p. 107
Saguramo p. 95
Shavnabada p. 116
Stepantsminda p. 414
Tamarisi p. 116
Tbilisi p. 58
Uplistsikhe p. 109

This chapter explores the centre of Georgia, west and south of Tbilisi, from the southern part of Mtskheta-Mtianeti region (see Chapter 10, p. 406-21 for the mountainous part) to Shida and Kvemo Kartli. They are all within easy reach of Tbilisi on a day trip.

It begins at Mtskheta, Georgia's former capital and UNESCO World Heritage Site, before visiting the country's most popular bean restaurant and the impressive national vine collection near Saguramo whose research vineyard holds over 400 varieties. Between visits to several natural winemakers – including two pioneering women – we explore Shida (Inner) Kartli before heading south towards Kvemo (Lower) Kartli's border with Armenia for important archæological sites. The hominid finds in Dmanisi from 1.77 million years ago place Georgia at the heart of the world's earliest culture.

The wide valley of the Mtkvari or Kura River is known for its agricultural generosity: fields of vegetables, fruit, sunflowers and other crops stretch for kilometres along the busy highway that runs east–west across the country. Sadly, most of Shida Kartli's northern border is today shared with the breakaway Tskhinvali region – also called South Ossetia – that is now off-limits to the Georgians. The large resettlement colonies that have been constructed to house some of its refugees emphasize just how close and problematic that situation is.

Jvari Monastery, above Mtskheta

Kartli has long featured in Georgia's wine history too. Atenuri, a wine from Ateni, was known in medieval times as the 'wine of kings'. The vines grow with character on the fertile, post-volcanic hills of the Trialeti Range. As in eastern Georgia, the summers here are long, hot and dry. They allow the grapes – and their stems – to ripen fully, making it possible to carry out whole-bunch maceration, though the tendency in Kartli is often for lighter, less structured wines, including some sparkling and *pétillant naturel*.

MTSKHETA

Mtskheta and Kartli have been at the heart of Georgia and its history from ancient times. Mtskheta was settled in the middle Bronze Age, around 3000 BC. Legend has it that it was founded by Mskhetos, Noah's great-great-great-grandson. The state of Kartli was created in the 4th century BC by one of Alexander the Great's generals. It formed part of Iberia, or Iveria, the Greeks' name for eastern Georgia. The area's political situations changed as often as the country's did, as waves of invaders and their cultures made their mark on Georgia's heartland. Mtskheta is where the Georgian King Mirian III was converted to Christianity by Saint Nino of Cappadocia in the 4th century AD.

Located at the confluence of two important rivers, and on the crossroads of Byzantine and Persian influences, Kartli developed a vibrant Christian culture; it was the only Kartvelian area with its own written language. Mtskheta held its position as the capital of Iberia from the 3rd to the 5th centuries AD, when Tbilisi took its place. Kartli also played an important role in the political and ethnic consolidation of the Georgians in the Middle Ages. Mtskheta remains the headquarters of the Georgian Orthodox Church today. In 1994 UNESCO declared Mtskheta and its monuments a World Heritage Site, so the area is now well preserved and should be high on any visitor's list of must-see places in Georgia.

The cathedral in the town centre, Svetitskhoveli, is one of Georgia's most sacred places. It stands on the site of earlier churches, including one made of wood in the 4th century AD and a three-nave basilica from 575 AD. Svetitskhoveli – or Cathedral of the Life-Giving Pillar – was built in 1010–29, incorporating the 6th-century church.

The name comes from the legend of two Georgian Jews sent to Jerusalem to decide Jesus' fate. They arrived too late, after the Crucifixion, but cast lots for the seamless tunic of Christ and brought it home to Georgia. Elioz Mtskheteli's sister, Sidonia, was so overcome by touching it that she died. Her grip on the sacred robe could not be loosened, and she had to be buried with it. A large Lebanese cedar grew from the tomb. When King Mirian converted to Christianity, he chose Sidonia's grave as the site for his church. He cut down the tree and made seven pillars from it as foundations for the church. The last pillar had magical properties and only returned to earth after Saint Nino prayed for a whole night. The pillar hovered in the air and was said to exude a sacred healing liquid, inspiring the cathedral's name.

Icon of Saint Nino in Mtskheta Cathedral

The magnificent cathedral is decorated with bas reliefs and contains precious icons and frescoes. Several Georgian kings were crowned and buried here. Only three tombs have been found, including those of King Vakhtang Gorgasali – the Wolf's Head – who founded Tbilisi, and Kings Erekle II and his son, Giorgi XII. Mtskheta is also where the Thirteen Assyrian Fathers first arrived in Georgia.

On the hill above Mtskheta is Jvari Monastery. Its panoramic position and the fine architecture of the 7th-century church make it an important destination. This is where Saint Nino first set up her cross, overlooking the pagan shrines of pre-Christian Mtskheta.

Opposite: Mtskheta Cathedral seen from across the river

On a more mundane level, there are food stalls along the street leading to Mtskheta's cathedral that sell good fruit leather and *chuchkhela*, the popular nut-filled 'candy' sticks.

Giorgi Barisashvili

WINE HISTORIAN
GIORGI BARISASHVILI

Giorgi 'Kvevri' Barisashvili is one of the leading experts on the history of wine in Georgia (see p. 25 for my interview with him). He's written books about wine made in the clay vessels that he prefers to spell as *kvevri* in English.

'Kvevri' as he likes to be called, has a fascinating collection of wine receptacles, old photographs and books. He's researched wine-related archælogical sites in Georgia and beyond and is a winemaker consultant to people making traditional wines. He lives in the centre of Mtskheta where his front garden is easy to spot: it's full of giant *kvevri*! He demonstrated how to drink from some of his collection of wine vessels. The ceramic *marani* he is using in the photo was used by families only on feast days.

Giorgi is a wonderful sharer of information about Georgia's wine history, but make an appointment to visit him, with interpreter. barisashvili@gmail.com

MUKHATGVERDI, MTSKHETA

RESTAURANT
SALOBIE

It may be hard to believe, but an eatery in the lay-by of a busy main road that's famous for selling stewed beans and dumplings is the most popular restaurant in Georgia. Salobie – even the name comes from *lobio*, or beans – is situated between Mtskheta and Tbilisi. Its vast hedge-lined car park is almost always full. The formula is simple: place and pay for your order, then sit at a table in the leafy terraces to wait for the food (it's most fun when the weather is good, but there are spaces indoors too). The kitchens are vast, the service is fast and efficient and the food is fresh and delicious.

Beans at Salobie

The stars on the menu have remained unchanged since Salobie opened in 1966. The famous beans come steaming in terracotta pots, with bread, salads and pickles available on the side. Large meat-and-broth *khinkali* have pliable dough so they're easy to eat correctly: by holding the dumpling from the stem (like an open umbrella), taking a cautious bite from the side rim to suck out the broth, and then biting into the meaty interior. Chargrilled pork *mtsvadi* and ground-meat kebabs are favourites too, with thin *lavash* bread and a loose tomato sauce (like a spicy juice) to pour into the wrapping around the meat.

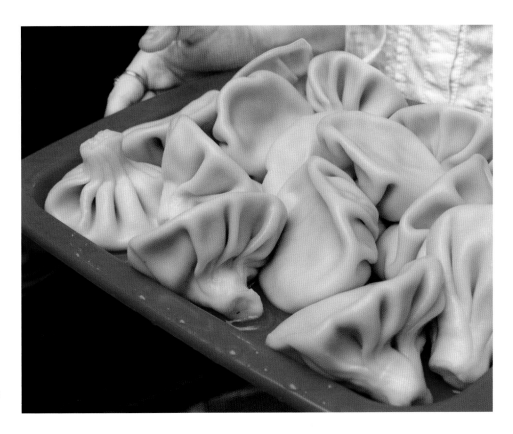

Khinkali are a speciality at Salobie

Beer and tarragon lemonade complete the picture. It's perfect for families and all ages. Salobie has been in the Togonidze family for three generations (Luarsab Togonidze is also a partner in Azarpesha and Polyphonia, see pp. 68 and 70 and a *tamada*, p. 29). It's the kind of relaxed, wholesome place you want to go back to as soon as you've left.
Tbilisi bypass road; tel: +995 555671977

JIGHAURA VILLAGE, SAGURAMO

VINE RESEARCH AND NURSERY
SRCA

One of the most impressive viticultural institutes I've seen in Georgia – or anywhere – is the Scientific-Research Centre of Agriculture (SRCA; formerly known as the National Centre for Grapevine and Fruit Tree Planting Materials). The centre operates on several levels. It houses the principal collection of native Georgian grapevines – about 437 of the over 500 known varieties – in ample vineyards covering 44 hectares in the valley near Saguramo (most Georgians refer to the centre as 'Saguramo'). The magnificent location, with a backdrop of mountains and the large Saguramo Nature Reserve nearby, provides a fitting setting for the precious vineyards. Many Georgian winemakers have explained how the rare variety collection was built up, vine by vine, by locating and taking cuttings from vines that had survived the Ottoman, phylloxera and Soviet eras. (Much of the collection has also been planted in other Georgian sites as prevention against disease or hail.) The collection was started in 2009.

The centre also reproduces the varieties to supply young vines to those wanting to re-establish them in areas where they have disappeared. During the Soviet era, Georgia's wine production involved less than a handful of varieties; only recently have efforts been made to expand the range again. In southern Georgia, where the Ottomans destroyed centuries-old vineyards, many varieties had all but disappeared. They are now being brought back with Saguramo's help.

Between 10 and 20 vines of each variety are planted in labelled rows to be studied; microvinifications analyse the wines' characteristics. The scientists have perfected a grafting system enabling them to propagate their cuttings. Rootstocks, germplasm and yeasts are studied, as are diseases and ways to resist them. The centre also works on international and table grapes and a myriad fruit varieties. There is a satellite weather station. The centre collaborates with many prestigious international research centres.

Top: A vineyard of Georgian varietals at SRCA

Bottom: Propagating vines, SRCA

Visits are possible by appointment and definitely of interest to wine enthusiasts and professionals. www.srca.gov.ge; info@srca.gov

CHARDAKHI

WINE, COOK
IAGO'S WINE: IAGO BITARISHVILI

Iago Bitarishvili is one of the natural winemakers who has most contributed to the growing popularity of Georgian *qvevri* wines. He was one of the first to bottle and sell his wines – and they are some of the best. And he and his wife, Marina Kurtanidze, quickly understood the power of sharing Georgia's culture of hospitality with their visitors. No one who has feasted under their pergola on meats grilled over vine prunings by Iago's father, and *khinkali* and vegetable dishes prepared by Marina and the women of the family, can forget that great experience. The couple have recently built a new tasting-dining room onto their cellar in the Mukhrani Valley.

"Wine tourism is incredibly important to us," Iago says. "There are no jobs available in these villages so it helps boost the sales from our bottles and it's a pleasure to offer home-cooked food with our wines." Iago began selling in 2003 but had always made some wine before that. His output has increased in recent years from 3,000 bottles in 2013 to almost 5,000 in 2015. "We have two hectares of vineyards – one is ours and one we rent – and we're not sure about getting bigger than that."

Iago Bitarishvili and qvevri

Iago is particularly known for his organic Chinuri, a white grape from Kartli. It has fine acidity and Iago works it in three versions: without skin contact; with 3 to 6 months of skin contact; and, most recently, as a naturally sparkling wine, or *pét nat*, shorthand for *pétillant naturel*. (See p. 112 for more on these wines.) Chinuri adapts admirably to all three, from the refreshing sparkler to the pure, mineral, skin-free version, to the more complex amber wine that retains its liveliness while accumulating layers of flavour, from warm spiced pears to hints of mint and honey.

Iago's wines are always clean and easy to drink. His cellar is unique: the bold striped rings around his *qvevri* necks remind me of the arches of the Great Mosque at Córdoba.

In addition to winemaking, Iago is involved in a national project to develop *qvevri* 'clusters', in which *qvevri* makers, viticulturists and winemakers will work together to promote and maintain this unique winemaking culture, which has been designated of Intangible Heritage by UNESCO. "I'll always be grateful to my father," Iago says. "He planted our vineyard fifty years ago, and it's the best present a parent could give his children!" Make a reservation to visit for a tasting with lunch or dinner, or a master-class on cooking or winemaking.
chardakhi@gmail.com; tel: +995 593352426

Marina Kurtanidze is the first woman in modern Georgia to make and bottle her own wine. She's married to Iago Bitarishvili (see previous pages) and helps run the family's winery. Like so many women in Georgia and beyond, she always has. She describes how the situation has recently changed for women in wine. "My husband and I both have other jobs but when it comes to our wine the whole family pitches in. Yet our wine is called 'Iago's Wine'. I mentioned that to a woman friend a few years ago who said: 'all the winemakers' wives are in the same situation. The men get all the glory. Let's make our own wine!' So Tea Melanashvili and I decided to do it together, beginning in 2012. We had to decide what style of wine we wanted as it was clearly not going to be done using our family vineyards."

Marina Kurtanidze

They were both fans of Mtsvane and decided to buy grapes from Kakheti. The wine is called ManDili, the word for the traditional scarf Georgian women use to cover their heads in church.

"Iago was supportive of our project," Marina says. "He's helped with technical knowledge when we've needed it. He takes our wine to fairs and even explains the important role women have always played in Georgian winemaking."

ManDili's first vintage was 2012 and produced 600 bottles. "We skipped 2013 because we were unknown so it was hard to sell the first lot, but in 2014 we were up to 1,000 and the demand is increasing. We're now buying grapes from a Kakhetian friend so we know how they're cultivated. The vines are 40 to 50 years old, and grow near Manavi, in western Kakheti. Our style? Very traditional: crushed grapes and six months of skin contact in *qvevri*."

Tasting the 2012 again in 2015, it had developed an amazing saffron-amber colour with an exotic nose of tea and apricots; the wine has real character with a subtle development over a strong backbone. It's an important wine in the chapter of women's winemaking too and is already inspiring other women to take to their *qvevri*.

ManDili wines are available at Ghvino Underground in Tbilisi (p. 67) and are being exported abroad. chardakhi@gmail.com; tel: +995 593352426. Marina generously shared three of her family recipes, which you'll find on the following pages.

*Opposite:
A* supra
*table at the
Bitarishvilis*

Walnut paste

NIGVZIS SAKMAZI   ნიგვზის საკმაზი

"This recipe is a cornerstone of much Georgian food, particularly in the central and western parts of the country," says Marina. "Each family has their own favourite recipe for it but the basic ingredients are good fresh walnuts, herbs, garlic and some spices. It's used on all sorts of vegetables, stirred into stews, and is a delicious condiment to have in the fridge to liven up hard-boiled eggs, cheese or cold meats." Use this as the basis for your own signature walnut paste, adding extra chilli, garlic, salt, herbs or spices to taste.

In Georgia tradition decrees that the walnuts should be pounded slowly by hand with the garlic and spices in a mortar and pestle, but a food processor makes an easy second choice if you don't have a good mortar.

Store the paste in an airtight jar in the fridge for 1–2 weeks, pressing a piece of plastic wrap right onto the paste to stop it oxidizing. You can also freeze this paste in small batches for later use.

For a great dipping sauce, combine 120ml/4fl oz/½ cup fresh pomegranate juice (the juice of about two pomegranates) with 120ml/4fl oz/½ cup of the paste.

MAKES **about 240ml/8fl oz/1 cup**
PREPARATION **10 minutes**

150g/5oz/1½ cups **walnut halves**
12g/⅓oz/3 **garlic cloves, or more to taste**
½ tsp **coriander seeds, crushed**
¼ tsp **ground fenugreek**
1 tsp **salt**
1 tbsp **chopped mint**
3 tbsp **chopped coriander/cilantro leaves**
1 tsp **minced dill**
fresh chilli, to taste
¼ cup **water**

Combine all the ingredients in the bowl of a food processor and pulse until you have an even paste. Some dishes are best with a more granular mixture while others call for a smoother texture – there are no rigid rules.

Store tightly wrapped with plastic wrap in the refrigerator for up to 2 weeks.

You can also freeze small batches of the paste, wrapped in foil for quick use at a later date.

This paste is quite concentrated and should always be loosened with a little water before being used, so follow individual recipes to see how much liquid is required.

Aubergine / eggplant rolls

NIGVZIANI BADRIJANI   ნიგვზიანი ბადრიჯანი

This classic recipe is found throughout Georgia as part of the vegetable starters for a *supra*. Small aubergines are sliced lengthwise, salted, rinsed and fried before being spread with walnut paste and rolled or folded. They're great with drinks before dinner too. If you don't have any walnut paste ready, make it while the aubergines/eggplants are being salted. By the way, the main reason to salt them nowadays is to reduce the amount of oil they absorb during frying. The bitterness has been bred out of most aubergines/eggplants.

MAKES **about 24**
PREPARATION **45 minutes**
  (including salting)
COOK **20 minutes**

500g / 1lb 2oz / about 7 small
  aubergines / eggplants
oil for frying
salt
1 recipe walnut paste
  (see pp. 100-101)
1 tbsp medium-hot red chilli
  pepper, minced (optional)
3 tbsp finely chopped basil
pomegranate seeds, to garnish

Wash the aubergines/eggplants and cut off their stems. Slice them lengthwise into 1-cm / ½-in slices, discarding the outer first and last slices. Sprinkle each slice with a little salt on both sides. Leave in a bowl for 30 minutes.

Rinse the slices very well under cold running water. Squeeze them in your hands to remove any excess water and pat dry with paper towels.

Heat about 1cm / ½in of oil in a frying pan. When it's hot enough (test this by dropping a small piece of bread or aubergine/eggplant in: it should immediately start to bubble and fry), lay the first batch of slices in, side by side. Don't crowd the pan or the oil will not be hot enough. Fry until golden, about 4 minutes per side. Remove to a paper towel and continue with the next batch, adding more oil as necessary.

Loosen the walnut paste with 2–3 tablespoons of water and stir in the red chilli and chopped basil.

When the aubergine/eggplant slices are cool, spread a spoonful of the walnut paste onto each slice, roll them up and decorate with pomegranate seeds or fresh herbs.

Aubergine / eggplant family style

BADRIJANI OJAKHURI   ბადრიჯანი ოჯახური

This colourful vegetable medley is a recipe from Marina's mother that stars aubergines/eggplants and sweet peppers. It goes wonderfully with grilled meats and *khachapuri*. For the tomato pulp, either peel and seed fresh tomatoes or strain imported canned plum tomatoes. The pulp should not be too juicy.

SERVES **6–8**
PREPARATION **25 minutes**
COOK **70 minutes**

900g / 2lb aubergine / eggplant
  (about 3 medium)
1 red pepper (about 150g / 5 oz)
1 yellow pepper (about 150g / 5 oz)
1 orange pepper (about 150g / 5 oz)
6 tbsp sunflower oil
1 tsp coriander seeds, crushed
15g / ½oz / 4 garlic cloves, or more
  to taste
480ml / 16fl oz / 2 cups chopped
  tomato pulp
30g / 1 oz / ½ cup chopped
  coriander / cilantro
30g / 1 oz / ½ cup chopped opal or
  green basil
15g / ½oz / ¼ cup chopped parsley
150g / 5 oz / 1½ cups walnut halves,
  ground
salt and freshly ground black
  pepper

Wash the aubergines/eggplants and, using a peeler, remove half of the peel, in long, alternating strips from top to bottom: they'll look like they're striped black and white. Cut the aubergines/eggplants into 2-cm/1-in cubes. Place them in a bowl and sprinkle lightly with salt. Set aside for 10 minutes.

Meanwhile, prepare the bell peppers. Wash, core and slice them into strips about 3cm/1½in long.

Rinse the aubergines/eggplants quickly in cold water. Shake off the excess water and turn them into a large frying or sauté pan with 3 tablespoons of the oil. Cover the pan and cook over medium heat, stirring and turning them occasionally, until they begin to brown evenly, about 25 minutes. When they're cooked through, remove them to a bowl.

Add 3 more tablespoons of oil to the pan with the peppers and coriander seed. Stir over medium heat until the peppers soften, about 20 minutes.

Stir the garlic into the chopped tomato pulp and add it to the pan with the peppers. Cook for 5 minutes before adding the herbs. Cook for a further 5 minutes before adding the aubergines/eggplants with their juices. When the vegetables are bubbling, stir in the ground walnuts.

Cook for 2–3 minutes more before turning off the heat. Check the seasoning, adding salt and freshly ground black pepper to taste. Let the vegetable mixture stand for at least 5 minutes before serving. Serve at room temperature or lightly chilled.

MUKHRANI

RESTAURANT, WINE
CHÂTEAU MUKHRANI

This historic, French-style wine château falls outside the focus of this book that, as I've explained, is about small family wineries working in traditional Georgian *qvevri*. Château Mukhrani, with its links to the royal Bagrationi dynasty and leading role in establishing European-style winemaking in Georgia, has played a part in the country's wine history: Prince Ivane Mukhranbatoni was influenced by his trip to Bordeaux and Champagne in the 1870s. The magnificent château (designed by French architects), with its well-tended gardens (originally designed by a Versailles gardener) and cellars with 60,000 barrels, is impressive. It offers many facilities, including a restaurant; there's also a wine bar in Tbilisi. www.chateaumukhrani.com

ON THE ROAD

Three of the principal roads in western Georgia converge at Khashuri's roundabout. That would be reason enough for street vendors in any country to hawk their wares. What makes this uniquely Georgian is the curious way that here, many people selling exactly the same things – from motor oil to

Nazuki
vendor

deck chairs – clump together in one short stretch of the road. How do they all make a living? On the road from Khashuri towards Surami in Imereti about 20 women on each side of the road stand precariously near the fast-moving traffic, waving what look like large shoe soles at the oncoming drivers. They are *nazuki*, a sort of sweetened bread that holds nostalgic sway over many Georgians. On my first trip there, my guide insisted on crossing to the far side of the road to get to her favourite vendor – with me in tow to take a photo – and we both risked our lives for what turned out to be a very uninspiring flat loaf painted with bland, spiced syrup. You've been warned!

GORI

Gori means hill and Gori's earliest fortifications were built on one: the Caucasian Iberians were besieged here in 65 BC by the Romans under Pompey the Great. King David the Builder established a city in 1123 in this strategic position on the main east–west route across Georgia; from the Middle Ages it was an important military stronghold. That didn't stop Gori being attacked through the centuries by Persians, Ottomans and Ossetians. The fortress was restored in 1774 under King Erekle II, then damaged badly in the 1920 earthquake. Most recently Gori was bombed and taken for 11 days in August 2008 by the Russians in the brief 2008 South Ossetian War. (It is very close to the border of the Tskhinvali region known as South Ossetia.)

Gori is the administrative capital of Shida Kartli, and has an imposing – if not overblown – town hall. Today the town is known as Joseph Stalin's birthplace. There is a museum dedicated to the dictator that I have not yet felt the urge to visit.

PATARA ATENI

WINE
GIORGI REVAZASHVILI'S MARANI

When I visit Giorgi Revazashvili at his home near Ateni, he's in the process of rebuilding his cellar and three large *qvevri* stand on the roof, wrapped to protect them from the rain before being buried. "They come from Imereti," the 24-year-old says proudly. Giorgi is one of the new generation of natural winemakers who are reclaiming their culture from the destruction of its recent history.

"Historically, Ateni was famous for grapes and Atenuri wine," says the tall, intense young man as he motions out over the landscape from our high vantage point at 720 metres (2,362 feet). "In Soviet times this was all apples, not vines any more, and recently many people have cut down whatever vineyards remained because of the low price of grapes." Giorgi wants to help relaunch his area. Only by making good, successful wines will the locals be inspired to follow.

Giorgi has less than one hectare of vines planted to three principal varieties: whites Chinuri and Goruli Mtsvane, and red Tavkveri. Atenuri, a historic wine named for this village, is a blend of Chinuri with Goruli Mtsvane (meaning 'green from Gori'). This Mtsvane has lots of fresh acidity and Atenuri is made by commercial wineries as a sparkling wine. Giorgi prefers it to be dry and still.

Tavkveri is another indigenous grape growing mainly in Kartli. It's light-bodied wine is bright, pale red with a floral nose and fresh flavours of hibiscus and cherries. It has a hint of spritz to it as is common with wines fermented in the cold Ateni autumn. (Giorgi is not currently doing long skin macerations on any of his wines.)

Giorgi's family vineyards average 40 years and are positioned high at 750 metres (2,460 feet). That's why his wines retain a lot of agreeable acidity: the big difference between day and night temperatures in summer, when the grapes are maturing, also helps the wines retain their perfumes. His vines are grown organically.

"That's what has always done here," he says as his 90-year-old grandfather appears on the terrace to greet the visitors. Giorgi towers above him but the old man is clearly proud of his grandson. He should be: since 2013, when Giorgi first started bottling, he has found importers in New York and Japan for some of the 1,000 bottles he's producing per year. He hopes to expand soon and add to his vineyards.
giorgirevazashvili@gmail.com

Top: Giorgi

Bottom: Giorgi's grandfather

DIDI ATENI

WINE AGRITOURISM
NIKA VACHEISHVILI'S MARANI

Ateni has long held a significant position in central Georgia, situated at a natural crossroads between the Lesser Caucasus and the wide Mtkvari River as it swings up and east from the south through Gori and Mtskheta towards Tbilisi. The Tana Gorge, behind Ateni Sioni church, was an important through route in earlier centuries. Ateni was developed by King Bagrat III and later by David the Builder, but irrigation pipes from the 1st century AD demonstrate the area's cultural importance much earlier. The very cold winters here allow the *qvevri* to undergo a unique cleaning process using ice from the river.

Nika Vacheishvili's fantastic property stands alone in this magnificent landscape, against a background of the craggy limestone of the Tana Gorge. It's a short drive from Ateni Sioni church. Nika Vacheishvili is a well-known figure in Georgia, an art scholar who served as the country's culture minister and now makes natural wines. Chinuri, Goruli Mtsvane, Budeshuri, Tavkveri and Atenuri Saperavi vines grow on terraces around the handsome house with its traditional wooden balcony.

The farm produces vegetables. In addition to his range of fine wines, Nika also sells cherry tincture and *chacha*. Visits, meals and tastings by appointment only. www.atenuri.ge, nvache68@yahoo.com, tel: +995 577270032

ATENI SIONI

It's the grape arbours you notice first in the roads around Ateni, with high pergolas in front of the houses that are used for wines made for family consumption. South of Gori the road leads towards the rugged Trialeti Range of the Lesser Caucasus, a landscape of limestone that closes around Ateni Gorge. Trialeti means 'a place of wandering', and its hills are thick with oak, beech and hornbeam; in summer the post-volcanic soils look arid. Nestled within the gorge is Ateni Sioni, a 7th-century church with beautiful pure lines. Its domed interior has eight columns and fine frescoes from the 11th century. The exterior is also in good condition, displaying rich carvings of animals and people. This is one of Georgia's loveliest churches, and well worth a detour.

UPLISTSIKHE

It's hard to imagine, as you scramble up and over the time-smoothed, pocked hilltop known as Uplistsikhe that in the Middle Ages it was home to 20,000 people, many of them artisans and merchants. These cave dwellings have ancient origins; they were carved from the stone in the first millennium BC. Uplistsikhe rises from the plain just a few kilometres from Gori, on what was once a key trade route from Byzantium to India and China. Now, like a giant sand sculpture half-erased by the waves, all that's left are tantalizing indications of a highly developed city. Here's a trace of the main avenue; that was the wine cellar; these pits were used for pagan rituals. A sharp-edged, 9th-century,

The view from Uplistsikhe

Uplistsikhe's caves and constructions are from different eras. The 9th- to 10th-century three-nave Christian basilica stands above much older rock carvings

three-church basilica stands at the top, dominating the organic swirls and hollows as rationally as stone and mortar can. It's even higher than Queen Tamar's Hall, an ample cave lower down that she never lived in.

The one thing the weather hasn't effaced is Uplistsikhe's strategic position. No wonder the citizens sheltered here during invasions. The wide views from the top stretch as far as the eye can see, while sheer rock drops precipitously down to the Mtkvari River below. There were moats too: they slowed but couldn't repel the 13th-century advances of Tamerlane, or Timur, and his conquering Mongols. Two centuries and several earthquakes later, the caves were fit only for shepherds harbouring from the rain.

GARIKULA

WINE, ABSINTHE
VINCENT JULIEN

Vincent's absinthe label

Vincent Julien was the first to bring the culture of naturally sparkling wines – called *pét nat* or *pétillant naturel* – from France to Georgia, and it's catching on. Several Georgian winemakers have followed suit. "These wines are made with the *méthode ancestrale* long used in the French countryside to make sparkling wines without added sugars or other alcohol," he says. Vincent also wanted to avoid using sulphites.

Vincent has recently created a cellar in Kakheti, at Sagarejo, 50 kilometres (31 miles) east of Tbilisi, but he's considered a Kartli producer because he vinifies grapes from Shida Kartli and makes wines with a friend at Garikula, 58 kilometres (36 miles) west of the capital.

"I buy organic grapes at Khandaki, between Ateni and Garikula, in an area known for its local whites, Goruli Mtsvane and Chinuri," he says. "Now I've built a cellar, I'll be doing the primary fermentation in *qvevri*, which is exciting." To make a *pét nat*, the wine is stopped from completing its fermentation and is bottled when the sugar content is still quite high and the wine is still fermenting. It gets 'locked' into the bottle as the fermentation continues. The CO_2 – the fermentation's natural by-product – remains, giving the wine its bubbles.

Vincent makes a personal wine, Kidev Erti, of Chinuri. "The name means 'one more' in Georgian: it's always nice to drink one more glass of it," he says. At Garikula Vincent makes a wine for his painter friend, Karaman Kutateladze, who runs the interesting Art Villa Garikula, an art centre with an annual modern art festival.

Vincent, who is originally from the Jura winemaking region, came to Georgia in 2006 as the director of classes at the French Embassy's cultural centre. "I had taught French as a foreign language and travelled a lot and I'd supplemented my earnings by pruning and harvesting in Burgundy and Champagne," he says. "I learned a lot!"

I first met Vincent at Ghvino Underground in Tbilisi (see p. 67), when the bottle he was holding caught my eye. Far from containing wine, this bottle is of absinthe, a drink that conjures the paintings of women with glazed looks by Pablo Picasso or Edgar Degas.

"I believe I'm the only absinthe producer in Georgia. The herbs for making it grow wild in the Caucasus – from *Artemisia absinthium* to fennel and green anise – so I gave it a try."

For the alcohol, Vincent uses triple-distilled Chinuri or Saperavi brandy. He blends the foraged plants and, after a short maceration, distils the liquid again. Other plants, including broom, colour the absinthe before it's aged, resulting in a drink that varies from green to yellow or light blue. "For now, I'm only selling in Georgia but interest is building!" Since the alcohol content is around 70% he recommends adding a little sugar, diluting the absinthe with ice-cold water and drinking it before dinner. "However, don't go beyond three glasses or you'll end up at 3 am spouting the poetry of Arthur Rimbaud." bonnaventure2002@yahoo.fr; www.garikula.com

KIKETI

WINE
TANINI; VINO

Kiketi village is in the Tbilisi district, but it's so close to Kvemo Kartli, I've brought Mariam Iosebidze into it too. This lovely young woman – and good friend – has created only the second Georgian winery to be run by a woman (after ManDili, see p. 99). Her uncle, Emzar Vasadze, produces his wine here in the cellar he built beside his wooden house and he's given Mariam two *qvevri* in it. He buys grapes from Kakheti for his wines, of Mtsvane, Rkatsiteli and Kartli Tavkveri, and has bought a vineyard there planted to Saperavi.

Mariam's first vintage was in 2014, of organic Tavkveri grapes she bought from Ateni, in Shida Kartli. "In Ateni they usually just crush the grapes and make the wines without skin contact, whereas in other parts of Kartli

Landscape near Kiketi

some people give the crushed grapes skin contact that lasts between two to three weeks. I wanted to do something in between," she says. Mariam used a destemmer but the grapes went into the *qvevri* with their skins. Two days after fermentation started, she began removing about half of the skins and, over the next five days, any skins that came to the surface were taken out. When she moved the wine from the big *qvevri* to a smaller one after fermentation, it was practically skin-free.

She has called her wine Vino: Mariam Iosebidze's Wine. "My *qvevri* can hold 570 litres so I'm able to make around 700 bottles," she says proudly a few weeks before her second harvest. I ask her to show me how she works using the traditional tools in the *qvevri*.

"The stick with layers of cherry bark on the end of it – it looks a bit like a rigid sponge – is for cleaning the *qvevri* at the end of the annual cycle; it's called *sartskhi*," she says. Hanging on the wall behind her is the *orshimo*, a scoop made from a dried-out gourd. "The stick with wooden spokes at the end is used to stir the fermenting grapes, and doesn't have a special name."

Mariam's god-daughter, Elene

Mariam's mother's family is originally from Racha, in the village near the exquisite church Nikortsminda (see pp. 384-85). "That village is around 1,100 metres in altitude – too high to cultivate grapes – but my great-grandfather grew them on a plot of family land in Bugeuli, near Ambrolauri, and would bring them to Nikortsminda to make into wine. "Unfortunately, during the difficult 1990s, our land was taken illegally and we have not been able to reclaim it. All that's left is a tiny parcel of about 500 square metres. It's overgrown and needs to be completely replanted but that's my dream and I hope soon to get started on it. I eventually want to make wine full time, it's my passion."

Mariam, who speaks English fluently, studied Japanese and International Relations with a focus on the Far East at the Tbilisi Free University. She went on to work for a company doing tours for Japanese people in Georgia but after a few months, she joined Living Roots, the tour company focused on traditional Georgian culture, foods and wines, run by Ia Tabagari and John Wurdeman of Pheasant's Tears (see pp. 166-68).

"I was really thrown into the natural wine movement and I soaked up as much information as I could from John and the winemakers I met at Ghvino Underground (see p. 67). They've been so supportive of my desire to make wine: it's not usual yet for women to do this in Georgia, but I'm sure that's about to change." mariamiosebidze@gmail.com

Opposite: Mariam Iosebidze with wine-making tools

TAMARISI (MARNEULI)

WINE
DASABAMI:
ZAZA DARSAVELIDZE

Zaza Darsavelidze picks me up in Tbilisi on the October afternoon I'm to visit his cellar in Kvemo Kartli. Zaza's a military man and he drives assertively out of town into the suddenly parched landscape south of the city. We're en route for Zaza's village, Tamarisi, but after a few minutes we stop at Shavnabada Monastery, positioned high on a rock looking back towards Tbilisi. Mama Gregori, in long black robes, proudly shows us the historic *qvevri* cellars. The monk is apologetic but they've just finished harvesting and he doesn't want me to take pictures. The handsome monastery is open to visitors, for those who wanting to see the cellars.

Shavnabada Monastery

We head south past a roadside shrine that prompts Zaza to say: "The giant statue of a woman that stands on the hill above Tbilisi is called Kartlis Deda, the Mother of Georgia. She holds a bowl of wine in one hand and a sword in the other. That's a double message: come as a friend and you'll share our wine; come as an enemy and you'll feel our sword. She tells her sons to defend their motherland. I'm a soldier and I fought in the Abkhazia war." He pauses. "It was very hard."

Dark clouds are forming but there's no rain. "This area has long summers," Zaza says. He's just finished harvesting and talks about the hot 2015 season. "We're at 300 to 400 metres (980-1,300 feet) above sea level, so our vineyards have enough breezes to cool the grapes and stop them from being 'cooked' by the sun. In winter it's very cold but we don't get much snow."

The light is starting to fade in Tamarisi, so we set off for the vineyards, reached on foot through their back garden. There are geese and chickens, and a vegetable patch whose summer abundance is over. Zaza's eight-year-old son, Saba, skips ahead to unlock the gate as we reach the vineyard.

"These are Rkatsiteli vines planted by my father 65 years ago," Zaza says of the neat rows. Grass grows underfoot and the plants look balanced and healthy. Their long arms send up evenly spaced canes; it's a refreshingly different style of viticulture from the competitive, high-density plantings so prevalent in France and even Italy. Zaza's late father was a winemaker and agronomist and had one hectare here. He planted whites Rkatsiteli and Mtsvane, and red Tavkveri. Six years ago Zaza added white Khikhvi.

"We only produce small quantities," he says. "In 2014 there were 2,300 bottles; in 2015 it was less than half that amount." Zaza bottles his wines under the Dasabami label and exports them to Japan and Australia. His usual annual output is around 2,500 bottles.

Zaza removes his shirt to do a bit of hoeing before sitting under a mulberry tree, where he pulls a bottle of *chacha* out from under a bush. His son runs to sit beside him. "I have three children," Zaza says. "Two teenage daughters and this young boy who I'm glad to say is following in my footsteps. He already has his own small *qvevri* in the cellar next to my big ones and he makes a little wine; he loves to help with the harvest too," he adds proudly, as he pours himself a small glassful.

We head back to the house to see the cellars before dinner. There are two *qvevri* cellars: one at ground level, outside, and another under the house. The largest *qvevri* holds 600 litres (132 gallons). "My family is from Imereti originally," Zaza says as we perch in the underground cellar to taste wine. "My grandfather came here 70 years ago, built the house and planted the vineyards. He dug up and brought very old *qvevri* with him, some of which are 300 years old." Zaza now buys his new *qvevri* from the potter Zaliko Bozhadze, in Imereti (see pp. 239-41). The tops of Zaza's *qvevri* are sealed with clay, with fresh mint and walnut branches stacked on top. "That's a traditional trick to keep ants and other insects away from the wine." I ask him when he started bottling, and why.

Top to bottom: Zaza hoeing; one of his vines; his tool collection

"I first bottled my wines in 2011. This is not a wine area any more but, like Meskheti in south-western Georgia, it was once a lively wine-producing region. During Soviet times all the private vineyards were confiscated and turned into 'factory' wines and since then it's all been destroyed. In Marneuli all they know about now is war." Zaza is currently the only producer in Kvemo Kartli bottling *qvevri* wines, though many people make unbottled wine for their families in other kinds of containers.

Zaza and Saba in the vineyard

"Luckily I met Ramaz Nikoladze (see pp. 262-65), the Imeretian winemaker, who tasted the wines and encouraged me to bottle them," he continues. "I think Ramaz has speeded up the *qvevri* wine world here by ten years. Without him it all would have been much slower to evolve. The same is true of John Wurdeman (p. 166): he's a wonderful ambassador for Georgia's wines."

Before dinner Saba wants me to taste his wine. He eagerly sets about removing the *qvevri*'s clay seal and scoops out a small glassful for each of us. Zaza and I sniff it and exchange looks: we're complimentary to the child but he's opened his *qvevri* so often the wine is practically vinegar. Saba drinks most of his.

During dinner we sample the 2014 Khikhvi, a Kakhetian grape. It's a deep golden-pink colour that reminds me of a natural Pinot Grigio. It had six months of skin contact and is still evolving, with long clean acidity and floral and mineral notes. The oldest wine he has is the 2012 Mtsvane. It's deep orange in colour, with an aromatic character and finesse. It goes well with the lovely meal Zaza's wife, Tea, has prepared for us and for Zaza's elderly mother.

Tea is originally from Racha so we're treated to an excellent *lobiani*, or bean pie, and to wild tree mushrooms flavoured with the family's walnuts and fenugreek, among other dishes. Zaza proposes a toast to the family, then he holds up his glass and says: "I don't like my wines, I love them! They're like children: even when they are problematic, we still adore them."

MENU

Tomato, red pepper and cucumber salad
Wild tree mushrooms with walnuts
Lobiani *bean pie from Racha*
Khachapuri
Aubergine/eggplant in walnut sauce
Fermented green beans
Cheese

Zaza's wife, Tea, at the dinner table

BOLNISI AND DMANISI

The carved-stone Bolnisi Sioni Church from the late 5th century is the oldest church in Georgia. Pagan and Christian symbols can be found inside the church, in carved stone pillars and capitals, and in relief sculptures. The inscription over the portal is the earliest extant example – in the Asomtavruli script – of written Georgian in Georgia (there is an earlier example in Palestine); the original is in the Georgian National Museum, in Tbilisi.

In medieval times, Dmanisi was the region's largest fortified town, an important commercial centre on a volcanic plateau at the crossroads of trading routes and rivers. The large town's remains occupy a 13-hectare site and include a citadel, baths, a palace and a 6th-century three-nave basilica. Beneath the ruins of the medieval town is a Lower Palæolithic site that is still being excavated and in which five hominid skulls from 1.77 million years ago have been found, giving this region one of the richest archæological patrimonies outside Africa. The small and small-brained hominids whose skulls were found died at different ages and predate Homo Erectus. The most significant finds – tools from 2 million years ago and the skulls – are on show in Tbilisi at the Georgian National Museum which now manages the site at Dmanisi. A Palæoanthropology Field School is held in summer here for students and anyone interested in these studies. www.dmanisi.ge

3. EAST TO KAKHETI

Akhmeta   p. 129
Alaverdi   p. 133
Artana   p. 142
Bakurtsikhe   p. 158
Bodbe   p. 179
Bodbiskhevi   p. 180
Davit-Gareja   p. 193
Dedoplistskaro   p. 180
Diklo   p. 129
Eniseli   p. 155
Gombori   p. 147
Gremi   p. 155

Ikalto   p. 145
Kardanakhi   p. 158
Khornabuji   p. 180
Kisiskhevi   p. 154
Kvareli   p. 125
Kvemo Alvani   p. 135
Kvemo Magharo   p. 181
Lagodekhi   p. 157
Laliskuri   p. 135
Lopota   p. 125
Manavi   p. 184
Mirzaani   p. 179

Napareuli   p. 125
Nekresi   p. 157
Sabue   p. 155
Sagarejo   p. 112
Shalauri   p. 152
Shuamta   p. 147
Sighnaghi   p. 159
Telavi   p. 151
Tusheti   p. 126
Vardisubani   p. 145
Zemo Alvani   p. 129

This chapter explores the largest region in Georgia and the one in which most wine – including traditional *qvevri* wine – is made. The long, wide Alazani River that runs south-east from the high mountains of Tusheti in the Greater Caucasus down through Kakheti's main valley on its way to Azerbaijan (and then the Caspian Sea) has determined the success and style of its agriculture and the course of its history. Kakheti formed part of Kartli-Iberia until the middle of the 8th century when it became a self-governing feudal principality. In 1105 King David the Builder conquered Kakheti and incorporated it into a united Georgian kingdom; there it remained until it fell during the Mongol invasions of the 13th century. It became an independent kingdom in the 1460s before coming under intermittent Persian rule in the following centuries.

Road vendor selling wild straw-berries

Today Kakheti is at the forefront of Georgian wine tourism, with offerings ranging from the family and independent winemakers working in *qvevri* – the focus of this book – to European-style château resorts. Between visits to over ten wineries here – including Alaverdi's historic monastery, where wine-making has taken place at least since 1011 – we visit a *qvevri* maker, explore two of the country's biggest food markets and travel to the distinctive towns of Telavi and Sighnaghi. Along the way are important cultural and historical sites – including the tomb of Saint Nino at Bodbe Monastery – and an extensive nature reserve on the border with Azerbaijan that is home to 150 species of bird.

The roads from Tbilisi and along the Alazani Valley are full of small bakeries and impromptu food stalls selling everything from just-picked yellow cherries (in June) to foraged oyster mushrooms (in autumn). There are butchers whose wares hang in muslin to keep off the flies, and dangling *churchkhela* – strings of nuts dipped in condensed fruit juice – that make chewy snacks for the drive. On clear days, they're all framed by the ever-present mountains that form Kakheti's stunning natural backdrop.

KAKHETI AND ITS WINES

Previous pages: John Wurdeman in the vineyard at Pheasant's Tears

In the *Encyclopædia Metropolitana*, published in London in the mid 1800s, Kakheti's current capital, Telavi, is described as "overlooking a beautiful valley, richly clothed in plantations of forest trees, many of them supporting vines which, in the time of vintage, hang in festoons from branch to branch weighed down by their clusters." If the grapes no longer hang from trees,

Harvest at Pheasant's Tears

they do still cover large swathes of the imposing Alazani Valley, and represent the region's most important natural currency.

Kakheti's annual turnover from wine production was $100 million in 2015 from vineyards owned by 20,000 farmers. Extensive vineyards are planted all along the valley, many of which were used in Soviet times for state-run collective wineries. Some have since been broken into parcels and offered to local people to rent or buy at advantageous prices. Others are farmed by the so-called 'wine factories' that produce vast quantities of inexpensive commercial wine for export. A tiny percentage of the whole is grown organically for wines made in *qvevri*.

Of Georgia's over 500 known and catalogued grape varieties, 88 are from Kakheti. Many are obscure and barely cultivated but that's not the case with three of the country's most popular and widely grown: the whites Kakhuri Mtsvane and Rkatsiteli, and the red Saperavi. Kakheti accounts for the lion's share of the yield of 100 million litres (*c.* 22 million gallons) produced in Georgia in 2015, with Rkatsiteli responsible for 55 percent and Saperavi for 30. Kakheti also has the largest number of Protected Designations of Origin (PDO) in the country, with 14 of the total 18.

Climate is a dominant feature in Kakhetian viticulture: far inland, away from the seas, the hot dry summers encourage the full ripening of the grapes – and their stems – which makes the whole-bunch style of maceration possible here. There's also a connection between Kakheti's terroir and its diet: this region favours meats and strong, sharp sheep's cheeses that go better with the deeper, more structured wines that are obtained through long macerations.

Kakheti's range of viticultural situations is diverse. The soils are variable but limestone and humus-carbonate are found throughout, as are sandstone and volcanic areas. There is some quartz amid the sandstone, and black sand from slate on the side of the valley nearest the mountains. Sediment cones also provide fertile bases for vines growing between 350 and 700 metres (1,500 to 3,000 feet) and over.

WINERY AND SPA STAYS

This chapter, like the rest of the book, is focused on visits to individual natural winemakers. However, there is so much wine activity in Kakheti that I've also included a few other wineries for historical reasons or because they offer accommodation. These include Château Eniseli-Bagrationi (pp. 155-56); Château Schuchmann (p. 154); Château Mere (p. 151).

Other wineries to stay in or visit: Hotel Twins Old Cellar Winery at Napareuli displays halved *qvevri* showing how wine is made inside the clay vessels: www.cellar.ge. Kvareli Eden Wine Spa luxury hotel and spa features 25 treatments and therapies from the grapes' natural properties: www.kvarelieden.ge. Lopota Lake Resort offers a relaxing place to recover from all the wine and food, with swimming pools, a lake and full-service spa: www.lopota.ge

KAKHETI FOOD AND HISTORY

A prosperous monarchy on the Silk Road from medieval times, Kakheti's fortunes rose and fell as it battled waves of aggressors. In the 14th century, Timur, the Turco-Mongol nomadic conqueror of the Eurasian Steppes, devastated the area. So too did the Safavid monarch, Shah Abbas (whose mother was Georgian), when he laid waste to the region in 1615. Tens of thousands of people were killed or deported, and Kakheti's population was decreased by two-thirds. The Kingdom of Kakheti was ruled by the Bagrationi family from the late 15th century. In 1762 King Erekle II Bagrationi (known as 'the Little Kakhetian') united the kingdoms of Kartli and Kakheti, allowing them in 1783 to become a protectorate of Catherine the Great's Russia. That didn't last long: the Russians soon withdrew their support and when the

King Erekle II in Telavi

Persians invaded Georgia in 1795, King Erekle was defeated and Tiflis (Tbilisi) razed to the ground. Soon afterwards, in 1801, the Russian tsar Paul I fully annexed Kartli-Kakheti and deposed the Bagrationi dynasty, ending its millenium-long history.

John Wurdeman V, of Pheasant's Tears winery (see p. 166) in Sighnaghi, theorizes that Kakheti's culinary preferences are linked to its history. "Georgia was mainly attacked from the east," he says. "Kiziqi, as the area around Sighnaghi was called, was a region of warriors who fought to defend this eastern 'gate' from the Arab Caliphates, Persians, Mongols, Khazars and more. As a result, the fighting men here were exempted from paying taxes and had no overlords. They paid their tax in blood. In times of peace, they were affluent and powerful; in times of war, they were battered.

"With these bands of men constantly traversing the Alazani Valley on guard against marauders, there wasn't time for the niceties of cooking, for making complex spice blends or sauces. What would men like that prefer? Meat on a stick! They could hunt, kill and roast. Today those dishes are still the favourites here, ideally cooked over fires of grape-vine prunings."

Kebabs and other roasted meats are hugely popular in Kakheti. You'll see – and smell – meats being grilled on impromptu barbecues around the region, including along the roadsides. Thanks to the transhumant Tushetians, the region is well stocked with mutton, goat and beef. Pork too is a favourite here – apart from in Tusheti, where it is neither eaten nor welcome. Any visitor to the meat sections of Kakheti's colourful markets (see Telavi, p. 151, and Bodbiskhevi, p. 180) will be amazed at the quantity and quality of the meats on offer, complete with stories about how and where the animals lived. Water buffalo live in southern areas of the region, providing some meat and the delicious yogurt that accompanies Kakhetian dishes so well. Like other less agricultural areas, the Pankisi Gorge – which is inhabited by the Kists, of Chechen origin – is known for its wonderful wildflower honeys.

Mtsvadi, meat on a stick

TUSHETI

Opposite: Autumn herds in the Alazani Valley near Telavi

Tusheti is a spectacular mountainous region in the North Caucausus where small villages at nearly 2,000 metres (6,562 feet) nestle in valleys surrounded by soaring peaks of up to 4,800 (15,748 feet). The Tushetians were effectively an autonomous regional group until the late 17th century. They divide into two main groups, the Chagma- and the Tsova-Tush. (The Tsova speak Bats, a Nakh language related to Chechen and Ingush, whereas the Chagma speak a Georgian dialect.)

Pastoralist near Alvani

Tushetians live in four principal valleys. The landscape is punctuated by historic tall stone watchtowers used to warn the valleys of invasions. Their remote location and independent spirit protected the Tushetians from full domination by the Kakhetian princes. Their recent history has been troubled: the Soviets threatened and disrupted their traditional lifestyle.

Tusheti is the most difficult place in Georgia to reach. It takes a five-hour drive up a perilous road to get there through a pass that's only open in summer. But it's beautiful and suits intrepid, fit adventurers who love the outdoors and the simple life. Tusheti is great for horse riding, hiking and camping. In summer, traditional mountain festivals welcome many Tushetians now living in the Alazani Valley, who keep strong cultural ties to their homelands.

Bordering Chechnya and Dagestan to its north and east, Tusheti has undergone many upheavals during the last century as Soviet and post-Soviet policies towards highland communities fluctuated. From the 1920s to '40s, the emphasis was on leaving the Tushetians in the high mountains, intensifying production there and fighting private property and wealth. Better-off Tushetians with large herds who employed pastoralists were deprived of voting rights for eight years and saw their herds limited to ten sheep, five cows, one horse and a donkey each, making it impossible to profit from the private economy. Anyone who resisted was killed, jailed or sent to Siberia.

By the 1950s and '60s, high mountain residents were forced down to the valley to work in collective factories as repressive, controlling measures were applied to the Tushetians. Refusing meant losing claims to pastureland. Down in the Alazani Valley villages, agro-cities with centralized planning were created. Some Tushetians stayed in the mountains to keep cultural traditions alive.

In a mid-1970s reversal, the government decided to resettle Tusheti's highlands for political and strategic reasons. Tourism began to be encouraged. A road fit for cars (albeit only 4 x 4s) was completed in 1981 and electricity was supplied to the high villages. Some families moved back up as the infrastructure improved.

Unfortunately, the end of the Soviet Union left highland Tusheti in a bitter-sweet situation. Tushetians regained their freedom to live where they wanted but highland services declined. The loss of electricity was crippling. The Alazani Valley offered them stability and better services. Those who remained faced other problems: after the political borders with Dagestan and Chechnya were closed, seasonal pasturelands became inaccessible.

Today, as tourism increases in Georgia, Tusheti's highlands offer remote guest houses and unspoiled highlands and are on UNESCO's Tentative World Heritage list. A WWF ecotourism project near Diklo focuses on sustainable honey and traditional carpet making to boost the local economy.

The Tushetian pastoralists try to continue their seasonal transhumance, alternating between summer highland and winter lowland pastures but it's harder now, with fewer services – electricity, water and vets – to facilitate their journeys.

ZEMO ALVANI

WINE
TSIKHELISHVILI WINES

Aleksi 'Lexo' Tsikhelishvili was born in Alvani, in the northern Alazani River Valley near Akhmeta. His grandparents were Tsova-Tushs and were originally pastoralists in the Tusheti highlands.

"I'm not sure why they moved down here in the early 20th century," says Lexo as we sit in his handsome house. "Maybe it was to avoid the harsh winters. But the Russians were also forcing the independent-minded highlanders down where they'd be easier to control. Many upper villages were abandoned, most disappeared with their names forgotten."

Before becoming a professional winemaker, Lexo worked variously as a vet, in a quarry and producing sun-dried apples for the Georgian army during Soviet times. What made him switch?

"My father made *qvevri* wines before that tradition started dying out in the 1960s," he says, as he

Lexo Tsikhelishvili

serves a white Mtsvane 2014 and slices of *kalti*: pungent Tushetian sheep's curd cheese. Despite its age, the deep amber wine feels young: with three months of skin contact it's rich, clean and has fine structure and tannins.

Lexo's ancient vines

"We always had some vines but in 1996 the government redistributed the Soviet collective vineyards and each Tushetian family was given half a hectare with a 49-year lease – after which we'll be allowed to buy the vineyards. My father-in-law and I each got some – for a total of one hectare."

The year 2009 was a turning point. "Before then I made family-style wine, in barrels. My friend, Soliko Tsaishvili, encouraged me to continue the *qvevri* tradition. We compared our wines. Microclimates and soils do vary but, using the same Rkatsiteli variety from the same valley, albeit 75 kilometres apart, the main difference was between barrels and *qvevri*." Lexo switched and now has seven *qvevri* buried outdoors; he produces around 3,000 bottles per year. In 2012 he bought another hectare (2½ acres) across the valley at Khodasheni.

Lexo currently makes three wines: Rkatsiteli, Mtsvane and Jghia (Jgia), a local red variety he found planted among the Rkatsiteli. He picks the whites first. "My vineyards were planted with 80 percent Rkatsiteli in 1982, during Soviet times, but we've found many minor varieties among it." Jghia is interesting, with good acidity and a nose of aromatic black pepper. He picks it when sugar levels are higher, in mid-October. Lexo exports his wines to many countries and sells at Ghvino Underground (see p. 67), among others.

Outside, the admirable 150 year-old vine that covers the yard's vast pergola is a good example of the vines that resisted phylloxera and helped save many ancient varieties throughout Georgia. "2009 was my first year working with *qvevri* but it seemed familiar to me, a link to my childhood. Soon I'll dig a new cellar three metres undergound for the *qvevri*: temperature is problematic in our hot summers and I want to keep my wines naturally cool and stable." alexi-57@mail.ru; tel: +995 551907959

WINE
LAGAZI WINES:
SHOTA LAGAZIDZE

Shota Lagazidze is a young natural winemaker: he made his first organic *qvevri* wines in 2015. Shota and his father, Eristo, built a cellar onto the family's lovely 1926 house in Zemo Alvani and Shota travels between there, Tbilisi and Sighnaghi. In 2013 he founded the Agri-Tourism Farms Association to help artisan producers and rural farmers improve communications and promotion. It currently has 30 members. He also worked at Ghvino

Underground where he met John Wurdeman and other winemakers.

Shota and his partner in Lagazi wines, Dato Pakhuridze, share a passion for wine. "Now we're aiming to sell it too," Shota says as we cross the Alazani Valley's expansive vineyards to Oboldziani, where the two have bought a half-hectare plot.

It's late autumn and Shota's first harvest is one week away. Most growers have finished harvesting and the guard they hire to discourage grape theft has left for the season. Shota and Dato's vines belonged to a vast, now-disbanded Soviet wine 'factory'. Their grapes are healthy and ripe.

"We have mainly Rkatsiteli," he says, tasting the rich, golden grapes. I notice different varieties amongst the Rkatsiteli, including violet-pink bunches of the increasingly popular Vardisperi Rkatsiteli and blackish-blue Jghia. Lagazi's first wine is Rkatsiteli 2015, along with 100 bottles of a Jghia-Saperavi blend. In 2016 they plan to bottle some Kakhuri Mtsvane too.

Like most people in the Alvani villages, Shota's family is Tushetian and he's worked many summers in the highlands, guiding visitors through the mountains to Khevsureti. Shota was my travelling companion for most of the research trips for this book, and often talked about Tusheti.

"Tushetians are pastoralists," he says. "Tushetian houses were built of stone to protect against their enemies and because there was little wood. Most were built by Dagestani stonemasons. When Tushetians moved down to the Alazani Valley, they lacked the skills for building wooden houses and hired carpenters from Racha in western Georgia.

Top to bottom: Shota's vineyard; his assorted grapes; the Lagazidze family

"Georgian people always fight for their freedom. Mountain people are wilder; in Tusheti 12 elders governed the local population but that didn't suit the Soviets who wanted centralized powers. People in the highlands were both rich and poor. My Tushetian great-grandfather, also named Eristo, was rich, with 2,000 sheep. In the mid 1930s, when the Soviets cracked down on private property and implemented collectivization in Tusheti, he was told to renounce his property or have it forcibly removed.

He refused and one night in 1936, the KGB came for him; he jumped from the balcony and fled. He spent seven years on the run, changing his name and going to work in Pshavi (a mountainous area south-west of Tusheti in today's Mtskheta-Mtianeti region).

"Sadly, a friend betrayed him, he was captured and told to 'admit' that the government had been right. He refused and was sent to Siberia. Meanwhile, my great-grandmother brought up her four children alone."

Shota's grandfather, Shota, was 20 when his father returned, but didn't recognize him when they crossed paths in the village. Eristo died soon afterwards from the deprivations of Siberia. Shota's grandfather married a Gurian gynæcologist and became an influential vet, following the animals' transhumance from summer to winter pastures.

"The Alvani area is too hot for the herds in summer, so they pass through in spring and autumn but in winter they are taken to the hills at Shiraki, in the Vashlovani National Park near Azerbaijan, that were awarded to them after the legendary battle at Bakhtrioni in 1659 when the Tushetians helped the Kakhetians fend off the Persians."

Shota was born in 1990 and grew up in what are often called the 'Black '90s', a period of corruption, political instability and lack of electricity and gas for most Georgians. He heard of people going to jail for listening to the Beatles. His father worked numerous jobs before the American Mercy Corps helped him buy 200 sheep. He is now head of Tusheti's Protected Landscape project, overseeing villages and agricultural areas in the highlands.

Top: Supra table in the Lagazidze home

Below: Room on the ground floor of the house

"I've grown up with these stories. They've made me determined to work for my family's future, and to help build sustainable rural tourism and the natural wines that are bringing so many interesting people and opportunities to Georgia." shotikolagazidze@gmail.com; tel: +995 551940217

ALAVERDI

In the new movement of Georgian *qvevri* wines of the last 15 years, no institution has become as well known or been as symbolically important as the Alaverdi Monastery. The rebirth of this ancient art – which never stopped or disappeared completely – assumes a different dimension when you see it being practised within the walls of a majestic 11th-century monastery. Their *qvevri* wines, bottled and sold under the "Since 1011" brand are exported internationally and the monastery remains a must-see destination for visitors to Georgia, both for religious culture and wine.

The earliest religious structures on the site date to the 6th century and are credited to Joseph of Alaverdi, one of the Thirteen Assyrian Fathers said to have come as missionaries from Mesopotamia. In the early 11th century, a new cathedral dedicated to Saint George was built here during Georgian unification by King Kvirike III of Kakheti. Alaverdi is a royal monastery and was used to crown the east-Georgian kings. It's a fine example of Georgian medieval architecture and was the country's tallest church until 2004 when Tbilisi's catheral was consecrated. The unadorned exterior reveals a frescoed interior though much of the painting was sadly lost

Top: Monastery's external wall with bee hives; bottom: vegetable garden inside the monastery

in the 19th century when the interior was heavy handedly white-washed during 'Russianization'. The church has undergone many periods of restoration. It was proposed as a UNESCO World Heritage Site in 2004.

Recent archæological digs, in which an early cellar of different-sized *qvevri* was found, have revealed that the monastery has been making wines

*Mama
Gerasim
in the
monastery's
wine cellar*

since at least the 8th century. Over 50 ancient *qvevri* have been discovered buried in the grounds.

The most recent chapter in the monastery's history started in 2005 when it became a functioning monastery again after the Soviet period. The 11th-century cellar was completely restructured and winemaking renewed. Today the wines are made by Father Gerasim, with the external help of winemaker Teimuraz Glonti.

"When Bishop Davit told me I could make wine in the monastery, I was speechless," Father Gerasim says enthusiastically as he shows us the monastery's *qvevri* room. "All my life I had wanted to make wine, on the outside too. When I decided to be a monk winemaker, I was afraid I'd feel lost in that big universe. To my surprise, all winemakers here have similar ideas. They have open-heartedly shared their experience with us. Beyond that you need hard work, but if the heart is pure… As for the grapes we use, our neighbours like to give their best grapes to the monastery but we are also buying vineyards now." Within the monastery walls, a vine 'collection' has been planted with over 70 local varieties.

We discuss the reception their wines have been receiving. "We know that *qvevri* wines are different from western styles and sometimes we're judged by people who are not familiar with ours," Father Gerasim says. "Personally I wouldn't want to judge something that was unfamiliar and that I didn't understand. That's why we like to take time to explain about this ancient method."

Bishop Davit takes up the theme: "How did Georgia manage to keep this method alive?" he asks. "Why is it not more in use? The *qvevri* tradition is about humility, not the promotion of individuals. It's an ancient tradition and wine was part of the sacred liturgy with roots at Alaverdi from the 6th century. Traditionally, each monk is allowed 500 grams per day of red wine. For us, the relationship with wine symbolizes a connection to God. We believe that man was formed from clay and returns to clay when he dies. In Hebrew, Adam means red earth, or clay, and it's in association with him that labouring for food – or farming – is first mentioned."

Bishop Davit continues: "We want to continue the 8,000-year tradition of winemaking because it is sacred. To us, wine is more than a beverage. Each monastery in Georgia had its own wine, cellar and vineyards. When we see monasteries in other countries, if we find *qvevri*, it shows they were Georgian monks."

At its peak, Alaverdi Monastery could accommodate 500 monks; today there are just five residents who are helped by nuns from a nearby convent as well as local volunteers. They make wine and honey, tend a large vegetable garden and prepare meals for the monastery's many guests.

In 2013 I attended a *supra* at Alaverdi to celebrate the second International Qvevri Symposium. It was a jolly affair, with monks and guests eating together in the large vaulted refectory. We were served Alaverdi's Rkatsiteli 2012 to accompany the many delicious dishes prepared by the nuns. The grapes ferment in *qvevri* with their stems and skins for six or more months of skin contact. The wine is unfiltered and has minimal sulphites. Alaverdi's wines include Rose Rkatsiteli, Kakhuri Mtsvane, Rkatsiteli, Kisi, Khikhvi and Saperavi. From the high table, the bishop led the toasts. One was "to Georgian wine and to Georgia, that has kept this tradition alive this long". After the meal the monks and guests convened in the monastery garden, swapping smartphone photos and exchanging email addresses.

The monastery has recently opened its Matsoni Café, beside the monastery's entrance gate. *Matsoni* is yogurt and the monastery's strain is apparently ancient. The lovely café serves *matsoni* with dried fruits or the monks' honey, *matsoni* ice cream, homemade pies and breads. It's open 10:00–18.00 in winter and 10:00–23:00 in summer. The cathedral is open to the public and contains many precious icons and reliquaries. Wine tours and tastings are possible but must be booked in advance and are better value for a group of eight rather than four people. www.since1011.com

THE LUNCH SUPRA MENU

Roast quail
Cold fried fish
Hot mushrooms
Nettle pkhali
Stuffed vine leaves
Tomato and cucumber salad
Bundles of sliced sulguni *cheese*
Aubergine salad
Khachapuri
Assorted fermented vegetables and flowers
Cheese

LALISKURI (LALIS QURI)

TUSHETIAN COOKING
DAREJANI ITCHIRAULI

Darejani Itchirauli is a lovely Tushetian woman who spent a morning with me cooking traditional recipes in her valley kitchen. From universal ingredients – flour, butter, cheese, potatoes – she created food that spoke of a different terroir and way of life.

"These are my grandmother's highland recipes," she says, kneading the dough for potato-filled *khinkali*. "We're from the Chagma-Tush branch of Tushetians, and we speak the local Georgian dialect." Darejani worked in California and also speaks some English. "Some ancestors came down from the mountains in the early 1800s, to land that had been awarded to the Tushetians in the 17th-century in return for their fearless fighting against the Persians in the 1659 Battle of Bakhtrioni." Many Tushetians still return to the high mountains in summer, keeping the ancient traditions alive.

Darejani sampling khinkali

"This is high-calorie food for people tending flocks or working outdoors," she says. "There wasn't much wheat in Tusheti so we had thin egg pancakes, *machkatebi*, filled with *khavisti* – melted cheese and butter – as our staple." There was also *khva*. Dark and intense in flavour, it's a thick roux with added cheese made from toasted barley flour blended with butter boiled in water.

Darejani spoke about contrasting Tushetian attitudes to pork. "Like most other Georgians, we're mainly Orthodox Christians. In Tusheti, pork is taboo, forbidden. They don't even look kindly on those who arrive with pork products. However, many Tushetians will eat pork down in the valleys; there are different customs here." Many Tushetians have biblical names; there may have been a Judaic influence on the area's feelings about pork just as there are Muslim influences from across the border in Chechnya.

As for beverages, in Tusheti herb-infused *chachas* are the favourites as well as *aluda*. It's brewed in local beer 'temples' from hops, barley and herbs, and is usually off-dry and low in alcohol. The brewing process involves incantations and prayers, and feels half-pagan, half-Christian.

Darejani sold honey in Tbilisi for years but stopped when the weights became too heavy. She is married to a priest. She chatted as she made *kotori*, the Tushetian version of *khachapuri*, which is stuffed with cheese and potato and cooked in a dry frying pan (they had no oil in Tusheti).

Opposite: Darejani's friend rolls out dough

Mosmula is unusual: plain boiled pasta enriched with onions and egg. It's fairly bland but perfect for a winter's breakfast. As she was making it, word spread in the neighbourhood. When the pot of *mosmula* was ready, local children lined up to get it before taking their steaming bowls on to the porch to eat. Darejani gives cooking lessons by appointment: tel: +995 599102944

Tushetian pancakes

MACHKATEBI მაჭკატები

These rustic egg pancakes filled with pan-melted cheese illustrate the kind of food that was needed by – and available to – the Tushetians living at high altitudes in the mountains. Like all comfort food, they hit the spot if you're heading out for a winter hike in the snow. The filling, of butter and cheese cooked together, is called *khavitsi*. It's so rich the pancakes can be cooked in an almost dry pan. The cheese used in Tusheti is farm cow's cheese. I use a mix of grated mozzarella, Swiss cheese and cheddar but you can experiment with your own favourites. Allow one or two pancakes per person.

MAKES **8 pancakes**
PREPARATION **10 minutes**
COOK **45 minutes**

2 large eggs
120 ml / 4 fl oz / ½ cup water
120 ml / 4 fl oz / ½ cup milk
1 tbsp cold-pressed vegetable oil
½ tsp salt
**100 g / 3 oz / ¾ cup plain/all-
  purpose flour**

FOR THE FILLING
**45 g / 1½ oz / 3 tbsp clarified or
  good-quality butter**
200 g / 6 oz / 2 cups grated cheese

Whisk the eggs with the water, milk and oil in a medium mixing bowl. Add the salt and flour and whisk again until you have a smooth, runny batter, the consistency of light pouring custard. If it's too thick, add a little more water.

Heat a heavy, non-stick, 20 cm / 8 in frying pan or skillet over medium to low heat. Pour a little oil onto a piece of folded paper towel and rub the inside of the pan (save the paper for the next pancake).

Pour about 60 ml / 2 fl oz / ¼ cup of batter into the centre of the pan and quickly swirl the batter around to make a large, thin pancake. Cook for about 1½–2 minutes, or until the pancake holds together and can be turned. It will be pale but may have some golden spots on it. Cook on the second side for a further 2–3 minutes or until the batter is cooked through. Remove the pancake to a plate and continue with the remaining batter, stacking the pancakes as you go.

In a small heavy skillet, heat the butter and stir in the cheese. Cook, stirring constantly for 5–6 minutes, or until the cheese has rendered some of its fat and is forming a stringy mass. Spoon some of the filling into the centre of a pancake and roll it up, tucking in the ends. Repeat with the remaining pancakes. Eat hot.

Opposite:

Top left: Swirling the batter

Top right: Melting the cheese and butter

*Bottom left and right: Forming the
filled pancakes*

Tushetian potato and cheese khinkali

TUSHURI KHINKALI   თუშური ხინკალი

These simple dumplings are a favourite in the high mountains of Tusheti. They're stuffed with a delicous filling of potato and cheese (or just potato, or just cheese, if you prefer). Read about *khinkali* (pp. 54-57) before you begin.

MAKES ABOUT **24**
PREPARATION **60 minutes**
COOK **10 minutes**

FOR THE DOUGH
260g / 9 oz / 2 cups plain/all-purpose flour
1 egg, at room temperature
120ml / 4 fl oz / ½ cup water
1 tsp salt

FOR THE FILLING
225g / 8 oz boiled potato, skin on
30g / 1 oz / 2 tbsp butter
110g / 4 oz / 1 cup grated cheddar or other cheese
½ tsp salt

Mix the dough ingredients together by hand until they form a ball (if necessary, add a little more flour or water). Turn it out onto a floured surface and knead for 4–5 minutes, or until the dough is smooth and elastic. Place the dough in a lightly oiled bowl and cover with a clean tea cloth while you prepare the filling.

Peel the potato once it's cool enough to handle. Grate it coarsely using a hand-held grater. Stir in the remaining ingredients, trying not to compact the mixture too much (if you are using cold potato, melt the butter first).

See pp. 56-57 for instructions on how to make and cook the *khinkali*. Serve them with lots of freshly ground black pepper.

ARTANA

WINE
KAKHA BERISHVILI

"As a child I wasn't given a choice: I had to become a musician," says Kakha Berishvili. "My parents and grandparents – not my teachers – helped me select which instrument I'd master. It was the violin but I never really loved it." Kakha was born into a family of musicians. Both parents were conductors. In Soviet times his mother worked at the Young Pioneer Palace for élite youths in Tbilisi. Kakha started playing aged six, studied at Tbilisi's Conservatoire, joined a TV orchestra and performed solos in Tbilisi concert halls during the Soviet period. He taught violin in Sighnaghi for several years. At 26 he decided to give up playing professionally, much to his parents' chagrin. "They had another vision for my life and wanted to send me to Russia to perfect my craft but I refused," he says.

"In my twenties I was at a crossroads. I loved spending time with my grandfathers – one a winemaker in Racha, the other a baker – and knew I wanted to do something outside the city. But those were difficult years in Georgia. I tried various things, became a potter, kept bees, made low-budget movies, wrote music for films…

"With some friends I set up a small movie studio in the 1990s and we made an ad in 1999 that won a prize at Cannes but the biggest problem back then was Georgia's lack of electricity. We were constantly in the dark. Whenever we bought a generator, it was immediately stolen. Some films were made in stages, whenever we could afford them, but by the time we neared the end, the actors were too old!" He laughs, shaking his head.

We're sitting in Kakha's eclectic, cluttered house in what was originally a small factory for painting wooden toys made in Siberia (the toys were then shipped back to Siberia, in what Stalin called the 'diversification of industrial life'). It's in a remote part of the countryside near Artana, a village on the north side of the Alazani River Valley in one of Kakheti's northernmost winemaking areas. Kakha's vineyards are in the foothills of the mountains as they begin to rise steeply towards Tusheti and Dagestan, near the Lopota River as it flows down to join the Alazani. He moved here in 2006. How did wine enter the picture?

"My father made wine in Tbilisi and planted a vineyard there but, three years later, when it could have given fruit, a development of high-rise buildings went ahead and it was destroyed." His father became a priest aged 40.

"My friends and I loved drinking wine but there was no good wine in those days. The only solution was to make it ourselves; lots of people started for that same reason." When Kakha was close to 40, he decided to become a winemaker. With three friends from the city, he invested in several plots of vineyards near Artana totalling one hectare (2½ acres). When the friends dropped out, Kakha kept going. "That was after the Soviet period, in about

2000, and great vineyards in Kakheti were very cheap as the large cooperatives had been broken up and there was lots of choice." He met Soliko Tsaishvili and found out about Elkana, the organic producers' association. "I needed some income and Soliko convinced me: 'If you don't sell your wine you'll be broke and have to go back to Tbilisi.' I took the plunge." He bottled his first wines in 2010 for the New Wine Fair. They sold.

Today he produces wines from two hectares (5 acres): the original hectare of 35-year-old vines he owns and another he rents nearby. He's recently bought some land to plant new vineyards. His lovely daughter Keti has moved to Artana to help run the winery and organize visits.

Kakha pruning winter vines

The vineyards are quite high, at 450 metres (1,476 feet), near the river and the Great Caucasus. Big night-to-day temperature differences there help the grapes maintain their perfumes. The soil is quite acid so the wines are fresh and lively. Kakha works organically, using bacteria instead of pesticides to combat predators. He makes Rkatsiteli and Saperavi in *qvevri* but is not wedded to long skin macerations.

"You have to taste the grapes and the wines to understand them. I was like a blind man at the start and asked the locals for guidance but they didn't know, so I just had to build my own experience. In 2015 the grapes were delicate, different and they needed a soft touch so I didn't macerate them: I trust my intuitions now."

His maximum production from those varieties is 2,000 bottles though sometimes he makes much less (he's pruning shorter now). He's planting Rose Rkatsiteli, Ghvinis Tetri and Kakhuri Mtsvivani in the new vineyards. He also produces *chacha* distilled from the winemaking residues.

It's early March and the evenings are chilly, so we move indoors to his bedroom-workroom to taste wine. A large cheese is brought out. The unfiltered orange Rkatsiteli 2014 has a great nose of tea and flowers, with fine acidity and tannins. The ruby Saperavi 2013 is silky, velvety and deep. I also taste the just-made 2015 vintage: it's young and fruity with lots of verve.

I notice a full beekeeper's outfit hanging on the wall near Kakha's violin case. He takes me into the garden by flashlight and shows me a set of hives.

He opens one and pulls out a large tray of honeycomb, the honey still inside it. "This is a project to help defend the world's bees sponsored by the Pentagon," he says, improbably. "Take it with you, you're here for another week, you can eat it as you go." ketevanberishvili@gmail.com

WINE
MARANI JUNIORS

While I was visiting Kakha Berishvili (see above), young men from the village turned up. Shota Iashagashvili, Vaxo Paghava and their friend Ika Gavasheli call themselves Marani Juniors and have just started making organic wines in Artana. "We were economists in Tbilisi but quit our bank jobs to come back to the village to make wine," Shota says. "Unfortunately our first crop of grapes was stolen from the vineyard before we could pick it but in 2014 we got there first!" Growers who don't live close to their vineyards often pool together and hire guards to camp in the vineyards until the grapes have been safely picked. The Juniors sell their wines at Ghvino Underground in Tbilisi (see p. 67) and plan to expand their operation with different varieties. maranijuniors@gmail.com

Excavated qvevri at Ikalto

IKALTO ACADEMY

This compact religious complex with monastery and academy is situated 9 kilometres (6 miles) from Telavi within a walled garden dominated by tall cypress trees. Its first church was founded in the 6th century by Saint Zenon, one of the Thirteen Assyrian Fathers. Two other churches were added later and in the 12th century an academy was also constructed, during the reign of King David the Builder. This included a refectory and winemaking facilities with *qvevri* rooms and grape-crushing stalls. Viticulture, chanting and winemaking were taught to the students along with more intellectual subjects: theology, rhetoric, astronomy, philosophy, geography and geometry.

The grape-crushing trough at Ikalto

Although the academy was in large part destroyed in 1616 when Persian invaders set it on fire, it's a fascinating place for wine lovers to visit, with ancient *qvevri* and a long, vaulted stone trough where the grapes were crushed still in evidence.

Ikalto has special significance for Georgians because the 12th-century poet Shota Rustaveli apparently studied here. He wrote *The Knight in the Panther's Skin*, Georgia's national epic.

VARDISUBANI

QVEVRI MAKER
ZAZA AND REMI KBILASHVILI

This *qvevri* maker's pottery is just outside Telavi on a country lane of independent houses. The heart of Zaza and Remi Kbilashvili's family business is their studio. Unusually it's located right under their house: they craft their *qvevri* in its cool, low-ceilinged semi-basement. When I visited in June, the batch of *qvevri* the men were making was almost finished and the space was crowded with high, round-bellied clay vessels. The house suggested a mother hen sitting on a clutch of eggs.

"My family has been making *qvevri* for at least five generations," says Zaza who, like his father, is a master *qvevri* maker. "We'll put 'necks' on these *qvevri* to finish them. Climate – and micro-climate – are very important. You can only make big *qvevri* in warm months but summers here are hot so we're careful to dry them slowly for two to three weeks before firing. You can't rush or cracks might appear." *Qvevri* can hold up to 2,000 litres of wine.

Top: The qvevri studio

Bottom: The kiln

The kiln is in the garden below the house, so the finished *qvevri* are carried there carefully on a trolley. The firing takes seven days using a wood fire, with just eight *qvevri* in the bunker-like kiln. After firing, while the *qvevri* are still warm, the men paint their interiors with beeswax.

"They shouldn't be too hot or the wax will burn," says Zaza as we visit the now-empty kiln. "We know by touch and experience how to do it. When it's done correctly, the wax impregnates the clay. The *qvevri* remain porous but the wax enters the clay's tiny pores to make the *qvevri* more hygienic and easy to clean. Air still passes through the *qvevri* walls yet the liquid doesn't escape."

"In the old days many potters made *qvevri* as most families produced wine," says his father, Remi. The Kbilashvilis are one of the last three families in Kaheti making *qvevri*.

They get their clay from a hill quarry 3 kilometres from the house. "An American lab tested samples and found unique minerals in this vein. We mix the clay with black slate sand for added structure: the *qvevri* are only 4 to 7 centimetres thick. Kakhetian clay is harder to work than Imeretian. Ours contains limestone which helps protect the wine from bacteria, but *qvevri* need annual cleaning."

"Being made in *qvevri* is beneficial for wine," says Zaza. "Clay's tannins are good for the stomach. We didn't have barrels or steel tanks before. Alternatives now exist but most Georgians still prefer *qvevri* for their family wines."

"The Soviets were against this tradition," says Remi. "*Qvevri* require more care and don't work for mass-produced wines. We weren't allowed to but we secretly continued making *qvevri*. Soviet ideology was against our traditions: we can't abandon our roots, languages and culture."

"Yes, tradition is key," Zaza agrees. "If from childhood you watch your father do this, it's in your blood. I respect my father for keeping this art alive."

"There's a lot of interest in our *qvevri* today," says Remi, with satisfaction. "This revival comes mainly from small cellars needing five or six *qvevri* but we're also now sending them abroad."

"*Qvevri* making has recently been granted world patrimony status by UNESCO," says Zaza proudly. "UNESCO filmed us working. *Qvevri* are a part of Georgian culture that no one can negate." tel: +995 555106090

RESTAURANT
NIKALA

One of eastern Georgia's best restaurants is on the Gombori Pass road between the magnificent Shuamta Forest and Telavi (look for wild mushroom and berry sellers); Nikala is on the right just before Château Mere. The restaurant, a series of self-contained rooms and covered outdoor tables, is positioned on a hillside, with a rooftop terrace facing the Caucasus. Chef Niko Kobiashvili is a wonderful character. In his chef's whites and short-order hat he runs the show. He began building the restaurant in 2000, when the road through the pass was closed.

"My Tbilisi customers took the longer route via Sighnaghi, but now it's much faster," he says, showing us into a private dining room. It's not fancy but spacious, with many chairs and a long table. "Georgian meals last hours and the toastmaster, or *tamada*, likes to set the rhythm of the toasting and drinking. That's easier if the groups are separate. People bring their own singers and if everyone is in the same room it's confusing. There's lots of ritual when Georgians eat."

Niko has always worked in restaurants. "My family were builders but I loved to cook. During Soviet times I was a chef in state-owned restaurants but afterwards few restaurants remained. In 2000, with some friends, I built a kitchen here with one big dining room." Why do customers drive far to eat here? "People in the cities are nostalgic about the country and our genuine ingredients," he says. "And people from around Kakheti want my farm produce and foraged wild foods." His family makes wine, grows vegetables and keeps animals.

The menu features seasonal ingredients: wild mushrooms in spring and autumn; hearty pork and lamb dishes in the cold winters; vibrant vegetables in summer; and lots of herbs and fruit sauces. "Kakhetian cuisine isn't spice-driven," he says, as a platter of wild oyster mushrooms fried in unrefined Kakhetian sunflower oil arrives. "The flavours come from the ingredients, herbs and garlic."

We've been served yogurt soup with caramelized onions; wild leeks; lamb *chakapuli* stew with tarragon; walnut-sauce aubergine/eggplant with pomegranate seeds; fermented green tomato; assorted cheeses; tomato and cucumber salad; aromatic herbs; and *khinkali* filled with curd cheese and butter (not on the menu but worth requesting

Top: Niko; bottom: aubergines

in advance). For dessert there are platters of fresh fruit and green walnuts boiled in sugar syrup. kobiashvililasha@yahoo.com; tel: +995 599198834

Lamb chakapuli

BATKNIS CHAKAPULI   ბატკნის ჩაქაფული

This fragrant and unusual stew features fresh tarragon as the defining herb as well as bitter greens such as radish tops, rocket/arugula or watercress. Make it when tarragon is fresh and plentiful. In Georgia *chakapuli* is often also made with veal and sometimes sees white wine added along with the water or broth. The Georgian method is usually to simply boil the meat in water but I prefer to brown it first for added flavour. If you don't have the fresh fruit, omit it! This is a fabulous stew.

SERVES **8–10 at a** *supra*
PREPARATION **30 minutes**
COOK **90 minutes**

2 tbsp sunflower oil

30g/1oz/2 tbsp butter

1.2kg/2lb 10 oz lean stewing lamb, cubed

260g/9oz/1 large onion, finely chopped

8g/¼ oz/2 garlic cloves

½ tsp coriander seeds, crushed

720ml/24fl oz/3 cups plain meat broth or water

1 bay leaf

¼ tsp ground chilli/cayenne

1 tsp salt

20g/¾oz tarragon, on the stems

120ml/4fl oz/½ cup green plum sauce (*tkemali*), see pp. 268-269

100g/3½oz/2 cups radish greens, rocket/arugula or watercress, cut in half

15g/½oz/½ cup fresh coriander/cilantro, chopped

1 tbsp chopped fresh dill

16 small green plums, large grapes or ripe gooseberries

freshly ground black pepper

Preheat the oven to 180°C/350°F/Gas 4. In a large casserole (Dutch oven), heat the oil and butter and brown the lamb in small batches over medium-high heat, removing the browned meat to a bowl. When all the meat has been browned and removed, stir the onion, garlic and coriander seed into the hot pan and cook, covered, for a further 5 minutes over low heat, stirring often. Add more oil if necessary. Return the meat to the pan and stir it into the onions.

Meanwhile heat the broth or water to boiling. Pour it over the meat, stirring well. Add the bay leaf, chilli and salt. Tie half of the tarragon stems together with thread and add to the stew. Cover the casserole and place in the centre of the preheated oven. Bake for 1¼ hours, or until the lamb is tender, stirring occasionally. Meanwhile, remove the leaves from the other tarragon stems and set aside.

When the lamb is tender, remove the casserole from the oven and return it to the stove over medium heat. Remove and discard the cooked tarragon stems. Stir the liquid around the edges of the casserole to catch all the brown cooking juices.

Stir in the plum sauce. Adjust seasoning, adding salt and freshly ground black pepper to taste. Stir in the greens and fresh herbs, including the reserved tarragon leaves. Add the fruit and cook for 2–3 minutes more, until the leaves have just wilted. Remove from the heat and serve.

VARDISUBANI

RESTAURANT, HOTEL, WINE CHÂTEAU MERE

This recently constructed 'château' hotel looks monumental from the outside but it comes alive when you're inside the colourful interior. The dining room reminds me of a Victorian parlour with its busy and eclectic mix of styles. The atmosphere is fun and the food abundant and good. There are 15 spacious rooms: most offer spectacular mountain views. Beside the pool is a *qvevri* cellar where Mere produces wines under the Winiveria label. This hotel is a sister to the Royal Batoni, across the valley near Nekresi. www.mere.ge

TELAVI

Telavi has a wonderful sprawling food market, or *bazari*, open daily from 8:00 to 16:00. It presents an eclectic mix of peoples, products and cultures and reflects the position Telavi held in the area, three times capital of the Kingdom of Kakheti. From the 16th century, while much of Georgia suffered a decline, Kakheti prospered thanks to its Astrakhan Silk Route links and to the influx of Armenian, Persian and Jewish communities.

The summer palace of Erekle II, king of united Kartli-Kakheti, is in Telavi. Erekle was considered a good ruler, able to stabilize his kingdom's economic and social problems, but in 1783 he placed it under the protection of Russia's Catherine the Great. This led to Georgia being incorporated into the Russian Empire. The king ruled for 54 years, and was wounded in battle 80 times.

The fascinating Giorgi Chubinashvili Telavi State History and Ethnographic Museum chronicles the history of Kakheti from the Bronze Age onwards. It's located in several rooms of King Erekle's summer palace (within the crenellated walls). Cholokashvili Street is Telavi's prettiest: recently it's been restored to its former grandeur with lacy balconies and colourful houses.

Telavi market

*Opposite:
The palace
wall in Telavi*

WHERE TO EAT, SHOP AND STAY   Chardatan Café – enjoy views of the Caucasus on a terrace beside a 900-year old plane tree at this café run by two young Tushetians. They sell the special beer, Alkhanaidze, that's only found in this area, with salads and grilled meats. The giant tree stands just beyond the equestrian statue of King Erekle II, near the town's magnificent palace walls. Chadari Street; tel: +995 599678686

Café Marleta – this lovely café-restaurant is in a house belonging to Sopo Gorgadze (see below). The walls are decorated with pictures and photographs that are anything but 'restaurant art'; Sopo's father, Malkhaz, is an accomplished painter. It's bohemian, with style. Bagrationi Street, 13; tel: +995 577722771. cafemarleta@gmail.com

Giorgi Tsankashvili is a beekeeper making honey in his back garden on a quiet street in Telavi, near the cheese farm of Sopo Gorgadze (see below). Tel: +995 592201842

For a hotel with character, Rcheuli Marani is part of a small chain in Georgia that chooses interesting buildings. The hotel has a decent restaurant, pretty wooden balconies and good views. www.rcheuli.ge

SHALAURI

CHEESE, HOME RESTAURANT
MARLETA'S FARM

Leo and Sopo

When two sophisticated city types uproot to the country to start a farm it doesn't always work. But Sophia Gorgadze and her husband, Levan Tsaguria, left Tbilisi a few years ago and never looked back. They built a house with a mountain view, milked a cow named Marleta (they named their café after her too, see above) and fell in love with cheesemaking.

"I've lived in New York, painted sets and produced films, and love focusing on challenging projects," the engaging Sopo, as she is known, says in fluent English. "We started with seven goats – seven of them – as there's no real tradition of goat's cheese in Georgia."

Levan – or Leo – took advanced courses and became the family's main cheesemaker. "I was an architect in Tbilisi, and had never produced food before, but it's become a passion," he says. Leo's delicious French-style cheeses use vegetable ash and other natural flavourings.

As the couple worked through the local bureaucracy's complex demands, they realized there were few provisions for small-scale cheesemakers. They established the

152 | KAKHETI

Artisan Cheesemakers Association of Georgia to help navigate laws geared to industrial production. (Slow Food has fought similar battles in other countries.)

"I've don't regret leaving the city," Sopo says as she sets the table for guests. "We have space here to offer wine and cheese tastings and Georgian dinners for those who want to experience eating with an artistic, cheese-making family." The cheeses – cow's and goat's – are sold in Tbilisi at the Georgian Basket (see p. 63). Sopo cooks dinners for groups with advance booking.

Some of the goat cheeses

Why did they choose Telavi? "Telavi was like a European capital under King Erekle II," she says. "It's not a provincial town but a proud small city with its own character, not far from Tbilisi. I've always loved it but some friends were shocked when we moved. In Georgia you must take charge of your destiny. The country's searching for its modern identity: ours is to live here, with our children, dogs and goats." marletasfarm@gmail.com; tel: +995 577722771

WINE
DAKISHVILI VINEYARD:
TELEDA VITA VINEA

Giorgi 'Gogi' Dakishvili is an accomplished winemaker and long-time champion of *qvevri* for winemaking. He produces organic wines under the Teleda Vita Vinea label with his sons, winemaker Temuri and the much younger Davit. Gogi is also a consultant nearby for the large German-owned winery, Schuchmann, where he has created a line of *qvevri* wines (see p. 154). Both cellars are in the Alazani Valley, where top Kakhetian wines are made. The Dakishvili's microzone is the Kondoli Valley, south-east of Telavi at 350 and 400 metres (1,148 and 1,312 feet).

I've visited the winery several times. Its *qvevri* cellar and tasting room overlook what the French call a *clos*: a wall-enclosed vineyard.

"Teleda is the ancient word for Telavi," says Gogi as we join the table for a *supra* dinner prepared by the family's women. "Temuri

Dakishvili vineyard

and I make Teleda wines from 80-year-old vines planted here by my grandfather, and from 50-year-old Kisi vines near Akhmeta." The Dakishvilis own 2½ hectares (6 acres) in three plots. All their wines are made in *qvevri*, including whites Rkatsiteli, Mtsvane and Kisi and a deep, spicy red Saperavi.

At dinner an amber Rkatsiteli 2013 accompanies fried aubergines rolled with garlic and coriander, flaky *khachapuri* and grilled meats. Gogi assumes

the role of toastmaster, or *tamada*, and gives at least ten toasts that evening. The wines and relaxed atmosphere lead to talk about winemaking: Gogi likes to maintain high standards. The conversation moves on to caring for *qvevri*. "Hygiene in the vineyard and in the cellars is key," he says.

I'm ready for more Rkatsiteli 2011. It's dry with a nose of honey and apricots, has good energy and tannins, and a pleasant note of bitterness that complements the food. As he fills my glass, Temuri smiles and says: "Some western white-wine lovers are unused to the tannins and flavours of

Supra *with the Dakish-vili family*

amber, Kakhetian-style Rkatsiteli wines but most develop a taste for them. It's still hard to make one's full living from wine in Georgia: many of even the most famous producers work part time in agritourism, restaurants, or other jobs. Luckily things are changing as wine tourism builds and the word spreads about our unique *qvevri* wines." The Dakishvili family offer wine and cheese tastings by appointment. www.vitavinea.ge

KISISKHEVI

WINE, HOTEL, RESTAURANT
SCHUCHMANN

This winery hotel offers a central location from which to take day trips to Kakheti's most important wine areas, towns and sights. The German-owned winery, founded by rail industrialist Burkhard Schuchmann in 2008, now includes a 20-room hotel, restaurant and tasting room within the winery complex. Guests can watch modern Georgian wines being made and take cooking classes. There's also a pool and a wine spa. The winery is open all year.

Winemaker Gogi Dakishvili (see above) is a fixture here and helped create a line of *qvevri* wines that bridge the gap between traditional Georgian wines and those with a more international style. The winery produces 1.5 million bottles: 30 percent are made in *qvevri*, making Schuchmann the largest producer of non-organic *qvevri* wines in Georgia. The estate owns

Gogi Dakishvili

120 hectares (297 acres) of vineyards and also buys grapes from local growers working to their specifications. www.schuchmann-wines.com

GREMI

Gremi was the medieval capital of the Kingdom of Kakheti, an important trading town on the Silk Road that was razed by the Persians in 1615. (Telavi became Kakheti's capital in the 17th century). Today Gremi's 16th-century Church of the Archangels – with beautiful complete frescoes – and citadel, or Royal Tower, remain and have been put onto the Tentative UNESCO World Heritage Site List.

SABUE VILLAGE

GUEST HOUSE, WINE, FRUIT COMPOTES
CHÂTEAU ENISELI-BAGRATIONI

Period furnishings in the Château Eniseli-Bagrationi

This guest house is ideal if you want to stay on an estate where wine and fruit products are made, close to Gremi. The Eniseli-Bagrationi property, built in the 19th century by Zakaria Jorjadze, offers a rare insight into Georgia's aristocratic past. French-trained Jorjadze was one of the first Georgian winemakers to incorporate European technology into wine production. His Saperavi won a gold medal in Brussels in 1888.

*Meri
Bagrationi*

*Fruit
compote*

"Zakaria lived in Tbilisi but ran his wine business from this, his summer house," says Meri Bagrationi, the current owner, as we tour an elegant property whose charm suggests a French wine château. Much of the interior is unchanged, with period furniture and large windows overlooking the gardens and vineyards.

The monumental *qvevri* cellar is not currently in use. Built in 1875, its 120 *qvevri* were damaged during Soviet times and are now being restored. "In the Communist era the winery was confiscated," Meri recounts. "Zakaria had two sons and a daughter, Nino Jorjadze. She remained in the house after the loss of the winemaking facilities." An educated, well-travelled aristocrat, Nino became a nurse during World War I. She took remarkable photos on the Caucasus front lines; some are displayed in the cellar and offer an insider's view of the war.

"The Communists built a huge national cognac factory here that became very famous," says Meri. Cognac is still made on the estate, as is wine. In 2003 Meri and her husband, Sandro Bagrationi – a descendant of the Jorjadze family and of the royal Bagrationi dynasty – bought the property. "It has taken so much work to bring the estate back to life," says Sandro. The young couple live in the house with their children and run the estate, producing high-volume wines primarily for the Russian market, not made in *qvevri*. They also make delicious artisan fruit 'compote'.

"This is an old Georgian tradition which every grandmother made in summer from home-grown fruit," Meri says as we watch women filling glass jars with the beautiful fruit and syrup. "Compote appears at Georgian meals either before or instead of wine; the sweet fruit drink is delightfully refreshing with our savoury food." Compotes are made by boiling fresh fruit in sugar syrup. The fruit and its syrup are served in glass jugs, diluted with water to taste. They're made from many varieties, including plum, peach, quince and Cornelian cherry. The cottage industry also produces jams and other fruit preserves. "My husband wanted to revive these still-popular traditions."

The Bagrationis have an attractive single-storey house on the grounds for six guests, with its own garden. The family also prepares delicious traditional Kakhetian food with advance booking. www.eniselibagrationi.ge

NEKRESI

On the eastern side of the Alazani River Valley, near Shilda, Nekresi is a cluster of buildings with pre-Christian origins. Its importance as a religious site dates from the 4th century when King Mirian III reinforced its defensive walls and his grandson, Trdat, built the first Christian church here. It's one of the oldest Christian buildings in Georgia. From here Mirian waged his holy war to establish Christianity as the state religion. Two centuries later, Nekresi was chosen by the missionary Abibos, one of the Thirteen Assyrian Fathers, as a stronghold against the Persian effort to convert the population to Zoroastrianism.

Other buildings added to the monastery complex over the next millennium include a 7th-century church with important 16th-century frescoes, and an 8th-century bishops's palace with a *qvevri* cellar behind it. The palace was ruined during incursions by the Persians and by Lezghins from nearby Dagestan. The churches have recently been restored, including some remarkable frescoes. Set in woods on the foothills of the higher Caucasus, Nekresi commands great views across the valley towards Kakheti. Access from below is by foot (a steep climb) or minibus from the car park.

LAGODEKHI NATIONAL PARK

Highway 5 cuts west–east across Georgia from Tbilisi, crossing the Alazani Valley between Tsnori (on the plain below Sighnaghi) and Lagodekhi before it turns south into Azerbaijan. Before Lagodekhi it passes through the Alazani wetlands, seasonally flooded woods that are home to many bird species.

North of the town, as the land rises into the mountains, is the expansive Lagodekhi National Park, positioned between Dagestan and Azerbaijan. This was Georgia's first nature reserve, set up in 1912 as a hunting area. Today it's divided between Strict and Managed Nature Reserves. The former is only accessible to researchers; the latter is open to the public and includes a well-organized visitor's centre and clearly marked trails for hiking and horse riding.

Primula in Lagodekhi

From beech forests to alpine zones, the park is an extraordinary showcase of Georgia's biodiversity, home to 150 species of birds, 53 mammals – including tur (a kind of goat), lynx, grey wolf and brown bear – and many others.

BAKURTSIKHE, KARDANAKHI

*Top: Soliko
Tsaishvili*

*Bottom:
Soliko
extracting
wine from a
qvevri*

Solomon 'Soliko' Tsaishvili has been one of the catalysts of the recent movement in Georgia to bottle natural *qvevri*-made wines. When I first met him in 2008 at Terra Madre in Turin, he was with Ramaz Nikoladze (see p. 262). They had a booth at the Slow Food event aimed at highlighting biodiversity and the global communities who are keeping food and winemaking traditions alive. A large poster with photos of the clay *qvevri* was pinned to the wall, and they stood proud but sheepish, unable to communicate as neither side spoke each other's language. There was a lot of buzz about them at the event: 'Have you seen, the Georgians who make their wines in clay jars are here?'

Like Ramaz in western Georgia, Soliko uncovered the potential from eastern Georgia by visiting villages seeking anyone making good wine from organic vineyards. He encouraged any likely candidates to start bottling and selling their wines; many now-famous producers began that way.

"The Slow Food Foundation *qvevri* project was one of the most successful Presidia in Europe; it helped make Georgia famous and was very important for natural wines," Soliko says.

Soliko describes his winemaking beginnings. "In Soviet Union times, there was no private property. You could make some wine for home use but weren't allowed to sell it. Large-scale wine was industrialized and if there hadn't been this family wine tradition, the craft of *qvevri* wines would have been lost." He shakes his head.

Soliko was a literary journalist in Tbilisi at the time, and bought grapes in Kakheti. He'd use glass jars to make 200 litres in the cellar of his building. His friends loved *supras* and wines. "In 2003 some of us decided to buy a place with vineyards in Kakheti and renew the *qvevri* tradition." Their first wines were bottled under the Prince Makashvili Cellar brand: this became Chveni Ghvino – Our Wine – in 2010.

"In Tbilisi we sourced grapes from different parts of Kakheti each year and liked Kardanakhi's best. Now we're five partners with five vineyards at Kardanakhi and three nearby at Bakurtsikhe, for a total of 5½ hectares," he says, climbing down the long ladder to the underground *qvevri* cellar. "We worked organically until 2015 but are now committed to biodynamics as interpreted by Nicolas Joly in France."

The vineyards are mainly Rkatsiteli, aged 16 to 46 years, planted at densities of 3,600 to 4,800 plants per hectare (2½ acres) at altitudes of between 320 and 400 metres (1,050 and 1,312 feet). Using around 10 *qvevri*, their annual production is about 7,000 bottles that are exported internationally. The wines are available in Tbilisi at Ghvino Underground, as Soliko is one of its founding partners (see p. 67). He doesn't usually do tastings in Kakheti.

"Our group consists of Merab Matiashvili, Davit Kapanadze, Irakli Pruidze, Velier Spa Triple A and me," he says as he uses a pipette to draw a deep amber Rkatsiteli from a *qvevri*. It's got a great nose and clean, fine tannins: a long, dynamic wine. "We're making three wines: Rkatsiteli, Rkatsiteli with Mtsvane and Khikhvi, and red Saperavi. But we're exploring other Kakhetian varieties with a Kakhetian wine club that's planting rare grapes. This kind of biodiversity is surely the future."
chvenigvino@hotmail.com; tel: +995 99117727; +995 577437028

SIGHNAGHI

After spending time in the lower Alazani Valley as it slopes down towards the river, it's exhilarating to navigate the tortuous 'S' bends up the mountain to Sighnaghi, one of Georgia's prettiest and most distinctive towns. Sighnaghi commands spectacular views of the Caucasus range, weather permitting. (I went there a dozen times before I was treated to that full view: the mountains often hide demurely behind veils of cloud or fog.) Winter's the best time to get the whole panorama, with snowy peaks as icing on the cake.

Street view of Sighnaghi

Sighnaghi was built and given an extensive defensive wall with 23 towers in the late 18th century by King Erekle II – 'the Little Kakhetian' – to defend its strategic position from marauding tribes. The city became a flourishing trading point on the Silk Route, a centre for artisan crafts of carpetmaking, leatherworking and wine.

In the 19th century, there were many wine cellars in Sighnaghi. Early photos show men and oxen transporting wine in swollen buffalo skins with goat skins used for smaller quantities. Country people came to buy or barter goods in the town's square.

Today Sighnaghi retains much of its charm, with attractive wooden houses featuring fretwork balconies. It's become a hub for new wine tourism with important cellars, restaurants, wine bars and hotels. (Unfortunately it's also a centre for noisy four-wheelers that incessantly buzz up and down its central streets.) Climate change is having its effect here too. Sighnaghi's ancient name, Kambechovani, meant 'land of the water buffalo'; today this area is dry and in, some areas, threatened with desertification. The warmer winters have attracted Georgia's first olive tree plantation, on the slopes below Sighnaghi.

The Historical-Ethnographic Museum of Sighnaghi has 16 works by painter Niko Pirosmani, whose birthplace was nearby at Mirzaani (see pp. 179-80).

WHERE TO EAT, DRINK AND STAY   These are places I've eaten and stayed in:

Sighnaghi overlooks the mountains

Nikala – go to this popular eatery for *khachapuri* cooked on a spit, great *khinkali* dumplings, fermented vegetables and kebabs. Home-cooked popular Georgian food, no frills but fun. Loloshvili, 4; tel +995 355189256

Tavaduri, with tables out in the small square in summer, is a fine place for well-cooked, traditional dishes sourced from local ingredients. Gzirishvili Street; tel +995 595142311.

Sanadimo – this restaurant has a panoramic terrace and unpretentious dishes. Tamar Mepe Street; tel +995 355230058

Hotel Kabadoni is at the top of the town; it is modern, spacious and has great views of the mountains www.kabadoni.ge.

Hotel Pirosmani is part of the Rcheuli group of four hotels that choose centrally located buildings of character: this one's in a main square, relaxed with roomy rooms www.rcheuli.ge.

Guest house Dzveli Ubani is at the lower end of the town, near the city gates in a quiet neighbourhood. Gorgasali Street, 8; tel +995595158780

Living Roots Ranch – the latest venture from Living Roots partners, John Wurdeman (of Pheasant's Tears) and Ia Tabagari, who run the Tbilisi-based food and wine tour company together. This small horse-riding ranch, with a cast of farm animals and big views, is high on the hill above Sighnaghi, about 1.5 kilometres from the town. It offers horse treks from 1 hour to multi-day tours. You can also ride down the mountain to the Pheasant's Tears vineyards and have a picnic along the way. Larger groups can be catered for with advance notice. Guest rooms are being added. info@travellivingroots.com

Street in Sighnaghi

Kedeli Brewing – John Wurdeman and Ia Tabagari (see above) are also collaborating on a new craft beer production project with American partners Annie Lucas and Doug Grimmes from MIR Corporation in Seattle. They plan to build and open the brewery by early 2017, making beer using wild hops from the Alazani Valley, local organic barley and other cereals.

WINE
KEROVANI WINERY

"Kerovani comes from *kera*, the Georgian word for family hearth, the household's focal point," says Archil Natsvlishvili, who owns and runs Kerovani winery. "And *keria* is the big candle that was always kept burning in the house from which other things could be lit. So Kerovani suggests deep symbolic links to the family ties that are so important to Georgians." Kerovani is located in a private house in the tiny streets above Sighnaghi's central square. Archil's aunt Tinatin Natsvlishvili, the director of the local music school, lives there.

To create the winery, Archil teamed up with his cousin Ilya Bezhashvili, who brought 25 years of winemaking experience and a vineyard to the project. "This was our grandfather's house; he'd be proud to see us mak-

ing wine here," says Archil as he shows me their handsome brick *qvevri* cellar and tasting room. "In his day there were no opportunities in the private sector and people were dependent on state jobs."

Ilya and Archil

The men have other careers and only started winemaking professionally in 2012. Archil works in Tbilisi as a telecoms software developer. Ilya has been an English-Georgian interpreter and translator since the 1980s. "In most Georgian villages people had family vineyards – even during Soviet times – but not in Sighnaghi as this isn't really a farming area," says Archil. "Shevardnadze's government decided to donate the co-operative vineyards to local families." The large state-owned vineyards were divided into rows of 3 x 100 metres (328 feet).

"Four rows were given to all adults except married women," Ilya explains. "My father, my married sister and her husband, and I formed three households and we got a total of 12 rows with a certificate of ownership."

Archil in the vineyard

"Not everyone wanted their share, so we bought another parcel quite inexpensively, bringing us to 28 rows, a total of 1.5 hectares," says Archil.

We drive 12 kilometres (7½ miles) to visit the vineyards in a gently sloping open landscape. It's June and the vines are in full leafy growth. The rows are farther apart than I'm used to seeing in Italy. "The Soviets used big tractors so the rows from that period are widely spaced," says Ilya. "These vineyards were planted in the 1960s and '70s so quite a lot of plants are missing too. Traditionally, new vines were created by running a long cane from an existing vine down into the soil and up again and waiting until it took root before cutting it free from the 'mother' plant."

"Like many older vineyards, ours is a field blend of different varieties, with Rkatsiteli the most prevalent," says Archil. We also spot some large-leafed Mtsvane with Buera, Rose Rkatsiteli and Saperavi. The pair work the vineyards organically, using only the 'Bordeaux mixture' (copper sulphate and slaked lime) as a treatment against bacteria. They vinify varieties separately and harvest in late September.

Opposite:
The cellars at
Kerovani

Currently they make four wines: Rkatsiteli, and a white field blend, both with six months of skin contact; and reds Saperavi and Cabernet Sauvignon, each with one month of skin contact. Their annual production is around 3,000 bottles. "There's lots of interest in Georgian wines now and grape prices are rising but not long ago the vines were being grubbed up to plant plums which are easier to cultivate," says Ilya. "We're planning new vineyards on land we've bought recently, of native varieties like Simonaseuli, a rare red grape." The winery is open to visitors by appointment for tastings and vineyard visits. ilya_bezhashvili@yahoo.com; www.kerovani.com

WINE, RESTAURANT
JOHN OKRUASHVILI:
OKRO'S WINES

John Okruashvili's house and *qvevri* cellar are high in Sighnaghi's old town at 850 metres (2,789 feet). John, who often shortens his surname to Okro, is currently increasing annual production from 10,000 to 15,000 bottles of *qvevri* wines under his Okro's Wines label. He's recently created handsome tasting rooms and a restaurant for those visiting the cellar. John explains his concept. "Usually in restaurants, you choose the food first and then pair the wine to it," he says. "Our idea is different: you'll taste our wines, decide which you want to eat with and we'll present a menu to suit those wines."

John and Jenny Okruashvili

John is doing the initial cooking himself to set the style for his cooks. His sister and partner, Jenny, is the manager.

This is quite a career switch for a telecoms consultant who plans international GSM computer networks. "Fifteen years ago, I wasn't sure I wanted to return to live in Georgia," John says in perfect English. "I'd studied at Southampton University and was working for Motorola in Iraq in 2004 when my Baghdad hotel was blown up and I had to leave. Back in Georgia, I set off on a quest for good wines, travelling through small villages almost like a stranger. The only wines were then being made in small amounts by families, often diluted with water, which seems crazy to us now! It turned out to be very difficult to find good wines. I decided to have a go myself: I was sure I could do better than that."

That first year, 2004, he bought 300 kilos (661 pounds) of Rkatsiteli grapes and crushed them himself. "It was brilliant!" he laughs. "The following year I made twice as much and by the third year I bought my first parcel of vineyards: 10 rows of 100 metres each."

Initially he made the wines in steel tanks but in 2009 he borrowed his first *qvevri*. By then he was bottling the wines and building a cellar. "We began to age our wines in *qvevri*, something not many others were doing then," he says as we sit in the tasting room with wines from different vintages. "Traditionally Georgians finished their wines before the next harvest. But I believe that ageing a wine in *qvevri* gives that wine soul." The estate's wines are aged for at least two – and ideally three – years before being sold. Rkatsiteli 2013 (tasted in autumn 2015) spent six months on the skins in *qvevri* before being racked, and a further three months in *qvevri* before being moved to stainless steel tanks; it was bottled in 2015. It has a deep amber colour and a clean, vibrant energy. Saperavi 2010 was grown down in the valley; it's very rich in the nose, rather saline, with fruits of cherry and plum in the palate too.

Old Kakhetian vine

There were many early challenges, from a shortage of corks in Georgia to the lack of a bottling plant – the last one went to a Turkish firm to bottle cola. Now that other natural winemakers are bottling their wines, those logistical problems have been resolved. The Okro winery has grown steadily with a second cellar 6 kilometres (4 miles) outside of Sighnaghi. Production is increasing, as are the vineyards, to 4.5 hectares (11 acres).

Many of John's grapes are grown at high altitudes of 750–850 metres (2,461–2,789 feet). "That helps them retain acidity and perfumes," he says. The Okruashvilis currently produce an interesting range of nine wines, from the obligatory Rkatsiteli and Saperavi to less familiar varieties including Budeshuri Saperavi (sometimes called Kashmi Saperavi), a more aromatic variety of Georgia's most popular red with oval berries and paler pulp. New plantings will yield whites Kakhuri Mtsvivani, Bodburi Chitistvala (or 'bird's eye'), Gvinis Tetra and an ancient red, Simonaseuli.

John is keen on experimentation and has recently begun making a late-harvest Saperavi using a system similar to icewine. "We leave the grapes on the plant until after the first frost in late November or December," he explains. The result is a not-too-sweet dessert wine with the clean freshness that characterizes the Okro wines. John and Jenny are also producing a trio of naturally sparkling wines (*pétillant naturel*) from Tsolikouri, Kakhuri Mtsvane and Rkatsiteli, as well as a pink Tavkveri Rosé they call the Sister's Wine. They are proud not to use any sulphites in their wines. info@okroswines.com

WINE, RESTAURANT
PHEASANT'S TEARS

In the glass-walled dining room at Pheasant's Tears restaurant, a *supra* dinner is taking place. Dishes of delicious food cover the long table from end to end, with more appearing from chef Gia Rokashvili's tiny kitchen all the time. The table is full of guests – Georgians and foreigners – and the wines are flowing, as they do here. Two women and three men sitting together at the table start to sing, a cappella, and the dissonant harmonies of a medieval Georgian polyphonic chant electrify the room. When it ends there's rapturous applause as the feast continues.

John H. Wurdeman V

A man with the look of a Viking stands up and his clear voice calls out above the chatter. There's a sparkle in his eyes and a glass of orange wine in his hand. "Friends! This is a toast to gratitude: gratitude for new friends meeting, for old friends seeing each other, and for being able to celebrate with good wine, good food and good company. *Gaumarjos!*" He raises his glass as the room answers: *gaumarjos!*

When John H. Wurdeman V first came to Georgia in 1995 as a young painter seeking inspiration, no one could have anticipated the important role this American polyglot would eventually play as a champion of Georgia's culture. Since then his passion for the country – and its unique musical, artistic and winemaking traditions – has turned him from enthusiastic fan into unofficial ambassador for all things Georgian. He tirelessly takes foreign guests around the country to share its customs. Several have changed their lives as a result, moving to Georgia to make wine, to sing in polyphonic groups – with John's wife and partner, Ketevan Mindorashvili – or open restaurants serving natural wines and foods. (Even to write books about them – I should know!)

He's a familiar presence on Georgian food and wine TV shows, known to everyone simply as John, or *Djoni*. At Pheasant's Tears, John and his partner in wine, Gela Patalashvili, have created a successful winery and restaurant that are magnets to visiting wine lovers. John has introduced Georgia's vignerons to international wine importers, winemakers and journalists, spreading the word – and the wines – far and wide. How did his Georgian journey begin? "When I first visited Georgia, I was a postgraduate painting student at the Surikov Institute in Moscow and fascinated by polyphonic music," he says. "Like flamenco music, its rigid traditions allow for a lot of freedom, and I'm drawn to the idea that the ancient can become cutting edge in art and other aspects of life." He's given a TED talk on the subject.

John, a lifelong vegetarian, was born in New Mexico to hippy parents. His father, John, a stone carver, runs the Lazare Gallery of Russian Art in Virginia with his current wife, Kathy. John's mother, Theresa, is a watercolour painter and art teacher.

John bought a house in Sighnaghi in 1996 and moved permanently in 1998. "In the late '90s, life here was necessarily simplified," he says. "The modern comforts we take for granted like electricity or gas had been stripped away during Georgia's wars and post-Communist period, so I painted when the sun came up and read by candlelight." Hearing singing outside his window one night in 1997, he followed. The singer was the young Ketevan – or Keto, as she's known – and within two years they were married. "Keto was travelling the country recording fast-disappearing traditions in Georgian folk music, so from 1999 to 2006 we made CDs, held

Carpets and artefacts at Pheasant's Tears

workshops and collected dances and songs for the archive." Keto, who runs Zedashe, a singing group, gives classes and performs internationally; she cooks and creates menus at their Tbilisi restaurant, Azarpesha (p. 68).

"Another fateful meeting changed my life again. I was painting in a vineyard when a young man on a noisy Soviet-era tractor stopped and invited me for dinner. I asked him to shut off the engine so we could talk. He replied the tractor had no starter motor and drove away." That was John's first encounter with Gela Patalashvili.

"When Gela next spoke to me he offered to give me two rows of his vineyard so I could make wine with my children, Lazare and Gvantsa. Again he invited me to dinner. I didn't want a vineyard and blew him off as a madman!" But Gela persisted. Finally, John accepted the grapes and Gela's winemaking lessons.

A supra in the restaurant

"I was forced to become a winemaker," John laughs. "The fermentation cycle was exciting and Gela was charming. And he kept inviting me to dinner." Gela comes from a farming family. He and his brother learned *qvevri* winemaking from their grandparents. They worked hard and were doing better than some of the other villagers.

"Gela said: 'I know you're passionate about polyphony and dance but wine culture is no less important. Many wines that travel abroad from here don't speak Georgian. We're losing our voice. You speak many languages and have friends throughout the world. I can make the wine but I need you to speak on its behalf, to tell Georgia's ancient wine story.' That's how it started!" John says.

Gela also convinced John to invest in a vineyard. "We didn't know anything about the natural wine movement; our ambition was to make something authentically, unapologetically Georgian. In 2007 we bought the rights to excavate old *qvevri* from abandoned villages – including some from the 1850s. We lit fires inside to sterilize and rewax them before plunging them back into the ground near our vineyard. Gela and his cousins then erected the cellar's walls around the *qvevri*."

Pheasant's Tears was born. (John overheard old men in the village discussing wine as they played backgammon. One said: "Only the best of wines can make a pheasant cry tears of joy!") Gela made the wines and John travelled the world as global interest in *qvevri* wines was beginning.

A decade has passed and the pair now produce many different organic *qvevri* wines from over 400 varieties of native Georgian grapes that they have planted in their vineyards. If Rkatsiteli, Mtsvane, Chinuri, Tavkveri and Saperavi take centre stage, Polyphony is an exciting, unique field blend of their complete vine collection.

Pheasant's Tears wines are served at top tables around the world while ever more people come to Georgia to follow the *qvevri* story. "Along the way they discover the fabulous food and hospitality in Georgia and don't want to leave," John says. Certainly, no one wants to leave Pheasant's Tears. Chef Gia's exceptional cooking and the warmth of the hospitality given by his wife, Tamriko, make it a uniquely personal and lively destination.

"What I love about this place is that we haven't forgotten our primary passions, it's all here!" John says. "Upstairs is Keto's music school for Georgian folk song and dance. Downstairs, next to the restaurant, Georgian antiques and carpets are on sale beside a roomful of my paintings. The Georgian feast is supposed to inspire dialogue and I'm happy this restaurant has helped do that about natural *qvevri* wines."

Gela and John have just completed a big new cellar in the valley – beside the original cellar – with panoramic views of vineyards and mountains. It's a great place for drinking wine and sharing experiences. (In 2017 Ketevan and John are opening a farm-driven restaurant there.) John's other projects in Georgia keep multiplying. In addition to being partners with Luarsab and Nino Togonidze in Tbilisi's Azarpesha restaurant (see p. 68), John and Keto are also involved in the group's new restaurant there, Polyphonia (see p. 70). He is a partner in Living Roots travel group (see p. 425) and has recently opened the Living Roots Ranch for horse riding outside Sighnaghi (see p. 161). There's also an artisan craft beer project getting underway, Kedeli Brewing (see p. 161). www.pheasantstears.com

CHEF GIA ROKASHVILI

Gia Rokashvili, the chef and gastronomic backbone of Pheasant's Tears restaurant, has the ability to produce unmistakably Georgian food from ingredients and combinations that don't always adhere to tradition. "Many Georgians feel that tradition shouldn't be changed in any way, that you can't add herbs to *khachapuri* because their ances-

tors didn't," he says, as he chops an enormous handful of purple basil to put in a vegetable dish. "I love to cook Georgian food but I don't want to be stuck in the 11th century. Throughout our history, we've had influences from many strong neighbours – from the Turks and Persians to the Greeks and other Mediterranean countries – and each has left their mark on Georgian cuisine. Think of the impact of the Spice Route bringing ingredients and ideas from Asia. To me they're all vibrantly alive in Georgian food today."

Like all the best self-taught chefs, Gia's natural palate guides him to create delicious dishes with huge flavour that remain balanced. "I always loved cooking and when I ran the grocery store in Sighnaghi, I enjoyed trying the new ingredients John and his friends

Chef Gia Rokashvili

brought." When Pheasant's Tears decided to offer food with its wines, John invited Gia to be the chef. That was an inspired move. Gia, his wife, Tamriko, and their wonderful team have made Pheasant's Tears restaurant one of the highlights of any trip to Georgia.

MENU

Water buffalo yogurt with pomegranate syrup
Tomato, cucumber and pale peppers salad
Wilted purslane
Rocket/arugula and barberry salad
Beets in green plum sauce with coriander/cilantro
Cooked green beans
Herbed, smoked aubergine/eggplant
Black-eyed beans with onion, mint and coriander/cilantro
Fried eggs and peppers
Khachapuri
Stewed lentils
Beef chakhokhbili
Coriander/cilantro chutney

Aubergine/eggplant ajapsandali

AJAPSANDALI   აჯაფსანდალი

This colourful vegetable stew resembles ratatouille but combines root and summer vegetables (and has no courgettes/zucchini). The vegetables cook together: cut them into good-size chunks so they retain their flavours and bite. What makes it so Georgian is the quantity of fresh herbs that bring it to life. The original recipe calls for a whole head of garlic, but I find that's too much unless you have fragrant fresh garlic, so just use as much as you like. *Ajapsandali* is as good cold as it is hot or warm.

SERVES **8–10** at a *supra*
PREPARATION **25 minutes**
COOK **45 minutes**

500g/1lb 2oz potatoes
300g/10oz carrots
30g/1oz/2 tbsp butter
6 tbsp sunflower oil
¼ tsp dried summer savory
  (*kondari*) or wild thyme
675g/1lb 8oz small aubergines/
  eggplants, sliced crosswise
450g/1lb tomatoes, peeled
2 red peppers, cut into bite-size
  chunks
115g/4oz smaller, pale green
  peppers, seeded and quartered
400g/14oz onions, chopped
30g/1oz garlic/8 garlic cloves,
  or to taste, roughly chopped
fresh green chilli, to taste
freshly ground black pepper
20g/⅔oz/½ cup purple and/or
  green basil, chopped
20g/⅔oz/½ cup coriander/
  cilantro, chopped
10g/⅓oz/¼ cup parsley, chopped
2 tbsp chopped fresh dill
salt

Peel and chop the potatoes and carrots into large, bite-size pieces. Heat the butter and oil with the *kondari* or thyme in a large heavy saucepan. Add the potatoes and carrots, cover, and cook them over medium heat for 10–15 minutes, or until they start to soften. Stir occasionally.

Add the aubergines/eggplants to the pan, stirring well. Cover and cook for 10 minutes. Slice the tomatoes. Add the red and green peppers, tomatoes, onions, garlic, chilli and 1 tsp salt and stir well. Cover. Cook over medium heat until the vegetables give up their juices, about 15 minutes. Stir occasionally to prevent sticking.

Test the aubergines/eggplants and potatoes for doneness. When they are tender, and the other vegetables seem cooked too, add the herbs. Stir them into the vegetables and cook for 5 minutes more. Remove from the heat. Allow the *ajapsandali* to stand for at least 5 minutes before serving hot or at room temperature.

Herbed oyster mushrooms

SOKO სოკო

Chef Gia loves to cook with wild foods, including the many varieties of wild mushrooms that appear in the woods and fields during the year in Kakheti. If you can't find oyster mushrooms, use your favourite varieties, or a mix of wild and cultivated mushrooms.

These mushrooms can be used as part of a *supra*, or eaten with eggs and toast for breakfast. For added kick, serve them with some *ajika* on the side (see pp. 334-335 and 392-393).

SERVES 4
PREPARATION 10 minutes
COOK 20 minutes

- 240g/1lb oyster or other mushrooms
- 8 spring onions/scallions
- 3 tbsp cold-pressed sunflower or extra virgin olive oil
- 8g/¼oz/2 garlic cloves, finely sliced
- 2cm/1in medium-hot fresh chilli
- 4 fresh sage leaves, torn in half
- 4 fresh mint leaves
- 2 sprigs fresh tarragon
- dried chilli/red pepper flakes
- salt and freshly ground black pepper

Clean the mushrooms by removing any dirt and wiping the caps and stems with moist paper towel. Cut the mushrooms into large chunks. Cut the spring onions/scallions into 10cm/4in lengths, using both white and green parts.

Heat the oil in a frying pan large enough to fit all the mushrooms. Sauté the spring onions/scallions for 3–4 minutes before adding the mushrooms. Cook the mushrooms over medium heat for 4–5 minutes, or until they begin to soften. Stir in the garlic, chilli piece and the herbs. Season with salt and pepper and cook until the mushrooms have given up their water and are beginning to brown.

Sprinkle lightly with dried chilli flakes before serving.

Wilted purslane salad

DANDURI   დანდური

Purslane (*Portulaca oleracea*) may seem like a weed to some but it's eaten in many countries as a delicacy and is found both cultivated and wild. Purslane is highly nutritious: extremely rich in omega-3 fatty acids, it also contains many vitamins. The vineyards of Kakheti are full of purslane – or *danduri* as the Georgians call it – so it's easy there to forage an armful and make this delicious salad. As with any plant growing low to the ground, purslane needs careful soaking in several changes of cold water to rid it of sand or grit. Add a tablespoonful of vinegar to the soaking water for extra disinfection if your purslane comes from the wild. Gia makes his purslane salad without oil as part of a *supra*, but add a few spoonfuls of good oil if you are serving it alone.

SERVES **6 at a** *supra*
PREPARATION **10 minutes**
COOK **10 minutes**

15g / ½oz / 4 garlic cloves, minced

200g / 7 oz purslane, washed, thickest stalks removed

3 tbsp fresh lemon juice or white wine vinegar

2 tbsp finely sliced spring onions / scallions, green and white parts

1 tbsp finely chopped dill

2 tbsp finely chopped coriander / cilantro

chilli / red pepper flakes

salt and freshly ground black pepper

Put the minced garlic into a small bowl with ½ cup water. Set aside.

Bring a large pan of water to the boil. Drop the purslane into the boiling water and blanch it for 2–3 minutes. Drain and refresh immediately under cold running water. Drain.

When the purslane is cool, turn it into a serving bowl. Toss it with the lemon juice or vinegar. Sprinkle with the spring onions and herbs, and with 1–2 tablespoons of the garlic in water mixture, to taste (save the rest for another dish). Season with salt and pepper. Mix well. Sprinkle with chilli flakes and serve.

Stewed sour cherries

ALUBLIS SHECHAMANDI   ალუბლის შეჭამანდი

The sour cherries were in season in June one year when I spent time in chef Gia's kitchen at Pheasant's Tears and he cooked some into a delicious zingy and tart compote (in the English use of the word), stewing them with sugar and freshly grated ginger. Use like a condiment at a *supra* with barbecued meats or stir them into yogurt for a quick dessert or breakfast. If you can't find sour cherries, use sweet cherries with just 2 tablespoons of sugar.

PREPARATION **10 minutes**
COOK **20–30 minutes**

60ml / 2fl oz / ¼ cup water
65g / 2 oz / ⅓ cup sugar
500g / 1lb 2 oz sour cherries, washed and pitted
1 tbsp grated fresh ginger root

Heat the water and sugar together in a heavy medium saucepan over low heat until the sugar dissolves.

Stir in the cherries and any juice they have made. Add the ginger, cover the pan and cook over medium heat for 10 minutes, or until the fruit is boiling. Lower the heat, and cook for 10–15 minutes more, or until the fruit is soft.

Allow to cool before serving.

QVEVRI-MADE CIDER
SAIDANAA CIDERI:
NATHAN MOSS

Nathan Moss is a well-travelled London hipster, complete with beard and foodie pedigree. He started eating sea urchins aged five, worked in Japan as a car mechanic and at the Landmark Hotel in London as a sound technician before being promoted to the brewery at Moorgate Conference Centre. Why did he move to Georgia? "I knew I wanted to live somewhere with good quality food and drink," he says. "Luckily it turned out to be Georgia."

In 2013 his godparents – Bristol choirmasters who teach Georgian folk songs – brought Nathan to Sighnaghi to attend Village Harmony, Patty Cuyler's influential singing workshop in world music. "I knew little about

wine so there was nothing to unlearn but I was blown away by Pheasant's Tears Kisi 2012," he says. "I wanted to do something in Georgia. I worked for several months at Pheasant's Tears, learning about natural wines and *qvevri*. With Jancis Robinson's book, *How to Taste*, I found out about acidity, tannins and sweetness. I missed cider but it isn't part of Georgia's culture. It got me thinking about the *qvevri* process."

Nathan researched craft cider. He bought two 220-litre (48-gallon) *qvevri* – they fit in his car – and borrowed a press. "I found sharp, sweet apples used

Cider apples at Saidanaa

for vinegar and bought 1,600 kilos. It's cold here so I waited until after Christmas for the fermentation to finish but the first result was pretty good. I want to make sparkling organic cider using the *méthode ancestrale* of spontaneous fermentation in *qvevri*, bottling it straight from my Sighnaghi garden. After all, Saidanaa Cideri means 'Where is this cider from?'"

Nathan's married to a Georgian architect, Nanouk Zaalishvili, and has no plans to leave. "I love it here and there's so much to do," he says. "Sighnaghi has just 1,500 residents: that's less than Dulwich College!" nathan@saidaanacideri.com

Alex Rodzianko

WINE
JSC CRADLE OF WINE

Paul Rodzianko is a businessman from Tuxedo Park, New York who came to Georgia in 2008. Chairman of the Hermitage Museum Foundation, Rodzianko's business activities focus on Russian-American links in culture, energy and environmental technology. He has worked too with an industrial winery in Kakheti, Teliani Valley.

Paul's son, Alex, first became interested in *qvevri* wines through John Wurdeman (see p. 166). Father and son decided to make wine, buying a house and building a cellar in

Sighnaghi. They own 9 hectares (22 acres) of vineyards in the Sighnaghi area at Ojio, Khashmi and Nukriani. Alex and Paul began working in *qvevri* and bottling their wines. They produce field blends from the older vineyards, as well as Rkatsiteli and Kakhuri Mtsvane.

In 2015 Alex started to train as a chef at New York's Culinary Institute. Paul continues the winemaking activities. www.facebook.com/cradleofwines

BODBE MONASTERY

Close to Sighnaghi is the stunning Bodbe Monastery where the remains of St Nino are enshrined; she is credited with bringing Christianity to Georgia in the 4th century. In the Middle Ages the kings of Kakheti were crowned at Bodbe. Recently it's been restored and is a memorable place to visit.

Today this tranquil oasis, strategically placed on a promontory overlooking the Alazani Valley, is run by nuns, has perfectly tended gardens and is open to the public. Its Pilgrim Refectory serves delicious savoury pies. Open daily 10:00 to 19:00. Tel: +995 595277107

A nun tends the vegetable garden at Bodbe

SOUTH-EAST OF SIGHNAGHI

Art lovers: the village of Mirzaani, a few kilometres south-east of Bodbe, was the birthplace of Niko Pirosmani (1862–1918), motifs from whose

iconic naive paintings are seen everywhere in Georgia. Pirosmani's house is now a small museum (open Tuesday to Sunday). On the third Saturday of October each year, on Pirosmani Day, the *supra* that was the subject of his paintings is recreated on the table within the museum.

If you prefer ancient ruins, the remains of Khornabuji Castle – or Queen Tamar's Castle – are perched high on a rock 3 kilometres from Dedoplistskaro. Ancient *qvevri* are still visible in this fortress that may have served Tamar in the early 13th century but whose origins are older. The strategic promontory was originally built on in the 1st century BC, and was first chronicled in the 5th century in the reign of Vakhtang 'the Wolf Head', the 32nd king of Iberia who founded Tbilisi and first imported silkworms into Georgia from India (see p. 181). It offers commanding views on clear days.

BODBISKHEVI MARKET

Butcher's stall at Bodbiskhevi market

This magnificent Sunday food market attracts people from Georgia and nearby Azerbaijan; it's eastern Georgia's largest market. I love wandering the lanes of everything from live chickens and squealing piglets to fresh vegetables, foraged greens, spices, walnuts, cheeses and hand-churned butter.

The butcher's section is one of the most powerful spectacles you'll see in Georgia, though not perhaps an easy sight for those used to the sanitized, supermarket image of meat. Here you are reminded, quite rightly, that our food comes thanks to the sacrifice of very real creatures. The meat from animals whose lives have been spent roaming the countryside and eating what they choose attracts the discerning eyes of those who will cook it.

I've often gone to Bodbiskhevi with chef Gia Rokashvili (see p. 169), who recounts the butchers' stories about the animals: where they lived, how old they were, who they belonged to. There's respect in the telling, the cooking and the eating of an animal that has lived a dignified life. Make sure you get there early in the morning to see the market at its best. Open Sundays 7:00 to 13:00.

Herb seller at Bodbiskhevi

KVEMO MAGHARO

HERBALIST, SILK WORMS
LAMARA BEZHASHVILI

The first time I met Lamara Bezhashvili, she greeted me with a hug, a warm smile and some leaves she had just plucked from her garden. Soon she was giving helpful hints about their curative powers: how a dried walnut-leaf tisane is antiseptic for tooth problems, or how boiling an onion with apple and potato cures a cough. She's a healer who seems immediately in tune with whomever she encounters.

Lamara's alchemy extends to other aspects of nature. She's keeping the ancient tradition of breeding silkworms alive. Her rambling garden contains a small hut filled with trays of millions of grey-green silkworms in various stages of development. They live on fresh mulberry leaves.

"Many people in this area once bred these caterpillars for their silk cocoons; this important cottage industry has now mostly been lost," Lamara says, as we watch the silkworms devour their leaves. "I'm keeping it going, working with local women to produce simple goods we can spin, weave and sell." She shows me how to pull the silk from inside a silkworm without killing it, like a magician pulling one endless glistening thread out of a hat.

Lunch is eaten at a pretty garden table under a mulberry tree. Here too, Lamara's transformational skills are evident. She's an expert fermenter and presents an array of fermented flowers and vegetables, from *jonjoli* and acacia blossoms to green tomatoes, string beans, garlic heads and

cucumbers. They're the perfect counterpoint to grilled lamb, potato *khinkali* and dressed eggs and are found on every Georgian table. The conversation moves from bread mothers and cheese starters to everyday family life. We may be in a garden of medicinal plants but the most restorative cure is to be with the radiant Lamara, drinking a toast to friendship. lamarabreshumi@yahoo.com; tel: +995 593965595

HOW TO FERMENT ACACIA OR *JONJOLI* BLOSSOMS

Jonjoli are the blossoms of the Caucasian or Colchis bladdernut tree (*Staphylea colchica*). Pick the flowers just before they start to open to avoid insects being inside. Leave the flowers on their tender stems. Rinse them in cold water and drain lightly. Sprinkle with salt and press them under a weight for two hours. Rinse lightly.

Place the flowers into a glass or ceramic jar with 1 tablespoon of salt per litre (1¾ pints) of volume. Press them tightly to avoid air bubbles. Add a little dried dill (optional) and seal the jars. Left in a warm, sunny place, the flowers will ferment in about two weeks. Store in a cool dark place. When well made, they'll keep for several months.

After you remove some of the flowers from the jar, refill it with water to reduce the intensity of the salt. Serve with white or spring onion, coriander/cilantro and cold-pressed sunflower oil.

JUNE *SUPRA* MENU

Fried aubergines with herbs and garlic
Baby potatoes
Fermented green beans
Potato khinkali *with pepper*
Grilled skewered meat
Hard-boiled eggs with tiny coriander seeds
Fermented acacia flowers, garlic and tomato

Opposite:
Supra *table at Lamara's*

Top: Lamara; centre: jonjoli blossoms two days before picking; bottom: fermented jonjoli

MANAVI

It's mid June and the growing season is in full swing. We turn through some pine trees along the main road between Tbilisi and Sighnaghi onto a dirt track. The grass reaches the car windows. At the top of the lane is a small cabin with a larger structure beside it. We're having lunch at Nikoloz 'Niki' Antadze's and he's doing the cooking.

Niki is one of the original gang of four natural winemakers that inspired so many others. His laid-back charm belies his determination and cultural approach to winemaking. He's rescuing ancient vines, working organically and finding new ways to vinify native grapes. Niki studied in Germany, taught German, translated books and plays and worked as a ski guide before that. Since 2012 he's concentrated on wine.

"I bought my first vineyard in 2006 and it seemed natural to make the

The table set in the unfinished cellar

wine organically, in clay *qvevri*," Niki says as he sprinkles herbs over a cold yogurt soup. "In 2008 Luca Gargano, an Italian importer, said he'd buy my wine if I bottled it. The only others working in *qvevri* then were Ramaz Nikoladze, Soliko Tsaishvili and Iago Bitarishvili."

We're having lunch in his unfinished *qvevri* cellar (it's since been completed), eating practically al fresco. Like a giant playhouse, Niki has mapped out the room with straw bales one metre high to provide the cellar's insulation, and added a wooden roof. "I'll build the walls from clay to allow the room to breathe, with windows to let in the cool north wind," he says. The cellar's starting point is the *qvevri* he's already buried. For our lunch Niki's improvised a table over the wine-filled *qvevri*, complete with chequered cloth.

We're on a south-facing hillside near the village of Manavi. "I chose this village because my mother's family are descendants of its former dukes," he says. "One vineyard's official name is Royal Cru and it was ours in the 1740s. There was a quasi-feudal set-up and Manavi's grapes went directly to the king. I also bought these vineyards because my great-aunt said it was a special place for Mtsvane. It's part of my family's oral history, like how to dye shirts or cook certain dishes."

Niki has been Tbilisi based but now spends more time in the one-room hut beside the cellar. "I also dream of making cheese and growing vegetables but it's hard work, you have to do it slowly." His vineyard commitments have grown rapidly. To the hectare (2½ acres) of vines planted in 1972, he's added two more he'll plant soon. He rents two hectares (5 acres) nearby, in Kakabeti, of 95-year-old Rkatsiteli vines and 20-year-old ungrafted Saperavi on a hilltop at 800 metres (2,625 feet); Giorgi Kupatadze wanted help keeping his family's historic vineyards alive.

Niki's fascinated by old vines. "So much of our vine heritage has been destroyed through disease or politics, and now there are only around 15 very old vineyards left in Georgia," he says. "You must be gentle and not push them too much if you want interesting grapes."

Niki's great-aunt would be proud of his results with Mtsvane – Georgian for green – as he's taken this grape to new heights in different styles. With six months of maceration, it produces a light amber wine of surprising complexity, with fine acidity and tannins, and notes of pears, tea and resin. He also makes Mtsvane without skin contact as it sometimes become overly aromatic. "I prefer the wine to be ethereal, full of fresh air," he says. "With skin contact, the wine becomes layered, structured and warming, with higher alcohol levels."

Niki under an old eating grape vine

His Rkatsiteli has remarkable depth. "I used 10 percent whole bunches with their stems for a small carbonic maceration," he says. "I'm surprised at how many fresh fruit aromas appeared during the long fermentation. The amber, macerated Rkatsiteli gives layers of flavour, including of spice and dried fruits." Niki intends to plant several old varieties – including Kakhuri Tetri (Kakhetian White).

We eat lunch sitting above the *qvevri*. He's buried 16 – for a capacity of 19 tonnes – and plans to add ten more. "I've found an old *qvevri* maker in Imereti with his own quarry. It's high-quality clay they mix with mountain sand using a donkey. The clay ages for one year before use: clay ferments too."

Lunch was a triumph. Niki produced a feast from his humble kitchen in the cabin's porch, with motley dogs and cats in attendance. Cold yogurt soup was followed by tarragon and egg tart, spinach *pkhali*, green beans with eggs, beef stew and salad. Desserts are rarely served in Georgia but Niki surprised us with a delicious cherry and meringue dessert from his mother's recipe. "I learned to cook from her and my grandmother. Ten percent of Georgian men can cook. They cook well but not often, mostly celebration food, especially the meats."

Tarragon and egg pie

TARKHUNIS GHVEZELI   ტარხუნის ღვეზელი

Tarragon is the star of this fragrant pie and adds an aromatic component to a *supra*. Here a richer dough works well but you could also use shortcrust pastry.

MAKES 1 28–30cm / 11–12 in pie
 (serves 8–12)
PREPARATION 1 hour (including
 dough rising)
COOK 45 minutes

FOR THE DOUGH

375g / 13 oz / 3 cups plain/all-
 purpose flour
½ tsp salt
¾ tsp quick-acting/instant yeast
1 egg, at room temperature
115g / 4 oz / ½ cup butter
150ml / 5 fl oz / ⅝ cup warm milk

FOR THE FILLING

450g / 1lb spring onions / scallions
150g / 5 oz / 1 cup onion, chopped
2 tbsp sunflower oil
60g / 2 oz / 1½ cups fresh tarragon
 leaves
1 tsp salt
5 hard-boiled eggs, chopped
60g / 2 oz / 4 tbsp butter
1 egg yolk, for topping the pie

Make the dough: mix the flour, salt and yeast in the bowl of a food processor. Beat the egg and butter into the warm milk. Pour them into the dry ingredients and process until the dough begins to form a ball. Knead or process for 2 minutes. Cover and leave to rise for 30 minutes at room temperature.

Slice the spring onions / scallions crosswise into 1-cm / ½-in pieces, separating the whites and greens. Sauté the onion in the oil over medium heat until translucent, 3–4 minutes. Stir in the whites of the spring onion / scallion and cook for 3 minutes. Add the greens and the tarragon leaves and cook for 3–4 minutes. Remove from the heat, sprinkle with the salt and set aside.

Place a heavy flat baking tray in the centre of the oven and preheat to 190°C / 375°F / Gas 5. Punch down the dough and divide it into two equal balls.

On the floured board, roll the first ball into a circle large enough to fit a 28–30 cm / 11–12 in flat baking pan. Place it in the pan. Press the dough evenly into the pan, leaving a slight overhang. Spread the onion and tarragon evenly over it, leaving a 2-cm / 1-in border of dough around the edges. Sprinkle the chopped eggs and black pepper on top and dot with butter (see small photo).

Roll out the second dough big enough to reach the pan's edges. Transfer it onto the pie; lightly wet the dough edges and crimp the pastry to seal, trimming off any excess. Beat the egg yolk with a little water and paint the pie top. Prick it with a fork. Bake until the pastry is golden brown, 30–35 minutes.

Green beans with eggs

MTSVANE LOBIO   მწვანე ლობით

This easy recipe is perfect for a relaxed summer's lunch when green beans and tomatoes are abundant and full of flavour.

SERVES **4–6**
PREPARATION **15 minutes**
COOK **30 minutes**

600g / 1lb 5 oz green, string or
   runner beans
4 tbsp extra virgin olive oil
30g / 1 oz / 2 tbsp butter
115g / 4 oz red onion, chopped
300g / 10 oz tomato, peeled, seeded
   and chopped
½ tsp coriander seeds, crushed
4 eggs, beaten
30g / 1 oz / ½ cup finely chopped
   coriander / cilantro
salt and freshly ground black
   pepper

Steam or boil the beans until they are cooked the way you like them. Remove the beans from the pan and refresh under cold running water. Chop them into 2-cm / 1-in pieces.

In a large frying pan, heat the oil with the butter. Stir in the onion and cook over low heat until the onion is sweet and starting to brown, about 6–7 minutes. Stir in the tomato and coriander seeds and cook for 3–4 minutes more to soften the tomato. Stir in the beans, raise the heat to medium, and cook until the beans are heated through.

Season the beaten eggs with salt and freshly ground black pepper and pour them onto the vegetables with the chopped herbs. Keep stirring until the eggs have set, about 3–4 minutes. Serve hot.

Chilled yogurt soup

MATSVNIS SHECHAMANDI   მაწვნის შეჭამანდი

Soups made with *matsoni*, or cow's-milk yogurt, are very popular in Georgia. Many are made with sautéed onions, rice and herbs and served hot. I fell in love with this cold yogurt soup; it's so refreshing on a hot summer's day. Use good-quality organic yogurt with a nice acid tang to it.

SERVES 4
PREPARATION 15 minutes

500g / 1lb 1 oz / 2 cups plain yogurt
240ml / 8fl oz / 1 cup water
85g / 3 oz very finely sliced and chopped cucumber
14g / ½oz / 2 spring onions / scallions, finely chopped, white and green parts
1 tbsb finely chopped coriander / cilantro
1 tbsp finely chopped dill
1 tsp finely chopped mint leaves
1 tsp finely chopped chives
½ tsp finely chopped medium-hot green chilli
salt and freshly ground black pepper

Whisk the yogurt with most of the water until smooth. The consistency should be creamy but soup-like. If necessary add a little more or less water.

Whisk in the remaining ingredients and season with salt and pepper.

Allow the soup to rest in the refrigerator for at least 30 minutes before serving to bring out the flavours of the herbs. Serve chilled.

DAVIT-GAREJA

Davit-Gareja is a group of cave monasteries built up a hillside on the border with Azerbaijan, near Kakheti's eastern border with Kvemo Kartli. This area was once covered with trees, but iron smelting in the 1st millennium BC and the Turks' determination to level the terrain in the 16th century led from deforestation to desertification.

The first monastery was founded here in the 6th century by Saint David, one of the Thirteen Assyrian Fathers. Others were added successively, carved into the sandstone hill with sophisticated systems for storing and sharing water and with terraced gardens. The cave-monasteries were decorated with beautiful frescoes, some of which remain today. In the 12th century, a school of fresco and manuscript painting was developed here: the complex became eastern Georgia's most important centre of culture and education. The monasteries of Udabno and Lavra are among the best restored; only three of over 20 monasteries are now in use. Ongoing work by archæologists, monks and art restorers is bringing others back to life.

The site is easily reached from Tbilisi and can be visited as a day trip. Go with someone who knows the way: the road is difficult and requires a 4x4 vehicle; the terrain attracts snakes in summer. Respect the dress code the monks request: men should wear trousers and women should cover their shoulders, arms, heads and legs.

Opposite:
Niki clearing
around old
vines

4. SOUTH-WEST TO SAMTSKHE-JAVAKHETI

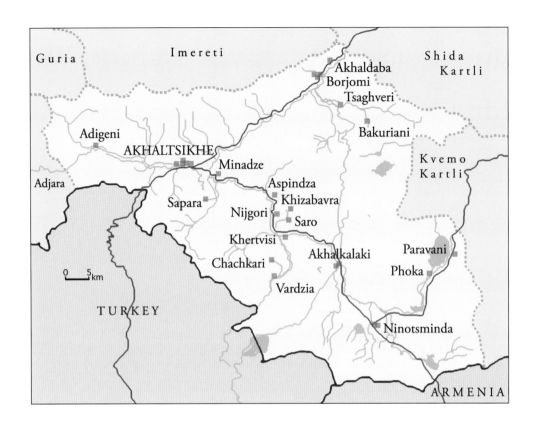

Akhaldaba   p. 231
Akhaltsikhe   p. 228
Aspindza   p. 212
Bakuriani   p. 231
Borjomi   p. 231
Chachkari   p. 206

Khertvisi   p. 211
Khizabavra   pp. 208, 226
Minadze   p. 210
Nijgori   p. 212
Paravani   pp. 194, 197

Phoka   p. 197
Sapara   p. 229
Saro   p. 228
Tsaghveri   p. 231
Vardzia   p. 200

This trip, to the southern borders with Armenia and Turkey, takes us through some of my favourite Georgian landscapes, from the high plateau of Javakheti to the majestic mountains of Vardzia and along the Mtkvari River valley to Akhaltsikhe. It also takes us to what was one of the world's earliest winemaking centres.

Here two regions – Samtskhe (in what is still called Meskheti) and Javakheti – are joined into one and their area's history has been carved in stone in the hidden cave city of Queen Tamara and the ancient vine terraces that were sacked by the Ottomans. 'King' Tamar's soldiers lived in the caves with their horses and drank wine crushed from the indigenous vines of a once-thriving village, Chachkari, whose three remaining families have been pushed to sell their centuries-old walnut trees to survive. Closer to Akhaltsikhe, volcanic valleys with what look like showered meteors give way to dramatic diagonals of stone where the bedrock has been forced from below.

The mountains are covered by slow-moving herds, and by colonies of wild mints and sages, broom and giant cow parsley, smokebush and evening primrose, perfect for hoopooes. They're peopled by small numbers of rural villagers who battle the elements to make their living but whose hospitality abounds. Their modest settings provided us with remarkably refined food: French-style cheeses made on an austere steppe by nuns in a convent, and a meal fit for a queen in the humble kitchen of a teacher. Special foods here include salted and smoked goose, potatoes and wheat. Until recently many people in the wine valleys lived semi-underground in stone houses built into the hillsides, with cellars for wine and stone terracing. A young winemaker's ambitious project offers hope for a revival of the area's wine culture and a more prosperous future; it's echoed by Georgian winemakers from other regions.

We drove this route (via Kvemo Kartli and the Paravani Lakes) in summer, when the mountain passes and the plateau were accessible. In colder seasons you can get to Samtskhe-Javakheti from Tbilisi via Borjomi and Akhaltsikhe.

PHOKA

CHEESE AND PRESERVES
PHOKA NUNNERY

Previous pages: Pastoralists with their herds on the Paravani Plateau

If you drive south from Tbilisi across Kvemo Kartli into Javakheti you reach the high volcanic Paravani Plateau whose long lakes stretch out among mountains that take on lavender tones in autumn's soft light. You pass sparse villages with haystacks taller than houses, neat cabbage and potato patches, and many dung-heaps. The only trees – stunted plums and apples – grow close to the houses. At over 2,000 metres (6,560 feet), we're above the treeline on expansive Alpine steppes that offer summer pastures for vast herds of sheep, goats and cattle.

Phoka Nunnery: A nun pulls her wheelbarrow past haystacks and drying dung

The winters are long and cold. Temperatures go down to between -20°C (-4°F) and -40°C (-40°F) when the animals need to be kept indoors, so supplies of hay are critical. Owing to the lack of wood, dung is an important heat source. Cow pats and manure are dried in summer along the rough stone walls and neatly stacked for winter use. Here, nothing is wasted.

Given the harshness of the climate, it's surprising to come upon one of Georgia's most famous nunneries close to the southern tip of Lake Paravani. Phoka Nunnery is a sacred place for followers of St Nino, the nation's patron saint who is credited with bringing Christianity to Georgia in the 4th century. The Eastern Orthodox Church recounts that the young Nino travelled from Cappadocia in central Turkey to preach and that she crossed into what was then the Georgian Kingdom of Iberia around 320 AD.

"We believe she came up through Armenia and arrived here on 1 June, on her way to Mtskheta, the country's capital at that time," explains Mother Shushaniki, one of 23 nuns currently living in the convent. "Legend has it that she cried on seeing snow for the first time. Before continuing her mission, she spent the night here and had a vision of a saint with a letter addressed to the pagan king."

The church was built in the 11th century. The monastery was opened in the 19th century and has gone through several renewals, most recently in 2000. It now includes ultra-modern buildings alongside the modest local dwelling and ancient church whose Byzantine-style mosaics were created by the nuns. Phoka continues to attract many pilgrims and visitors. The nuns run a local school, work in the community and produce a range of goods, including cloisonné enamel icons, preserves, honey and cheese.

"There had been a long tradition of cheesemaking in this area as the missionaries sent by the Pope in Rome brought that culture in the 17th century," says Mother Shushaniki. "In 1992, when the monastery opened in its modern guise, we started experimenting and in 2010 began selling our cheeses. We've expanded the repertoire with recipes learned at several Benedictine monasteries in France and from internet masterclasses in production and ageing. We currently keep ten cows, and two of us make the cheeses from their milk. We can produce plenty of cheese but have nowhere nearby to sell many. So we've developed some special cheeses that mature over time, like the Javakhetian blue-mould cheese using vegetable ash that is aged for 45 days."

The Phoka cheeses are well-known in Georgia and are now sold in Tbilisi (see p. 63) as well as from the attractive little shop inside the monastery. The range includes 11 cheeses in many shapes and styles. The shop is like a jewel box, with dainty piles of cookies and truffles, chocolates neatly wrapped with Japanese papers, and jars of honey from their own hives. The nuns' unusual preserves include green *ajika*; strawberry jam with chillies; blackberry jam with rose petals; grated seabuckthorn; and Cornelian cherry. www.phokanunnery.ge

Produce at Phoka Nunnery: top: cheese; bottom: sweetmeats

VARDZIA

The medieval cave city of Vardzia is the beacon that attracts visitors to this remote but stunning part of Georgia, close to the border with Armenia. Begun in the 12th century by King Giorgi III as a strategically placed fortification, Vardzia became a vast monastery and military complex under his daughter, Tamara. The hidden city was dug from the tufa rock at over 1,300 metres (4,265 feet) above sea level, and commands the Mtkvari River valley.

It is said that during times of war, the city could hold up to 10,000 soldiers, 600 horses and many more people. Each room had running water and was lit by torches. The armies trained and hid in the city during the day, sweeping down to surprise and vanquish their enemies by night. Wine was an important part of monastic and military life as Vardzia's 25 cellars attest, with over 185 *qvevri* buried within them. Originally much of the maze of tunnels, rooms and 13 churches was spread over 19 floors, and was not visible from the valley below. The violent earthquake of 1283 damaged and filled many of the caves: the mountainside nearest the valley broke away, revealing the caves' existence. Recent work has reopened about 40 percent of the city to visitors. Wear robust hiking shoes: the path through Vardzia is steep in parts and quite challenging.

WHERE TO EAT AND STAY A couple of kilometres past Vardzia, Valodia's Cottage is a modest but enterprising hotel surrounded by impressive vegetable and beautiful flower gardens. On summer evenings you eat dinner outside by the river. Tel: +995 59 9114506. At Vardzia Resort, a newly completed high-level complex across the valley from Vardzia there's a good restaurant specializing in grilled foods, including *khachapuri* on a spit and barbecued meats. www.vardziaresort.com

OUR MEAL AT VALODIA

Meskhetian Pie (layered with melted butter)
Kinkhali *filled with cheese, with caramelized onions*
Tomato and cucumber salad
Khachapuri
Beef and tomato stew
Ajapsandali *(tomato, aubergine, lots of peppers)*
Cheese
River trout
Mulberry brandy

Opposite: Vardzia's cave city with one of its many churches (the arches with the bells)

Beef and tomato stew

CHASHUSHULI ჩაშუშული

At Valodia's Cottage in summer you eat dinner outdoors beside the river. They prepare a simple beef, onion and tomato stew that inspired this one, with clean flavours and aromatic herbs. In Georgia it would probably be cooked on top of the stove, but I find it easier to bake it in the oven. If you make this in summer, use fresh ripe tomatoes you've peeled and seeded. Otherwise use Italian peeled plum or cherry tomatoes. There's just a hint of heat from the chilli in this stew, it's not supposed to be too fiery. This stew is also made with chicken, when it's known as *chakhokhbili*.

SERVES 3–4, more in a *supra*
PREPARATION **20 minutes**
COOK **90–120 minutes**

40g / 1½oz / 3 tbsp butter
225g / 8 oz / 1½ cups chopped onion
450g / 1lb stewing beef, cut into
    3cm / 1¼ in cubes
1 tsp ground fenugreek
10g / ⅓ oz / 3 garlic cloves, finely
    chopped
480ml / 16fl oz / 2 cups water or
    plain meat broth
1 tsp salt
240ml / 8fl oz / 1 cup tomato pulp,
    fresh or canned (without juice)
finely chopped medium-hot fresh
    chilli, to taste
30g / 1 oz fresh coriander / cilantro,
    tied into a bunch

TO FINISH
10g / ⅓oz / ¼ cup chopped fresh
    coriander / cilantro
10g / ⅓oz / ¼ cup chopped basil,
    purple and green
2 tbsp chopped fresh parsley

Preheat the oven to 180°C / 350°F / Gas 4.

In a heavy, cast-iron or other ovenproof casserole (Dutch oven), melt half the butter. Stir in the onions and cook over low heat until translucent, 7 minutes.

Turn the onions onto a side plate and add the remaining butter to the pan.

Stir in the meat, raise the heat and brown the beef on all sides in small batches. When all the meat is browned, return it to the pan with the onions, the fenugreek and half of the garlic. Cook for a minute more.

Add the water, salt and tomato pulp and bring the mixture to the boil. Add the chilli. Remove from the heat, pushing the bunch of coriander into the middle of the stew.

Cover the casserole and place in the centre of the preheated oven. Cook, stirring occasionally, for 70–90 minutes or until the meat is tender but not dry.

Remove the stew from the oven. Pull out the coriander bouquet, squeezing it against a spoon to extract all the flavour; discard. Stir in the chopped fresh herbs and remaining garlic, and allow to stand for 5 minutes before serving.

Grilled meatballs

KABABI ქაბაბი

Barbecued meats are great favourites in Georgia, as are kebabs made of ground meats with herbs and spices. If you don't have a barbecue, cook them on the grill or under the broiler. Use any mix of meats – lamb, beef and / or pork for these. The barberries give a lovely hit of sour-sweet fruit but if you can't find them use dried sour cherries or cranberries, cut into quarters. If possible, crush your own coriander seeds: the result will be much more fragrant. You can add some chilli to spice them up, but I like the aromatic quality of the coriander seed and cumin to come through.

MAKES **10 meatballs**
PREPARATION **80 minutes (including rest)**
COOK **15–20 minutes**

225g / 8 oz ground beef
225g / 8 oz ground pork
1 egg
4g / ⅛ oz / 1 clove garlic, chopped
2 tbsp dried barberries
¼ tsp ground cumin
⅓ tsp coriander seeds, crushed
15g / ½ oz / ⅓ cup finely chopped fresh coriander / cilantro (including stems)
60g / 2 oz / ½ cup onion, finely chopped
30g / 1 oz / ⅓ cup plain / unseasoned breadcrumbs
½ tsp salt
freshly ground black pepper
10 slices streaky bacon

Combine all the ingredients except the bacon in a medium bowl. Mix well, cover and refrigerate for at least one hour.

Preheat grill / broiler to 270°C / 500°F.

Divide the meat mixture into ten. One handful at a time, form them into compact oval balls, squeezing to stop them from crumbling. Thread the balls onto skewers that will fit in your grill / broiler.

Wrap one slice of bacon tightly around each ball so the bacon doesn't overlap, as in the small photo.

Place the skewers about 12cm / 5in from the heat source and grill for a total of 14–18 minutes, turning the balls three times (or use your barbecue).

Check for doneness: the meat should be cooked through. Serve as part of a *supra* or alone, with salad and crusty bread.

CHACHKARI

Fence, dog, house, woman in Chachkari

You reach the high village of Chachkari by taking the narrow road that passes below Vardzia, through the Vardzia car park and along the river, and then climbing up, around and behind it (on the right-hand side if you are facing Vardzia's mountain). It's a steep, rocky road that's accessible by rugged vehicle or walkable in hiking boots (but be careful: I fell there in smoother walking shoes).

The small village stretches towards the interior of the mountain with pale tufa rock formations on either side that protect and hide it. It's now only inhabited by the old folk of three families but once was home to three generations of fourteen families. Modest animal pens are delineated by pole and wire fences and crumbling stone walls; fruit trees of former orchards are unkempt. In June I spotted self-seeded marijuana amidst the wildflowers, and encountered noisy dogs, a few chickens and a couple of old men tending their vegetables. It may be semi-abandoned now, but Chachkari's historical importance shouldn't be underestimated.

"Chachkari is the oldest village in this area and predates 12th-century Vardzia by hundreds of years," says Giorgi Natenadze, whose family origi-nated here, as he leads us though a meadow towards an ancient vine. "This was a highly developed centre of viticulture and these hillsides were covered

with terraces of vines. In the 16th century, under Ottoman rule, the villagers were rich and
paid high taxes. Despite the shortage of direct
sun, the mountains retain heat and Chachkari
was usually the first to harvest its grapes. The
village produced wine, walnuts, vegetables
and honey for the inhabitants of Vardzia."
The city was minutes away but hidden underground and its thousands of inhabitants
needed daily supplies; Chachkari provided
them through tunnels and secret entrances
reached from above.

A senior resident of Chachkari

We clamber across a stream to where a
300-year-old vine, thicker than the tree it's
planted beside, twists and disappears up into
the tree's foliage. At its feet is a little cave
room, dug from the rock. It's just tall enough
to stand in, and contains a large stone trough where the grapes were once
pressed by foot; the juice ran down through a hole at its base to be collected.

"Unlike in Vardzia, this village had many
such presses, and *qvevri* for making and storing the wine," Giorgi says. "Some wine was
transported in animal skins to *qvevri* buried
inside Vardzia's caves. The Ethnographical
Museum in Tbilisi has 70 houses from different Georgian regions; one is from this village."

Today Chachkari's survival depends on the
renewed interest in Georgia's wine history. But
the challenges it faces are many and, in some
cases, brutal. As we were wandering through
the village we heard the high-pitched sound of
chainsaws cutting wood. Giorgi let out a cry
and, calling Shota to go with him, started running towards the noise. When I reached them
I found a scene of devastation. In the centre of
the village, a group of foreign workers were
cutting down a 300-year-old walnut tree.
Giorgi pleaded with them to stop but it was
too late: other magnificent walnut trees had
already been felled and a vast tractor truck

*Giorgi and Shota Lagazidze try to
stop more walnut trees from being
felled*

had crushed a hillside's worth of stone-wall terracing to get to them.

"This is a crime I've been trying to prevent," said Giorgi, almost in tears.
"These ancient, irreplaceable trees are being sold to the Turkish and Italian
furniture industry by unscrupulous dealers who come to these rural areas,

offer the old people a handful of dollars and destroy the villages' culture and ecosystems. I offered the villagers money not to do this but they are easily bullied and this is the result." The men listened, shrugged their shoulders and continued cutting. We came away depressed and shocked at the loss of this natural patrimony.

KHIZABAVRA VALLEY

WINE
FROM NATENADZE'S
WINE CELLAR

View of the Paravani Valley

Opposite: Giorgi Natenadze with the ancient stone terraces below Khizabavra

Giorgi Natenadze has a dream. This dynamic young man's ambition is to relaunch the native viticulture of Meskheti, the part of south-western Georgia now called Samtskhe that has been sidelined for over 100 years.

"This was once a thriving wine-producing region before the Ottoman Turks occupied it in the 16th century and stayed for almost 400 years," he says as we drive from Vardzia towards Akhaltsikhe, following the meandering Mtkvari River. On either side of the valley, sometimes for long stretches at a time, the linear rhythm of ancient stone-wall terracing can be seen on the mountain-sides, though most are now abandoned and overgrown. Before the occupation, Meskheti was much larger and included what is now the northern part of Turkey, from Armenia to the Black Sea.

"Meskheti was one of the world's oldest winemaking areas and viticulture led the economy here," he says. "The Ottoman occupation ended that. 1,100 – or 80 percent – of the villages in these mountains were razed, sixth-century terraces were wrecked, vines were grubbed up and the locals were given the choice of demolishing their cellars or being killed." Despite that, in the 16th century 10,000 tons of grapes of seven colours were sent from Aspindza to Turkey for making into juice. But winemaking traditions were lost. As recently as 2005 the only wines being produced in the area were made domestically, by crushing grapes with sugar and water.

Part of Giorgi's project is to renew the terraces. He and his partner have so far acquired 32 hectares of terraced land from the government and are working with skilled masons to rebuild the volcanic basalt dry-stone walls.

"These black rocks are key to the terroir's success as they hold the sun's heat for 24 hours," he says. "They were quarried from higher in the mountains and brought here centuries ago, as was the soil that fills the terraces and the water needed for irrigation in this drought-prone area. The re-habilitation is an expensive undertaking but investing here in a 10

Giorgi Natenadze at the base of the 300-year-old vine in Chachkari

to 15 year cultural project will bring life back to the communities and help regenerate this very poor area." Giorgi is replanting the vineyards with native Meskhetian varieties.

"Most indigenous Georgian grape varieties came from Meskheti but most disappeared during our country's turbulent history," he says. Giorgi acts like a detective, following leads to seek out any surviving native vines. "Sometimes I see a Meskhetian surname in another part of Georgia. I phone the family and ask if they took a vine cutting with them when they moved. You'd be surprised how many did." He takes GPS readings and cuttings of any he finds.

Closer to home, Giorgi scans the countryside around Akhaltsikhe, where his cellar is located, looking for abandoned castles, woods or houses where vines may have been left unattended. We visit one in the hamlet of Minadze. Behind a crumbling house that's thick with wild roses, a spiralling 250-year-old vine climbs over a poplar tree.

"To reach the grapes I have to get up to the vines's top canes where it naturally produces its fruit." He scrambles up like a young boy, coming down minutes later with his hand full of grapes. Giorgi's collection of local vines now comprises 44 varieties planted in a half-hectare vineyard near his home. Of these, 24 have been identified as Meskhetian while others are being DNA-tested. He'll name those without identities using the family name or village where he found the vines.

In 2013 Giorgi began microvinifications of this collection, sometimes making only one litre of wine from each variety, to taste and compare them. His cellar is full of wines bottled under his label 'From Natenadze's Wine Cellar'.

Meskhuri, a red variety, was his first wine. He made 920 bottles of it in 2009 and 900 in 2012. It's got a lovely nose of raspberries and an exotic flavour with lively acidity and attractive tannins. Other varieties he's working with are Meskhetian Mtsvane, the early-harvesting white Samariobo and white Tskhenis Dzudzu which translates literally as horse breast. He runs a wine shop in the square in front of Akhaltsikhe's fortress where both natural and larger-scale wines are sold.

Khertvisi, one of Georgia's most spectacular fortresses. Legend has it that Khertvisi was one of the first fortresses that Alexander the Great came upon in Georgia

Giorgi knows he can't change the local wine culture alone. He helped establish the Georgian Traditional Wine Association of Samtskhe-Javakheti to restore local wines and train young people in good winemaking practice. This will improve family wines and stimulate agritourism. It's helping attract winemakers from further afield. John Wurdeman of Pheasant's Tears (see p. 166) has planted vines near the Khertvisi fortress with the French organic winemaker, Thierry Puzelat, from the Loire. Zurab Topuridze (p. 283), the Gurian winemaker, is also launching a project here.

Looking at the now-barren terraces through Giorgi's eyes, the hillsides become green and the vines laden with grapes and potential. "A Greek writer came here in the seventh century and described its beauty and the many colours of the grapes he saw growing. At that time we exported wines to Persia, Egypt, Athens and even Rome. When I started, everyone told me I was crazy, that it couldn't be done. But we've started sending Meskhetian wines out into the world again." www.natenadze.company

NIJGORI, ASPINDZA

COOK
MAKVALA ASPANIDZE

Still feeling exhilarated about Giorgi's vineyards (and upset about Chachkari's walnut trees), we turn from the Mtkvari Valley road into Makvala Aspanidze's narrow driveway. Inside the gates is a familiar rural setting: haystacks, woodpiles and flat circular baskets of stoned plums drying in the sun. A few chickens peck at the grass around her single-storey house of grey stone and rough mortar; they scatter as she comes to greet us.

Makvala's interior makes an unforgettable impression. The main front room runs the width of the house and includes an area with three neatly made single beds, a small dining table with chairs, a modest kitchenette and a storage area for grains and seeds. What makes this three-in-one still more unusual is that the roofbeams seem, at some point, to have been raised and the internal walls partly removed. The result is more like a theatre set than a conventional house, particularly as we discover that Makvala now lives here alone. There are more rooms to the back, including Makvala's bedroom. Beside her bed, a wood-burning stove heats the house and can be used for cooking (see p. 8).

Makvala's kitchenette comprises a work table covered with a rose-motif waterproof cloth; a four-burner stove and oven running on bottled gas; plus a few standing cabinets for dishes and foods. There's no sink because there's no running water in her house. She fills several buckets and bowls in the kitchen from a well in the back garden.

From this simple kitchen Makvala has produced some of the most re-fined, unusual and delicious meals I've had the pleasure of eating in Georgia. She's an outstanding cook and has collected many ancient recipes. When I asked if she had thought of writing a cookbook, she replied that she's too tired: between tending to the animals and her vegetable plot and teaching Georgian literature in the village school she has enough on her plate. "We work like the oxen that plough the land," she says.

Makvala was born in Saro, a village higher up the mountain. "This low-er area near the river grew the vegetables and fruits for the upper villages," she says as she begins to work the dough for her exceptional *khachapuri*, made with multi-layered pastry like filo. "Up in Saro everything was baked in the *purne*, the small building where ten or fifteen families would pool their wood and make enough breads for two weeks. It was built of clay and stones and had two floors, the lower for the fire and the upper for the oven. Now each family has its own."

Makvala is a resourceful cook and, like most Georgians, is used to fora-ging for seasonal mushrooms, berries and wild greens for cooking and medicinal use. She prefers to preserve them through sun-drying rather than by fermenting and pickling. The family eats the main meal in the evening,

Opposite: Makvala stretching the dough for Meskhetian khachapuri

which is never more than two dishes unless they are preparing a *supra* or for guests.

"Everything is cooked fresh each day as I don't like eating leftovers," she says. "I don't have time to cook more than that as I leave at 6 am to go to work and also have to do the 'male' jobs, like chopping firewood, picking fruit and spraying the vegetables." She's unhappy about the seeds and hybrids that are now available as modern vegetables and fruits have less flavour than the local foods she grew up eating. "Even the tomatoes and potatoes are much less good than before."

Drying plums

As she cooks she recounts stories from her university student days in Tbilisi, and of receiving weekly parcels of food from home to share with her flatmates. She explains how hard it is to dry mulberries, the virtues of the local pork – which has pure white fat – and the goose *khinkali* dumplings that are traditional to this area, and that feature finely chopped smoked and salted goose meat similar to ham.

For our lunch, Makvala prepares a group of unusual dishes. The centrepiece is the fine, inimitable *khachapuri* whose dough is folded over and over with melted butter to make it flaky (see p. 213). There's also *tutmaji* pasta 'soup' and *qaisapa* fruit condiment (see pp. 222-25 for recipes). Her other dishes are harder to replicate because the ingredients may not be easy to come by, but I'm describing them for those who may want to give them a try.

Shechamandi. This recipe calls for dried stinging nettles (pick them early in the season, using gloves!). Makvala takes two handfuls of dried nettles (called *tchintchari*) that were picked in spring. She chops them roughly as she brings a panful of water to the boil (enough to cover the nettles by 5cm/2in). Cook the nettles, uncovered, for about 10 minutes. Wash half an espresso-cupful of cracked wheat in cold water, drain and add to the nettles; simmer for about 30 minutes. Add more water as necessary to keep the mixture wet: the consistency should be of a loose stew. When the wheat is almost tender, pound 2 cloves of garlic in a mortar with a good pinch of salt. Make a little roux of 2 tablespoons of flour and water in a teacup and add it to the nettle

Above: Dried nettles

Below: The nettles being cooked

mixture, stirring to integrate the flour well throughout. Add the garlic and continue stirring for another 2 to 3 minutes over medium heat. The sauce will have thickened. Finally whisk in a well-beaten egg, cook for a couple more minutes, stirring all the time. Remove from the heat and serve immediately.

Tklapi –
*home-made
fruit leather*

Tklapi. Instead of dessert we were offered rolled sheets of Makvala's
home-made fruit leather, or *tklapi,* made of two types of plums and mulberries. "They must be boiled for a full day, starting at 5 am, stirring often to
prevent sticking. You don't add extra sugar, just the natural sweetness of
the fruit, but they should never be super-sweet anyway, a bit of tartness is
part of their character. When the fruit is cooked and reduced (you can test
it on your arm to see if it sets), add a little flour to the mixture, and boil it
for another few minutes before straining it onto a moistened flat wooden
surface and spreading it thinly and evenly in a large circle to allow it to
cool and dry. It should be thin enough to see the light through it when it's
finished." makvalaaspanidze@gmail.com

MAKVALA'S MENU

Layered penovani *or Meskhetian* khachapuri
Small potato khinkali
Tutmaji, *like two-textured pasta*
Qaisapa: *boiled sun-dried fruits with sautéed onions*
Shechamandi: *stinging nettles with cracked wheat*
Bakmasi: *boiled mulberry juice syrup (Good for the stomach)*
Cheese: *stringy*
Tklapi: *home-made fruit leather*
Raspberry compote cordial, diluted with water

Makvala Aspanidze's front room includes three beds and a dining table

Meskhetian khachapuri

MESKHURI KHACHAPURI   მესხური ხაჭაპური

The buttery, layered dough of Meskhetian, or *penovani khachapuri* speaks of the Ottoman influence in southern Georgia. Makvala makes an elaborate version using an unleavened flour and water dough that she stretches as thin and as wide as strudel, painting its layers with melted butter. The result is a light, airy dough somewhere between puff pastry and filo. To stretch it this thin she uses a customized round, raised board (*pekhshumi*) and a tapered rolling pin (*ukhlavi*). She also stretches the dough by throwing it in the air.

I tried to recreate her ethereal dough, but mine just wasn't as fine as hers. The most similar result came from ready-made, all-butter puff pastry. It's quick and easy and produces an elegant pie. Use a mixture of your favourite cheeses, including mozzarella, cheddar, cottage cheese, feta and Emmental to bring more flavour.

SERVES 4
PREPARATION **10 minutes**
COOK **30 minutes**

1 roll ready-made all-butter puff pastry, chilled
75g / 1½oz / ⅔ cup grated or crumbled cheeses (see above)
80g / 3oz / ¾ cup grated firm / pizza mozzarella
1 egg yolk

Preheat the oven to 220°C / 425°F / Gas Mark 7. Place a heavy flat baking tray in the centre of the oven while the oven is preheating.

Unroll the dough and cut it into a square about 22cm / 9in on each side. Let it sit at room temperature on a lightly floured board while you prepare the cheese. (Refrigerate the remaining dough and use it for something else.)

Combine the cheeses, including the mozzarella, in a mixing bowl. Spread the cheese in an even layer onto the dough square. Pick up two opposing corners of the dough and bring them into the centre, pinching them together to hold. Repeat with the remaining corners. The parcel will look like a closed envelope with slightly higher outer edges. Pinch the seams of the envelope together so that it doesn't come apart during baking. Turn the bread over onto a sheet of parchment paper.

Paint the top with the beaten egg yolk. Slide the bread onto the preheated baking tray in the oven. Bake for 25–30 minutes, or until the top is a deep golden brown. Cut into pieces and serve hot.

Small potato khinkali dumplings

KARTOPILIS KHINKALI   კარტოფილის ხინკალი

These delicious small dumplings are stuffed simply with mashed potato and served with onions cooked in butter so slowly they caramelise. I've usually encountered them in the south of Georgia.

These *khinkali* are made with the simplest dough – just flour and water – and the amounts of flour you'll need may vary to make a dough that's pliable enough to roll out without sticking. See the Master Recipe on pp. 55-57.

MAKES **about 18**
PREPARATION **35 minutes**
COOK **30 minutes**

350g / 12 oz potato, peel on
30g / 1 oz / 2 tbsp butter

FOR THE DOUGH
200g / 7 oz / 1¾ cups plan/all-
     purpose flour
120ml / 4 fl oz / ½ cup water
½ tsp salt

FOR THE ONIONS
115g / 4 oz / ½ cup high-quality or
     clarified butter
170g / 6 oz / 1¼ cups chopped onion
salt

Boil the potato until it's just soft. Strain, peel and mash it with the 30g / 1 oz of butter. Salt to taste. Set aside.

Make the dough by following the instructions on p. 55.

Prepare the onions: in a heavy-bottomed, small saucepan, melt the butter. Stir in the onions and cook, over low to very low heat, until the onions and butter are starting to turn golden-brown. Check to make sure the onions are not cooking too fast: the butter should be lightly bubbling and the whole process should take 20–30 minutes. Swirl the pan every few minutes.

When the colour begins to deepen, swirl it more often, removing the pan from the heat if the colour deepens too much. You're looking for a rich nut brown. Don't let it burn! You'll be rewarded with delicious sweet-tasting onions. As soon as the onions are done (left), remove the pan from the heat.

Make the *khinkali*, following the instructions on pp. 56-57. Roll the dough out about 6mm / ¼ in thick initially and use a small cutter 5.5cm / 2¼ in in diameter to form the dough circles. Roll them out further before filling them with the potato mixture.

Serve the boiled *khinkali* with the bowl of hot buttered onions on the side.

Noodle and yogurt soup

TUTMAJI   თუთმაჯი

This fascinating dish is made using the humblest ingredients but thanks to some culinary imagination the result is an unusual soup with two textures. A simple flour and water dough similar to pasta's is fashioned into two shapes and each is cooked differently before being brought together in a yogurt broth. This dish should be eaten hot. It will add a talking point to a *supra* spread. They say it will also cure a hangover.

SERVES 4–6
PREPARATION 30 minutes
COOK 20 minutes

220 g / 8 oz / 1½ cups plain/all-purpose flour
120 ml / 4 fl oz / ½ cup water
60 g / 2 oz / 4 tbsp clarified butter
75 g / 2½ oz / ½ cup finely chopped onion
120 ml / 4 fl oz / ½ cup plain yogurt
salt

The pasta noodles (top), ropes (bottom right), and chunky pieces (bottom left)

Mix the flour and water together to form a fairly stiff dough. Knead it on a lightly floured surface for 3–4 minutes or until the dough is smooth and doesn't stick. Divide the dough ball into two pieces. Cover one in plastic wrap while you work the other.

Roll the first piece of dough into a circle about 6 mm / ¼ in thick. Sprinkle it with flour. Cut it into four strips, horizontally. Stack the strips and slice them crosswise to produce short noodles about 1.5 cm / ½ in wide. Sprinkle with flour as you break them into individual noodles.

Roll the remaining dough into several ropes the thickness of fat pencils. Cut each rope crosswise to form small chunky pieces about 1.5 cm / ½ in long. Sprinkle them with a little flour.

Melt the butter in a medium frying pan over low to medium heat and, when it's bubbling, add the chunky dough pieces to the butter, tossing them until they're golden brown. This will take about 15 minutes. Bring 720 ml / 24 fl oz / 3 cups of water to the boil in a medium saucepan. Add the onions to the pan with the dough chunks and cook, stirring often, until the onion is translucent, 5–6 minutes.

When the water boils, stir in 1½ teaspoons salt and the noodles. When the water comes back to the boil and the noodles come to the surface, stir in the yogurt and cook for a couple of minutes more. Stir in the onion mixture, taste for seasoning and serve.

Stewed fruits and onions

QAISAPA   ყაისაფა

"This dish is always the first to be served at a wedding," says Makvala. Qaisapa makes for an interesting addition to the *supra* table, bringing the surprise of caramelized onions to a compote of stewed dried fruits. Makvala sun-dries her own fruits – plums, apples, pears, peaches – but it's easy to make with whatever naturally dried fruits you can find. Dried fruits vary in how much liquid they will absorb so add a little more water if necessary. The result should be quite juicy. The important thing is to use a small, heavy saucepan to cook the onions in the butter, and to watch them carefully to make sure they don't burn.

SERVES **6–8 as a condiment**
PREPARATION **5 minutes**
COOK **45 minutes**

40g / 1½oz / ½ cup dried apple slices
40g / 1½oz / ½ cup dried pear slices
50g / 1¾oz / ½ cup stoned dried plums or prunes
720ml / 24fl oz / 3 cups water
60g / 2oz / 4 tbsp clarified butter
115g / 4oz / ¾ cup finely chopped onion
¼ tsp salt

Chop the fruit slices into halves or quarters. Put them in a medium saucepan with the water.

Cover the pan and cook over low heat, stirring often until the fruit is soft and cooked, about 45 minutes.

While the fruit is cooking, heat the butter in a small, heavy saucepan. Stir in the onions and cook over low heat for about 20 minutes, or until they turn a deep golden brown. Keep shaking or stirring the pan every few minutes, especially as the onions start to colour as there is a fine line between browned and burned!

When the fruit is soft and the plums are falling apart stir the onions into the fruit and mix well.

Season lightly with salt. Remove from the heat and serve warm.

ANIMAL WISDOM

I was high in the mountain village of Khizabavra at dusk when I heard the unmistakable sounds of a herd of animals approaching. A large group of sheep with a few goats was heading towards a crossroads in the village that had paths leading away from it in several directions. I asked which way the animals would go as I wanted to photograph them. The answer was: several.

Sure enough, in small groups, the sheep broke away from the pack and headed confidently towards different parts of the village. A small group came down the path towards me, and then peeled off, in twos and threes, left and right, to disappear through the open ground-floor doors of the houses around me. They were greeted by women, children and dogs. Without needing to be prompted, each animal knew who it belonged to and where it lived. The shepherd who had been with them all day followed on his horse, with a dog or two to accompany him, but by then his charges were all safely inside their stalls for the night.

UPPER KHIZABAVRA, NEAR SARO, ASPINDZA

CHEESE
NANA DATASHVILI

Nana Datashvili and her partner, Temure Plachiashvili, run a dairy and are responsible for bringing a new and unexpected type of cheesemaking to Georgia.

"We have twenty cows in the mountains above the Mtkvari River valley, ten kilometres from the Turkish border," says Nana who is a trained veteri-

narian and also runs and teaches at the village school in Khizabavra, on the other side of the valley from the dairy. I was delighted to find that Nana speaks Italian, so we were able to converse easily.

"We had been wanting to do a farm exchange and some Italian cheesemakers came to visit us. We made friends and now they come every summer. They have helped us set up our dairy and taught us to make cheese in the style of Parmigiano-Reggiano." Most Georgian cheese is made fresh daily, and consumed within a few days. Much of the tradition of long-ageing cheese has been lost in Georgia.

"We are now ageing our cheese for 90 days as they do in Italy, using only the milk of our pasture-fed herd," she says. The cheese, called Battista after their Italian dairyman friend, has won prizes in Tbilisi, where it is sold at the Cheese House (see p. 63) and in several restaurants in the capital. "We've recently also

Nana Datashvili

started making a cheese with Saperavi, the Georgian red wine, that is dark red outside and white within. This is a poor area, and it's hard to make a living here but we've found a way to make an income from cheesemaking by differentiating ourselves from the others." Dairy visits by appointment only. datashvili71@mail.ru; tel: +995 595518041

AKHALTSIKHE

Akhaltsikhe is the capital of Samtskhe-Javakheti region, and is a mere 22 kilometres from the Turkish border. Its monumental fortified citadel, Rabati, was begun in the 13th century and still dominates the city from its high perch (in Georgian: *akhal* = new, *tsikhe* = castle). The aristocratic complex has recently been restored (like new) and includes a mosque, minaret, church and synagogue. They confirm Akhaltsikhe's reputation for religious and ethnic tolerance as the city was divided between Christians, Jews, Ukrainians, Russians, Georgians and Armenians from the 17th century. The area still has a large Armenian population.

In the 18th century, Akhaltsikhe was the centre for the Circassian slave trade. It was a melting pot of cultures, with gold, silk, metalwork and wine all significant for commerce. A vineyard has recently been planted inside the fortress walls that testifies to the importance of the grape in Meskhetian history.

The castle complex also houses the Ivane Javakhishvili Samtskhe-Javakheti Historical Museum. Findings here date from the Palæolithic and Early Bronze Ages, with metal work and ceramic burial urns showing the impact of Hittite culture on Meskheti. The attractive museum is worth visiting, with jewellery, ceram-ics, wine jars and domestic pottery, including some from the Roman and mediæval periods.

Vines planted within Akhaltsikhe's citadel

WHERE TO STAY   I stayed at the recently modernized Hotel Gino Wellness Rabath, within the citadel walls, a perfect location for visiting the citadel. www.gino.ge
The Lomsia Hotel is another high-end choice, just outide of the citadel. These hotels have adequate restaurants; there are not many good restaurants in the town. www.lomsia.ge
WHAT TO SEE   A short drive south-east from Akhaltsikhe (reached from the road that goes towards Vardzia) is the fortified Sapara Monastery complex with the remains of a palace and several churches hidden in the hills. The largest church is intact and stands dramatically positioned above the gorge. It is dedicated to its founder, St Saba, and retains well-preserved 14th-century Byzantine frescoes. The complex was abandoned in the 16th century under the Ottoman expansion but the monastery is now active again.

BORJOMI

From Akhaltsikhe it's an easy drive along the verdant Mtkvari River valley north to Borjomi, Georgia's most famous town for mineral waters and natural spas. (Bottles of the naturally carbonated, fairly salty mineral water are sold throughout Georgia.) It's a lovely place to spend a few days relaxing and taking the waters and recently some of the historic spas have been modernized and upgraded. Chekhov, Tchaikovsky and the Russian royal family were among the most famous guests to be enthusiastic about taking the waters here, as was Stalin.

To the west of the town, the Borjomi-Kharagauli National Park is one of Europe's largest nature reserves, with 76,000 hectares of native forest and alpine meadows. It was established in 1935 and offers facilities for hiking, fauna and birdwatching. The reserve, which has long been under the supervision of the WWF, is home to 55 species of mammal and 95 of birds.

WHERE TO STAY   If you want to pamper yourself, the Borjomi Rixos is a new luxury hotel and spa near the elegant 1890s Romanov Palace, which is now the residence of the President of Georgia. www.borjomi.rixos.com. They're in Likani, on the south-western outskirts of Borjomi. The IHG Crowne Plaza is more central, near the thermal baths. www.IHG.com

If you're driving north from Borjomi towards Tbilisi and are feeling hungry, stop in Akhaldaba. There's a cluster of small restaurants famous for simply grilled meats and Imeretian *khachapuri* along the road. My favourite is Phorea, otherwise known by the woman owner's name, Tsitso.

BAKURIANI

From Borjomi the road going south-east to Tsaghveri along the Borjomula River leads up to Bakuriani, one of Georgia's most important ski resorts. The well-equipped winter resort is 25 kilometres from Borjomi, at 1,700 metres (5,575 feet) in the Trialeti range. If you're there in summer, these scenic mountain pastures have lovely trails for hiking. The resort offers high-end hotels with spa facilities as well as rooms to rent in private houses for less money and a more authentic experience.

Opposite:
The Mtkvari
River near
Borjomi

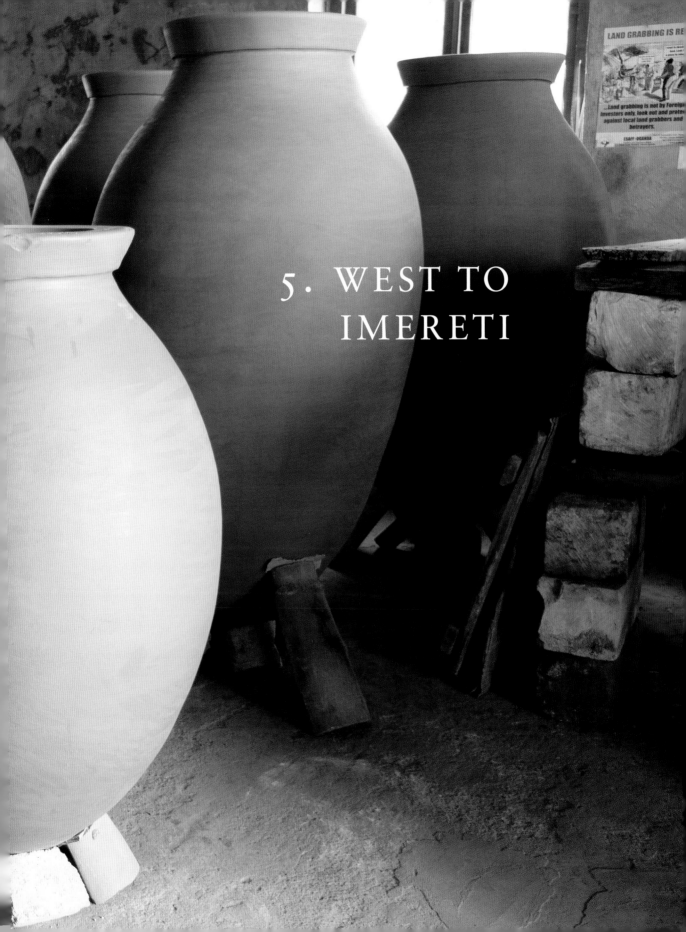

5. WEST TO IMERETI

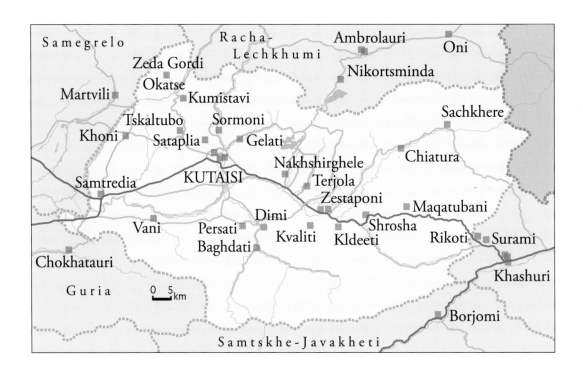

Baghdati   p. 272
Chiatura   p. 275
Dimi   p. 272
Gelati   p. 276
Kldeeti   p. 248
Kumistavi   p. 275
Kutaisi   p. 273

Kvaliti   p. 249
Maqatubani   p. 239
Nakhshirghele   p. 262
Okatse   p. 275
Persati   p. 276
Rikoti   p. 235
Sataplia   p. 275

Shrosha   p. 235
Sormoni   p. 276
Terjola   p. 258
Tskaltubo   p. 275
Vani   p. 276
Zeda Gordi   p. 275
Zestaponi   p. 249

Driving west from Tbilisi, you can't help but notice when you get to Imereti. The main road passes through a tunnel under the Rikoti Pass and comes out into another world as it winds through gentle hills and valleys. It's a rural landscape of small farms and vineyards that reflects the area's more stable, sedentary history.

Imereti is one of Georgia's main winemaking centres and this chapter focuses on several of its top natural wine producers. It begins at the beginning: with a visit to a celebrated *qvevri* maker who produces the giant vessels for winemaking by hand from local clay. Imereti's red clay is apparent as soon as you cross from Tbilisi into the Imeretian hills: at Shrosha potters display and sell their wares along the main road, from huge *qvevri* and *toné* ovens to small dishes and pots for cooking beans and local cornbread. Imeretians are great hosts and are often characterized as light-hearted, with a good sense of humour.

Clay water jug with vine leaf

Imereti's limestone bedrock provides the setting for some of Georgia's most exciting natural wonders, including caves and underwater lakes surrounded by stalactites. The region is punctuated with waterfalls and thermal springs that remain popular with those in search of natural cures. The climate in Imereti is warmer and more humid than in eastern Georgia, and there's a lot more rain.

Kutaisi, once the capital of the Kingdom of Georgia, still demonstrates that grandeur in its cathedral, theatres and other imposing public buildings. This was the domain of David the Builder, the medieval king who unified Georgia and launched its Golden Age with important churches and academies at Gelati, which today are included in UNESCO's World Heritage Sites. Above Kutaisi, a small cemetery called the 'Pantheon' is the final resting place for many of the country's most creative intellectuals, including the Imeretian composer Meliton Balanchivadze (1862–1937), father of the groundbreaking choreographer, George Balanchine (1904-1983).

FOOD AND WINE

Previous pages: Qvevri studio of Zaliko Bozhadze

The food in Imereti is western Georgian, with a focus on corn instead of wheat and distinctive vegetable cookery; its complex use of nuts and subtle spices reflects past connections with Byzantium and the Spice and Silk Routes. In general the food is lighter here than in eastern Georgia. Walnut pastes flavoured with marigold petals, Imeretian *khachapuri*, pomegranates and reduced blackberry sauces are staples on the menu in this agricultural area of small farms and holdings. If walnuts feature in many of the recipes, so do their leaves: they're often used to line the clay dishes in which cornbread is baked, both to stop the bread from sticking and to impart a deeper flavour. This area is rich in fruits, from cherries and plums to the currently popular kiwi and feijoa. In the summer season you'll find vendors along the roads selling baskets of raspberries, blackberries, wild apricots and forest mushrooms as well as local honeys and fruit preserves.

Above:
Cæsar's
mushrooms

Below:
Cheese

Imeretian *khachapuri* is probaly the most famous of the iconic cheese-filled breads commonly eaten across the country. It has a thin crust made using either yeast, bicarbonate of soda or yogurt (*matsoni*) as a starter for the flour and water mixture (see p. 50). In the old days, a mother-in-law would ask her son's new bride to make *khachapuri* as a test to see if she would be a good wife.

Cheese is another defining feature of the cuisine here and locals use Imeretian – or *imeruli*, the Georgian adjective – cheeses to give their breads character. This white, curd-based cheese is springy to the touch and normally made of cow's milk. It's quite mild, with a milky sweetness and pleasantly sour note that defines the flavour of a well-made *khachapuri*.

The cheese is often produced domestically every day by anyone with a cow or two (that's most people outside the cities). Otherwise it's sold fresh – one to two days old – in discs 3 to 7 centimetres (1 to 3 inches) thick that can weigh anything from 0.5 to 1.5 kilos (1 to 3 lbs). These cheeses tend to be heavy in water, with a salt content of around 5 percent, so the cooks shred or crumble and then squeeze them by hand to remove the excess moisture before adding them to their dishes.

Imeretian wines are often lighter in body, have less extraction, lower alcohol and brighter acidity than their eastern counterparts, as if to mirror the more delicate food. Imereti is the second most important wine-producing region after Kakheti and the most important in western Georgia. There are many native varieties, but the preferred white grapes here are Tsolikouri, Krakhuna and Tsitska. Otskhanuri Sapere is the primary red; Aladasturi, Argvetuli Sapere, Chkhaveri and Dzelshavi are also popular, though less common. The soils and altitudes vary a lot in Imereti, as do the micro-zones, with small vineyards located on high slopes, mid slopes and in the valleys. The most commonly found soils are yellow and red clay over lime bedrock, but flint is also often found and can confer a distinct, smoky character to some of the wines.

The only AOC in Imereti is Sviri, which is based on Tsolikouri. This white grape has thick skins that help defend against the fungal infections that are prevalent in humid western Georgia. Tsolikouri produces medium- to full-bodied wines, with soft acidity and notes of yellow fruits and minerals; it is usually harvested in mid-October.

When making Imeretian wines in the traditional way, small amounts of *chacha* (skins, stems and seeds) are added to the fresh must during the alcoholic fermentation. The classic Imeretian style is to destem the grapes, place them in a *qvevri* with 15–20 per cent of the skins for one or two months before racking the juice into another *qvevri* for further ageing. However, many of today's independent producers are experimenting with their styles and produce wines in a full range from those with no skin contact to those with prolonged, full skin contact.

AN IMERETIAN TOAST

All of our invaders – whether Persian, Arab, Mongol or Turk – thought that our strength came from the vines. They killed us and burned our vines but we didn't die, and neither did the vines. This is a toast to our ancestors and to the children of the new generations.

Sifting corn meal at Kutaisi market

MAQATUBANI

QVEVRI POTTER
ZALIKO BOZHADZE

The Qvevri-Maker's Tale: "To make a *qvevri*, you start at the pointed bottom," says Zaliko Bozhadze, one of Georgia's most famous and acclaimed master potters. "That's the only part that's done on a potter's wheel. Then you work up from there, a little clay at a time, adding about 15 to 20 centimetres per day in the summer when it's hot, but only 20 centimetres every three days when the weather is cool or rainy." A *qvevri* is, in effect, a giant coil pot and the potter learns by experience how much he can add in a day and still maintain the strength and tension needed to hold the shape and weight of the clay that is to come. After all, the *qvevri* walls are only about 4 centimetres (1½ inches) thick, and no armature or other material helps the clay maintain its smooth egg shape. "It takes about three months to build a large *qvevri*, so we work on several simultaneously, to bring them all up together."

Rati Bozhadze

Zaliko has three sons who help in the family business; Rati works alongside him in the studio. "This craft is in my blood," Zaliko says as he presses and turns a short baton of clay into the upper edge of a half-built *qvevri*, moving dextrously around the large pot as he does so. "My father and grandfather made *qvevri* and I started when I was about six, making small pots alongside my father. Now my sons are involved too but this is a job you can only do if you're passionate about it." Zaliko has lots of passion and he's passed it onto the many great winemakers who use his *qvevri* in their cellars in Georgia, Italy, France and beyond.

The Bozhadze's workshop produces *qvevri* and *toné* – the large cylindrical ovens that the best traditional Georgian bread is baked in. The workshop is easy to spot on the main road into Imereti: if you're coming from Tbilisi it's on the right-hand side after the Rikoti Pass tunnel, as the road snakes through the hills (you can't miss the cluster of *qvevri* and *toné* on the grassy verge above the buildings). Pull in and you'll find the family working in the studio or kiln just a few steps down from the road.

Toné *in the kiln*

Opposite: Zaliko making a qvevri

This area, called Maqatubani, is known for its red clay. That's the secret to Zaliko's great *qvevri*. The most suitable, purest type of clay is only found in two or three areas in Georgia, in Imereti and in Kakheti. The potters mix their own clay, adding sand as needed to get the correct consistency.

Once the *qvevri* are finished they are 'signed' with a stamp that will identify them even after firing. They are then allowed to dry naturally for between two to four weeks before being fired, a dozen or so at a time, to prevent cracks forming. The kiln is a separate building facing the studio. The *qvevri* are stacked at the back of the vaulted chamber, raised off the ground on a kind of scaffold so the wood embers can be pushed below them for the heat. A row of *toné* ovens is placed in front of the *qvevri* before the front of the kiln is bricked up and closed completely, with only a space left at the bottom for the long, burning logs the men push along the ground into the kiln.

"The big *qvevri* take four to six days to be fired, and we keep the fire going for all that time as the high heat must constantly fill the kiln's chamber," Zaliko explains as he re-enacts the procedure for me in the kiln building. "Once the fire has finished, we leave everything untouched for two days

Zaliko waxes the inside of the hot qvevri

– until the front wall is cool enough to touch – before dismantling the wall and 'freeing' the objects inside." (See photo of the firing on p. 24).

The final stage of preparation takes place while the *qvevri* are still hot, and the whole team has to be ready to act quickly, for time is of the essence. Each hot *qvevri* (again, it's all done by touch and experience) is moved down to a lower terrace where it is painted on the inside with pure, heated beeswax in liquid form.

Zaliko Bozhadze

"The temperature has to be just right as when the wax is applied to a hot *qvevri*, it gets pulled into the inner pores of the clay walls and forms a membrane. If it's too hot, the wax burns. This is not like a glaze: the wax does not seal the inside in a layer. These *qvevri* will be scrubbed many times in their lives and the wax has to remain, so the wax is encouraged to travel inside the clay's structure, sealing it to some extent, though a small amount of air will still be able to pass. That passage of air is key to *qvevri* winemaking. Pure beeswax has a waterproofing and a sterilizing effect, as the ancient Egyptians discovered."

I timed one of my visits to coincide with the waxing and the air was filled with a delicious scent of honey. Once the *qvevri* have been waxed and checked for any cracks or defects that would allow wine to escape, they are ready to be transported to their new homes. *Qvevri* are made in many sizes, from giant to small, to accommodate each winemaker's needs.

"In the old days the *qvevri* were often given a protective outer coating of limestone, sand and water when they were lowered into the ground, but today that's more likely to be concrete with a wire armature that makes them easier to transport," he says. *Qvevri* and their makers are included on UNESCO's Intangible Cultural Heritage List. qvevri.maqatubani@yahoo.com; tel: +995 555171296

MAQATUBANI

RESTAURANT
ZGAPARI RIVER RESTAURANT

On the main road towards Kutaisi, coming from the east, just a short distance past Zaliko Bozhadze's *qvevri* pottery is a steep, sharp left turn with several large signs. One points down a narrow road to Zgapari River Restaurant (you can't miss it as the road leads to the restaurant's car park by the Dzirula River). The dining rooms are raised up a storey, with several outdoor terraces for warm-weather meals.

This family-run restaurant specializes in the 10 to 15 varieties of mushrooms that are found in the surrounding woods, as well as many wild greens, berries, vegetables and fruits. Fermented plants here can include borage, bladdernut blossoms (*jonjoli*), nettle, wild leeks and garlic.

Of the mushrooms, the golden crown must go to the sun-yellow Cæsar (*Amanita cæsarea*). They appear from early summer to mid-autumn and are served at the restaurant simply placed in sizzling-hot clay dishes to be cooked. In Italy they are called *ovoli* and are usually eaten raw, but in Georgia they're served hot.

(Note: If you like to forage for mushrooms, make sure you always check your finds with an expert before eating them. In its closed, egg-shaped vulva state, *Amanita cæsarea* can sometimes be mistaken for its deadly cousin, *Amanita muscaria*. Never eat an Amanita that is not completely open.)

Ekala, greenbrier (*Smilax excelsa*), is a climber with spinach-like leaves whose young shoots are edible; it grows in the area. It's found in at least two seasons, spring and early autumn. It's served fresh as a *pkhali*: blanched and dressed with a light walnut and coriander sauce, usually without vinegar, often with subtle chilli and fresh or dried *kondari* (a herb like a wild thyme). Young chard leaves or sorrel are also prepared this way. Being on the river, customers travel here to eat locally caught fish – fried or grilled – as well as quail or chicken. As with so many Georgian restaurants, this is a great place to come in a group so you can taste all the seasonal specialities. We were once served a whole roast goat stuffed with a whole chicken here!

OUR AUTUMN LUNCH MENU

Cæsar mushrooms
Elarji: *cornmeal with smoked cheese*
Wild leeks with walnut sauce
Roast chicken with sour blackberry sauce
Crisp jonjoli *with white onions and coriander*
Grilled river fish
Tkemali

Opposite:
Zgapari
River
Restaurant
lunch

Duck with blackberry sauce

IKHVI MAQVLIT   იხვი მაყვლით

At Zgapari Restaurant I love the roast chicken in blackberry sauce. Here's my own take on it for when blackberries are plentiful (frozen berries can also be used). It features duck breasts, though chicken breasts or pork fillet/tenderloin work well too. The meat is marinated for several hours or overnight before being cooked.

MAKES **2 duck breasts**
PREPARATION **35 mins, plus 4–12**
 hours marinating time
COOK **30 mins**

2 boneless duck breasts, skin on

FOR THE MARINADE
8g / ¼ oz / 2 garlic cloves, minced
½ tsp coriander seeds, crushed
½ tsp grated fresh ginger
½ tsp salt
⅛ tsp chilli/red pepper flakes
3 tbsp fresh blackberry juice

FOR THE SAUCE
225g / 8 oz / 2 cups blackberries
¼ cup water
¼ tsp coriander seeds, crushed
¼ tsp ground fenugreek
2 tbsp chopped fresh coriander /
 cilantro
1 tbsp chopped fresh mint
¼ tsp salt
2 tbsp lemon juice
12 blackberries, to garnish

Using a sharp knife, score the duck skin in 1cm / ½ in rows in a diamond pattern (don't cut into the meat). Pat dry with a paper towel. Put the breasts into a small resealable plastic bag. Mix the marinade ingredients and rub them over the duck in the bag. (If you are cooking the berries after this step, add the juice to the marinade later.) Close the bag and refrigerate for several hours.

Cook the blackberries with the water in a small stainless steel saucepan, covered, over low heat. (If the berries are small and dry, you may need to add a little more water.) Cook until the fruit is soft, 10 minutes. Remove from the heat and push the berries and their juice through a sieve, discarding the seeds. Add the spices, herbs and salt to the juice and mix.

Have the duck at room temperature before cooking. Heat a heavy skillet (with a lid). Place the duck breasts in the hot pan, skin-side down, and cook over high heat until the skin is golden, 4 minutes. Turn the duck and cook for a further 3 minutes.

Remove the duck from the pan. Discard all but about 2 tablespoons of the fat. Reduce the heat to medium-low. Pour in the lemon juice and 180ml / 6 fl oz / ¾ cup of the blackberry sauce and stir to scrape up the duck's cooking juices. Return the duck to the pan and spoon the sauce over it. Cover and simmer for 8–10 minutes (for medium-rare). Add the remaining berries for the last few minutes. Allow the duck to stand for 10 minutes. Slice diagonally. Serve with the sauce and berries.

Leeks with walnut paste

PRASI პრასი

In Georgia the thin, wild leeks that are foraged in spring are one of the year's most prized foods (see below). They're served in many ways, including with walnut paste. In the absence of the wild version, here's an easy and delicious way to bring winter leeks to life: just blanch them and toss with the paste. Make sure your leeks are well cleaned of any sand by soaking them in a large bowl of cold water for 10 minutes before cooking. Use the green and white parts of the leeks. Make a cut lengthwise along each leek, cutting only to the centre. Then cut them crosswise into 2-cm/1-in slices.

SERVES 4–6 at a *supra*
PREPARATION **15 minutes**
COOK **5 minutes**

400g/14oz/3½ cups sliced leeks
   (see notes above)
40g/1½oz/3 tbsp walnut paste
   (see pp. 100-101)
2 tbsp water
1 tbsp finely chopped fresh
   coriander/cilantro
chilli/red pepper flakes, optional
salt and freshly ground black
   pepper

Bring a medium saucepan of water to the boil. Drop the leeks into it and boil for 5 minutes, until the leeks are just soft. Drain over a bowl to catch the cooking water (use it in a soup or stew). Let the leeks cool in the strainer or colander.

In a cup, mix the walnut paste with the water and stir well for a minute or two (this will help release the walnuts' flavour). Add the fresh coriander.

Turn the cool leeks into a serving bowl. Stir in the paste and mix well. Taste for seasoning, adding a pinch of optional chilli flakes, salt and pepper to taste.

KLDEETI

Amiran Vepkhvadze, a lawyer by profession, makes two wines from Imeretian grapes he grows organically outside the village of Kldeeti, between Shorapani and Zestaponi. "I used to sell my grapes to large wine 'factories', as so many people around here do, but after meeting Ramaz Nikoladze (see p. 262), who has been the catalyst in this area for encouraging us to produce organic *qvevri*-made wines, I started making and bottling my own wines in 2009," he says as we stand under a high pergola in his vineyard, around the corner from his house and cellar. This training system, called *olikhnari*, is traditional to Otskhanuri Sapere, a local variety of red grape. "Even though it is quite tricky to prune, it helps the grapes mature and keeps them raised well off the ground, away from the natural humidity we have in this part of Imereti that Otskhanuri easily falls prey to."

Amiran beside his vineyard

His well-structured wine has very deep colour, firm tannins and lively acidity, with flavours of berries and cherries. It is fermented on the skins and aged for nine months, all in *qvevri*. Otskhanuri Sapere is an ancient variety from the Kolkheti family and it's characterized as being partway between a wild and domesticated vine. It is sometimes used to darken wines made from less deeply coloured grapes.

Amiran also produces a white from Krakhuna, another indigenous Imeretian variety that makes fruity wines, often with lovely notes of pears, with fresh acidity. It has been known in Imereti since at least the 18th century. He is in the process of expanding his vineyards from his current 2 hectares and has recently planted new vineyards of Otskhanuri, Tsitska and Tsolikouri that will begin to yield grapes in 2016. We went to take a look at the new vineyard on a very windy September day. With characteristically Imeretian humour he peopled the field with children as he declared: "I'm pleased. Our soft, yellow-orange clay and water have produced such strong, healthy one-year-olds!" Amiran exports the wines to Europe, Japan and the USA; currently his annual production is around 4,000 bottles. vefxvadzea@mail.ru; tel: +995 591643654

ZESTAPONI

Zestaponi is situated at the eastern end of the Kolkheti Plateau and has ancient roots in Georgian history. It sits on the banks of the River Kvirila. In Soviet times, Zestaponi was an industrial centre with several heavy metal factories and still processes large quantities of manganese ore that is taken from the area by train for export.

There are several ancient sites and churches in the surrounding area including at Shorapani, the 'Sarapanis' that Jason and the Argonauts were said to have approached in Greek mythology.

KVALITI

WINE
KVALITI: ARCHIL GUNIAVA

"In this village, when a baby is born, it doesn't matter what the parents want, that child is already a winemaker," says Archil Guniava with a wry smile as we walk along a hedge-lined lane in the village towards his vineyards. The village, Kvaliti, is a few minutes' drive south-west of Zestaponi, one of the region's largest towns, and is in the heart of wine country at 250 metres (820 feet) above sea level. Unlike in France or California, where that phrase suggests large expanses of delineated vine monoculture, in most areas of rural Georgia vineyards are interspersed with houses, orchards, animal shelters and vegetable gardens. Wine has always been considered an integral part of the family larder, and one of the most important 'foods' at the dining table.

"In our village nobody stopped making wine during or after the Soviet era, even if they could have been punished for it," Archil says as we sit in his *qvevri* cellar. "Selling wine wasn't forbidden in Soviet times but then, it wasn't allowed either, and there were always people trying to catch us at it and throw our villagers in jail. But that didn't deter us," he says proudly. "Of course the wines that were being made in those days may not have lived up to today's standards as there was a certain amount of sugar being added but it was the only income most people around here had."

Archil's grandfather was brought up near Kvaliti and he and Archil's great-grandfather sold large quantities of wine they transported in buffalo or sheep skins – the latter being as much as one strong man could carry. When Archil's grandfather moved to the house Archil now lives in, he brought 5 tons' capacity of *qvevri* with him (his four siblings also each got the same amount) and set up their business selling wine.

"In Soviet times the government took grapes from us and the quality was not important as the Russians bought large quantities of low-grade

Archil Guniva's cellar contains buried qvevri *of many sizes*

wine with added sugar. But here we always kept one sugar-free *qvevri* for the family's use, as well as a smaller one with just grape juice for religious days."

Archil had a career in forestry and had no ambitions to make wines to sell. But in 2010 he met Ramaz Nikoladze (see p. 262), the wine producer whose cellar is just 20 kilometres (12 miles) from Kvaliti, and everything changed.

"Ramaz was looking in western Georgia for people making wines the traditional way in *qvevri* and he invited me to visit him. After I saw his organic vineyards and *qvevri* I decided to give it a try. I had heard too that the goverment was backing traditional Georgian winemaking." His parents

Archil in his vineyard

Opposite: Archil with his sons, Vakho and Nikoloz

have retired from selling wine themselves but Archil has brought new life to their cellars and today exports wine to Japan, Europe and the USA. He still works in forestry but runs the winery now with his wife, Tsiuri Makhatadze, and four children.

Currently his production, from under 1 hectare of vineyards near the family's home, is around 2,000 bottles per year, divided between two wines. The white, Tsolikouri Kvaliti, is a fine example of this quintessentially Imeretian grape. The red, of Otskhanuri Sapere, is a blend of red and white grapes: Archil feels the red is too heavy on its own. His is light-bodied and refreshing, and goes well with food. He plans to increase production gradually but says most people in the area have even fewer vineyards.

"My neighbours don't understand why I work so hard to avoid pesticides and other chemicals," he says. "But last year their vineyards were rained out while mine seem to have done so well thanks to their boosted natural defences." He laughs as we walk across the yard from the cellar to the dining room. "My father and grandfather can't quite believe that we won't be jailed any more for selling wine," he says. "And my grandmother is very surprised at all the attention our old-fashioned *qvevri* are receiving – the very same *qvevri* that caused such problems in Soviet times."

After our visit to the cellar, where I sample wines directly from the *qvevri* under the watchful eyes of three generations of the Guniava family, we walk to dinner across the yard and up the house's outer staircase – a typically Imeretian architectural feature. In a luminous room completely filled by a large oval table, a *supra* is being set out. The women come and go with ever more dishes to fill the table before we sit down.

I ask Tsiuri about one of the vegetable dishes that looked like a green mash. "That's wild green *pkhali*," she says. "Imeretian women are used to – and skilled at – finding wild greens in the meadows. In the old days, when a girl was born they would say: she has arrived to find *pkhali* in the fields. To make this type of *pkhali*, the most tender parts of seven or eight different plants – including wild violet leaves, stinging nettles, borage, beet greens, chard and spinach – are blanched, drained and chopped very finely. Then a walnut sauce is stirred into them and they're served cold or at room temperature." Imereti is famous for its *pkhali*, made from many green vegetables dressed with walnut or hazelnut sauces. "Hazelnuts are cheaper for those who don't have their own walnut trees."

Tsiuri's chicken with sour plum sauce

Our lunch also included a home-reared, free-range chicken that had been roasted in a pan with salt and oil. It was served in a very garlicky, sour green plum sauce loosened with a little water. The white Tsolikouri and blend of red Otskhanuri Sapere with Tsolikouri from 2014 accompanied them all splendidly. archilguniavawinecellar@gmail.com; tel: +995 599534295

THE LUNCH

Green bean pkhali
Wild green pkhali
Imeretian khachapuri
Chicken with sour plum sauce
Roasted chicken
Tomato and cucumber salad
Home made breads
Local cheeses
Grilled river fish
Tkemali

Opposite:
The supra
table at the
Guniavas',
with Archil's
son, Nikoloz

Vegetables with walnut paste

PKHALI   ფხალი

Pkhali are vegetables dressed with herbed walnut paste. They're often made using leafy greens – from spinach and chard to beet greens and foraged leaves – but are also popular made from green beans. The consistency varies from firm and paté-like to looser. I cook green vegetables quickly to maintain their colours and flavours, but some Georgians prefer to cook them for longer.

SERVES **4–6 as part of a** *supra*
PREPARATION **10 minutes**
COOK **10 minutes**

LEAFY GREENS PKHALI

600g / 1lb 5 oz leafy greens, washed
  and roughly chopped
120ml / 4fl oz / ½ cup water
50g / 1¾oz / ¼ cup walnut paste
  (see p. 101)
1 tbsp white wine vinegar or lemon
  juice
½ tsp ground marigold petals
1 tbsp finely chopped coriander /
  cilantro
1 tbsp finely chopped parsley
salt and black pepper
pomegranate seeds, to decorate

Push all the greens and the water into a saucepan. Cook, covered, stirring occasionally, until they wilt down and are cooked to your preference. When cool enough to handle, squeeze the greens with your hands to remove the excess liquid. (Save the cooking water.) Chop the greens finely.

Mix the walnut paste with the vinegar or lemon juice, spices and herbs. If the sauce is very thick, stir in a spoonful of the reserved cooking liquid.

Mix the greens with the walnut sauce. Taste for seasoning. Form into small balls and decorate with the pomegranate. Serve cool or at room temperature.

GREEN BEAN PKHALI

350g / 12 oz green beans, stem ends
  removed
3 tbsp walnut paste (see p. 101)
½ tsp ground marigold petals
2 tbsp water
1 tbsp finely chopped fresh dill
1 tbsp finely chopped fresh basil
pomegranate seeds, to decorate

Steam the green beans until tender. Immediately refresh them under cold water. Drain well. Place half the beans in the bowl of a hand blender and process to a purée. Chop the rest into 2-cm / 1-in pieces.

Mix the walnut paste with the ground marigold and water to blend. Stir in the herbs. Add the sauce to the puréed beans. Taste for seasoning. Stir the purée into the chopped beans. Mix well. Form the beans into ovals and decorate with pomegranate seeds.

TERJOLA

WINE
TERJOLA WINES:
GOGITA MAKARIDZE

A good number of today's best-known natural winemakers in Georgia are over 40 (some are over 50) and most have spent their working lives in other professions – from the tech industries to music, teaching or the law. Over the last five to 10 years, they've found themselves unexpectedly bottling and selling wine and taking a new direction in their lives and careers. Another cluster are under 30, the really new generation, who are just starting out now and who certainly represent the future of Georgia's potential in wine.

In between are a handful of producers, really just a very few, who are now in their 30s. These young people were born in the last years of the Soviet regime, and grew up during Georgia's 'Black '90s' of the post-Soviet era when there was very little of anything for them, including opportunities, money, electricity, heat and sometimes even food.

Gogita Makaridze turned 30 in 2014 and is a great example of someone who had to think outside of the box to invent a project for himself and his peers. "I was always interested in viticulture as my father had a vine nursery, and I started making wines when I was very young," he says. "I had a job in the financial department of the local town hall. That's where I met Ramaz Nikoladze in 2009 who is from the same area. He came in asking if anyone had vineyards and would be interested in joining an association of organic producers, Elkana. I was."

From there Gogita founded a cooperative of 10 producers aged between 25 and 38, including two women. They decided to pool their resources as none could independently afford the tractor, cellar and other equipment needed to become bottlers. By banding together they were able to apply for funding from the EU's Agriculture and Rural Development programme (ENPARD).

Top: Gogita with his grandfather's vine

Bottom: Corn grows beside the vineyard

"We were approved and received 35,000 euros to get started," he says. "The coop has enabled us to pool our existing vineyards and even plant some new ones, for a total of 5 hectares. The proviso was that we had to form one single brand of wine, Terjola Wines. Since then we've expanded our production from 700 to 3,000 bottles and we're now exporting to Japan and other countries." They also joined the Kvevri Wine Association and sell their wines at Ghvino Underground in Tbilisi (see p. 67).

We walked around the Makaridze's house into the vineyard that Gogita's grandfather had planted before World War II. Only 20 plants remain from that period, gnarled and twisted by time, but Gogita has planted new vineyards of the local black grape, Otskhanuri Sapere, which does best when trained onto high trellises. Despite its many branches Otskhanuri yields only about 1.5 to 2 kilos (3 to 4½ lbs) per plant.

"We're only at 130 metres (427 feet) here and it's very hot and dry in the summers but our mix of limestone and clay retains water in the heat," he says. "I'm also planting an unusual variety of yellow Tsitska that is sweeter and has smaller bunches than its greener namesake. Ours is better for making dry wines, while the 'normal' Tsitska has higher acidity and is more suited to sparkling wines."

Currently the coop is making four wines: two whites and two reds. Tsitska and a blend of Tsitska and Tsolikouri are the whites; Otskhanuri Sapere and Aladasturi the reds. Aladasturi is preva-

Gogita with his father under the vine trellis

lent in Guria and on the Gurian border with Imereti. It's a late-harvesting variety of the Kolkheti family that is also served as a table grape. It's fast climbing and high growing and is often used for shade on pergolas around houses. Their project includes holding back some of their wine to be aged before selling.

Gogita is pleased to have women in the cooperative. "In Georgia's past, 150 years ago, women were traditionally not allowed near the vines or the cellars, and in some places it may still be like that. Happily we don't feel that way at all!"

We made our way into the house to taste the wines in preparation for the *supra* that Gogita's mother and other women in the family were cooking. The dinner with Gogita Makaridze's family was a complex mix of flavours and sensations: raw, pickled, fresh, sour, roasted, stewed, fermented, baked, tannic, nutty, sweet, all at the same table, and the wines went so well with them. I particularly loved the *chakapuli* veal stew: the meat was flavourful and tender and was given a sour tang by tiny pickled plums the size of hazelnuts, with spring onions, dill, coriander and tarragon. At the end of the meal, after what seemed like hours of wonderful eating and drinking, the serving dishes were just as full as they had been at the start: the women had continually replenished them. *Didi madloba*! (Thank you very much!)
gogitater@mail.ru

The meal was exceptional and it also brought me some good luck: the photograph I took of Gogita's mother, Naili Basiladze, bringing food to the supra table won a prestigious prize from the International Association of Culinary Professionals (IACP): the Culinary Trust Award for Food Photography that Makes a Difference. I gave the photo this title: In Caucasian Georgia Abundant Hospitality Defines and Defends the Country's Culture.

The menu consisted of stuffed peppers and aubergines with walnut sauce; chakapuli veal stew; fermented jonjoli; lightly acidic red plum sauce; excellent white cornbread; cheese; local quail with mushrooms; farm tomatoes; home-reared small chickens; barbecued pork at the very end when everyone was full, followed by khachapuri.

NAKHSHIRGHELE

WINE
NIKOLADZEEBIS MARANI:
RAMAZ NIKOLADZE

What is wine?" Ramaz Nikoladze savours the question as he pauses in his efforts to prise open the clay seal of a buried *qvevri*. "You have a grape, you crush it and wait. But you must do it with your heart, not your head – though sometimes you need your head too," he adds wryly. The opening of a *qvevri* is a ritual that often takes place with spectators gathered and an air of celebration and suspense. Before he built his new indoor cellar in 2015, Ramaz followed the customs of his part of the country by burying his *qvevri* outdoors, covered only with a makeshift roof to keep the worst of the rain off. The neck was all you saw poking up from the ground, with a large stone over its wooden cover. To remove the clay seal takes strength and precision. When it's done, and the wine appears just below the surface, there's a round of applause. Now Ramaz looks serious: he scoops out the first glassful of amber liquid, takes a sniff and then a big sip. His eyes are closed but he's smiling. "Yes, *this* is a wine."

We're in the garden of the Nikoladze house in the rural village of Nakhshirghele, a few kilometres east of Kutaisi. Ramaz and his family have been making wines here for as long as he can remember, working from vineyards of white Tsolikouri and Tsitska that his grandfather planted. As the freshly opened wine is shared and enjoyed, the conversation moves from plans for the future to reminiscences of the past. Ramaz is one of the most influential natural winemakers in Georgia and is responsible for helping to launch its 'new' *qvevri* wine revolution.

"The movement, if we can call it that, started in several regions at once: Kakheti, Kartli and here in western Georgia too," he says. "A handful of crazy people decided to make their own wines. There was a literature specialist, a linguist, a violinist, even an artist, and we all had the same desire, though we didn't know each other at the time.

"I had always made wine with my family members. We sold some in bulk but I was young – 22 or 23 – and wanted to do something by myself. I started experimenting by ageing a few demijohns for a year or two to see how they'd taste. I never imagined I could bottle wine to sell. After all, the situation was very difficult in the '90s. The big 'industrial' wineries controlled who could sell wines in restaurants and wine shops and anyway we were completely unknown."

One day in 2004 a friend invited himself over for dinner and brought a guest, a Japanese food journalist, Natsu Shimamura, the founder of a Slow Food chapter in Japan. "She saw me open a *qvevri*, and tasted our wines and food," Ramaz says. "A few weeks later I got an invitation to Terra Madre, Slow Food's event in Turin, dedicated to indigenous food-making communities around the world. They were interested in *qvevri* tradition."

The Slow Food Foundation for Biodiversity helps to sustain unique food and wine production methods that are at risk of becoming extinct by forming what it calls 'Presidia': groups of producers who are maintaining that tradition and might be in need of assistance or sponsorship to keep their work going.

"That was what pushed us to seek out other growers," Ramaz says. "Soliko Tsaishvili (see p. 158) went looking in Kakheti, his native wine region in eastern Georgia, and I took up the search here in Imereti."

He travelled around the villages, tasting family wines and talking to their makers. "I wanted to make sure they worked their vineyards organically and were motivated enough to join us." Soon Ramaz was able to form a group of five Imeretian producers wanting to bottle their wines to partner with five from Kakheti. The Presidium was made.

"Some of the growers were sceptical initially, but we needed help to promote our project and to buy small equipment for bottling, that sort of thing. We went on to present the Presidium's wines at Terra Madre in Turin, in 2006 and 2008. In the meantime, it helped establish a network within Georgia. That's how I met John Wurdeman from Pheasant's Tears (see p. 166) and producers from different parts of the country."

Ramaz scoops wine from the newly opened qvevri

Ramaz is committed to organic principles in the vineyard, working without the use of chemicals, herbicides or pesticides. He's pretty hardline about this: "We believe that what matters is the life of the soil and the plants. We grow vegetables among our vines: we don't want to eat or drink anything poisonous." Ramaz helps to educate the locals about the perils of chemical sprays but gets frustrated if they aren't prepared to make changes over time. "Where is your honour? Or your sincerity?" he asks them. If they still won't abandon the chemicals, he stops dealing with them.

Recently Ramaz and his wife, Nestan, have moved to a house of their own a few kilometres away from the family village with a newly built covered *qvevri* cellar, but he still comes back to help his father and brother work their vineyards. He makes three wines from the local whites: monovarietals from Tsolikouri and Tsitska, plus a blend of the two. Each is produced in two versions: with skin contact and without. He has almost one hectare of vineyards, producing 2,000 bottles, but that will increase when his newly planted vines start yielding fruit, in 2017 or 2018.

In 2012 Ramaz was one of the founding members of Ghvino

Ramaz Nikoladze

Underground, the natural wine bar in Tbilisi (see p. 67) that is run cooperatively by a group of natural winemakers. "We talked about needing somewhere to show our wines. Should it be a bar or a shop? The group consisted of Kakha Berishvili, Soliko Tsaishvili, the Jakeli brothers, John Wurdeman, Nika Bakhia, Niki Antadze and me. We liked the first place we found for rent and just decided to go for it, fixing it up ourselves by hand. It was Georgia's first natural wine bar and has turned out to be a key part of the whole project and a hub for both winemakers and enthusiasts. We offer a large assortment of our kinds of wines and can help visitors link up with the producers." Ramaz worked as the bar's manager for several years and has helped inspire a new generation of young men and women to make their own wines. He continues to help new winemakers to get started, like Giorgi Simonguliashvili: he's given him the use of a *qvevri* in the new cellar until he gets his own set-up. Ramaz is tired of working in the city and now hopes to be able to spend more time in his village vineyards and working as an enologist with other producers.

In 2015 I was asked by *Decanter Magazine* to select just one wine I had drunk that year for the special 40th anniversary issue. I chose a 2013 Tsolikouri made by Ramaz. Here's what I wrote about it: "I love wines that make you question the status quo. This beautiful amber-coloured wine is made – as many of Georgia's best wines are – in *qvevri* (large traditional clay vessels buried in the ground). Ramaz Nikoladze produces it from 100-year-old Tsolikouri vines in the Imereti hills, with three months of stem-free skin contact. The wine's exotic notes of spice, apricots and tea ride with exciting energy to a finely tannic, elegant finale and go just wonderfully with food.'

Ramaz's wife, Nestan Kravishvili, is an inspiring cook and generous host. She prepares her food in a small kitchen-house in the garden of their main house, as is the tradition in many Imeretian families. "Imereti is not as rich as Kakheti because people didn't have as much land here," she says as she starts to prepare her beans for *lobio*. "There were smaller gardens and most people lived on whatever vegetables and crops they could grow. They supplemented that diet with foraged foods like greens, fruits and mushrooms."

In Imereti, as in most parts of western Georgia, dishes are given added complexity with the use of spices, herbs and nuts. They're usually still ground by hand in mortars and pestles. Nestan's mortar is made of tight-grained wood and the pestle she inherited from her grandmother is of volcanic stone. (She pounds her coffee in a walnut-wood mortar.) Nestan pounds the *lobio* seasoning – including nuts, herbs, garlic and spices – in it for many minutes to release all the flavours.

"We use a lot of walnuts, even in dishes such as stewed *lobio*. And we prefer to eat those dishes with cornbread, *mchadi*, rather than wheat bread; corn's a staple in Imereti. The cornbread is made from ground white corn [yellow corn here is just for animals] and traditionally cooked in clay dishes called *ketsi* that are often lined with walnut leaves for added flavour. The dishes are heated to white-hot on a wood-burning stove before the cornmeal is added, and then they are stacked, with some hot embers on the top, so that many portions can be ready at once. Sometimes they are cooked in the fireplace." Her *mchadi* is oval in shape and enriched with cheese. It's slightly crunchy on the outside and quite delicious.

Ramaz harvesting with his family

Nestan's bean recipe also includes a thick, dark syrup she makes by boiling and reducing the cooking water from the plums she uses for her sour plum sauce, *tkemali*. It adds a sour tang and complements the warmth of the nuts and spices.

"Beans have long been grown here, with some varieties originally coming from Armenia," she explains. "*Lobio* is an important dish in this part of the country. When there is a death in the family and there's no time to prepare food, *lobio* is cooked by the neighbours who bring it over when they come to sit with the bereaved. No meat is consumed in Imereti when someone dies. A candle is lit for the person who has departed and when it has burned down, the family eats. Miniature *khachapuri* called *kokori* are also made and distributed at this *sakurtkhi supra*. They say Kakhetians can't live without meat; well, for us westerners, it's beans we rely on."
georgianslowfood@yahoo.com; tel: +995 551944841

Beans with walnuts and spices

LOBIO I   ლობიო

Nestan Nikoladze's wonderfully complex bean recipe includes pounded walnuts and the dried petals and fresh leaves of the orange French marigold plant, *Tagetes patula*, see p. 41. The leaves are more pungent, with a distinct, vegetal note that gives these beans an extra dimension. Nestan works all the flavouring ingredients in her mortar and pestle. That's the best way, but a food processor also produces a great result.

SERVES **4–6 or more at a** *supra*
PREPARATION **40 minutes, plus 12
 hours soaking**
COOK **90–180 minutes**

350g / 12 oz / 2 cups dried Borlotti
  or other fine-skinned beans
1 tsp ground marigold petals
½ tsp dry *kondari* (summer
  savory) or delicate thyme
¼ tsp ground chilli/cayenne
30g / 1 oz / ½ cup chopped fresh
  coriander / cilantro
200g / 7 oz / 1½ cups chopped
  onion
30g / 1 oz / 2 tbsp butter
1 tbsp marigold petals
½ tsp coriander seed, crushed
12g / ⅓ oz / 3 garlic cloves
2 tbsp chopped fresh parsley
2 tbsp finely chopped celery or
  celeriac leaf
5 or 6 fresh French marigold leaves
115g / 4 oz / 1 cup ground walnuts
½ tsp ground fenugreek
1 tsp salt
3 tbsp sour plum sauce or lemon
  juice
French marigold leaves, to garnish

Soak the beans overnight in good clean water (filtered, if possible). Drain, rinse well and turn the beans into a large saucepan. Cover them with two fingers of water and bring to the boil. After about 15 minutes, when the beans start producing foam, pour the beans and water into a colander and rinse the beans again. Cover them with fresh water and boil for 45 minutes, skimming off any foam that appears.

Stir in the ground marigold, *kondari* or thyme, chilli, half of the chopped coriander / cilantro and half of the onions. Continue cooking until the beans are tender, anything from 30 to 60 minutes more. Add more water as necessary to keep the beans covered by two fingers. Meanwhile, sauté the remaining onion in the butter until light gold.

Using a mortar and pestle, pound the marigold petals with the coriander seed. Add the garlic and pound again. Add the parsley, celery leaf, marigold leaves and remaining coriander, pounding until the mixture is like a paste. Add the ground walnuts, fenugreek and salt. (Alternatively, place all the ingredients in the bowl of a food processor and process to a rough paste.)

Stir the paste into the beans with the sautéed onions and the sour plum sauce or lemon juice. Cook for 10 minutes more, mixing well. Taste for seasoning. Serve hot or at room temperature, garnished with marigold leaves.

Tkemali sour plum sauce

TKEMALI   ტყემალი

Sour sauce made from fresh plums, *tkemali*, underpins many dishes in Georgia. You can find bottled *tkemali* but it's very easy to make. The classic version is made from small, green unripe plums prevalent in Georgia. Other plums can be used (as long as they're not over-ripe) as their skins contain enough acidity to give the sauce its characteristic tang. Mint may not be as traditional in this sauce as coriander/cilantro and dill, but include it for added verve. This sauce will keep in the fridge for a few days. It's not intended for long preservation but can also be frozen. This sauce is often paired with beets for a sweet and sour dish.

MAKES **600ml / 28fl oz / 2½ cups**
PREP **20 minutes**
COOK **20 minutes**

600g / 1lb 5oz fresh plums, rinsed
120ml / 4fl oz / ½ cup water
¾ tsp coriander seeds
¼ tsp fennel seeds
12g / ⅓oz / 3 garlic cloves, minced
fresh chilli to taste (optional),
    finely chopped
30g / 1oz / ¾ cup finely chopped
    fresh herbs: a few sprigs each of
    fresh mint, coriander / cilantro
    and dill
½ tsp salt

Cook the plums and water gently in a stainless steel saucepan, covered, until they're soft, about 15 minutes. Turn the plums and their juices into a sieve set over a large bowl.

Pound the seeds with a pinch of the salt using a pestle and mortar. Add the garlic, optional chilli and remaining salt and crush them with the spices.

When the plums are cool enough to handle, push them through the sieve, discarding the pits but forcing the skins through with the pulp.

Stir the spiced garlic paste and fresh herbs into the plum purée. Mix well and correct the seasoning. The sauce should be aromatic and sour. It will keep for several days in the refrigerator.

BEETS WITH SOUR PLUM SAUCE   ჭარხალი ტყემლით

SERVES **6–8 at a** *supra*
PREPARATION **10 minutes**

600g / 1lb 5oz / 4½ cups beets
120ml / 4fl oz / ½ cup sour plum
    sauce (see above)
2 tbsp chopped fresh coriander /
    cilantro
salt and pepper

Use finely chopped cooked beets without vinegar for this recipe.

Mix the beets, sauce and herbs together in a bowl. Season to taste. Add some pomegranate seeds if you like. Serve cool.

Spiced walnut paste

BAZHE I   ბაჟე

This complex paste flavoured with many delicate spices goes well with beets and other simple vegetables or hard-boiled eggs. Nestan pounds her ingredients using a mortar and pestle but you can make a quicker version in a food processor.

MAKES **about 240ml / 8fl oz/1 cup**
PREPARATION **15 minutes**

200g/7 oz/2 cups walnut halves
8g/¼oz/2 garlic cloves
1 tsp salt
½ tsp coriander seeds, crushed
1 tsp ground marigold petals
½ tsp ground cinnamon
¼ tsp ground chilli/cayenne
½ tsp ground fenugreek
⅛ tsp ground cumin
large pinch of grated nutmeg
pinch of ground cloves
80ml/2½fl oz/⅓ cup water

Place all the ingredients in the bowl of a food processor with the water and pulse to obtain a thick paste. Store in the refrigerator for one week covered tightly with plastic wrap to prevent the nuts from oxidizing.

BEETS WITH SPICED WALNUT PASTE   ჭარხალი ნიგვზით

MAKES **12**
PREPARATION **15 minutes**

6 small beetroot/beets, boiled and peeled (about 360g/12 oz)
120ml/4fl oz/½ cup spiced walnut paste (see above)
3 tbsp water

Cut each beet in half. Scoop out a small hollow in the cut side of each half.

Mix the walnut paste with the water. The sauce should be stiff enough to hold together without running, but not too solid. Add more water if necessary. Spoon the paste into the hollow in each beet half, spreading it evenly. Arrange on a serving dish and serve cool or at room temperature.

Didimi and
his wife Endi
at harvest

DIMI

WINE
I AM DIDIMI

Didimi Maghlakelidze lives in Dimi village on the southern side of the wide Rioni River plain south of Kutaisi, close to the large town, Baghdati. To get there you drive across the Ajameti Reserve, a centre of managed biodiversity with forests containing centuries-old trees.

I am fortunate to visit the charming Didimi on the day he and his wife and friends are harvesting their high-pergola Krakhuna (Krahuna) vines. With his nephew Ramaz Nikoladze's help he's been bottling since 2011 – and his wines are always in demand – but Didimi says he's thinking of scaling back.

"I'm getting too old," he says, though that doesn't stop him from working tirelessly to gather the high grape bunches. The vineyard is right behind their house, through a little cornfield that was being picked over by a clutch of chickens.

Doug Wregg, of Les Caves de Pyrene in London, describes white Krakhuna as 'the Riesling of Georgia'. Certainly its aromatic edge, minerality and dry backbone when it's made in *qvevri* make for a delicious wine that has earned Didimi many loyal followers in Ghvino Underground and beyond – despite the very small quantities the men produce. He also grows white Tsolikouri and two local red varieties, Dzelshavi and Aladasturi.

For enquiries, contact Ramaz Nikoladze (see p. 265).

BAGHDATI

Gaioz Sopromadze is a winemaker living in the town of Baghdati. He was one of the first members of the Slow Food Qvevri Presidium organized by Ramaz Nikoladze (see p. 262). His wines, of Tsolikouri and Chkhaveri, are produced from family vineyards and made in outdoor *qvevri*. The family offers simple meals of local foods while several bedrooms are available for those wanting to try Georgian agritourism. goga-sopromadze@mail.ru; tel: +995 595786131

COLCHIS, JASON AND THE GOLDEN FLEECE

In the highlands of Svaneti and Racha, shepherds used to secure sheepskins across the waters of some rivers to sift and catch tiny filaments of gold. This is thought to be the basis for the ancient Greek myth about Jason and the Golden Fleece. In the 13th century BC, Jason set out from Greece for the land of Colchis (Kolkheti), the ancient kingdom that corresponds roughly to western Georgia, including Samegrelo and the coastal parts of Abkhazia, Guria and Adjara. In their boat, the Argo, Jason and his Argonauts rowed from Greece across the Black Sea and up the Phasis River (today's Rioni, it runs between Samegrelo and Guria) to the city of King Aeëtes, thought to be Kutaisi or Vani. Before Jason could claim the Golden Fleece, he was set three tasks by Aeëtes. Princess Medea, his daughter, is said to have been born in Cutatisium, or Kutaisi. She fell in love with Jason and used her knowledge of narcotic plants to help him accomplish the tasks and to win both the Fleece and her hand in marriage. Did she use some of the marijuana that grows wild in the Caucasian mountains to do it?

KUTAISI

Kutaisi is the most important city in western Georgia, and is believed to have been the capital of the ancient Kingdom of Colchis (Kolkheti) that Jason and his Argonauts set out for. The Golden Fleece may have been housed here before the Greeks removed it. The city remained the Kingdom of Imereti's capital until 1508 when it was captured by Selim I, Sultan of the Ottoman Empire. In the 17th century, the Imeretian kings repeatedly sought help from the Russians to liberate them from Ottoman rule, but it was not until 1770 that King Solomon I managed to do so, with the help of Catherine the Great. In the early 19th-century, Kutaisi was the centre of Georgian winemaking and of its trading.

Kutaisi still radiates an atmosphere of culture, especially in the heart of the old town (the outskirts are less inspiring). Kutaisi has one of the most attractive central squares in Georgia, dominated by the Mekhishvili State Opera Theatre and the large fountain-sculpture in front of it that features early ironwork animals like those from the steppes. Kutaisi State Historical Museum is one of the country's most important museums and has many artefacts connected to wine and food. The Pantheon Cemetery, high on a hill overlooking the city, is worth visiting to see the sculptural headstones of Georgia's intellectuals and artists, including Kutaisi's most famous com-poser, Meliton Balanchivadze, father of the pioneering choreographer, George Balanchine.

The Rioni River runs through the town, with leafy residential neighbourhoods covering the hills on both banks. Kutaisi had a thriving Jewish community until 1917 when many left. Kutaisi has a large covered market whose central space resembles a souk. Here vendors sell different grades of cornmeal piled into pyramids for making local breads, and many qualities of walnuts and hazelnuts for the region's famous sauces.

Kutaisi's magnificent Bagrati Cathedral, on the Ukimerioni Hill, is dedicated to the Dormition of Mary, and was begun in the early 11th century by King Bagrat III. The monumental medieval building suffered repeatedly over the centuries, and in 1692 was partly destroyed by an Ottoman explosion when the dome and ceiling caved in. Reconstruction has been going on since the 1950s; until 2012 it had no roof and priests gave sermons in the open air. In 1994 Bagrati – like Gelati (see p. 276) – was added to UNESCO's World Heritage Sites; its status was questioned when the cathedral underwent major reconstruction in 2008 under President Saakashvili – including a new roof – that has brought the church back into use.

Top: Kutaisi's Bagrati Cathedral

Bottom: Central square in Kutaisi with the Mekhishvili State Opera Theatre in the background

On a more contemporary note: As you drive towards the centre of Kutaisi from the direction of Tbilisi, you can't help but be startled by what looks like a giant glass and concrete 'eye' peering out from the ground. This controversial architect-designed domed Parliament building has been the seat of Georgia's parliament since 2012 – a move that has earned both praise and criticism. The government has been keen to devolve the power from Tbilisi (where the rest of the government remains) to the western part of Georgia, in homage to its important past. Certainly they're trying to dispel the dismal post-Soviet aura that abandoned factories and social housing projects still conjur, but this design has not been universally applauded. Kutaisi Airport has recently been upgraded and now hosts international flights to Russia, Europe and beyond (including a new direct line to and from Milan).

WHERE TO EAT. Rcheuli Palace Hotel, which is one of a group of characterful hotels in other parts of Georgia, has a large dining room and serves well-cooked traditional dishes if you specify that's what you want and pre-order them. www.rcheuli.ge

Of the city's restaurants, Bar-Restaurant Palaty is the best known and serves some interesting fusion dishes in an informal setting with live music. Pushkini Street; tel: +995 431243380

NATURAL AND ARCHÆOLOGICAL SITES IN IMERETI

Imereti's geological karst formation, with ancient strata of red clay, soluble limestone and other rocks, continues to reveal caves and other natural wonders.

In 1984 a large series of natural caves – the Prometheus Caves – was discovered near Kumistavi filled with exceptional rock formations, from stalactites and stalagmites to petrified waterfalls, underground rivers and lakes that have been scenically lit and made accessible by foot or boat.

A few kilometres south-east from there, the Sataplia cave in the Sataplia Natural Reserve (Sataplia means 'place of honey') is notable for dramatic underground rock formations and for the 120 million year-old dinosaur footprints that have been discovered there. This has been a national reserve since 1935 but it's recently undergone a modern facelift with the addition of viewing platforms and visitor centres.

In the area around the spa town of Tskaltubo, naturally hot radon-carbonate mineral springs were very popular in Soviet times, including with Joseph Stalin, as some of the murals that remain illustrate. If people seeking cures there have dropped from 125,000 in Soviet times to just 700, it's still worth a visit. Some of the former health sanatoriums are now being used to house refugees from Abkhazia.

In the top, north-western corner of Imereti, near the villages of Zeda and Kveda Gordi, are the Okatse Canyon and Kinchkha where some of the country's most spectacular waterfalls are situated, now with panoramic walkways and routes. It takes about an hour to drive there from Kutaisi. Check weather conditions before going up.

North-east of Zestaponi, near Chiatura is the Katskhi Pillar. Like an eagle's nest, this 40-metre (132-feet) natural limestone monolith, or 'pillar', is topped by two tiny churches that are amongst the earliest in the world, from the 5th and 6th centuries. They were inhabited by hermit monks. One has a cellar with eight large wine *qvevri* still visible in the ground.

SORMONI

Three of my favourite local wine-makers have told me that this is one of the neighbourhood restaurants they like best, as it serves unpretentious dishes using high-quality ingredients. It's a Soviet-era restaurant in the small village of Sormoni (due north of Kutaisi, near Rioni). Sormona is not far from the Gelati Monastery so it's a useful place to stop before or after a visit there.

Ancient qvevri *found during an excavation at Gelati Monastery*

GELATI MONASTERY

A wonder of Georgia's Golden Age, Gelati is a medieval monastery complex with three churches begun in 1106 by King David IV of the Bagrationi dynasty (David the Builder). Gelati was one of the most significant cultural centres of Georgia. Education was very important to the enlightened King David and during his reign a number of schools and academies were established. Gelati's Academy – like that in Kakheti at Ikalto (see p. 145) – employed some of the most celebrated Georgian theologians, philosophers, scholars and scientists of the age. It has revealed many ancient *qvevri*. Despite being attacked over the centuries, Gelati is very well preserved and contains beautiful frescoes, mosaics and manuscripts. King David died in 1125 and, at his behest, is buried under the gatehouse to the Academy. Gelati is a UNESCO World Heritage Site.

VANI

Vani (or Surium as it was probably called in ancient times) was a centre of ancient Colchis (Kolkheti) from the 8th to the 1st century BC and will be of interest to lovers of archæology. Its site and museum, near the border with Guria, show many of the finest artefacts from Colchis, including intricate gold jewellery (though some of the best finds are now housed in the National Museum in Tbilisi). In the 4th century BC, people were buried in clay *qvevri*, as findings from this site attest.

PERSATI

Ének Peterson is an American cellist and singer who came to Georgia to study polyphonic music in 2014 and never left. She works at Ghvino Underground and has recently begun making wine from 180 15-year-old vines she bought in 2015, in the village next to Baghdati. enek.peterson@gmail.com

Opposite: Part of Gelati Monastery

6. THE BLACK SEA COAST: GURIA AND ADJARA

Acharistskali p. 315
Bakhmaro p. 283
Batumi p. 310
Chokhatauri p. 283
Dablatsikhe p. 283
Dvabzu p. 294

Goderdzi p. 311
Gonio p. 314
Keda p. 314
Khulo p. 281
Kobuleti p. 298
Kvashta p. 314

Ozurgeti pp. 283, 294
Sakvavistke p. 283
Sarpi p. 311
Shekvetili p. 283
Tsikhisdziri p. 298
Ureki p. 283

This chapter travels down along the Black Sea through Guria and Adjara. These half-mountainous coastal regions start rising near the sea and are covered in lush greenery that thrives in their humid, subtropical climate and predominantly clay soils. It rarely freezes near the coast but it often rains, so citrus, tea, corn, beans, soft fruit, persimmons, hazelnuts and tobacco are the favoured crops, while bamboo and invasive creepers grow wild along the roadsides. Farther inland the mountains reach over 2,000 metres (6,562 feet), with spectacular scenery and high villages of log cabins that offer winter snow and sports. When the weather allows, the Adjarian road between Batumi and Akhaltsikhe via Khulo enables scenic access to Samtskhe-Javakheti through the mountains near the border with Turkey.

Wooden Gurian house

The food in these coastal regions is often spicier than elsewhere in Georgia with chillies making a regular appearance on the menu, as they do in Samegrelo. Cornbread takes precedence over wheat at the table, and seafood is understandably popular. In both regions home cooks shared some of their most iconic recipes with me: Christmas 'egg' *khachapuri* and hazelnut-dressed salad in Guria, and an Adjarian cheese pie that resembles rococo lasagne, its layers of ruffled dough alternating with butter and cheese. Eggs simmered in a buttery compote of tomatoes and onions and novel ways to serve roasted fish are other specialities offered by three generations of women in an Adjarian family.

Guria and Adjara were once part of the ancient Kingdom of Colchis, or Kolkheti, that stretched all along the eastern shores of the Black Sea. Vines were cultivated here from very early times but several centuries of Ottoman domination in Adjara, and the devastation caused by phylloxera and mildew in Guria, brought an end to most large-scale viticulture. Luckily the picture is changing, as a visit to Zurab Topuridze, Guria's best-known natural winemaker, demonstrates. His vineyards are planted on steep hillsides with a distant view of the sea.

A night spent at a family guest house provides insight into contemporary life in Guria. We make a stop on the coast at Kobuleti to see the beach and a colourful market before reaching Batumi, the Black Sea port and resort town where fresh seafood is always on the menu. Since the loss of the Abkhazia coastline further north in 1993, the sea frontage from Samegrelo, Guria and Adjara are what remain to Georgia and, within these, Batumi is the most attractive port of call. A trip inland for lunch at a wonderful restaurant, the Adjarian Wine House in the low hills of the Adjarian interior, concludes this chapter.

Previous pages: The Black Sea at Kobuleti

GURIA

Gurian landscape

Like Adjara, this region was part of the ancient Kingdom of Colchis (Kolkheti). It was invaded by the Ottoman Turks in the 15th century but their presence in Guria was sporadic and Gurians were more able to resist their influence; the Turks remained in Adjara for over 300 years.

In the Middle Ages Guria was controlled by powerful feudal landowners whose domains were worked by tithed peasants. The lords often battled with their counterparts in Samegrelo and Imereti. Legend has it that the Gurians were very skilled at training hunting dogs for the noblemen's pleasure.

Much of the coastal area was marshy and malarial until the early 20th century when the swamps were drained; until then most people lived in villages in the hills. The prevalence of eucalyptus trees along the coast helps keep excess water levels down.

In the 19th century Guria boasted many varieties of vines – for both table grapes and wines – but phylloxera destroyed many of the region's vineyards. In Soviet times there were small commercial vineyards of Tsolikouri and tea plantations, as well as small family vineyards for home consumption. Most were ripped out to grow food in the 'black' post-Soviet 1990s.

ECOTOURISM IN GURIA

Today, rural Guria relies on agriculture and tourism for its primary income. Ecotourism is well suited to this unspoiled area, within easy reach of sea and mountains. Mount Gomi, just 17 kilometres (11 miles) from Ozurgeti, offers winter sports such as snowboarding and great hiking in summer. Bakhmaro, at 2,000 metres (6,562 feet) in the mountains on the Adjarian border, is known for its clean air and is popular for those with bronchial problems. It's also the source of a pure mineral water. Its wooden

A goat waits at a Soviet bus stop

houses, with lacy balustrades and peaked roofs, are reminiscent of the Alps. Up the coast from Kobuleti are the seaside towns of Ureki and Shekvetili. They're close to the expansive Kolkheti National Park, an unspoiled nature reserve of wetlands, woodlands and biodiversity that can be visited by canoe, on horseback and on foot.

SAKVAVISTKE (NEAR DABLATSIKHE)

WINE
IBERIELI WINE CELLAR:
ZURAB TOPURIDZE

Zurab Topuridze is Guria's most influential natural winemaker. He's also the environmental operations manager of a large oil company, has six children and speaks great English. His vineyards and *qvevri* cellar are in the heart of Guria, in the hills between the mountains and the sea, near Chokhatauri. Zurab and his wife, Tamar, have 8 hectares of vineyards here: 1 hectare with vines aged 5 to 15 years, and 7 hectares of younger vines. Some grow on steep terraces he has carved from the hillsides heavy in volcanic clay. Zurab is best known for Chkhaveri, a light-bodied Gurian red (sometimes described as pink) from which he produces elegant, organic white and rosy dry wines with lots of character. Zurab's family is originally from Samegrelo but Tamar is from Guria. They didn't start off as winemakers.

"We were living in Tbilisi but in 1992, after we got married, we began visiting Tamar's family and that's when I first discovered Guria," Zurab says. "I'm a geologist by profession and this was the only part of Georgia I didn't know." Tamar's family lives in a small village, Sakvavistke, near Dablatsikhe, that was known for its Chkhaveri. The connection was recorded in books on Georgian viticulture.

"This was a curious twist of fate," Zurab says. "In the late 1930s my Megrelian grandfather, Sardion Topuridze, who was a captain in the

Russian army, avoided capture by the KGB by fleeing from western Georgia to Kvemo Kartli, an hour south-west of Tbilisi." Sardion was an agronomist and took cuttings of Chkhaveri, his favourite grape from the west, to plant in Bolnisi. Zurab grew up watching him tend those and a couple of other varieties.

"To me Chkhaveri was an almost mystical grape. I loved it because of its pink colour and because we would always harvest it long after the others, even in Kartli. When I discovered that Chkhaveri was historically linked to Tamar's family's village, I saw it as a sign that we had to do something with it." That was in 2000.

The couple bought a modest house near Tamar's parents and decided to plant a vineyard. They searched the neighbourhood and found a few Chkhaveri vines growing in a nearby village. The first vines came from there and were planted in 2001 along with local red varieties Jani and Skhilatubani in two small plots near the houses. Three years later, Zurab discovered a large, uncultivated plot higher up the mountain at 450 metres (1,476 feet).

"It was a huge 7-hectare piece of pasture land with no human impact: it hadn't been cultivated or sprayed but it wasn't forest either. From up there you can see the Black Sea, and it's south facing which helps to dry out some of the area's high humidity. In Guria that's like having water in the desert. Chkhaveri is not afraid of the heat. Gurians like to joke that even a passing bird's shadow is too much shade for this sun-loving variety."

He leased the land from the government, terraced the slopes and in 2008 planted 5,000 robust baby Chkhaveri plants. Then he waited for three years to get the first grapes. Unfortunately things were not quite what they seemed. "It was a nasty shock to discover that what I had been sold as Chkhaveri turned out to be Cabernet Sauvignon! The nursery made a big mistake," he says, shaking his head. "We lost a lot of time and money but decided to replant, so in a few years we'll finally have plenty of the right grapes." Initially Zurab was just happy to be reinstating this historic variety but soon word got out about the delicious Chkhaveri he was making.

Top: Mevlud Tsintsadze with his precious car

Bottom: The qvevri cellar

"Creating a business from wine wasn't part of the early plan, not consciously, at least," he says. "Sure, my family and friends can consume a lot of wine, maybe even two tons of grapes' worth per year. But two more tons? That was stretching even our large appetite for wine."

Zurab pours me another glass of the distinctive rose-madder dry wine with an intriguing hint of smokiness. "You have to understand the history of this grape," Zurab says. "From the mid 1960s to the end of the 1970s the Communists liked to drink bottled semi-sweet Chkhaveri. At the time it was considered a rare wine and you could only get it if you had relatives or friends high up in the Communist party. People remembered its prized status." The Gurians who made it privately for their families produced Chkhaveri as a dry wine but commercially the semi-sweet was in demand.

At home, most families focused more on Tsolikouri which was easier to cultivate and less susceptible to mildew.

"Chkhaveri requires twice as much effort in the vineyard but I'm more of a viticulturist than an enologist, so I enjoy that challenge." Producing it in *qvevri* as a dry wine, Zurab ferments the Chkhaveri grapes on 10 to 15 percent of their skins for 20 days to obtain the delicious pink wine.

"It's a very late-ripening grape so we pick in November and, as the cellar is up at 270 metres (886 feet), we sometimes have trouble keeping the fermentation going because of the cold."

In some vintages the wine has an attractive hint of smokiness. "Many late-harvesting west-Georgian grapes have it in some years, but not

Top: Zurab's terraced vineyards; bottom: the family

always," Zurab explains. "We're still not sure why but it may be that the vines absorb some smoke from the air when people heat their houses with fireplaces." Whatever the reason, it goes particularly well with the area's smoked cheeses and sausages.

The Topuridzes' shift into wine selling came in 2010 when their friend Soliko Tsaishvili, the winemaker from Kakheti (see p. 158), invited Zurab to send some samples. "I thought they just wanted free wine to share with their friends, but after tasting it Soliko called and invited me to present the

Chkhaveri at a wine festival. I was the only person they knew who was making it." It proved to be very popular. "There were lines around my booth so I thought, 'Why not bottle and try to sell it?' That same year it won a national wine prize." His other wines include a light-bodied, perfumed Saperavi with a lovely raspberry colour.

Zurab's success with Chkhaveri has inspired others to plant the grape in Guria. "I'm delighted to have helped relaunch this winemaking area. In the past, Guria was known for over 60 varieties of red grapes and 40 of white, though not all were intended for winemaking. But after the Soviet period Guria was forgotten as a winemaking area because citrus fruits, tea and hazelnuts took over as crops here. The same is true of Samegrelo and Adjara: these regions were not considered strategic viticultural areas and no investments were made in their appellations. That's changing now."

Elene Topuridze with roast chicken

Zurab enjoys teaching other growers in his area about organic viticulture and encouraging new producers to work without pesticides. He's also expanded his own wine production to include new projects in Guria (with an experimental collection of over 40 Gurian varieties planted), Kakheti and Meskheti, near Vardzia.

The Topuridzes' current output is 8,000 bottles. They export their wines abroad and are looking forward to building the business more as the new vines come into full production. The cellar and vineyards in Guria can be visited by appointment. I spent a lively morning in Tamar's kitchen in Tbilisi as she and the children prepared our delicious Gurian *supra* lunch. Some of her recipes are on the following pages. www.iberieli.com

SUPRA LUNCH

Roast village chicken with hazelnut-coriander paste
Gurian Christmas khachapuri
Imeretian khachapuri
Chicken kharcho
'Backcombed' aubergine/eggplants
Fermented vegetables
Cornbread
Devilled eggs
Cucumber and tomato salad with hazelnut dressing

Opposite:
Zurab adds
the finishing
touches to the
supra *table*

Gurian Christmas khachapuri

GURULI GHVEZELI   გურული ღვეზელი

This special bread is made in all Gurian houses on Christmas day and contains hard-boiled eggs in addition to the usual *khachapuri* cheese filling. It's popular throughout the Christmas and New Year season and is sometimes baked with a coin or nut inside. The person who gets the hidden treasure will have a prosperous new year.

   This can be baked either as small, individual breads or as one larger bread. The bread's shape changes too, into a rounded crescent or half circle. I love the addition of the eggs as it makes a more substantial bread with an extra dimension. Perfect for lunch with a salad all year long.

FOR METHOD AND INGREDIENTS,
SEE MASTER RECIPE PP. **51-53**

The baked khachapuri

Following the Master Recipe, make the dough as described, for 1 or 2 breads. Prepare the cheeses for the filling. You'll need 2 hard-boiled eggs for every 225 g / 8 oz of cheese. (You won't need to add any raw egg to the cheese.)

When the dough has risen, roll it out into a circle or oval 30 cm / 12 in wide on a piece of parchment paper. Distribute the cheese evenly over half of the circle. Top with sliced egg and some ground black pepper. Cover the filling with the other half of the dough, pinching it all along the border to seal it. Fold the sealed edge in, onto the bread. Using the paper to help you, turn the bread over, hiding the seams underneath. Shape the bread into a crescent, folding the pointed tips under to seal them.

Beat an egg yolk with a teaspoon of water and paint it evenly over the top of the bread. Prick a few small air holes in the dough with a fork.

Slide the bread onto the preheated heavy baking tray in the oven and bake until the top is golden, about 25–30 minutes (smaller breads will take less time). Rub the top with 1 tablespoon butter while still hot. Slice the bread into slices crosswise to serve.

'Backcombed' aubergines/eggplant

ACHECHILI BADRIJANI   აჩეჩილი ბადრიჯანი

There is no limit to the imaginative ways the Georgians have of serving aubergines/eggplant. Here the fruit – for it is a fruit – is baked until soft (fry it in oil for a heavier version) before being 'backcombed' or shredded with a fork and flavoured with nuts and herbs. It makes a great salad accompaniment. If you prefer, use hazelnuts instead of walnuts.

SERVES **6–8**
PREPARATION **15 minutes**
COOK **40 minutes**

4 medium aubergines/eggplants, washed (about 1.2kg/2lb 10oz)

3 tbsp sunflower oil

75g/2½oz/½ cup mild white onion, minced

8g/¼oz/2 garlic cloves, minced

30g/1oz/½ cup chopped coriander/cilantro leaves

1 tsp ground marigold petals

1 tsp ground fenugreek

1 tsp coriander seeds, crushed

¼ tspn dried chilli, or to taste

6 tbsp ground walnuts or hazelnuts

15g/½oz/¼ cup chopped fresh basil

salt

Preheat the oven to 190°C/375°F/Gas 5.

Slice the aubergines/eggplants lengthwise into 1.5-cm/½-in slices. Lay them on a flat baking tray, painting a little oil onto each slice. Bake until soft, turning occasionally, about 15 minutes. Allow to cool.

Transfer the aubergine/eggplant slices to a bowl and, using a fork, shred the pulp lengthwise. Combine the other ingredients in a small bowl before stirring them into the aubergine/eggplant. Mix well. Salt to taste and let the dish sit for 15 minutes before serving to allow the flavours to develop. Serve at room temperature.

Hazelnut paste

TKHILIS SAKMAZI   თხილის საკმაზი

The Gurians are famous for the hazelnuts that now cover a large part of the region, having replaced both vineyards and tea bushes as a cash crop. Hazelnuts may be less prized than walnuts in most of the country but they provide interesting variations on some of the best-loved recipes.

Think of this rather dry paste as a concentrate to be diluted before use with whatever is best suited to the dish: water for a light salad or oil for painting onto a roasting chicken. Taste a few of your hazelnuts before making the paste to be sure they are fresh and not bitter.

To make a tasty but light dressing for the cucumber and tomato salad that appears on every Georgian *supra* table, stir 2 tablespoons of water into 2 tablespoons of paste in a small bowl, mix well and pour over the salad. That will be sufficient for 2 to 3 people; increase the quantities for a bigger salad.

MAKES 240ml / 8fl oz / 1 cup
PREPARATION 10 minutes

110g / 4oz / 1 cup hazelnuts, roughly chopped
12 g / ⅓oz / 3 garlic cloves
1 tsp salt
25g / ⅔oz / ½ cup chopped coriander / cilantro leaves
fresh chilli, to taste

Place all the ingredients in the bowl of a food processor and pulse until a thick paste has been obtained. (Note: whole hazelnuts get stuck easily on the blades of the machine, so it's best to chop them coarsely before you process them.)

Store the paste in the refrigerator covered closely with plastic wrap to stop oxidation. It will keep for a week or more. You can also freeze it in small batches for later use.

DVABZU VILLAGE

GUEST HOUSE
GURIIS KHIBLI

Naziko Javelidze runs a family guest house whose name means 'Gurian Charm' from her home in the countryside village of Dvabzu, about 6 km (4 m) from Guria's capital, Ozurgeti, and 20 km (12 m) from the sea. It's a relaxed rural area with houses fenced off around gardens, vegetable patches and enclosures for a few domestic animals. Naziko has three pigs and a cow in her care plus a handful of chickens. Outside her gate, a family of speckled pigs run free, enjoying the little ditched canal that flows from a spring past her front garden. The stream is called Stolocro and means 'river of a hundred fishes'.

*Naziko
Javelidze*

Naziko's house can accommodate several guests on the first floor in simple homey rooms, with two bathrooms on the landing to share. Down on the ground floor, at the back of the house, is her large kitchen in a separate small building just a few steps from the dining room and its more formal furnishings. Naziko's cook, Maia Askurava, prepares fresh cheese and several dishes for the evening's *supra*.

We eat in the dining room with the women, a male neighbour and Naziko's son, Vakhtang Koroshinadze, who is the *tamada* for the evening. He explains how toasting is practised in their area.

"The first toast is always to peace here in Guria," he says as we raise our glasses of local Chkhaveri. "The second is to god who gives us sunrise and sunset so that we can sleep and rest. We thank god for everything: bless this house and give us good health! *Gaumarjos!*" A few minutes later, as the meal is underway and conversation is flowing, comes the third toast, to the guest 'who is always welcome'.

During dinner, Naziko's son recounts the difficult history of their village and this part of the region before independence in 1918.

"We Gurians always wanted to be free, to have a revolution, and as punishment our area was ravaged by the Russians. Many villages were destroyed, the people and the animals all killed. From 1905 to 1918 the Russian army lived here to control the area and Dvabzu, a Russian word meaning 'two flies', was coined for this place as only two flies were left after all the destruction. After the war, anyone who had been able to escape came back and in 1918 Georgia became an independent country. So here's a toast to our homeland, to Georgia, which like god is only one. We must work harder to improve our country and keep it independent." nazijavelidze@ yahoo.com; tel +995 599787516

Lobio, *stewed herbed beans*
Guruli ghvezeli: *Gurian* khachapuri
Guruli satsivi: *cold chicken with
walnut sauce*
Shredded carrot salad
Tomato and cucumber salad
Fried fish
Home-made cheese
Fermented vegetables

Maia Askurava

THE GURIAN HOUSE

In the marvellous Ethnographic Museum in Tbilisi, there is a perfectly preserved original three-roomed Gurian house from 150 years ago. It belonged
to the equivalent of a middle-class family. It's made entirely of wood and
is raised about one metre off the ground on large stones, both for ventila-
tion and to stop the damp from rising. Each room in the house is positioned
around a central fireplace and has its own door to the yard: the living room,
young people's room and old people's room. The house is luminous and airy,
with a balcony for sitting outdoors in hot weather. All cooking was done in
an external kitchen.

As I drove around the gentle hills of the Gurian countryside, I was fascinated by some of the houses I saw, made of diverse building materials from
the Soviet and post-Soviet eras, including aluminium cladding (see overleaf).
Each has a well-tended lawn around it, a personalized wrought-iron fence
and, usually, a vegetable garden, small orchard and vine arbour. Pigs, cows
and goats roam freely along the roads during the daytime, as do geese and
ducks.

*Overleaf:
Four styles of
Gurian house*

ADJARA

Driving down the coast from Guria, you travel through Kobuleti's Bird and Nature Reserve before arriving at the town, with its wide bay frontage on the sea (see pp. 278-79). The beaches here are sandy and uncluttered. In the town's interior, a large open and covered food market makes a stop worthwhile. Just 7 km (4 m) south of the town, on the coast at Tsikhisdziri, are the ruins of Petra, a 6th-century Byzantine stone fortress that commanded views of both sea and land. It was considered impenetrable in its day and is also thought to be the 'Demonian Kingdom's Castle' mentioned in Shota Rustaveli's epic 12th-century poem, *The Knight in the Panther's Skin*.

The Ottoman Turks invaded most of western Georgia but later retreated from every region except Abkhazia and Adjara, where they remained for 100 years more. A large part of the population in these areas converted to Islam. In food terms that has meant less pork and more goat. Farming goats and sheep here is lucrative: during Muslim festivals the animals are sold across the border in Turkey. Adjarian cuisine reflects other Turkish influences: layered pastry, stuffed vine leaves, variations on the kebab and recognizably Turkish desserts.

From Kobuleti we drive up into the hills overlooking the sea along winding narrow roads overgrown with lush vegetation: eucalyptus, palm, bamboo, flowering vines and all manner of fruit trees. We're visiting a family of talented cooks.

ABOVE KOBULETI

HOME COOKS
TINA MIKELADZE
LIA ZOIDZE

I spend a wonderful day in Tina Mikeladze and Lia Zoidze's house watching and learning from three generations of women in their family. They don't usually cook for guests, but as friends of friends, they generously agreed to open their kitchen for me. Tina is Lia's mother. Lana Nikolashvili is Lia's daughter-in-law and has just given birth to a baby boy when we visit. Four generations live in this spacious wooden Adjarian-style house in the low hills above Kobuleti, in an exotically perfumed garden with a distant view of the Black Sea. We're surrounded by tall ferns, citrus and loquat trees, zinnias and black-eyed Susans. A cat snoozes on a woodpile. The ground floor is reserved for agricultural and pantry purposes; the upper floor is for living. A wooden porch covers two sides of the house.

I love the peaceful atmosphere in their home. In one corner of the large room that moves from living to dining room and then into kitchen, a TV shows the Indian soap operas that are all the rage in Georgia now. The young baby sleeps beside his great-grandmother, Tina, as she sits and works, patiently pounding spices with her pestle and mortar or carefully chopping a large pile of onions. Lia works mainly on the elaborate *achma* pie, while the lovely young Lana helps the older women prepare the tomatoes as she waits to give her baby his next feed.

Tina explains the importance of a good pestle stone, asking me to hold it. I'm startled by how dense and heavy the black river stone is, yet perfectly rounded at one end. "This stone was given to me by my mother, as it was given to her by hers. Many Georgian dishes feature ingredients that have been hand pounded, so the pestle is a key tool. If you find a stone that fits your palm, you treasure it and keep it safely: it's a family heirloom." (See p. 48.)

Lia, who has the dramatic looks of a Greek actress, is a housewife and lives here while her husband runs a food shop in Kobuleti specializing in ice cream. The women decided to prepare several traditional recipes: *chirbuli*, eggs cooked in an aromatic tomato-based sauce; *iakhni*, a beef stew enriched with walnuts and marigold; and the exquisite *achma*, an intricately layered cheese pie. Like home-made lasagne but with ruffled layers, *achma* takes several hours to produce if you start from scratch, but it's a show-stopper if you want to impress your guests with a unique, labour-of-love kind of dish. Its crispy top and soft cheesy centre are unique. Once the meal was cooked and laid out on what I feel is one of the most beautiful *supra* tables I've seen (see p. 31), out came a 2-litre cola bottle filled with Tsolikouri made at Zestaponi. And with that came the toasts and the celebration of a family's traditional food culture. It was an honour to be part of them.

Lana cooking with her husband's grandmother, Tina

Eggs with onions and tomatoes

CHIRBULI   ჩირბული

This rich, satisfying dish envelops the eggs in a complex sauce of tomatoes, herbs and caramelized onions. The onions need long, slow cooking to sweeten, so don't rush them. Use good-quality or clarified butter that has not had water added to it. Use fresh tomatoes when they're plentiful and ripe, or use canned tomatoes, though the yield is low once you strain out the juice. Make *chirbuli* as part of a *supra*, or serve it alone for a great brunch.

SERVES 3–6
PREPARATION **20 minutes**
COOK **60 minutes**

115g / 4 oz / 8 tbsp butter
400g / 14 oz white onion, minced
550g / 1lb 4 oz / 3 large tomatoes
   (or 3 x 400g / 14 oz cans plum
   tomatoes)
4g / ⅛ oz / 1 garlic clove, minced
1½ tsp salt
¼ tsp dried chilli, finely chopped,
   or to taste
½ tsp coriander seeds, crushed
15g / ½ oz / scant ½ cup finely
   chopped coriander / cilantro
7 eggs

Melt the butter in a small, heavy saucepan. Stir in the onions and cook over low heat until the butter is a rich gold and the onions are trans-lucent and turning gold. Stir often. This can take 45 minutes or more, so keep a careful eye on the onions to prevent them burning (a heat diffuser helps if the onions are cooking too fast).

Meanwhile, drop fresh tomatoes into a bowl of boiling water for a minute before peeling off the skins. Discard the seeds and juice (save those for soup). Squeeze the tomato pulp to rid it of excess juice. If you're using canned tomatoes, strain them, discarding the juice. You should have about 360ml / 12fl oz / 1½ cups of pulp. Using a blender or processor, purée the pulp. (You may want to strain out the seeds if you're using canned tomatoes.)

Combine the garlic, salt, chilli and crushed coriander seeds. Stir in the fresh coriander / cilantro. When the onions are done, heat the tomato purée in a large frying pan. Stir in the herb and spice mixture. Add the onions and their butter. Cook for 5 minutes, tasting to correct the seasoning.

Ten minutes before you want to eat, carefully slide the eggs into the bubbling sauce, one at a time, keeping their edges apart (see opposite). Cover the pan and cook over medium heat for 7 to 9 minutes, or until the eggs have poached in the sauce. Serve each egg with some of the sauce.

Chicken and walnut stew

KATMIS KHARCHO   ქათმის ხარჩო

Kharcho or *kharsho* is the name given to several dishes in western Georgia. One is a beef soup with tomato, rice and walnuts. This *kharcho* – usually made with chicken or beef – instead features a delicately spiced nut sauce with marigold petals. It's one of my favourite Georgian meat recipes. The sauce looks like it contains lots of cream, but none is added: the creaminess comes from the ground walnuts. Use high-quality whole nuts and grind them just before using to stop them oxidizing or becoming bitter. This recipe can be adapted to whatever chicken pieces you prefer, but I like using thighs and drumsticks as they become tender and juicy cooked this way. There should be lots of the delicious sauce to spoon over the meat and soak up with bread. Serve this dish hot or cold.

SERVES 3–6

PREPARATION **20 minutes**

COOK **55 minutes**

800g / 1lb 8 oz / 6 chicken thighs on
   the bone
3 tbsp sunflower oil
150g / 5 oz / 1 cup finely chopped
   white onion
170g / 6 oz / 1½ cups walnut halves
1 tsp ground fenugreek
1 tbsp marigold petals
1 tbsp ground marigold petals
1 tsp coriander seeds, crushed
8g / ¼ oz / 2 garlic cloves, chopped
1 tsp salt

Trim the chicken of any excess fat, leaving a little of the skin on each piece. Heat the oil in a large heavy saucepan and add the onion, cooking for 3 to 4 minutes until the onion starts to soften.

Add the chicken, turning the pieces every few minutes until the raw edges are gone. Cover the pan tightly and cook over medium heat, turning occasionally, for 30 minutes.

In the bowl of a food processor, combine the walnuts with the spices, garlic and salt. Pulse the processor until the walnuts are finely ground.

Add 480ml / 16fl oz / 2 cups cold water and process until the mix is well blended.

Pour the walnut mixture into the saucepan with the chicken. If necessary, add another cupful of water so the chicken is just covered by the liquid. Lower the heat and cook for 15 minutes, stirring occasionally.

Remove from the heat and allow to stand for 10 minutes before serving.

Achma (baked layered pasta)

ACHMA   აჩმა

Achma comes from Adjara and Abkhazia and is all about texture. It's like baroque lasagne: sheets of thin, ruffled pasta layered with butter and cheese. *Achma* takes time to prepare, so make it for a *supra* when its sumptuous layers, crisp top and subtle flavours will complement more colourful dishes. It's not usually made to be eaten alone. The pasta sheets need to be very thin and are most easily rolled out by hand. Most of the eight layers are boiled before being ruched or gathered. High quality butter – that has no added water or other stabilizers – is clarified and cooked until it's a rich gold and is used to paint each layer of the dough. (Less pure butter burns much more easily.) The Georgians use crumbled fresh cow's farm cheese but if you can't find that, a mixture of drained cottage cheese, cheddar and firm pizza mozzarella will make a tasty substitute. (For a more decisive flavour, add a little Parmigiano Reggiano to the mix.)

SERVES 12-16 at a *supra*
PREPARATION 105 minutes plus
 dough resting time
COOK 40 minutes

FOR THE DOUGH
4 eggs, at room temperature
420 g / 15 oz / 3½ cups plain /
 all-purpose flour
1 tsp salt

FOR THE FILLING
170 g / 5 oz / 10 tbsp clarified butter
400 g / 14 oz mixed cheeses, grated
 or crumbled
salt and freshly ground black
 pepper

Mix the dough ingredients together into a ball in a food processor or by hand. Knead steadily on a lighty floured surface for 8 minutes, or until the dough is silky and elastic. Cover with plastic wrap and refrigerate for at least 30 minutes.

Heat the butter in a small heavy saucepan. It must simmer very slowly for 20-30 minutes without burning to get a nutty flavour. If it starts to turn deep gold immediately remove it from the heat and cool the bottom of the pan. Don't let it burn! (I use a heat diffuser or simmer ring on my stove to keep the butter from cooking too fast.) Using a pastry brush, butter the inside of a 30 cm / 12 in x 25 cm / 10 in rectangular baking dish at least 6.5 cm / 2½ in deep.

Bring a large pan of salted water to the boil. Place a large bowl of cold water in the sink. Divide the dough into 8 equal pieces. Cover 4 while you work on the first balls.

Preheat the oven to 190°C / 375°F / Gas 5.

Roll out the first dough ball to the size of the dish. Lay it in the bottom of the dish, trimming any

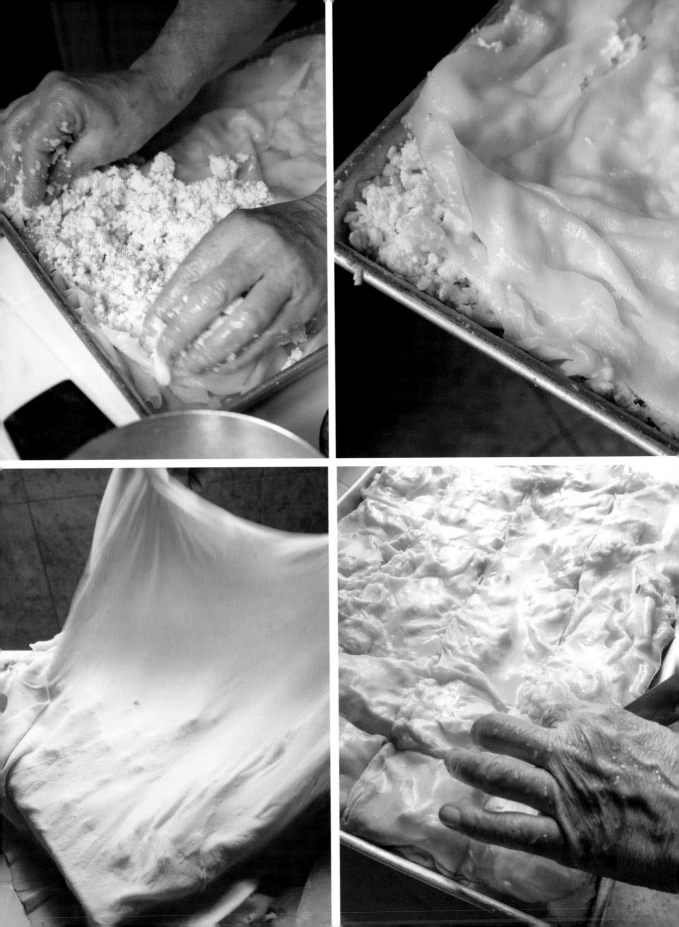

The finished achma

excess. Paint evenly with the melted butter. Roll out the second ball paper-thin, bigger than the dish size. Drop the sheet of pasta into the boiling water and cook for 3 minutes. Remove it from the pan and refresh in the cold water, rinsing it well to remove any excess starch. Don't worry if the pasta splits. Squeeze out the excess water with your hands. Open up the sheet again and arrange it in the dish, ruffling it to fit it into one layer. Paint it with the butter.

Roll out, boil and rinse the third layer, arranging it over the other layers. Brush lightly with butter and spread half of the cheese over it in an even layer. Season with freshly ground black pepper and salt if your cheese is not very salty.

Repeat the rolling out, cooking and rinsing for the fourth, fifth and sixth layers, painting them lightly with the butter. Top the sixth layer with the remaining cheese in an even layer. Season with pepper and optional salt.

Repeat the process with the seventh layer, brushing it lightly with the butter. Roll out the final layer but don't boil it. Instead, use it to cover the whole pan like a flat bedspread, tucking the edges down inside of the pan. Paint the top with butter before carefully cutting the pie into 12 or 16 pieces with a sharp knife. Paint a little more butter into the cracks between the squares. Bake for 40 minutes or until the top is browned and crisp. If the top is not browning enough, you can always run it under the grill or broiler for a couple of minutes before serving. Eat *achma* hot.

Previous page:

Lia Zoidze rolls out a layer of dough

Opposite:

Top left: Spreading the cheese

Top right: Adding more layers

Bottom left: The top layer is fitted over the pan

Bottom right: Cutting out the squares before baking

Fish baked with walnuts

TEVZI   თევზი

Along the Black Sea coast, baked fish is given added taste by herbed pastes of walnuts or hazelnuts. This easy recipe works with almost any delicate whole fish that has a cavity that can be filled, like sea bream or sea bass. The locals often cover the fish with untreated lemon or walnut leaves during baking to keep it moist and for extra flavour. If you don't have the leaves, bake the fish with a piece of parchment paper loosely placed over it.

SERVES 2-3
PREPARATION 15 minutes
COOK 20-30 minutes

650g / 1lb 7 oz fish, scaled and
  gutted
a handful of walnut or lemon
  leaves
2 tbsp sunflower or extra virgin
  olive oil

FOR THE PASTE
100g / 3½oz / 1 cup walnut halves or
  hazelnuts
20g / ⅔oz / ½ cup coriander /
  cilantro
8g / ¼oz / 2 garlic cloves
½ tsp coriander seeds, crushed
1 tbsp white wine vinegar
½ tsp salt
medium-hot chilli, to taste

Rinse the inside of the fish to remove any bitter organs or veins. Pat the fish dry. Rinse the leaves thoroughly.

Spread the bottom of a baking dish with a spoonful of the oil and arrange the fish in it in one layer.

Preheat the oven to 200°C / 400°F / Gas 6.

Make the paste by putting all the ingredients in the bowl of a food processor and pulsing until a coarse paste is reached. (If you are using hazelnuts, chop them roughly before putting them in the processor.)

Fill the cavities of the fish with half of the paste, reserving the rest. Drizzle the fish with the remaining oil and cover it with the leaves or parchment paper.

Bake the fish in the oven for 20-30 minutes, or until it's cooked to your liking. Meanwhile, add a few spoonfuls of water to the remaining paste and pulse it again to make a smoother sauce.

Serve the fish with the paste and with the sauce on the side.

BATUMI

Batumi, Georgia's most important Black Sea port, is the capital of the Autonomous Republic of Adjara and Georgia's second-largest city. It was a Greek trading colony in the 2nd-century BC, a Roman port under Hadrian, and was fought over against the Ottomans many times between the 15th and the 19th centuries. The port played a key role in the early 20th century when, after the 1918 Armistice, British troops came to Batumi to protect the then independent Georgia and the Caspian oilfields from the Bolsheviks and Germany. They remained for two years; when they left, the Bolsheviks invaded and annexed Georgia. Just before the Bolsheviks arrived in Batumi, Turkey decided to occupy the city. In the very short war that followed – of just a few days – the Georgians fought the Turks in the streets of Batumi and liberated the city.

Batumi clocktower

Today Batumi offers an appealing mix of faded *fin-de-siècle* grandeur and out-to-impress modernity. It feels different from the rest of Georgia and fun to explore. Now that Sokhumi, the other once-popular resort town up the coast in Abkhazia, is out of bounds for Georgians, Batumi – and, to a lesser extent Poti – are the main coastal resorts in the country.

In addition to being the western terminus for the Baku railway line that has been so important for oil shipping, Batumi has long been a popular resort for northerners in search of the sun, and it has retained some of that old-world charm in its seafront palaces and handsome residential areas.

It's been brought up to date with modern technology and art museums, amusement parks and festivals: jazz in July, *cinéma d'auteur* in September.

Anyone interested in the archæology of wine will find a visit to the State Museum of Adjara interesting: it contains a big vine fossil from 1 million years ago, as well as many clay wine vessels that underline this part of the world's role in the history of wine. On a more spirited note, the town's clock tower – or Chacha Tower – is said to spout *chacha* at 7 pm every evening from its fountain (bring your own cup and keep your fingers crossed).

Batumi's a great place to walk or cycle, whether along the 6 kilometres (4 miles) of landscaped seafront promenade that was first designed in the

1880s – the Bulvari – or through the atmospheric streets of the centre, with their myriad restaurants, bars, nightspots and hotels. For food lovers, the fish and food markets are colourful and worth exploring, with spices and other dry goods on sale to take home.

The panoramic Batumi Botanical Garden on the coast 9 kilometres (6 miles) north of the harbour was laid out in the 1880s and opened in 1912 by a Russian botanist. It was one of the largest botanical gardens in the former Soviet Union and specialises in local subtropical plants.

Batumi is a busy commercial port, home to merchant and fishing boats as well as an oil refinery. If it's swimming you're after, there are better places for bathing a few kilometres outside of the town on both sides, with stony or gravel beaches. (There's a nice beach just before you reach the Turkish border at Sarpi.) The backdrop to the town are the magnificent mountains of the vast Mtirala National Park, with pristine rivers and lush valleys of subtropical plants that are well suited to hiking, birdwatching and other forms of ecotourism. Those in search of winter sports can drive just two hours from Batumi to the recently constructed Goderdzi Ski Resort, on the road that leads from Batumi towards Akhaltsikhe in Samtskhe-Javakheti region. www.goderdzi.com. www.tourismadjara.ge

Seafront at Batumi

THE BLACK SEA

The Black Sea's water is a mix of fresh water from rivers and rainfall with the saline water of the Mediterranean (via the Ægean Sea) that is pulled into the Black Sea thanks to a strong undertow current. The Black Sea's unique characteristic is that these two strata of waters don't really blend, so the top layer remains lightly saline (about 17 percent as opposed to the Mediterranean's 35 percent) while from a depth of about 50–100 metres (164–328 feet) the water's salinity increases. The bottom layer, below 200 metres (656 feet) – and around 90 percent of the sea's volume – is technically anoxic, or oxygen free, as there are no deep currents; it's inhabited only by plankton. The sea is nutrient rich despite these unusual strata. Pollution levels are being reduced now that there are more controls on industry around the basin of the Sea.

Batumi fish market

The Black Sea was navigated by every sea-going people, from the Thracians to the Byzantines, Goths, Venetians, Tatars and Ottomans. Today it is used for trade, commercial fishing and tourism. You can take cruise boats from Batumi (or Poti, up the coast) to Romania, Bulgaria and other points around the Black Sea.

EATING SEAFOOD IN BATUMI

Unfortunately, most of the small local fishing boats have been banished by the interests and financial power of the large commercial fishing fleets, so there's no real possibility of buying the catch of the day from individual fishermen as you can throughout the Mediterranean. But this is still the best place in Georgia for very fresh seafood, and the town's daily fish market (see below) is small but fun to visit. (There's also another fishy part in the larger market, across the main road from the fish market, where there is a room for seafood and, in particular, the smoked fish that is very popular here.
The fish – mainly oily fish such as mackerel – arrives frozen and is smoked in Georgia.)

Batumi: smoked fish market

The Black Sea is less saline than the Mediterranean, and the fish differ in flavour here too. In shallower waters, there are Black Sea horse mackerel, grey and red mullet, molluscs, delicious black mussels and crab. (The native but highly invasive striped zebra mussel is tiny and best avoided.) Deeper waters offer breeding grounds for Thornback skate, Black Sea turbot, gurnard and dogfish.

BATUMI FISH MARKET

The newly refurbished fish market is on Gogebashvili Street, near a gas station and a big industrial oil depot. Don't be put off by this unprepossessing location, the market is clean and jolly with lots of women hawking their seafood. If you're hankering for fresh fish for lunch or dinner, select and buy it from the seven or eight stalls in the market. The women will gut and clean your purchases. Take them next door (on the right, if you're facing the sea) to one of two small restaurants that offer simple cooking styles – grilling, boiling or frying – and vegetables or other dishes to complement the seafood. For a special treat, look for the legendary Black Sea turbot. It has hard 'stones' on its back (don't try eating those or you'll break your teeth) but is deliciously meaty and fine. When they are in season, small mussels are also a delicacy here.

Balagani 1 Fish and Grill

Balagani 1 Fish and Grill is the one on the left. Izgara Grill is on the right. They both have small menus that include corn bread, fried potatoes (real and delicious) and salads. Our fish came with a jazzy, loose sauce of walnuts, coriander, garlic, chilli and water. Wash the meal down with beer or tarragon lemonade, or the syrupy fruit compote everyone in Georgia seems to love. These small restaurants are always open during market hours (during daylight), so you can just turn up, buy your fish and they'll cook it. Tel: +995 591951466

Other restaurants: Okros Tevzi (Golden Fish) has a large terrace by the sea and features seafood. Tamari Avenue, 5; tel: +995 422251807. Fanfan has a hip interior, with eclectic decor and a European feel. The food's eclectic too, but it can make a change from too much *khachapuri*. Ninoshvili

St, 27; tel: +995 591150051. Marseille is a more traditional affair, with Georgian food, a summer courtyard and a website! www.batumirestaurantmarseille.com

Megrul-Lazuri is a few kilometres north of the city, on the main highway, with a lovely large terrace and good Megrelian and Adjarian food. Tbilisi Highway (E70), 16, Makhinjauri; tel: +995 422253066

I stayed at the Batumi World Palace, a comfortable and well-placed hotel close to the Chacha Clock Tower. www.batumiworldpalace.com

SOUTH OF BATUMI

Batumi and the coastal region around it were subjected to battles and occupations from Neolithic times. Access to the Black Sea was fought over by everyone from the Greeks and Romans to the Persians, Genovese and Ottoman Turks. Vestiges of these civilizations remain throughout Georgia. Gonio-Apsaros, a fortress 15 km (9 m) south of Batumi, was a Roman fortified city mentioned by Pliny. Its ruins are still being excavated; some of the artefacts found within it are displayed in the Gonio-Apsaros Museum inside the handsome cren-

Top: Gonio-Apsaros Fortress

Bottom: Sarpi

ellated walls of the town. They're visible from the main road. Many tourists come too to enjoy the cleaner beaches at this point of the coast, just a few kilometres north of the Turkish border at Sarpi.

KVASHTA VILLAGE

Bichiko Diasamidze and his son, Jambul, are traditional bagpipe players and makers in the Keda region, near the border with Samtskhe-Javakheti. The women in the family – Tina and Maia – are wonderful cooks and will produce traditional Adjarian meals for guests with advance notice. Tel: +995 593658081

ACHARISTSKALI

About 15 kilometres (9 miles) east of Batumi, on the road towards Keda

RESTAURANT
ADJARIAN WINE HOUSE

and Akhaltsikhe as it follows the Acharistskali River valley and starts to climb towards the mountains, is one of the most lovely restaurants in western Georgia. The Adjarian Wine House is a wide stone and brick building, with attractive reception and dining rooms and ample winemaking cellars. In summer there are canopied tables set out in the garden overlooking a vineyard and surrounded by trees, or a terraced stone tower on which to eat.

The handsome wine house was built on the remains of an 18th-century winery and opened in 2010 as the Georgian equivalent to a small French château, with an emphasis on Adjarian cuisine. I love the food here (the wine is of an international style, despite some being made from local Chkhaveri grapes). For me, it is the range of delicious and unusual dishes that make the visit stand out.

There are many dishes on offer, some of which show a tie with Turkish food, including *zedavri*, a shredded

Adjarian Wine House

cucumber salad with yogurt, and *sarma*, rolled chard leaves stuffed with rice and meat. Georgian touches make others memorable: kebabs here are served with tangy, fiery green plum sauce; *borano*, a local cheese, is fried in pools of browned – almost caramelized – butter, and mixed with potatoes; *mkhali* (like *pkhali*) here are crushed green beans tossed with vinegar, walnuts and herbs. I get out of the habit of eating dessert when I'm in Georgia as they are rarely on offer, but it's well worth saving room for the sweet *baklava* made in a nearby family bakery. www.awh.ge

Adjarian khachapuri

ADJARULI KHACHAPURI   აჭარული ხაჭაპური

A highlight at the Adjarian Wine House is this open-faced cheese bread, with its bright yellow egg yolk at the centre, the most iconic dish from the Autonomous Republic of Adjara. Adjarian (or Adjaran) *khachapuri* is a favourite throughout Georgia, and involves participation from the diners who stir the egg into the hot cheese to finish its cooking. The edges of this *khachapuri* are quite thick. The diner breaks off a chunk by hand and dips it into the eggy cheese. I like the version where the dough edges are enriched with grated cheese before baking.

**FOR METHOD AND INGREDIENTS,
SEE MASTER RECIPE PP. 51-52**

Follow the Master Recipe for *khachapuri* using the yeast dough on page 51. You will need one egg for the centre of each *khachapuri* made with 225g/8oz flour, and 15g/½oz/1 tbsp soft butter for serving the bread.

After the yeast has risen, preheat the oven to 170°C/325°F/Gas 3. Place a flat, heavy metal baking sheet on a rack in the centre of the oven.

Punch the dough down, turn it out onto a lightly floured surface and knead for a minute to form an even ball. Roll it into a circle 30cm/12in in diameter on a piece of baking paper. Sprinkle 3 tablespoons of the grated cheese along the top and bottom edges of the dough and roll them in towards the centre to form a boat shape with pointed ends. Pinch the dough to stop it unfolding.

Fill the centre of the 'boat' with the remaining cheese mixture. Bake until the crust is golden and the cheese is bubbling, about 25 minutes. Carefully slide a raw egg into the centre of the bread and put it back into the oven for 2 to 3 minutes more. The yolk should still be runny.

Remove from the oven and put the butter on top of the egg. Serve immediately, stirring the egg into the hot cheese and butter.

7. WEST TO SAMEGRELO

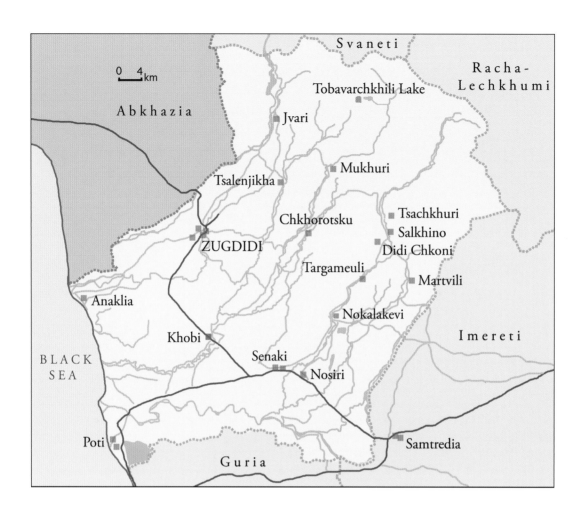

Anaklia   p. 340
Didi Chkoni   p. 325
Jvari   p. 356
Martvili   p. 324
Mukhuri   p. 324

Nokalakevi   p. 340
Nosiri   p. 340
Poti   p. 340
Salkhino   p. 325
Senaki   p. 340

Targameuli   p. 328
Tobavarchkhili Lake   p. 324
Tsachkhuri   p. 327
Zugdidi   p. 341

This trip explores the coastal region of Samegrelo, or Megrelia, that was so important for trade with Asia and the West, on both the Silk and Spice Routes. It visits Martvili for food and wine, where a group of young natural winemakers are inspiring a renaissance of local red Ojaleshi grapes. There are recipes collected from other parts of the region too. Megrelian food is fiery and exotic, and is some of the country's most distinct.

Samegrelo formed the central part of the ancient Kingdom of Colchis (c.13th century BC–164 BC) which has been described as 'the earliest Georgian political unit'. Colchis featured prominently in Græco-Roman mythology as the land of the Golden Fleece to which Jason and the Argonauts sailed. To the Greeks this area constituted 'the farthest world', the easternmost point of their known map, where the sun rose. In the Middle Ages it became part of the unified Kingdom of Georgia and was long ruled by the Dadiani family before being absorbed into the Russian Empire and, later, the Soviet Union. Samegrelo is now administered jointly with Upper – or

Megrelian hazelnuts

Zemo – Svaneti, the high mountainous region. It also borders the secessionist Autonomous Republic of Abkhazia and has taken in tens of thousands of refugees from that region since the wars of 1992–93 and 2008. Like the Svans in Svaneti, people from Samegrelo speak their own language – Megrelian – but write in Georgian.

Samegrelo, like Guria and Adjara, has a subtropical climate, with frequent rain and steamy summers along the often marshy coastlands. It's mainly flat near the Black Sea and around the wide estuary of the Rioni River – western Georgia's main river – as it is at the mouth of the Enguri River, near the Abkhazian border. Tea, citrus, feijoa, hazelnuts, corn and soya are the crops grown here. The central and northern parts of the region climb steadily towards Svaneti, some of the highest parts of the Caucasus, and road travellers bound for Svaneti invariably pass through Samegrelo to get there.

That's fine with me: two of my favourite restaurants in Georgia are here – in Zugdidi, and outside of Senaki at Nosiri – so it's always a pleasure to stop on the way up or down from the mountains to eat traditional Megrelian fare. Even better is to eat in a family with home-grown, home-cooked food!

If it's coastal time you're after, Poti – built near the ancient Greek colony of Phasis – is today a busy industrial port with naval and military bases, though there are still some lovely neighbourhoods around the centre. Beaches, sun loungers and cocktails can be found further north up the coast at Anaklia, a recently developed seaside resort.

Previous pages: Martvili Chkondidi Church and Monastery

MEGRELIAN FOOD

The food in Samegrelo is spicier (and hotter) than in eastern parts of Georgia. Chillies are often used to jazz up sauces and flavour meats. Spicy sausages and kebabs make an appearance, as do stews stained saffron-yellow by French marigold petals. It's not just about heat. If Imeretian-style *khachapuri* cheese bread is already an exercise in indulgence – with its ooz-

Megrelian
khachapuri

ing cheese centre and just-baked crust – the Megrelian version is even more voluptuous, with an extra layer of golden cheese on top. Megrelians love roast suckling pig on feast days but focus their energies on assorted vegetables too, often cooked in clay pots. To cool the palate are fresh, ricotta-like cheeses enlivened with mint, and plenty of aromatic herbs and greens. Walnuts, hazelnuts and cornbreads also balance those richer, spicier dishes. Stretched-curd *sulguni* cheese is made of buffalo or cow's milk and is sometimes smoked. *Elarji*, an elastic blend of hot corn-meal and *sulguni*, is another of the region's best-loved staples. *Ajika*, in red and green versions, is a hot chilli paste with a complex mix of spices that most families blend to their own tastes. Pre-made *ajika* is available in markets and shops throughout Georgia and is a great condiment to bring home: add a small amount to a dish or sauce for unmistakably Georgian character.

One dish that is popular with the Georgians – and that's particularly recommended for nursing a hangover – is *kutchmatchi*, a robust spiced stew of assorted organ meats and walnuts that is most effective washed down with a few glasses of *chacha*, they say.

THE MEGRELIAN HOUSE

The Megrelians are known to be house-proud. Their one- or two-storey houses are often set within neatly cut lawns, with nothing growing too close to obscure their beauty. An external staircase leads to the upper rooms. Today the Megrelian house is often a square, wooden building with a full-length balcony along the front onto which the rooms open.

It wasn't always that way, as a visit to the Ethnographic Museum in Tbilisi shows. The Samegrelo House is one of the first you encounter in the museum's fascinating grounds. It was transported from Samegrelo in 1976, in the early years of the museum's life. The one-room wooden house is from the mid 19th century, when people in the country lived simply, without windows or a chimney.

"The fire was always lit in the middle of the room so it was smoky inside," says my young museum guide, who is wearing the long, plain traditional dress of that period. "The women sat on the right and the men on the left. There were rituals too, as when a new bride entered the husband's house for the first time. She had to walk around the fire three times and touch the chain hanging over the fire that held the cooking pots. Only then did she become a full member of his clan."

The family cooked on one side of the house and slept on a wide raised dais along the other. This kind of *sajalabo*, or house for a large family, could hold three generations, sometimes with thirty people living together. The single sleeping platform was divided between men on one side and women on the other, with the eldest members sleeping near the outer walls. The rest of the family slept in descending order of age, with the babies in the middle. If a couple wanted privacy they went outdoors to a small, raised wicker house that doubled as a barn or storage room.

The Megrelians lived like this until the mid 1800s, when a newer model of house – the *oda* – was adopted. This had windows and a chimney and was raised on legs. If it was built near an old *sajalabo*, that became the kitchen and the family lived in the new *oda*. The walls were hung with carpets and music was an important part of family life. Today the most common configuration is to have a small house – which is used as a kitchen – next to the main living house. "They say that a Megrelian woman always starts cleaning her house from the outside, from the yard, and then goes inside. The exterior is very important to them."

Megrelian house in the Ethnographic Museum in Tbilisi

TO SEE IN SAMEGRELO

This region has many natural features, or national monuments – like caves and waterfalls – that are fun to visit, especially in the foothills of the Caucasus. The Georgians have begun developing some of the best sites for tourism. Mukhuri has mineral waters that never freeze, even in −25°C (−13°F) winter temperatures. From there, in summer, adventurous hikers can trek 45 kilometres (28 miles) up into the mountains to the remote Tobavarchkhili Lake, an Alpine lake at nearly 3,000 metres (9,483 feet), and one of the most stunning scenic spots in northern Samegrelo, on the border with Svaneti. A less time-consuming and challenging alternative is to take a jeep for the first 30 kilometres (18 miles) and walk the last 10 (6) to the lakes. Martvili has an impressive natural canyon (see below).

Megrelian country road

Between Senaki and Martvili, at Nokalakevi are the ruins of an ancient royal town and fortress of Colchis known to Byzantine historians as Archæopolis and to Georgian chroniclers as Tsikhegoji, the fortress of Kuji. It's situated on the Tekhuri River and played an important part in 6th-century wars between the Byzantines and Sasanians.

Much of the coastal region of Samegrelo is still marshland and home to many varieties of birds, insects and plants in the large Kolkheti National Park Reserve, inland from Poti on the Rioni River.

MARTVILI

Martvili has a busy Friday market that's worth a visit, with many producers from the area hawking their wares. It also contains a beautiful church and monastery situated on a high hill at the edge of town that you now reach by climbing a steep staircase. The carved stone Chkondidi church was built in the 10th century over the remains of an earlier 7th-century church (see pp. 318-19). It contains frescoes from the 14th to the 17th centuries. It's home to several monks and is surrounded by a small contemplative garden on what was already a sacred site in pre-Christian times. The attractive Givi Eliava Martvili Local Museum has recently been renovated and contains important archæological finds from the area and domestic objects of wood and basketry as well as fabulous artefacts from the noble Dadiani family, including clothing, saddles and personal belongings. Outdoors is a vineyard with a collection of rare Megrelian varieties.

Didi Chkoni market

Four kilometres (2½ miles) north of Martvili (take the road towards Gachedili), there is a sign on the left towards the spectacular Martvili Canyon, with the Dadiani waterfall and boat tours available, as well as dinosaur footprints and Colchic forest. The countryside around Martvili is known for its caves and waterfalls – especially at Toba, Oniore and Abasha.

DIDI CHKONI

This small town has a lively Sunday market when the farmers and local people from the surrounding countryside bring their produce, animals and wares to sell.

SALKHINO

Salkhino – meaning 'for the feast' – was the summer residence of the noble Dadiani family, Samegrelo's ruling feudal landowners whose seat was in Zugdidi (see p. 341). It's situated 15 km (9 m) north-west of Martvili, on the Tekhuri River. The Summer Palace, or 'Qvevri' Palace as the Dadianis liked to call it, was constructed on the site of a more modest royal residence by Levan Dadiani, who ruled from 1804 to 1840. Construction materials were hauled to the site by peasants with 100 pairs of oxen and buffalo yoked to sledges. The great hall on the lower floor had sunken *qvevri* and a monumental fireplace with a sculpture of Bacchus seated on the mantelpiece. The walls were panelled with oak and chestnut. The Salkhino complex included a large wine cellar, 35 metres long and 10 metres wide (115 x 33 feet). As the historian Iona Meunargia put it: "The idea of building a palace of this kind, on this spot, could only have come to a prince such as Levan Dadiani, who spent all his life feasting and singing." The palace was gutted in Soviet times and is not currently open to the public but you can visit the lovely small church beside it and the park with vineyards planted in the local limestone-rich soils. There is a working monastery too.

Apart from the grounds, with their tree-framed vista of the mountains, Salkhino is interesting for its contribution to local wine history and connection to Prince Charles Louis Napoléon Achille Murat, Napoléon Bonaparte's great-nephew.

Murat (1847–95), who was born in New Jersey to an American mother and a French father, met and married Princess Salome Dadiani in Paris. He became a lieutenant in the French army posted to Algeria. After the French aristocracy was abolished, he and his wife moved to Samegrelo where he set up several businesses, including a winery. He found local varieties growing up trees and determined to 'rebrand' them by training them in the French manner. Not only did he import French varieties into Georgia but he also produced local Megrelian Ojaleshi in a more organized commercial way, successfully exporting it to France. Some historians credit him with helping

Avenue at Salkhino

to save this important variety. After Murat's untimely death, Salome took over the farming and wine production herself, becoming one of the first Georgian women to run such a large company and to help sell her own products (trading was considered shameful for noble-women). In 1912 their Ojaleshi won a gold medal at a French wine fair. During Soviet times the Dadiani's large vineyards were destroyed. Today the Patriarch's resident monks produce Ojaleshi wine from Salkhino's more recent vineyards and run the refurbished 18th-century *qvevri* cellar that once relied on oxen to transport the grapes.

Vine detail of Salkhino entrance gate

TSACHKHURI

From Salkhino we drive a few kilometres farther up into the hills to the tiny church and monastery at Tsachkhuri. "On a clear day from up here you can see all of Samegrelo," says Zaza Gagua of Vino M'ARTville (see p. 328) as we scan the view down towards the sea, "and it was all once a tea-growing area. This is a very strong place, with a stong legend. Each Easter Tuesday people from all over Georgia who can't have children bring cradles up to this monastery and pray here, in the hope of being able to conceive. The whole village opens its doors and five to ten thousand people come and are welcomed."

The lovely small church is situated beside a water spring, and has grape-themed decorations inside. As we admire the tranquil surroundings where a few cows graze peacefully in the shade of a large tree, Zaza talks about a rare grape variety, Machkvaturi.

"This local red grape was used by monasteries but its production was stopped during Soviet times when monks were forbidden from making wine. The Christian priests gave this wine to those who came for mass. The Machkvaturi grape cluster's shape was said to be like a phallus, so it became a fertility symbol and demonstrates an interesting cross between pagan and Christian customs in this

Metal door at Tsachkhuri Church

pre-Christian place. We've planted some so soon we'll be able to check what shape it really is!"

I waited in the cool of the shade near the church as Zaza and the others went to seek out a nearby waterfall. It was Sunday and people from the village came up to pray in the church. Many walked all around the outside of the church, touching the walls and kissing them. It reminded me of something Zaza had said earlier: "We Georgians 'feel' our history so deeply, we'll never stop fighting for our independence. If possible we'll work to get Abkhazia back too. It's still part of our country."

TARGAMEULI

WINE
VINO M'ARTVILLE

From the market town of Martvili, it's a short drive north into the country to Nika Partsvania and Zaza Gagua's *marani*, or cellar, beside Nika's house in the small village of Targameuli.

They bottle their wines under the 'Vino M'ARTville' label. The young men are partners in one of the most ambitious wine projects in western Georgia. Zaza is the winemaker, Nika a traditional vine grower who also raises young vine plants in his nursery. With their other partners (Malkhaz Gabunia and Grigol Tvalodze), they began exploring the possibility of bringing native grape varieties back to Samegrelo.

"This region has an ancient history of winemaking yet recently it had all but disappeared," says Zaza as we sit in the shade on the porch of their small cellar building in the village of Targameuli, near Martvili. "We started in 2012 with an idea to make natural wines from the local red Ojaleshi grape that's been very popular in Russia as a semi-sweet wine since before Soviet times. We bought grapes from local growers and decided to make a dry red wine from it, the first dry Ojaleshi to be bottled." Zaza's grandfather made wine in the traditional way and hoped the younger generation would follow suit.

By 2014, when a larger commercial winery in the area was competing for the grapes, their price at harvest doubled and were almost out of the young men's reach. "We decided we'd have to grow our own grapes to be safe," Zaza says. "We also wanted to control how the vines were being cultivated, so we planted our first half-hectare here in limestone-rich soils, at an altitude of 250 metres (820 feet)." The first planting was of 1,400 vines; in 2015, 400 more vines were planted.

We walk through the village to their vineyard. As the young vines begin fruiting for the first time, they've been underplanted with green beans. "Growing vegetables among the vines can help the soil," Zaza says. The microclimate is favourable here, with cooling winds coming down from the mountains in summer that help increase the grapes' aromas.

"In translation, Ojaleshi means 'vine growing up a tree' and these vines do perform best when trained high onto pergolas," Nika says. "Ojaleshi is said to be 'as strong as mountain people' and was one of the dominant varieties in Samegrelo, particularly when grown on the hillsides rather than in the valleys. Some old vines were capable of producing over 30kg (66lbs) of grapes per plant." Ojaleshi is rich in colour and has high acidity and tannins, perfect for long ageing. Its flavours of plums, berries and subtle smoke give it a lot of character, especially when it's harvested after the first snowfall. "Ojaleshi ripens very late, sometimes not until November or December, but they say the frost helps the flavour. It's a thick-skinned grape but is rather dry: you need 3.5kg (9lbs) of grapes to produce each litre of juice. There's another grape called Ojaleshi in Racha-Lechkhumi, but it's different."

When grape prices fell in the late 19th century due to phylloxera and other diseases, the locals planted hybrids like Isabella or Odessa and were encouraged to grow hazelnuts and corn instead of grapes. That explains today's shortage of vines despite the increased demand.

"Local nurseries are grafting Ojaleshi onto existing rootstock and also exporting the plants – even to Abkhazia – as the Russian demand is very strong," Nika says. "Georgia's National Wine Agency is interested in expanding the Ojaleshi presence in Samegrelo and has sponsored some plantings. Despite our tiny output – only a few hundred bottles in some years – we've been able to export our wines and have proved that there is a market for high quality dry Ojaleshi in Europe and Australia."

From left to right: Zaza and Keto Gagua and Nika Partsvania outside the cellar

Nika Partsvania in a recently planted vineyard

The four friends now work together on the project. Future plans are to diversify and experiment with other ancient grapes. "Before phylloxera there were sixty Megrelian varieties, so we're hoping to revive as many as possible over time with the help of the state vine nursery at Saguramo (see pp. 95-96)," says Zaza. "We're near the Imeretian border so we're also making small quantities of white Tsolikouri." Indeed, they made just 140 bottles of Tsolikouri 2014. A lovely light amber in colour, it was made with skin contact: fermented for one month with whole skins in steel tanks

with wild yeasts and no sulfites added. The Ojaleshi – of which they made 480 bottles in 2014 – is fermented in open casks and then moved into steel after that. They're considering moving on to *qvevri* but think that only one part would be made that way, with the rest remaining in steel. For now, the important thing is to increase production as the bottles are few and the demand is growing fast.

Zaza and his lovely wife, Keto Ninidze, moved to Martvili from Tbilisi to open Oda, a natural-wine cellar and Megrelian family restaurant in their traditional wooden house from the 1930s.

Before visiting Nika and Zaza's vineyards, we spent several relaxed hours with their families at Nika's house while lunch was being prepared. It's a rural setting, with pigs snoozing in the shady lanes and cows wandering as their fancy takes them.

Behind the house, several wooden structures have been erected in the garden, set in a hazelnut grove and surrounded by assorted fruit trees including cherry, persimmon and plum. The lopsided chicken coop is up on stilts with a ladder leading to its door; the chickens are free

Top:
A pig relaxes in a lane

Bottom:
Nona stirs the ghomi

and elected that evening to sleep in the cherry tree rather than inside the coop. Behind it is the wooden outhouse. The family's water is not plumbed into the house but comes from a well situated in the middle of the garden, with a canopy roof over it of corrugated iron with space for washing dishes and clothes. A larger wooden structure is built onto even higher legs, this time with a human-scale ladder to reach it. This is for drying corn and other vegetables.

Smoke is streaming out of the *patskha*, a small hut made of woven hazelnut branches that looks like a room-shaped basket. This is where most of the cooking takes place, over an open fire lit on the hut's dirt floor. A chicken is roasted over it on a long wooden stake, and later Nika's relative, Nona Siordia, stirs the *ghomi* – loose white cornmeal like polenta – in an iron cauldron there. Indoors, *khachapuri* is baked in a portable oven set on a chair, while the spiced *kharcho* stew simmers on the stove.

Keto Ninidze, Zaza's Gurian wife, is a philologist who is starting to write about wine. She talks to me about Samegrelo as she helps cook the food for the *supra* lunch that's being held in the *marani*.

"Megrelians like intense flavours," she says. "Maybe because this area was swampy

Meat on a stick: chicken roasted over the open fire

and suffered from malaria in the past, a lot of chilli was used to boost the immune system. They never had much wheat so they preferred to eat cornmeal especially with dishes like roast chicken. You almost always get *ghomi* at meals in Samegrelo. Sometimes cheese is stirred into it, as in *elarji*. Maize is the staple starch here, and is traditionally eaten with the hands.

"We're very close to Imereti but in central Samegrelo there is creamier, fatter milk and also buffalo milk, so some of the cheeses are richer." I couldn't resist asking about the region's famous *khachapuri*: Why do the Megrelians put cheese on top of theirs? Keto smiles as she answers. "Firstly because we have more good cheese and secondly because we want them to be unique!"

A refreshing note is provided by two cheese dishes made with mint. Nadughi sees a fresh curd cheese like ricotta blended into a paste with mint, water and a little salt. That's used to fill paper-thin slices of *sulguni* cheese. In gebzhalia, *sulguni* is sliced a little thicker into strips that are bathed in a mixture of mint, fresh coriander/cilantro and yogurt or milk.

The women – with some help from the men – serve the memorable feast on a traditional low table and stools in the *marani*, with the assembled company tasting and eating at what we might think of as a child's table, surrounded by wine jugs. All the food cooked directly over the wood fire had exceptional flavour with an exotic, smoky quality. www.facebook.com/vinomartville; vinomartville@gmail.com

Spicy green and red pepper ajika

AJIKA აჯიკა

These Megrelian *ajika* – like intense salsas – are best made in summer. They're quick and easy to prepare. Serve them at a *supra* like relish or add them to marinades for fish or poultry. Stored in clean, airtight jars in the refrigerator, they will keep for a week or two.

MAKES **480ml / 1 pint / 2 cups**
PREPARATION **20 minutes**

GREEN AJIKA მწვანე აჯიკა

200g / 7 oz / 1 green bell pepper
150g / 5 oz medium-hot green chilli
  peppers
15g / ½oz / 4 garlic cloves
30g / 1 oz / ½ cup fresh
  coriander / cilantro
20g / ⅔oz / ⅓ cup parsley
20g / ⅔oz / ⅓ cup celery leaves
20g / ⅔oz / ⅓ cup basil leaves
1 tbsp chopped fresh dill
1 tbsp coriander seeds
1 tbsp ground fenugreek
2 tsp salt

Wearing rubber gloves, remove the stems, seeds and membranes from the bell and chilli peppers. (Save and dry the chilli seeds for later use.) Chop roughly.

Place all the ingredients in the bowl of a food processor and process until the mixture resembles a pesto. Transfer to a clean glass jar and store in the refrigerator.

RED AJIKA წითელი აჯიკა

450g / 1lb / 4 medium tomatoes,
  peeled
225g / 8 oz red bell pepper
115g / 4 oz medium-hot red
  chillies
45g / 1½oz / 12 garlic cloves
1 tbsp dried marigold petals
½ tsp ground fenugreek
2 tsp coriander seeds, crushed
2 tsp salt

Cut open the tomatoes and remove the seeds and juice (save the juice in a bowl for another use). Wearing rubber gloves, remove the stems, seeds and membranes from the chillies. (Save and dry the seeds from the chillies for other recipes.) Chop roughly.

Place all the ingredients in the bowl of a food processor and process until the mixture resembles a thick salsa. Transfer to a clean glass jar and store in the refrigerator.

Megrelian khachapuri

MEGRULI KHACHAPURI მეგრული ხაჭაპური

Samegrelo's version of *khachapuri* is the richest and most indulgent and is popular throughout Georgia. Megrelian *khachapuri* has grated cheese on top as well as inside the bread. It's absolutely delicious and looks great when it's golden and gooey, right out of the oven. Use either kind of dough from the Master Recipe.

FOR METHOD AND INGREDIENTS,
SEE MASTER RECIPE PP. 50-53

Megrelian khachapuri

Follow the steps for Imeretian *khachapuri* in the Master Recipe, filling the dough with all but 3 tablespoons of the grated cheese for each *khachapuri* you are making. Mix the reserved cheese with the remaining half egg.

When the bread has been formed, spoon or paint the top with the egg and cheese mixture. Make an air hole in the centre and bake as for the Imeretian bread until the top is golden brown.

Opposite: Nona spoons egg and cheese on the top of her khachapuri

Cold chicken with spiced walnut sauce

SATSIVI საცივი

This dish is usually eaten at New Year's when the extended family is gathered around the *supra* table. It's traditionally made using a whole boiled turkey or chicken with its bones. It's cooled and served cold with a delicious spiced walnut sauce: *tsivi* means cold in Georgian. The sumptuous, subtle sauce is finer in texture than the herbed version so it's better suited to poached fowl. Use it on leftover cold turkey, hard-boiled eggs or vegetables. For a quicker version, use boneless chicken or turkey breasts gently poached to keep them moist and tender.

SERVES 2 or 4–6 as part of a *supra*
PREPARATION 15 minutes
COOK 20–30 minutes

400g / 14 oz chicken (2 boneless breasts, skin removed)

FOR THE SAUCE
720 ml / 24 fl oz / 3 cups water or chicken broth
1 bay leaf
sprig of fresh thyme
2 cloves
85 g / 3 oz / ⅔ cup finely chopped onion
1 tbsp vegetable oil
30 g / 1 oz / 2 tbsp butter
85 g / 3 oz / ⅔ cup ground walnuts
4 g / ⅛ oz / 1 garlic clove, chopped
½ tsp white wine vinegar
⅛ tsp ground cinnamon
pinch of ground cloves
1 tsp ground marigold petals
¼ tsp coriander seeds, crushed
pinch of chilli / cayenne flakes
½ tsp salt
360 ml / 10 fl oz / 1½ cups poaching liquid

Arrange the chicken breasts in a medium saucepan in one layer. Add the cold water or broth, bay leaf, thyme and cloves: there should be enough liquid to cover the meat. If not, add more. Gently bring the liquid to the boil over low heat. This should take 10 to 15 minutes.

As soon as the water boils, lower the heat and simmer gently for a further 10–15 minutes, or until a meat thermometer inserted in the thickest part of the breast reaches 74°C / 165°F. Remove the chicken from the pan and set aside to cool.

Refrigerate if you are not going to eat it right away. Strain the poaching liquid and reserve.

Sauté the onions in the oil and butter in a small saucepan over medium to low heat until the onions are translucent, 5–6 minutes.

Turn them into the bowl of a blender or food processor and process until smooth. Add the remaining sauce ingredients and process again until the sauce is smooth. Taste for seasoning.

Push the sauce through a medium-mesh sieve to remove the rougher pieces of walnut. Refrigerate for at least one hour.

Slice the chicken into rounds, arrange it on a pretty serving dish and pour the sauce over it. Serve cold.

NOSIRI (OUTSIDE SENAKI)

RESTAURANT
NOSIRI

This lovely Megrelian restaurant is on the main road (No. 1) between Kutaisi and Zugdidi at Nosiri, south-east of the large town of Senaki, which has an Ethnographical Museum and some monuments, and is within easy reach too of the ruins at Nokalakevi (see p. 324).

The restaurant seems like an oasis along the bland but busy commercial road: you enter through a large stone gate into a shady garden with bungalow huts around it, each with a dining table inside. Many Georgian families prefer to eat separately from one another so they can toast in privacy. Meals in restaurants like these can go on for several hours if the group of family and friends is numerous, so each table can go at its own pace.

There's a large kitchen in another building at the back, with a wide wood-burning oven – like a vast pizza oven – where many of the dishes are cooked, from the iconic Megrelian *khachapuri* to *tchvishtari* – cheesy cornbread – and vegetables or stews in clay bowls. Our meal also included herbed beans, home-fermented vegetables and greens spiced with walnut paste. I love the food and atmosphere

Nosiri lunch table

here and am always happy to come back. www.facebook.com/pages/Senaki-Nosiri-Restoraniegrisi/ 798069920258863; tel: +995 592408080

POTI AND ANAKLIA

Poti is currently Georgia's largest port and an industrial centre, though it has some pretty buildings in the centre. It was founded by the ancient Greeks on the River Phasis (today's Rioni) and took its name. Jason and the Argonauts navigated this river in their quest for the Golden Fleece in Colchis (see p. 273). At that time, the sea reached much farther inland. Poti was an important port along the Silk Road in pre-Christian times. More recently it was used by the Ottomans, including for their trade in Circassian girl slaves (one fifth of Constantinople's population in 1609 consisted of slaves). Alexandre Dumas, in his *Adventures in the Caucasus*, tells a diverting tale of the week he spent in Poti in 1858 on his way out of the Caucasus (after an icy night lost on his horse and hounded by wolves), during which he shot a pig and other exploits. Finally, as he leaves Poti by sea, Dumas looks back at "...a wonderful view of the two great mountain ranges of the Caucasus reaching out like arms to embrace the Black Sea".

Anaklia, a historic port near the border with the now out-of-reach Abkhazia, has recently seen new developments including a large resort area with hotels. The town, at the mouth of the Enguri River as it reaches the Black Sea, still harbours the remains of its 1703 fortress.

Future plans for both Poti and Anaklia are attracting huge investments from the Chinese working to speed up trade routes between China and Europe. By building deep-water ports here, they will be able to bypass Istanbul, cutting two to three weeks off the shipping times.

ZUGDIDI

Zugdidi is 25 kilometres (16 miles) from the Black Sea and was a key merchant city when the roads to Abkhazia were open, benefitting from the silk trade and other commerce. That border is now shut but Zugdidi remains the closest town to the Russian-occupied region. It is hosting thousands of refugees from Abkhazia, many of whom travel daily into the occupied territories to work their land or tend their flocks.

Dadiani Palace in Zugdidi

Historically, Zugdidi was home to the powerful Dadiani dynasty that came to prominence in the 12th century when they were given the hereditary title of Dukes of Odishi, the name for medieval Samegrelo. The Dadiani served at the court of the kings of Georgia and became the most powerful feudal family in western Georgia. For centuries they fought with the kings of Imereti, jostling for position in the western part of the country, and finally were recognized as princes of Odishi by the Ottoman Empire in the 16th century. They maintained their dominant status until the 19th century when Georgia was absorbed by the Russian Empire.

Today one of the Dadiani Palaces in Zugdidi is open to the public and hosts a museum containing the accoutrements of their reign, including finds from archæological digs in Colchis, gilded French furniture, a fine collection of 6,000 books belonging to Napoléon Bonaparte (obtained through marriage), and one of Napoléon's original bronze death masks. It also contains what is believed to be Saintt Mariam's robe. The handsome palace is set in its own grounds with a pretty botanical garden beside it that's worth strolling through on a hot summer's day.

The church behind the palace is active. We visited on a holiday, Saint Mariam's birthday on 21 September, when all the children and old men wore their Sunday best and sat in the park listening to the mass being broadcast from the church on large speakers.

Diaroni
Restaurant
Mendzel is a lively place to eat Megrelian food in the town centre, Kostava, 34; tel: +995 571541515.

RESTAURANT DIARONI

Time your visit to Zugdidi to coincide with lunch or dinner. Diaroni is the best restaurant in Zugdidi, and to my mind one of the best in Georgia, and well worth a visit if you're on your way up or down from Svaneti. I've eaten here many times and have never been disappointed. When I last went, they were preparing to move next door to bigger, more airy dining rooms with new kitchens. The current interior is of dark wood with very little daylight, but the food and atmosphere more than make up for that.

Diaroni specializes in hearty, delicious home cooking. That's because the large, busy kitchen is full of women (and a few men) who cook as they would for their families. It's a popular spot so the food on the large menu is always fresh and cooked to order. I was honoured to be allowed into Diaroni's kitchens, to be able to watch and learn a few of their great recipes from Nani Kozmava and Nargiza Tsimintia, among others. Some of these are on the following pages.

Diaroni is a perfect example of how skilled Georgian cooks balance their menus. Their salty, chilli-hot young veal ribs are cooled by minty, milky *sulguni* cheese balls, and complemented by fluffy yet crisp *tchvishtari*, a high cheesy cornbread that's baked to order but worth the wait. *Kharcho*, a veal stew with complex yet subtle Megrelian spices (including a hint of cinnamon), is a great match for *elarji*, the stringy polenta with cheese. Diaroni is also known for its many vegetable dishes. There are always several sauces too, from a thin coriander/cilantro green to a hotter red sauce of tomato, chilli and paprika, as well as the ubiquitous plum. Meunargia Street, 9; tel: +995 577443302

Top: Nani Kozmava in the kitchen

Bottom: Diaroni's fermented vegetables

MENU

Baby ribs with spicy red paste
Lobio *beans with walnuts*
Fermented vegetables
Kharcho *with chicken*
Tchvishtari: *baked cornmeal with cheese*
Megrelian khachapuri
Beets in spicy walnut paste
Green bean pkhali
Aubergine/eggplant with walnut sauce
Elarji
Assorted sauces

Spicy ribs

TSKHARE NEKNEBI   ცხარე ნეკნები

Diaroni restaurant is famous for its delicate veal ribs. Since ribs these fine are hard to find in other countries, I sometimes prepare this recipe using baby back pork ribs (they're also known as loin ribs), as in the small photograph. For added flavour, marinate the meat several hours before cooking the ribs. *Ajika* is the spicy, chilli-hot paste that's very popular in western Georgia. Make your own (see pp. 334-35) or buy dry red *ajika* ready-made from Georgian food importers.

SERVES 4–6
PREPARATION 15 minutes
COOK 90 minutes

900g / 2lb pork or veal ribs (see above)

FOR THE MARINADE
80ml / 3fl oz / ⅓ cup mayonnaise
2 tbsp cold-pressed oil
1 tbsp dry *ajika* or 2 tbsp wet *ajika* (see above)
1 tsp minced garlic
1 tsp minced medium-hot fresh chilli, or to taste
onion, to garnish

Place the ribs in a large mixing bowl. Make the marinade by mixing all the ingredients together. Spoon or paint it over the ribs to coat them on both sides. Cover the bowl with plastic wrap and refrigerate for several hours or overnight. Remove the ribs from the refrigerator an hour before you start to cook them.

Preheat the oven to 170°C / 325°F / Gas 3.

Place the ribs in a baking tray in the centre of the oven and roast for 60–75 minutes, or until the meat is tender.

Serve with rings of raw onion as a garnish.

Cheesy cornbread

TCHVISHTARI   ჭვიშტარი

This cheese-enriched cornbread is a great addition to the *supra* table but is delicious alone too. It's quick and easy to make and can be adapted to include your favourite cheeses. In Georgia freshly made cow's milk cheese is used, with some added *sulguni* on top, but firm pizza mozzarella works well too. Make it in a heavy skillet or baking pan.

SERVES **6–8**
PREPARATION **15 minutes**
COOK **30–35 minutes**

240ml / 8fl oz / 1 cup plain yogurt
1 egg
60g / 2oz / 4 tbsp butter, at room temperature
225g / 8oz mild cheddar, grated
150g / 5oz / 1 cup fine polenta or cornflour, white or yellow
¼ tsp baking soda
100g / 3½oz mozzarella, grated or diced
butter for the pan

Butter a 20cm / 8in skillet. Preheat the oven to 180°C / 350°F / Gas 4.

In the bowl of a food processor, blend the yogurt with the egg, butter and cheddar until smooth. Add the polenta and baking soda and process again.

Spoon the mixture into the centre of the skillet, patting it evenly into a disc but leaving a 2-cm / 1-in trough around the edge – between the edge of the pan and the mixture. (This is to avoid the butter running over the edge of the pan during baking.)

Dot the top of the disc with the mozzarella, patting it lightly into the polenta mixture. Bake for 30 to 35 minutes, or until the sides are golden brown. For a more golden top, place the pan under a grill for a few minutes before serving.

Serve in wedges from the pan or transfer the cornbread to a platter before cutting. It's best eaten piping hot.

Cornmeal with cheese

ELARJI ელარჯი

Cornmeal (polenta) is a staple in Samegrelo and it's often cooked alone – *ghomi* – to accompany meat and vegetables. When cheese is added to *ghomi* it becomes *elarji* and is served as a side dish. I love Diaroni's *elarji*: they use white cornmeal and add *sulguni* cheese while it's hot. The result is amazingly elastic. It's spooned onto small plates and goes wonderfully with the restaurant's spicy foods. Mozzarella makes a good substitute for *sulguni* and you can use fine-grain yellow cornmeal or polenta if the white variety is not available. Serve your *elarji* piping hot. For classic cornmeal, the meal to water ratio is 1:4, but if your cornmeal packet gives other instructions, follow those.

SERVES **6–8**
PREPARATION **5 minutes**
COOK **40 minutes**

960 ml / 1 qt / 4 cups water
170 g / 6 oz / 1 cup fine cornmeal or
    polenta
225 g / 8 oz / 1½ cups diced firm
    pizza mozzarella
1 tsp salt

Nargiza's elarji

Bring the water to the boil in a medium, heavy saucepan. Pour the cornmeal into the water in a steady stream, whisking to stop it forming lumps. Continue whisking as the water comes back to the boil. Set the pan over low heat – or use a heat diffuser – and cook the cornmeal slowly but steadily, stirring thoroughly with a wooden spatula every five minutes. Be careful: if the meal gets too hot it may spit. Continue cooking and stirring until the cornmeal is cooked, about 30 minutes.

When the cornmeal is ready, add the salt and cheese, stirring over low heat to blend the cheese. Continue stirring (the mixture will start to be very elastic) until all the cheese has melted, 7–8 minutes. Serve immediately.

This dish is best eaten hot but if you have any left over, cut it into thick slices to grill or sauté at another meal.

Opposite: Nargiza Tsimintia making
elarji *in Diaroni's kitchen*

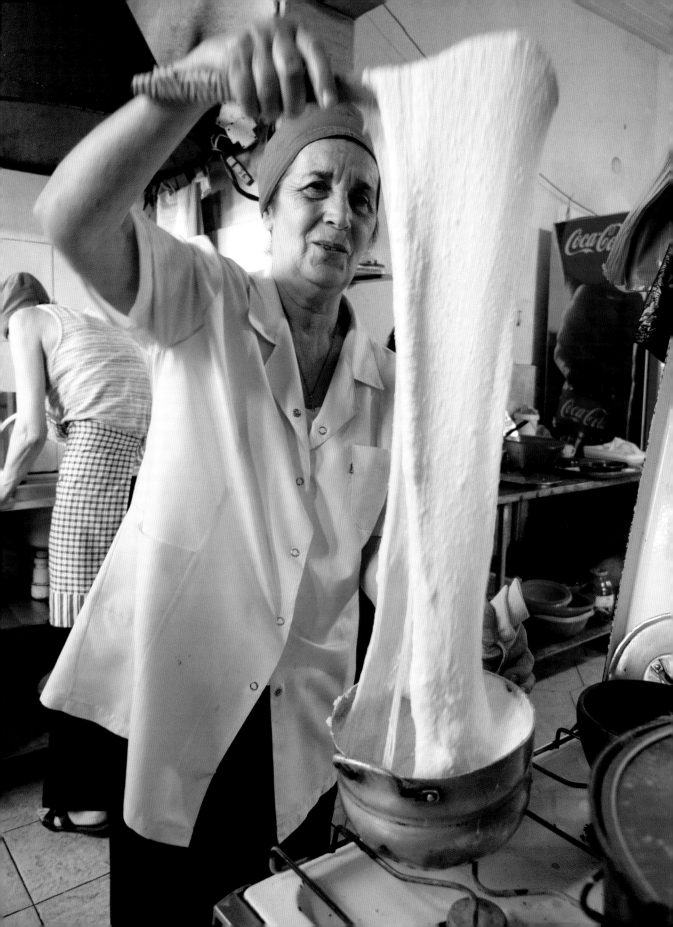

Chicken with nut sauce

BAZHE 2   ბაჟე

Bazhe is a nut sauce and can be made from walnuts, hazelnuts or almonds, though walnuts are the most usual. This quick and easy sauce goes wonderfully with roast or grilled chicken but can also be used on eggs or potatoes. Use a whole roast chicken or individual pieces, as I have. The sauce can be served hot or cold. Store leftover sauce in the refrigerator for 1 week.

SERVES 4–5
MAKES **about 1½ cups of sauce**
PREPARATION **15 minutes**
COOK **45 minutes**

900g / 2lb chicken pieces, skin on
2 tbsp extra virgin olive oil
hot paprika / cayenne
dried summer savory (*kondari*)
  or wild thyme
freshly ground black pepper

FOR THE SAUCE
100g / 3½oz / 1 cup walnut halves
8g / ¼oz / 2 garlic cloves
½ tsp coriander seeds, crushed
1½ tsp ground marigold petals
½ tsp ground fenugreek
pinch of chilli / red pepper flakes or
  ½ tsp hot paprika
½ tsp salt
1½ tsp white wine vinegar
175ml / 6fl oz / ¾ cup water

Arrange the chicken pieces in a baking pan (on a raised roasting rack if you prefer) and spread the oil over them. Sprinkle with the paprika, dried herbs and black pepper. Allow to rest while the oven heats up.

Preheat the oven to 190°C / 375°F / Gas 5.

Place the chicken in the centre of the oven and roast until done, about 40–45 minutes. Baste the chicken every 10 or 15 minutes with the pan juices.

Meanwhile, make the sauce. Place the walnuts, garlic and dried spices in the food processor (or pound them using a mortar and pestle). When the walnuts are evenly ground, add the remaining sauce ingredients and process to a fine sauce. (If you prefer it thinner, add more water.) Taste to correct seasoning and allow the sauce to rest for 10 or 15 minutes before using.

Arrange the cooked chicken on a platter and serve the sauce in a bowl on the side or poured onto the chicken.

8. NORTH-WEST TO SVANETI

RUSSIAN FEDERATION

0 _ 5 km

Abkhazia

Ushba
Ushkhvanari
Becho MESTIA
                    Adishi
Khaishi   Hatsvali
                         Zhibiani
                    Ushguli Chvibiani

                Lentekhi

Samegrelo

Racha-Lechkhumi

Adishi   p. 372
Becho   p. 360
Chvibiani   p. 374

Hatsvali   p. 372
Mestia   p. 371
Ushba   p. 370

Ushguli   p. 373
Ushkhvanari   p. 360
Zhibiani   p. 373

This chapter travels up to Svaneti, one of Georgia's most remote and fascinating high-mountain regions. Unlike Kazbegi, which can be accessed pretty quickly from Tbilisi (see p. 409), driving to Svaneti requires time: there may only be 136 kilometres (85 miles) from Zugdidi to Mestia – the main town in Upper, or Zemo, Svaneti – but it can take close to four hours. (Lower, or Kvemo, Svaneti is nearer to Racha and generally lower in altitude.) It's a long climb on an ever-winding road that follows the course of the Enguri, or Inguri, River as it descends from the giddy heights of the Greater Caucasus, where the glacier-covered mountains reach up to 5,201 metres (17,060 feet), to the Black Sea at Anaklia.

Good weather helps. On a clear day you see panoramic expanses of lakes, mountain peaks, pastures and painterly landscapes, in which clusters of stone houses are punctuated by the tall mediæval watchtowers called *koshki* that were built for Svanetian families' defence. On cloudy or rainy days, when these views disappear from sight, you'd be forgiven for wondering what all the fuss was about. Rockfalls and foreshortened vistas dampen the whole experience.

The first time I travelled to Svaneti, it rained constantly and I left after four days feeling I'd seen enough to last me. I went again in good weather and fell in love with the place, its people and its food. The open landscape makes all the difference. The mountains are wonderful for horse riding and trekking. (I haven't been in winter but Svaneti also offers modern ski resorts.) There are plenty of cultural activities too, with ethnographic museums and churches. The Svans celebrate many festivals, some religious, some agricultural.

Getting a feel for the rhythm of daily life in the valleys was the most fascinating aspect of my trips. The rural villages, with their colourful cast of people, cows, pigs, chickens and dogs offer scenes of what western Europe must have been like a century or more ago. Here nothing is wasted, not the space in a garden to grow an extra cabbage or a row of potatoes, nor the heat of a cow in the stable or its dung. Animals know where they can wander in the day and where to return at night. When the chill closes in after dark, life shifts indoors to rooms with fireplaces and long communal tables, warming food and song. I came away with some of these recipes, taught to me by the strong and admirable women of Upper Svaneti.

ON SVANETIAN FOOD

No wine is made in Svaneti as it's much too high for growing grapes but spirits are popular here, distilled from apples or even bread. High-mountain food culture is fascinating. Summer months allow for the growing of some vegetables and, despite being far less isolated than in the past, the Svan women pickle, ferment and preserve whatever they gather in the orchards, meadows and woods. Nettles and spring herbs are dried for later use.

Previous pages: View from the road to Mestia near Zeda Luha

Berries and other fruits are made into jams or into the astringent and sour sauces that accompany so many Georgian meals.

The Svans cook on black iron stoves whose ovens and hotplates are heated by burning wood. These time-honoured cookers are the heart of each household, often holding centre stage in large kitchens where members of the extended family assemble to cook, eat and stay warm. Visitors can share in these intimate experiences by staying at the many guest houses that have sprung up in the area, as a way to bring in extra income and to compensate for a lack of many 'official' restaurants. The families often bake and cook wholesome rural fare for their guests.

Flavourful potatoes play an important role here especially when they're mashed and paired with stringy local cow's cheeses in the remarkably elastic *tashmujabi*. Georgia's quintessential flat cheese breads – here called *teesh-dvar* – are taken to new heights when filled instead with millet or spiced meat, *kubdari*. Local cheeses of cow or sheep's milk are made by hand daily by most families; some cheeses are smoked.

Svanetian food is sometimes humble but never dull. Georgians are crazy for Svanetian salt, *svanuri marili*, which is a blend of spices and local herbs with salt and is used to flavour so many dishes here, from potatoes to cheese pies and meats.

There's wonderful honey to be found in Svaneti. The best way to get it is to stop at the stands of the roadside sellers who bring their bees up for the summer flowerings in what's known as nomadic beekeeping. You can't miss their brightly coloured hives as you drive up past the vast Inguri Dam and its lake, north of Jvari.

SVANETI: A SHORT HISTORY

The high mountains of the Greater Caucasus that delineate Georgia's northern borders hold pride of place in many Georgian hearts. So do the communities of ethnic mountain folk who have long inhabited these remote, cold and geographically challenging areas; the isolation has helped maintain their culture for thousands of years. Upper Svaneti is one of the favourites, with over 170 tall mediæval towers and mostly unspoiled villages maintaining many ancient customs of the country. The area is now a UNESCO World Heritage Site.

In its early history Svaneti had ties with the Sumerians and was a source of important metals – including gold and the copper that was necessary for making bronze – for Bronze-Age Colchis. (The Golden Fleece is said to have come from here or from the high mountains of Racha, see p. 378). Later, the province was caught between the interests of the Byzantines and the Persians. Svanetia became part of the Kingdom of Abkhazia and, in the 11th century, was incorporated into the Kingdom of Georgia. Its religious heyday came during Queen Tamar's reign; legend has it that she visited the duchy annually in the early 1200s.

Opposite: Women prepare lunch at Charkviani Guest House Chvibiani Ushguli

Thanks to their role as defenders of Georgia's northern borders the Svans were, in the main, a free people. Yet the area was known for its warring factions and dynastic feuds when it was controlled by the Dadeshkeliani princes from the 11th century to the 19th. Despite being a Russian protectorate from 1833, Upper Svaneti retained its autonomy until 1857 when the Russians deployed troops against the province after Prince Constantine Dadeshkeliani stabbed a Russian administrator to death. The anti-Soviet Svanetian uprising in 1921 was unsuccessful. After an avalanche in 1987 killed many schoolchildren, the Soviets forced 2,500 families to resettle in lower regions, many in eastern Georgia, in a traumatic episode of 'eco-emigration'. Since then Svaneti has suffered economic and other hardships but recently there's been some revitalization thanks to tourism and more peaceful conditions.

Statue of Queen Tamar, Mestia

The Svans, an ethnic subgroup of Georgians, speak a distinct, unwritten Svan language but study official Georgian in school. (Svan, Georgian and Laz are all members of the South Caucasian or Kartvelian family of languages.) Svan is in danger of dying out but is maintained in the area's complex and distinct polyphonic songs.

Until 1934 Upper Svaneti could only be reached by a path which was closed during winter. This isolation helped preserve both its architecture and its way of life. Today access is possible both by road and air.

SVANETI: SILK ROADS AND STONE TOWERS

Svaneti, like other parts of the northern Caucasus, was at times a section of the Silk Road from China as it worked its way from Asia to the Black Sea and the ancient trading port of Phasis (today's Poti). In the 6th century, as Persia and Byzantium fought for control of these important trade routes, the Byzantine Emperor Justinian pushed the routes up through the high mountains in order to avoid his Persian foes. Elaborate defensive walls were constructed to shelter and defend the caravans from local mountain tribes. Mestia was one point along the route that passed through Ushguli before moving down to Lower Svaneti and Kutaisi. Some time later, Christian missionaries established monasteries in Svaneti and settlements grew around the churches. After 1453, and the fall of Constantinople, the Silk Road across the North Caucasus ceased to be used.

Opposite: Oxen pull felled trees in the Upper Becho Valley

The 170 defensive towers called *koshki* that characterize the Svanetian landscape date from the 9th to 12th centuries. They could accommodate cattle – and sometimes kitchens – on the ground floor. Many had no doors to reach the upper floors: you climbed a ladder and entered through a small window positioned 5 or 6 metres (16 or 20 feet) off the ground. Once that ladder was pulled inside, it was practically impossible to gain access to them. The towers protected residents from attack by foreign invaders or from the local blood feuds that were common between the villages. During times of religious persecution many icons and precious items from other parts of Georgia were brought here for safekeeping; some of these remain in private houses.

Today the battle that Svaneti needs to fight is no longer against its old foes, be they Mongols, Chechens, Kabardins, Russians, Circassians or more local tribes. The challenge now is to handle the peaceful but powerful invasion of tourists responsibly, to minimise the risk of changing Svaneti's unique character. Luckily the rise in numbers of private guest houses has forestalled the development of large hotels and so far the balance between residents and visitors remains positive.

BECHO VALLEY

I've stayed in the Becho Valley on each of my trips to Svaneti. About 20 minutes by car from Mestia, this valley leads up towards Mount Ushba and its glacier, at 4,700 metres (15,419 feet), and in clear weather is dominated by Ushba's curvilinear peak. The road follows the narrow but fast-flowing Dolra River with clusters of humble farms and log cabins along its way, some grouped into small villages.

Pigs and other animals roam freely in the paths between the houses, each with a barn and woodpile attached. In some, heaps of dung outside small windows in the barns point to animals being stabled indoors. Most animals, however, seem to be free during the day and brought back into the safety of pens at night, sometimes accompanied by small children or village youths with their dogs. There are nocturnal predators – like wolves and bears – in these areas. In spring and summer, the open meadows are filled with wild-flowers and with lazy grazing cows. There are several family guest houses and small hotels in this valley, some of which offer wonderful food.

USHKHVANARI, BECHO

Opposite: Svanetian towers punctuate the landscape on the road between Mestia and Becho

COOK, GUEST HOUSE
KHAVA AND
JENAR KVITSIANI

Halfway up the Becho Valley between the main road to Mestia and Mount Ushba is the rural village of Ushkhvanari. Jenar Kvitsiani's guest house is a large house on the right as you go up towards the mountains. A short track leads to it.

Jenar and her sister, Nestani, live with their mother, Khava Gurchiani, and have turned their home into a guest house. It's recently been enlarged:

the rooms are simple with great views of the mountains. Be sure to visit the kitchen where Khava (who is the main cook) has her domain. She is a talented baker of the iconic *kubdari* breads that Svaneti is famous for, and does it all on and in her old black iron wood-burning stove. Watching her for several hours as she made three types of local stuffed breads gave an intimate view into how the women prepare food here. This skilled cook uses the same dough base for each of her versions of the flat, filled breads, and relies on her experienced touch to test their consistency and doneness. There are no oven thermometers here! Beyond the now familiar cheese-filled *khachapuri* (in one of my favourite versions), I love her spiced-meat *kubdari*, and the unusual bread filled with chopped and herbed millet.

She also makes a wonderful dish from stinging nettles, *tchintchari mkhali* (in eastern Georgian, these sorts of chopped and seasoned vegetables dishes are called *pkhali*). She takes a bucketful of the wild greens, boils them for 15 minutes, and then squeezes and chops them. To this she adds finely chopped white onion – raw or sautéed, pounded coriander seeds, fresh mint, parsley, coriander/cilantro and a hint of chilli. Plus the special spiced Svaneti salt the Georgians are passionate about (see recipe p. 370).

The first meal I had here was memorable for being a compilation of traditional Svanetian dishes. During my second stay the women branched out into less local fare. It was good but disappointing for anyone interested in native cuisine, so specify that you'd prefer Svanetian recipes at their generous lunch and dinner spreads. jenari.becho@gmail.com; tel: +995 599139072

Evening in the Becho Valley

KHAVA GURCHIANI'S STORY

Khava Gurchiani and her daughters opened their guest house in 2006; they were the second family in the Becho Valley to do so. As Khava cooked, she told her family's story. It's a revealing account of the upheavals so many people faced in the border regions between Georgia and the USSR.

Khava was born in Etseri village in 1938, in the valley next to Becho. Her future husband, Levan Kvitsiani, was born in Becho in 1935 but when he was seven he moved with his mother and sister north of Svaneti to Kabardino-Balkaria, on the Russian side of the Caucasus. Many villages in Kabardino-Balkaria were empty after the mass deportations and migrations of Turkic peoples that had been taking place there in the 1860s and again in 1937 and 1944 (when the Balkars were almost all deported to Kazakhstan and Siberia). Svans were encouraged to move up to the now-empty farms and work the land and live there. When, in 1957, Khrushchev permitted the deportees and their descendants to return to their native lands, many Svans decided to move back to Svaneti. Levan's family did so in 1957.

Khava Gurchiani with her kubdari *breads*

"At that time the government helped Georgians return to their homelands," says Khava. "Levan was given 10,000 *maneti* to buy some land and build a house, the very house we are cooking in today." Khava and Levan were married in 1968 and have five children, four daughters and one son. Levan's surname, Kvitsiani, derives from the Svan word, *kvets*, or wheat. Becho was famous for growing native varieties of wheat.

The Svans were not the only people to be allowed to settle in Kabardino-Balkaria. The North Ossetians also went there but, when the original Balkars returned in the late 1950s, the North Ossetians were reluctant to leave, leading to more conflict.

Spiced meat bread

KUBDARI   კუბდარი

This is one of the most delicious filled breads of all. *Kubdari* is a Svanetian speciality and is baked filled with lightly spiced chunks of tender pork and/or beef mixed with onions and herbs. A meal in inself, it also admirably complements the vegetable dishes at a *supra*.

Follow the Master Recipe for the yeast dough for 2 breads and method on pp. 51-52. In Svaneti, the salt used would be Svanetian salt – enriched with spices, see p. 370 – but this recipe already includes most of those spices.

Khava starts her breads cooking on the top of her wood-burning stove and oven, so make sure to follow the instructions about preheating a heavy metal baking tray as you preheat your oven.

SERVES **8–16**
PREPARATION **40 minutes**
COOK **45 minutes**

Master Recipe for yeast dough for 2 breads, pp. 51-52

FILLING FOR **2** BREADS

400g / 14 oz lean pork or beef fillet / tenderloin

30g / 1 oz / 2 tbsp butter

75g / 2½ oz / ½ cup finely chopped onion

4g / 1 garlic clove, finely chopped

⅛ tsp ground chilli, or to taste

1 tbsp tomato paste

½ tsp ground fenugreek

¼ tsp coriander seeds, crushed

⅛ tsp ground cumin

1 tsp fresh dill, minced

½ tsp salt or Svanetian salt

2 tbsp minced fresh coriander / cilantro

1 tbsp sunflower oil

2 tbsp water

butter, for the bread top

While your dough is rising, make the filling. Cut the meat into small, bite-size or smaller diced pieces, removing any fat.

Heat the butter in a small heavy saucepan and gently sauté the onion until it starts to become translucent, 6–7 minutes. Stir in the garlic and chilli and cook for 2–3 minutes more. Remove from the heat and stir in the tomato paste and dry spices. Stir the onion mixture into the meat with the remaining ingredients and mix well. Refrigerate until you're ready to use.

Place a heavy baking tray in the centre of the oven and preheat the oven to 180°C / 350°F / Gas 4 at least 15 minutes before you want to bake the breads.

Divide the dough and filling in half and form the breads following the instructions on p. 52.

Bake on the preheated baking tray for 30–35 minutes, or until the top begins to brown and the meat is cooked through. Remove from the oven and immediately spread a little butter all over the top and sides of the bread to keep it soft. Serve hot, sliced into wedges.

Cooked and raw salad

SALATI   სალათი

The Georgians are imaginative about their vegetables and make unusual salads in which some of the ingredients are both cooked and raw. This one is like a polyphonic riff on a grated carrot salad. There's something enticing about the different textures of cooked and raw bell peppers, or the crunch of fresh spring onions contrasting with the seductive sweetness of roasted onions. This is a very adaptable salad, so don't worry too much about exact measurements.

SERVES **8**
PREPARATION **30 minutes**
COOK **45 minutes**

THE ROASTED VEGETABLES
2 medium red onions peeled
4 tbsp cold-pressed oil
1 medium aubergine / eggplant, cut lengthwise into 1.5-cm / ½-in slices
1 red bell pepper, seeded and quartered
1 yellow bell pepper, seeded and quartered

THE RAW VEGETABLES
400g / 14 oz carrots
1 yellow bell pepper
1 red bell pepper
4 spring onions / scallions, whites and greens, sliced into rings
15g / ⅓oz / ¼ cup chopped fresh coriander / cilantro
135g / 4½oz / 1¼ cups walnut halves
1 tsp ground fenugreek
½ tsp coriander seeds, crushed
fresh medium-hot chilli (to taste), finely chopped
240ml / 8fl oz / 1 cup plain yogurt or sour cream
salt and ground black pepper

Preheat the oven to 200°C / 400°F / Gas 6.

Slice the red onions into eighths, from tops to roots. Toss them in a small baking pan with 2 tablespoons of the oil. Paint the other roasting vegetables with the remaining oil and arrange them on a flat baking tray (it's fine if some of the peppers sit on the aubergines / eggplants). Place both trays in the oven and bake for 15 minutes. Turn the vegetables, making sure the onions are evenly oiled. Continue cooking until the aubergines / eggplants are just starting to become golden, around 20 minutes more. Remove the trays from the oven. The onions should be soft and sweet: if they're still firm, cook them for another 10 minutes or until they sweeten but don't let them burn. When the vegetables are cool, cut them into thin slices.

Meanwhile, prepare the raw vegetables. Using a medium grater or food processor, grate the carrots into a large bowl. Slice the peppers into thin strips. They should retain their crunch. Mix them into the carrots with the spring onions / scallions and fresh coriander / cilantro. Stir in the roasted vegetables.

Make the sauce by grinding the walnuts with the spices, chilli and yogurt or sour cream in a food processor. If it seems too thick, add a little water. Season with salt and pepper.

Mix the sauce into the salad and allow it to rest for at least 30 minutes in the refrigerator before serving.

Braised meatballs

GUPTA   გუფთა

These substantial meatballs, from Grand Hotel Ushba (see overleaf), are perfect for a cold winter's day in the mountains (or the city). They're the size of a small apple, so two make a good-sized main course. Serve in small bowls with their cooking liquid and some of the cabbage. At a *supra* one per person should be plenty.

MAKES **about 15**
PREPARATION **35 minutes**
COOK **75 minutes**

100g / 3½oz / ½ cup uncooked white rice or 1 cup cooked rice
150g / 5 oz / 1 cup roughly chopped onion
2 eggs
1 tsp coriander seeds, crushed
½ tsp ground fenugreek
1 tsp salt
¼ tsp black pepper
450g / 1lb ground beef
450g / 1lb ground pork
1 small head of white, green or spring cabbage
1 440g / 14 oz can tomato passata or crushed tomatoes
1lt / 1qt / 4 cups beef, chicken or vegetable stock
2 bay leaves
20g / ⅔oz / ½ cup coarsely chopped fresh coriander / cilantro
1 tsp salt

Cook the rice according to package instructions. While the rice is cooking, prepare the other ingredients. Cool the rice before adding it.

In a food processor, process the onion and eggs with the spices until smooth. Add the rice and process again. Add half of each type of meat and process again. The mixture will be thick. If your processor is big enough, add the rest of the meat and process. If not, turn the mixture into a large mixing bowl and add the remaining meats by hand. Mix well. Preheat the oven to 180°C / 350°F / Gas 4.

Form the meat into about 15 balls 6cm / 2½inches in diameter. Line a deep, heavy casserole/Dutch oven with one layer of cabbage leaves. Add a layer of the balls, placing them carefully to keep them separate from each other. Cover each ball with a piece of cabbage (use the cabbage to keep the balls from touching each other). Make a second layer of meatballs and cover with cabbage leaves. Tuck the bay leaves into opposite sides of the pan.

Heat the tomato passata with a generous half of the stock until simmering. Pour it carefully into the casserole. The liquid should just cover the meatballs. If you need more, add the rest of the stock with more water as necessary. Cover the casserole and place in the centre of the preheated oven. Bake for 1 hour (about halfway through, check that the meatballs are submerged. If they aren't, add more liquid or put a dish over the meatballs inside the casserole to keep them down). Serve hot, with or without the cabbage.

BECHO VALLEY

RESTAURANT, HOTEL
GRAND HOTEL USHBA

At the top end of the Becho Valley is hotel and restaurant Grand Hotel Ushba, a small rural affair despite its grandiose name. The hotel is off the main track, surrounded by hillsides of wild yellow azaleas and magnificent views of the mountains. Its Scandinavian owner's æsthetic of country chic, pale pine furniture and thick duvets provides a cosy place to stay and offers a great base to hike or ride from. The communal dining room hosts meals for residents and non-residents (if you book ahead), prepared in the small kitchen at the back. The cooking is shared by several people, one of whom is Meri Guledali. Meri's a fine chef, and divides her time between the hotel and teaching at the local school. I asked her what people ate during the long cold winters. "Everyone here spends the summer and autumn preparing for winter," she says. "We store vegetables in root cellars and make preserves from fruits. We also make a lot of fermented vegetables, from cabbages to cucumbers. We always have good supplies of dairy products and of course we butcher the pigs in winter too." She describes one of her favourite winter preserves, fermented cabbage and beets. "You slice a whole white cabbage, stir it with a minced red chilli, a large spoonful of vinegar and another of salt. Then you boil four beetroot/beets. You slice them too, mix them with the cabbage, and pack them into sterilized jars. Add garlic, bay leaves and dried dill. Then pour in the beets' cooking water, but don't fill the jars too full or they'll spill over during fermentation. After about a week at room temperature the cabbage will be tender. Then you can store the jars in a cool place for several months."

Top: Meri Guledali

Bottom: Grand Hotel Ushba dining room

In Svaneti, each family makes its own salt (*svanuri marili*), but you can enrich your salt, Svanetian style, by adding some or all of these spices and herbs to good quality sea or mineral salt: ground caraway seed; dried red chilli; ground coriander seed; dried dill; ground blue fenugreek; dried garlic; ground marigold petals; black pepper; dried thyme. Use on meats, barbecues and to flavour vegetable dishes. Kept in an airtight jar, this salt will last for months. (See p. 368 for Meri's meatballs.) www.grandhotelushba.com

MESTIA

Mikheil Khegiani Svan House Museum, Mestia

In Svaneti, all roads lead to Mestia. This small but busy town is where everyone meets and hangs out. Its central streets, with their cafés with free wifi and open terraces, are always filled with hikers, campers, mountain climbers and just plain tourists stopping in on their way up or down the mountain valleys for food, drink and information. Café Laila, in Seti Square, is a main hub; it's open till late, and popular for everything from coffee to dinner. Tel: +995 577577677

GETTING THERE For those in a hurry there's an airport at Mestia with flights to and from major Georgian cities; trains and *marshrutkas* (small local buses) to Zugdidi from Tbilisi are available, followed by a ride in a *marshrutka* up the mountain to Svaneti.

MUSEUMS Mestia has two memorable museums. For me the most fascinating is the Mikheil Khegiani Svan House Museum. Named after a famous mountaineer, it's signposted from Mestia's central square, Setis Moedani, and is a few minutes' walk from there. Inside the 14th-century stone house, the large main room retains the carved wooden stalls that held livestock in winter and that surrounded the family's living area. It includes a hearth fire, bench and throne-like armchair for the *pater familias*. Legend has it that Svanetian wives were chosen on the basis of how much weight they were able to carry up the steep mountain tracks. The family slept in cubicles above the animals to conserve as much heat as possible. Beside the cooking area were storage chests for flour and boiled meats. A Svan tower stands nearby and is also open to visitors.

The Svaneti Museum of History and Ethnography is also worth visiting: it's housed in a modern building that was refurbished in 2013 and contains important collections of local and Georgian icons and artefacts.

SKI SLOPES AND GLACIERS

Hatsvali Ski Station is just 8 kilometres (5 miles) south of Mestia and was opened in 2010. It has several slopes and good access from Mestia. The slopes are usually open from December to April. Tetnuldi Ski Resort is further afield, east of Mestia, and is Georgia's second-largest ski station (after Gudauri, see p. 414). The ski slopes range from 1,600–3,165 metres (5,250–10,384 feet) on the mountain whose peak is at 4,858 metres (15,938 feet), near the border with Kabardino-Balkaria. www.tetnuldi.com Information about all of Georgia's ski resorts can be found on www.skigeorgia.ge. The village of Adishi, positioned beside a glacier, is located several kilometres from Mount Tetnuldi, and has four churches. www.svanetitrekking.ge is a good source of information about the area and its many opportunities for visiters.

View of Mount Ushba from the Becho Valley

USHGULI

We weren't lucky with the weather on the day we drove the endless 50 kilometres (32 miles) from Mestia up to Ushguli, Europe's highest permanently inhabited cluster of villages, situated at over 2,200 metres (7,218 feet). Normally that wouldn't matter too much but in June, after weeks of non-stop rain, the dirt road that leads up the Enguri River gorge – which is anyway only open three months of the year – was even more perilous and uncomfortable than usual. We bumped and gasped as rivulets turned into gushing torrents and washed over the rocky, narrow road before dropping steeply to the river below us. When we finally made it, the big views of the peaks that people rave about were hidden in the clouds. (On a clear day, they include Georgia's highest peak: Mount Shkhara, at 5,068 metres/16,628 feet.)

Ushguli woman sits at the base of a tower

Yet that trip to Ushguli and those hours spent in a Jeep crawling past isolated rural farms, imposing mediæval towers and banks of wild flowers whose colours were saturated in the wet grey, were unforgettable. (From the car window I spotted wild orchids, geraniums, honeysuckle, viburnum, wild yellow azaleas, orange poppies, campanula and many others.)

After lunch (see next pages) we visited the intimate church and monastery of Lamaria, above the highest Ushguli village, Zhibiani. The 10th-century church is built with a swallow-domed roof structure typical of Darbazi. It contains a painted fresco of the crucifixion in the small, vaulted chapel and several icons on tables within. The monastery was abandoned until recently. Lamaria is the northernmost Georgian church and a mere stone's throw from the Russian border. Two Svan towers stand nearby. They're known as Tamar's towers, for the area enjoyed a religious heyday during Queen Tamar's reign; the queen is said to have visited often. In Soviet times the Russians mounted large satellite dishes on these precious towers; happily, they've since been removed. In those days, when people faced the death penalty if even one little icon was found in their possession, the Ushguli villagers hid many important religious relics that, thanks to their bravery, still survive today. Ushguli and its 20 ancient Svan towers are now protected by the UNESCO World Heritage status they have held since 1996. There are several small ethnographic museums dotted around this part of Svaneti. They're often kept closed unless someone wants to visit, so ask the locals for the keys.

USHGULI-CHVIBIANI

The reception when we arrived at Chvibiani was memorable. We were ushered down a muddy track into the guest house of Laert Charkviani, where a roaring fire and fully laid table greeted us. As the people I travelled with settled around it, exchanging stories of the tortuous trip with friends from the other Jeep, I made my way to the kitchen where the women of the household were putting the finishing touches to our lunch (see photo p. 357). Actually, feast is a better word to describe this abundant, remarkable meal.

Lela Kobalia, Liana Meshkia and Marika Gigani had prepared a triumphant *supra*. The table was quickly filled with dishes of mushrooms stewed with red peppers (see recipe on p. 376); grilled pork strewn with raw onion rings and dill; sliced cucumber and tomato; cheese balls with mint and milk; and home-made corn bread sprinkled with cheese. The women were pulling freshly baked *kubdari* (spicy meat breads) out of the small wood-burning oven, and cutting their cheesy *khachapuris* into wedges. These were served with steaming bowls of vegetable soup. At the stove, they battled with *tashmujabi*, mashed potatoes stirred with stringy cheese, to divide the mass into portions. It was elastic and delicious. A dark jelly served in small bowls was made from the most intense and fragrant blackcurrants I've ever tasted.

Opposite: Iron wood-burning stoves are used throughout Svaneti

Below: Battling the tashmujabi

Mushrooms and red peppers

SOKO TSITELI TSITSAKIT   სოკო წითელი წიწაკით

Mushrooms are found in the meadows and woods in Svaneti in early summer and autumn, before the weather turns too cold. This is a nice way to give a Georgian twist to a mix of wild and cultivated mushrooms.

SERVES 4–6
PREPARATION **15 minutes**
COOK **25 minutes**

750g / 1½lb mixed mushrooms, wild and cultivated
150g / 5oz / 1 cup chopped onion
3 tbsp cold-pressed oil
1 large red bell pepper, cut into large dice
¼ tsp dried summer savory or mild thyme
½ tsp coriander seeds, crushed
½ tsp ground fenugreek
¼ tsp chilli/red pepper flakes
120ml / 4fl oz / 1 cup peeled canned tomatoes and their juice, roughly chopped
8g / ¼oz / 2 garlic cloves, chopped
20g / ⅔oz / ½ cup mixed chopped fresh herbs: parsley, basil and coriander/cilantro
1 tsp salt or Svanetian salt (see p. 370)
freshly ground black pepper

Clean the mushrooms, wiping them with a damp cloth as necessary to remove any soil. Leave small mushrooms whole; cut larger ones in half. The mushroom pieces should be big for this recipe.

In a large, non-stick frying pan, sauté the onion in the oil for 5–6 minutes until it starts to soften and become translucent. Stir in the bell pepper, dry herbs, spices and chilli. Cook for 2–3 minutes. Add the mushrooms and cook over medium heat, stirring often, until the mushrooms start to brown and release some of their moisture, about 5 minutes.

Stir in the tomatoes with their juice, the garlic and the fresh herbs. Mix well, season with salt and pepper, and cook until the mushrooms are soft, about 10 minutes. Serve hot, at room temperature or chilled.

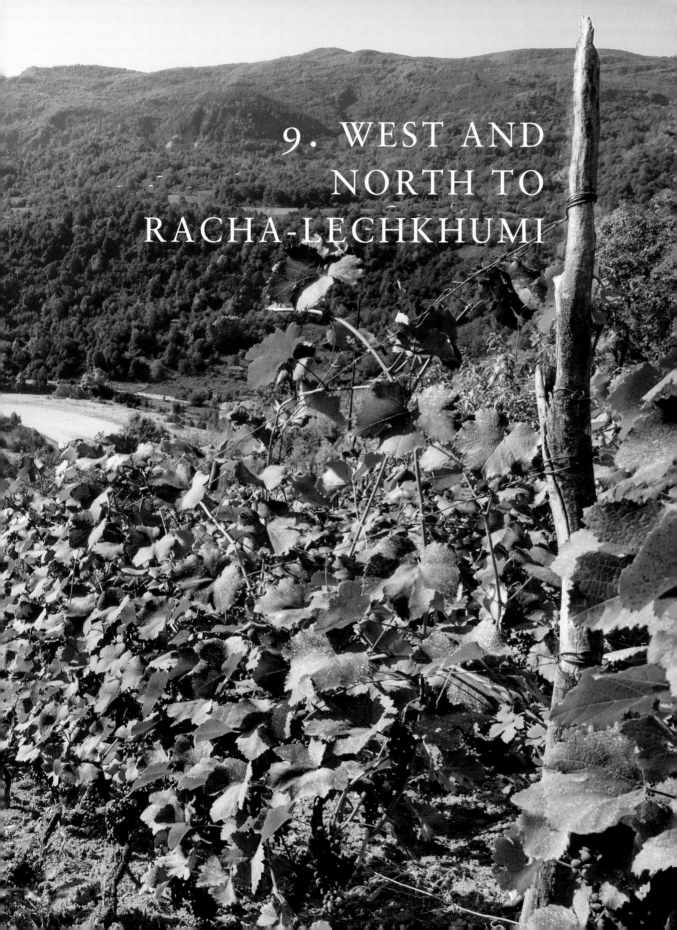

9. WEST AND NORTH TO RACHA-LECHKHUMI

Ambrolauri   p. 382   Khvanchkara   p. 382   Patara Chorjo   p. 387
Bostana   p. 382   Nikortsminda   p. 384   Tsageri   p. 382
Dzirageuli   p. 394   Okureshi   p. 382   Tsesi   p. 386
Isunderi   p. 382   Oni   p. 400

R acha-Lechkhumi is off the main tourist beat yet it offers stunning, wide-angle landscapes of forests, mountains and some vineyards. The peaks may be less high than those of Upper Svaneti or Kazbegi but the feel here is intimate yet wild. This sparsely populated region includes Racha, Lechkhumi and Lower (or Kvemo) Svaneti. (Today, eastern Racha is flanked by Tskhinvali, or South Ossetia, that is currently off limits for Georgians and tourists.)

The drive from the valleys around Kutaisi up the gently rising hills until you reach the 'entrance' to Racha shows the geographical reasons for the divisions: the region begins beyond a range of monumental limestone cliffs. It's an intensely wooded area, with fewer villages or farms. Forestry and woodworking are ubiquitous here; when people from other regions want wooden houses built they come to Racha to recruit their carpenters. Racha's houses are usually built of wood, and often have high and solid wooden fencing around them, unlike the airy wrought iron of Imereti and Guria. These houses look as if they've had to defend themselves from predators, probably of the four-legged kind. This is a perfect region for the adventurous outdoorsy type, with the possibility of trekking, climbing, rafting and other nature-based sports. There are caves throughout the region that are well worth exploring.

Typical Racha house

Historically, Racha was part of the ancient Kingdoms of Colchis and Iberia. It became a duchy within the unified Georgian Kingdom in 1090. The next six centuries were spent feuding with rival clans and monarchies as the status of duchy came and went. In 1789 the duchy was definitively abolished as the region was subordinated to the Kingdom of Imereti. During Soviet times some of the region was exploited for industrial production of coal and other geological resources – including arsenic – but most have since been abandoned, leaving some areas feeling underdeveloped. Tourism and wine are beginning to bolster the region's fortunes in a more sustainable way.

Previous pages: Murad Vatsadze's steep vineyards overlook the Rioni River valley

The winemaking area is concentrated along the slopes of the Rioni River, where a famous red is made, Khvanchkara. Many families make wine for home consumption but as yet little bottling is being done. Racha's enormous winemaking potential is just beginning to be directed towards well-made artisan dry wines. Experienced winemakers from other Georgian regions are interested in investing here, so there may well be promising results in the next few years.

The food in the region offers a few unique ingredients, like the smoked local ham that flavours many of the bean dishes here. The coveted hams are produced from pigs that mostly live free in the forests or are raised by families; they're in demand throughout the country. The beans too express their myriad differences in variety and terroir: they grow well in Racha-Lechkhumi and are always on the menu, stewed or used as a filling for *lobiani* breads. There are wild mushrooms in the woods and pastures, and mountains of potatoes. The region's legendary culture of hospitality is alive and well, as any traveller who ventures into a kitchen or dining room here can attest. Legend has it that in the mountains some Rachans left the door of a special room open for an unexpected guest, with food on the table. If the food was eaten it was cause for celebration.

Barakoni Church

GRAPE VARIETIES OF THE REGION

There are two main wine areas. One is for the very limited production of the red Usakhelauri grape, grown in the Tsageri district on the slopes of the Tskhenistskali River near Okureshi, Aubi and Isunderi in western Lechkhumi, close to the borders with Imereti and Samegrelo. This grape is also known as Okureshuli in central and eastern Racha. It is believed to have been domesticated from a wild forest vine fairly recently. Ojaleshi Orbeluri (nothing to do with Samegrelo's Ojaleshi) and white Tsolikouri are also found in this area.

The other is in the central part of the region, on the slopes leading to the Rioni River around Ambrolauri. Here the principal varieties are the reds Aleksandrouli and Mujuretuli that are blended into the popular and abundantly produced Khvanchkara, the region's most celebrated wine. (In its semi-sweet incarnation it's claimed to have been Stalin's favourite.) The best villages for the production of Khvanchkara are Chorjo, Tola, Bostana and Khvanchkara, all to the west of Ambrolauri on the northern side of the Rioni with south-facing slopes. Other vines here include white Rachuli Tetra, but there are also many other little-known native varieties.

AMBROLAURI

Opposite: Lunch at Izolda Dvali's guest house (see p. 394)

Ambrolauri is the capital of the region, situated on the Rioni River at 550 metres (1,800 feet) above sea level. It's a quiet provincial town – much of it fairly modern – that's centrally placed if you're visiting the area, with little to attract or cater to tourists. I stayed in one of its few hotels, the Metekhara Hotel, Gamsakhurdia Street, 2; tel: +995 599181464.

NIKORTSMINDA

If you are driving to Racha from Imereti, don't miss Nikortsminda; it's just off the main road, a few kilometres after you pass the large Shaori Reservoir. This is one of the most beautiful churches in Georgia. Dedicated to St Nicholas the Miracle-worker, the small church was built between 1010 and 1014 by King Bagrat III. It's a gem, inside and out: the pale external walls are carved with intricate natural designs, many of them based on the vine and other plants. The tower, with its conical roof over a drum above the crossing, is typical of the Georgian cross-dome style. Inside, the church was decorated in fresco, painted it seems by the 16th-century masters who also worked on Gelati (see p. 276). Despite being damaged in the devastating 1991 earthquake, Nikortsminda was restored and is today one of the jewels in Georgia's crown.

Ambrolauri is surrounded by woods and oversized limestone rocks with canyon-like passages cut through them for the roads. A few kilometres outside of Ambrolauri, on the road towards Oni, is the lovely Orthodox church known as Barakoni in Tsesi. It was built in 1753 and commissioned by Rostom, the ruler of Racha. Despite suffering in Soviet times and then in the 1991 earthquake, the church is worth visiting. (See p. 382.)

AMBROLAURI

HAM
TAMAZ NATMELADZE

I meet Tamaz Natmeladze out of season. It's a still-warm afternoon in September and Tamaz is neither smoking his hams – known as *lori* here – nor does he have any left: the precious pork has all been sold for the year. He's waiting until the cold sets in to start preparing for next year's production.

It may be the wrong time of year but I'm keen to find out firsthand how the process works. The smokehouse is a small wooden shack in the garden of Tamaz's large house in the suburbs of Ambrolauri. As is usual in rural Georgia, the garden is really an orchard, with various fruit trees and a few rows of tomatoes that are down to their last fruits. He shows us the (black) interior of the shack as he explains how he makes his hams. "After the pig has been slaughtered and cleaned of its organs, we butterfly it and salt the whole animal for ten days on wooden boards in another space. In winter the temperature is naturally low here, so it's like a huge refrigerator."

Tamaz outside the smokehouse

After 10 days, the half-carcasses are washed before being hung in the smokehouse for three days to dry out – without fire or smoke. Ten can be smoked at one time, hung up on hooks in the small hut. "Here in Upper Racha they are hung from the neck but in Lower Racha in a few villages it's by the hind leg," he says. "Each animal weighs between 20 and 30 kilos." The fire is then lit, using the wood from fruit trees including plum, apple, cherry and pear as well as hornbeam *(tskhrila)* and beech *(tsipeli)*.

"For the first week we keep the fire gentle but steady, without letting it smoke, so the meat is slowly cooked at low temperatures. In that first week, as the meat is being heated it loses its excess liquids and some of the fat." Over the next three to five weeks, depending on the size of the animals, the fire is lit every morning and made to smoke using sawdust but is put out at night when temperatures drop to near freezing. "In this way the pork is almost cold-smoked. The lower part, nearest the fire, is ready before the top, so we cut that off and sell it first, before the hams are finished."

In 2014–15 Tamaz smoke-cured 1.5 tons of pork. Some gets sold locally but there is a lot of demand from restaurants in Tbilisi as well as private customers. That explains why he runs out in just a few months. Where do the pigs come from? "I used to rear the pigs myself, but now I source 30 to 50 pigs from nearby villages where they are free to roam the forests, grubbing for acorns, berries and other wild foods. Some come from farms too, where the pigs live outdoors, of course." The pigs are local varieties, some from Svaneti and Kakheti, others that have been crossed with pigs from Ukraine and Russia. There used to be wild boar in the forests but they were all hunted; a few are slowly coming back.

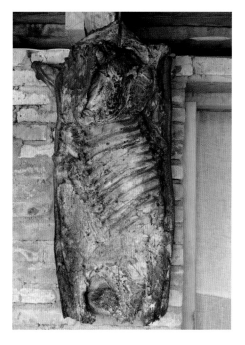

Smoked Rachan pork

Once the ham is ready it can be eaten as is or boiled. It is not traditionally an ingredient in the local bean pies; belly fat is usually used for that, smoked or unsmoked. Is there a tradition here of making hams unsmoked? "No, but some are done that way in Kakheti," he says, offering me an apple from his tree. How do you store the hams? "If you live in the city it's best to keep them in the fridge or in a cool dry place – not the cellar." We thank him and leave, without any ham but with a handful of fruit to see us on our way.

Rustaveli Street, 62; tel: +995599423174

PATARA CHORJO

WINE
MURAD VATSADZE

The white grapes are being harvested when we take the main road out of Ambrolauri heading west. We turn off to the right after a few minutes, onto a dirt road so steep I'm glad we're in a four-wheel drive. Murad Vatsadze lives at the top, in a large house that accommodates several generations of his family. The yard, lively with the usual country cast of dogs, cats and chickens, is on a flat terrace. Right behind it, fanning down and up as they follow the vertiginous profile of the mountain, are rows of vines interspersed with fruit trees. The position of these vineyards is breathtaking and as close to 'heroic' viticulture as I've seen in Georgia: all the work here must be done by hand on rocky, limestone and yellow clay so steep it's hard to keep upright. In the valley far below, the Rioni River flashes silver as it rounds a bend (see photograph pp. 378-79).

Members of the family – women as well as men – take it in turns to haul full buckets of yellow-green and greener grapes into the cellar at the side of the house. Meanwhile Murad's father, Murtaz, offers us the first of many refreshments that day, small glasses of *chacha* served on a bright floral tray in the shade of a walnut tree.

"The earliest vineyard here is over 100 years old but there are some from the 1930s on the left," he says as he offers a first toast. "Others are 30 years old. Up top we've got Aleksandrouli and Mujuretuli (Mudzhuretuli), the red grapes we blend into Khvanchkara, our region's special semi-sweet red wine." Indeed, the red grapes are ripening on the vines: it's the end of September and they've still got two weeks to go. "It's not just gathering the grapes that's hard," says Murad as he checks some of the new arrivals. "We

Our supra *lunch in Murad's cellar*

do everything from the pruning to the spraying moving up and down the steep rows on foot."

Racha is one of the regions where the new movement in winemaking – which is really a return to the old ways – has been slow to gather momentum. That's partly because bottling can seem expensive if you're used to selling your home-made wines in large quantities for local weddings, funerals and other events at very reasonable prices. It's also because Racha-Lechkhumi seems remote from the buzz of Kakheti or Tbilisi. If this area suffered fewer invasions over the centuries it's partly just because it's off the beaten track.

Today that's something of a handicap. Since the Soviet era this part of the country has struggled: Soviet mines were closed and tourism here is for those wanting to get away from it all. Quality wine could help change that pattern – as it has in other areas – and producers like Murad are being encouraged by some of the better-known winemakers from other Georgian regions to cultivate their vines organically and bottle their wines. Yet here the allure remains strong of systemic sprays that may have made the viticulturists' lives easier in the short term. As happened in Europe in the mid to late 20th century, the sales pitch for these products has been relentless from the multinational companies that produce them and, in remote rural areas, farmers need convincing that life might be better if they stopped using them.

In the *marani*, or cellar, Murad crushes the green grapes with a hand-cranked press like a laundry wringer. The fruit falls into a long wooden pressing box, or *satsnakheli*, resembling a canoe where the grapes were stamped on by foot until a few

Murad at work in the marani *where he crushes the grapes*

years ago. "We'll leave the crushed berries in here for three days, until the fermentation starts naturally, before letting them flow out of the hole in the

bottom directly into the *churi* in the back of the *marani*," he says. *Churi* is the local name for *qvevri*. After two to three weeks, when the fermentation has ceased, the *churi* are closed. They change the *churi* containers twice before spring, when the wine will be ready to drink. "It's the same process for the reds," he says. "We don't use long skin contact on them either and anyway we don't have enough space or *churi* to do that." The white grapes are Tsulukidzis Tetra (also known as Rachuli Tetra), Tsolikouri and Mtsvane. From their single hectare of vineyards the family produce three wines from the five varieties: a Mtsvane-Tsolikouri blend; Tsulukidzis; and the red Khvanchkara.

When the crushing is done, it's time for lunch. Murad's mother, Makvala, and his wife, Sopiko, have laid a colourful *supra* table for us right inside the *marani*, beside an open door looking out on to the garden. They have no running water in the house but they have prepared a feast. There are large pitchers of deep blue-black Khvanchkara to go with some of the finest roast chicken I've ever had, home-grown cucumbers and tomatoes, bread and cheese, preserved syrupy figs and a dish of fiery red *ajika*. (See p. 392 for recipe.)

As we eat and drink (I'm not sure how many times that pitcher was refilled, but we couldn't stop drinking that joyous, semi-dry fruity wine with its pure berry flavours), Murtaz talks about the old days. "In Soviet times Khvanchkara was still a great wine, and they drank it at all the special occasions; it was known as the best in the whole Soviet Union," he says proudly. "But now it's being produced industrially in the valley and it's of very low quality. Few families still make it the way we do." At that, he proposes another toast. The toasts that day included one to women: a table without women is poor, and lacking in something. Another was to those who have left us: there is no family without someone who has died. And to the Patriarch Ilia II: "He has the trust of 90 percent of the Georgian people, so let's drink to his long life." Tel: +995 599384413

*Top:
Murad's father,
Murtaz*

*Bottom:
chacha*

*Opposite:
Murad's mother,
Makvala, pensive after lunch*

Cooked ajika

AJIKA   აჯიკა

Every cook in Georgia makes their own *ajika*, an intense paste of vegetables, spices and herbs that is usually red or green, and hot. Small amounts of *ajika* are used to flavour other dishes such as marinades, grilled meats, beans or vegetables. Some are so fierce from the chillies that just a tiny spoonful is enough to add character to a recipe; others are cooler and can be used as a condiment at the table. It depends on how hot you want yours to be: start with one or two fresh chillies of medium heat. You can always add more.

Makvala's brilliant red *ajika* is unusual in being made from cooked carrots, beets and bell peppers. It's sweet and not too fiery and is delicious spooned onto *khachapuri* or barbecued meat. Make a batch and keep it in the refrigerator for two weeks or more. Bring out a bowlful at mealtimes, as you would any other condiment or dip. Use your food processor to slice the carrots and beets. And use a delicately flavoured, cold-pressed oil that won't dominate the *ajika's* taste.

MAKES **1 litre/1 quart**
PREPARATION **35 minutes**
COOK **90 minutes**

450g/1lb carrots, thinly sliced

450g/1lb raw beets, thinly sliced

600g/1lb 5oz red bell peppers,
   roughly chopped

2 fresh red chillies (semi-hot),
   sliced, or to taste

240ml/8fl oz/1 cup grapeseed or
   other neutral oil

115g/4oz/½ cup tomato paste

1 tbsp ground fenugreek

¾ tsp coriander seed, crushed

1½ tsp salt

12g/⅓oz/3 garlic cloves, chopped

Cook the carrots, beets, peppers and chillies with the oil in a large heavy saucepan over low heat for 15 minutes, covered, stirring often to prevent the vegetables from sticking or browning. Once the vegetables begin to steam, raise the heat to medium and boil for a further 30 minutes. Taste the vegetables to see if the chillies are hot enough; if necessary, add more. Cover again and cook for another 45 minutes. Remove from the heat.

Stir in the remaining ingredients and make a thick purée using a hand blender or food processor. Taste for seasoning. If the mixture is very hot (from the chillies) don't worry! Just add less to your marinades or sauces.

Spoon the mixture into sterile glass jars, pushing the *ajika* down evenly to avoid air bubbles. Allow to cool completely, top with oil, then cover and refrigerate. This *ajika* should keep for at least two weeks.

DZIRAGEULI VILLAGE

COOK, GUEST HOUSE
DIOMIDE DVALI CHÂTEAU DIO

This family guest house is to the west of Ambrolauri, not far from the town, at 1,200 metres (3,940 feet) above sea level. It's on the northern side of the main road. Through a country gate, in a pretty vineyard-garden with great views out over the Rioni Valley, Izolda Dvali runs a guest house for up to 25 people and will also cook for groups and give cooking lessons if you book in advance. It's worth it. She's a fine cook and lively hostess and can demonstrate how traditional foods are prepared in Racha. Meals can be arranged even if you're not staying at Izo's house.

There are two kitchens. One is in the main house, indoors. The other is at the bottom of the garden by a vine-covered pergola. Here the food is cooked over an open fire in an outdoor hut that can also be used as a smokehouse. (It's right beside a small cabin with pretty wooden fretwork on its porch that would make the perfect summer house for one or two people.) "This is a traditional Racha kitchen, separate from the main house," she says as she lines shallow clay bowls with walnut leaves for her cornbread, *mchadi*. They stop the bottom from burning and give the bread a distinct flavour. "We prepare large amounts of food for our *supras* here, with smoked hams and cornbread cooked right beside the open fire so they take on a smoky taste. The most important dishes in Racha are improved by being cooked this way."

Izolda Dvali

Lobio, dried beans, are one of the region's favourite dishes. "This is the best place for growing beans, that's why they're traditional here," she says. "We like to cultivate many varieties. They're planted in April and harvested in mid-August. Climate and soil are what matter: they need sun but moisture too."

At the markets in the region many varieties of bean are on sale, either fresh in autumn or dried during the rest of the year. Izo's ample *supra* spread (see photograph p. 383) also included bread stuffed with beet greens (see recipe p. 396) as well as roasted chicken, smoked local ham, stuffed peppers, sour plum sauces and her fine herbed beans (recipe p. 399). diomidedvali@gmail.com; tel: +995 557590779

Opposite: The wooden cabin is shaded by an ancient grapewine

Beet-green bread

MKHLOVANI მხლოვანი

Breads stuffed with wild and cultivated greens are popular in the mountainous regions of Georgia, including in nearby Ossetia. Beet greens and their stems are nutritious and taste great yet they're all too often thrown away. If you can't find them, substitute fresh rainbow or Swiss chard, or use part spinach. For the dough, and to form the bread, follow the Master Recipes on pp. 51-53. This bread works well with both the yeast and the yogurt doughs. The quantity of filling given here is for one bread.

SERVES **6–8**
PREPARATION **40 minutes**
 **(plus 90 minutes salting / dough
 rising)**
COOK **20 minutes plus 35 minutes
 baking time**

FOR THE FILLING
**450g / 1lb beet greens, chard
 and / or spinach, with their stems**
1½ tsp salt
45g / 1½oz / 3 tbsp butter, melted

The buttered beet greens

Make the dough for one bread from the Master Recipes. While it is rising, prepare the filling.

Pick through the beet greens and stems carefullly, washing them in several changes of water to remove any sand. Spin or pat dry to remove excess water. Chop roughly. Sprinkle lightly with the salt and place in a colander for 1 hour.

Rinse the greens in cold water and shake them to remove the excess liquid. Push them into a medium saucepan, over medium heat, and cover. You want to wilt the leaves quickly so they'll be easier to work with. As soon as they have wilted, remove them from the pan to a bowl, leaving any liquid, and toss with the butter.

Place a flat, heavy baking tray on a rack in the centre of the oven and preheat to 170°C / 325°F / Gas 3.

Follow the Master Recipe on p. 52 for filling and baking the bread.

*Opposite: Izolda's beet-green bread,
with her* lobiani *behind*

Beans stewed with herbs

LOBIO 2 ლობიო

Lobio, or beans, are prepared in hundreds of ways in Georgia and feature at almost every meal. They are at their best when cooked over a wood fire like Izo's, but they also benefit from being baked or simmered gently in traditional Georgian clay pots. Although the Georgians favour dark, kidney-shaped beans, I find it's more effective to use thin-skinned beans whose skins almost dissolve when cooked. So don't be afraid to use Borlotti or other premium beans as they'll make the texture and flavour better. This recipe adds vibrant fresh herbs to the mix: half are added during cooking and the rest at the end. See pp. 266 for a spicier version that also includes walnuts. The Georgians always serve fermented or pickled vegetables or flowers when they serve *lobio*, as a counterpoint.

SERVES 4–6
PREPARATION **25 minutes, plus 12 hours soaking**
COOK **90–180 minutes**

350g / 12 oz / 2 cups dried kidney, Borlotti or other beans

200g / 7 oz / 1½ cups chopped onion

2 tbsp dried marigold petals, or ground marigold petals

15g / ½ oz / 4 garlic cloves, chopped

30g / 1 oz / ½ cup chopped fresh coriander / cilantro

¼ tsp dried summer savory *(kondari)* or thyme

1 tsp salt

¼ tsp dried chilli / red pepper flakes

30g / 1 oz / ½ cup chopped fresh herbs, a mix of mint, green and purple basil, summer savory, celery leaves and parsley

Soak the beans overnight in good clean water (filtered, if possible). Drain, rinse well and turn the beans into a large saucepan. Cover them with two fingers of water and bring to the boil. After about 15 minutes, when the beans start producing foam, pour the beans and water into a colander and rinse the beans again. Cover them with fresh water and boil for 1 hour, skimming off any foam that appears.

Add the onions, marigold petals and half of the garlic and chopped coriander / cilantro to the beans. Stir in the dried summer savory or thyme, salt and chilli. Continue cooking until the beans are soft – anything from 30 to 60 minutes or more. If the water gets low, add more to keep the beans covered by about two fingers of water.

When the beans are soft and beginning to fall apart, taste them for salt and chilli, adding more if necessary (the chillies should only add a subtle hint of heat). Stir in the remaining herbs and garlic and cook gently for 10 minutes more. Check for seasoning again before serving.

ONI

Sun on the synagogue at Oni

This tranquil small town is situated at 830 metres (2,723 feet) on the Rioni River as it starts its way down from the high Caucasus towards the Black Sea. It is said to have been founded in the 2nd century BC by the Iberian King Parnajom. Its roots are much earlier: artefacts have been found here from the Bronze Age, and from the Kingdom of Colchis from the third to sixth centuries BC. By the Middle Ages it was a busy merchant town located on the crossroads between Imereti, Kartli, western Racha and the north Caucasus. The town was fought over by the kings of Imereti and the princes of Racha.

Oni's handsome 1880s synagogue is evidence of the town's once large and powerful Jewish community, third in size after Tbilisi and Kutaisi. Today, a few Jewish families still remain in Oni. The synagogue was designed by a Polish architect working with Greek Jewish builders from Thessaloniki.

This area has suffered from avalanches and earthquakes. The most recent was in 1991 when an earthquake measuring 6.9 on the Richter scale caused damage to the local infrastructure and to the Racha Regional Museum, home to the most important archæological finds in the area.

COOK, GUEST HOUSE
HOTEL GALLERY

This guest house is located on a leafy street near Onis's town centre. It started taking in guests in 2000 and was enlarged in 2008. The family also serves home-cooked food.

Elene Magrakvelidze runs the guest house with her husband Temuri who is an able carpenter and enthusiastic about the sporting activities available in the area. Behind the house is a garden that produces fruits, some vegetables and flowers. There's a shady grape arbour too. The cook, Lia Maisuradze, is skilled in the local dishes and her food is worth making a trip to Oni for, even if it's just for lunch (always call ahead to book). Lia prepares her traditional dishes on the free-standing black iron wood-burning stove in the kitchen. nikagugeshashvili@gmail.com; tel: +995 593660884

OUR LUNCH AT ONI

Lobiani: *bean-filled bread*
Chicken with garlic: shkmeruli
Fried cornbread
Lobio *in a big clay pot*
Beets with plum sauce
String beans
Smoked Racha ham
Khachapuri
Cheese

Supra *table at Hotel Gallery*

Lobiani: bean-filled bread

LOBIANI   ლობიანი

This filled bread is a cornerstone of every Rachan meal. *Lobiani*'s most often served with a traditional filling of plain, mashed or puréed thin-skinned beans. Some Rachans add the fat from locally smoked hams to the beans for a distinctive smoky taste. You can get that extra layer of flavour using Speck, smoked prosciutto from northern Italy, as below. If you prefer your pie vegetarian, use plain beans or the herbed beans from the recipe on p. 398. Follow the Master Recipe on pp. 51-53 for the dough, and for how to fill and bake the bread. If you're in a hurry, use drained and rinsed canned Borlotti or kidney beans. This recipe is enough to fill one bread.

SERVES **6-8**
PREPARATION **30 minutes (plus 90 minutes for dough rising)**
COOK **25 minutes**

FOR THE BEAN FILLING
720ml / 24fl oz / 3 cups plain cooked beans (plus some cooking liquid)
60g / 2oz / 4 tbsp butter
6 paper-thin slices Speck, chopped
salt

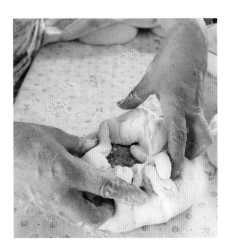

Prepare the dough for 1 bread on p. 51. While it is rising, make the filling.

Mash or purée the beans by pushing them through a sieve or using a hand processor or crusher. The purée should be fairly stiff – like mashed potatoes – but if it seems too dry, add a few spoonfuls of the bean cooking water.

In a small non-stick frying pan, melt the butter over medium heat. Add the beans and the optional Speck. Cook for 5 or 6 minutes, stirring frequently, until the beans are heated through. Taste for seasoning and allow to cool before filling the bread.

Place a heavy baking tray in the centre of the oven. Preheat the oven to 180°C / 350°F / Gas 4.

Follow the instructions on p. 52 for filling and baking the bread, painting the top with a little beaten egg before baking. Bake for 25–30 minutes, or until the top is light gold. Rub the top of the bread with butter as soon as it's out of the oven. Serve hot.

Lia Maisuradze making lobiani: *opposite, she tops her dough with beans; left, she closes the beans into the dough*

Grilled chicken with garlic sauce

SHKMERULI   შქმერული

Here's one for garlic lovers. This is an easy and delicious version of the popular Georgian dish in which chicken is baked and then topped with chopped garlic in milk. Here the chicken is marinated with garlic for a few hours before being grilled and then served with a garlic and sour-cream based sauce. It's particularly good when fresh, young garlic is in season, delivering all the garlic's fragrance without the cloying pungency of old garlic. It's easy to double for more people, just use whichever chicken pieces you like best.

SERVES 4
PREPARATION **20 minutes plus marinating time**
COOK **30 minutes**

750g / 1lb 10oz chicken thighs or legs, with skin on

FOR THE MARINADE
20g / ¾oz / 5 garlic cloves, chopped
3 tbsp groundnut or sunflower oil
1 tsp coriander seeds, crushed

FOR THE SAUCE:
120ml / 4fl oz / ½ cup chicken broth or stock
12g / ⅓oz / 3 garlic cloves, finely chopped
½ tsp salt
180ml / 6fl oz / ¾ cup sour cream

In a deep bowl, toss the chicken pieces with the marinade. Cover with plastic wrap and allow to sit for several hours or overnight in the refrigerator.

Preheat your grill or broiler. Grill or broil the chicken until the skin is golden and the meat is cooked through, about 10–12 minutes per side. Make sure you put a piece of foil or a tray under the chicken to catch the cooking juices (discard any uncooked, leftover marinade that may have raw chicken juices in it). Remove the chicken to a warm serving dish.

Add the chicken broth or stock to the chicken cooking juices and stir to loosen them from the pan. Pour them into a small saucepan through a strainer. Stir in the chopped fresh garlic, salt and sour cream and heat gently to simmering point. Taste for seasoning. Spoon some of the sauce over the chicken and serve the rest in a small bowl on the side.

10. NORTH TO KAZBEGI AND UPPER MTSKHETA-MTIANETI

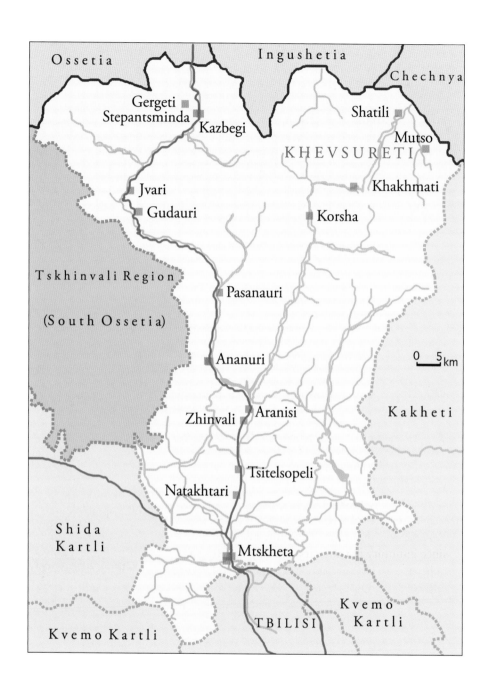

Ananuri p. 410
Aranisi p. 411
Gergeti p. 420
Gudauri p. 414
Jvari p. 409

Kazbegi p. 414
Khevsureti p. 411
Mtskheta p. 409
Mutso p. 411
Natakhtari p. 410

Pasanauri p. 410
Shatili p. 411
Stepantsminda p. 414
Tsitelsopeli p. 410
Zhinvali p. 410

This chapter explores Kazbegi, the highland area of Mtskheta-Mtianeti region that can be visited from Tbilisi as a self-contained trip. (For the southern part and the town of Mtskheta, see chapter 2, pp. 88-119.) It travels up the Georgian Military Highway through a soaring landscape at over 2,000 metres (6,652 feet) towards Stepantsminda, the town with panoramic views of Mount Kazbek that's just a few kilometres from the borders with North Ossetia and Ingushetia. In good weather the resort town can be reached in three to four hours from Tbilisi, making these peaks more readily accessible than Svaneti or Tusheti.

After leaving Mtskheta, the highway heads north towards the Zhinvali Dam, passing the turn-off that leads north-east to the highlands of Khevsureti. It winds upwards past the ski resort at Gudauri and through the unspoiled Kazbegi Nature Reserve, popular with nature lovers, trekkers and mountaineers.

This is one of my favourite parts of Georgia. The majestic mountains here – in some of the highest parts of the Greater Caucasus – are breathtaking yet you never lose sight of the relationship Georgians have with nature. On a steep mountainside across a dramatic gorge, the ground appears dotted with white rocks. Look more closely and they're sheep, hundreds of them, spread out across the landscape led by shepherds on horseback with dogs to guard against wild predators. Sheep and cattle roam the highland pastures for many months of the year (though over-grazing has led to erosion in some places). The area is sparsely populated, with few villages as the road rises in leaps and twists through lunar fields of rock and giant stones. Plan to travel up in daylight for the views.

The Georgian Military Highway travels north by north-west from near Tbilisi all the way to Vladikavkaz in Russia. The route has been known since antiquity but was first used by the Russians only in 1769; it was rebuilt as a more modern road in the 1860s. On its way up it skirts the invisible – but uncrossable – border with Tskhinvali region, the occupied territory to its west known as South Ossetia, only two kilometres away at the closest point. That's just before it passes the Russian-Georgian Friendship Monument, built in the 1980s to commemorate a century of ties.

Russian-Georgian Friendship Monument

Previous pages: Dawn on Mount Kazbek with the Gergeti Trinity Church still in shadow

It's a rough road in parts, particularly in the highest stretches between the Jvari Pass (at 2,370 metres/7,776 feet) and Stepantsminda. Severe weather can close the upper sections but in principle it's open all year to allow heavy goods vehicles from Armenia, Azerbaijan, Iran and Turkey access to Russia, as the long queues of trucks at the border often demonstrate. (Unlike Georgians, Armenians require no visa to travel to Russia.) The road offers panoramic scenery, some tortuous hairpin bends and is kept up so as to allow access to the mountains (in suitable vehicles) in winter as in summer.

FOOD

No wine is made in these areas for the altitudes are too high to grow grapes, but you'll be offered grain-distilled spirits, fruit-based alcohols and barley beer. There's wholesome, warming food to be found in hearty *khinkali* dumplings or cheese- and potato-filled breads. Cabbage, potatoes and river trout are abundant, as are lamb and other meats and cheeses from the many herds that pasture here in summer. Nomadic beekeepers produce wonderful honey in the mountains.

EATING EN ROUTE

Khinkali dumplings and other simple dishes are available in lots of little taverns along the route, from Natakhtari to Pasanauri, if you get hungry before starting the climb. At Tsitelsopeli, Patiosani Katsis Dukani, or the Righteous Man's tavern, is just off the Military Highway and offers straightforward affordable Georgian village food sourced from local ingredients. It's on the west side of the road and is open all year. Tel: +995 593491324

ANANURI

Ananuri sits at the edge of the reservoir

As you drive up and around the large Aragvi Reservoir that was created in 1985 when the Soviet-era Zhinvali Dam was built to supply hydro-electric

power, you can't miss the imposing fortress and church complex at Ananuri. It once stood in a commanding position along the road above the village, which was relocated before the dam was built. (Original plans for the dam would have flooded the fortress too but luckily a public outcry blocked them.)

The crenellated fortress walls enclose what was the stronghold of the chivalrous but violent Dukes of Aragvi, a feudal dynasty that ruled the area from the 13th century. Many battles were fought here. The larger, brick church was built in the 17th century. The carvings on its exterior walls show Persian influence; they feature a large cross flanked by grape vines (being eaten by deer), as well as angels, dragons and lions. A Khevsuretian square-section defensive tower also still stands within the fortress walls.

KHEVSURETI

Khevsureti is reached from the Georgian Military Highway by turning east at Aranisi, south of the Zhinvali Dam, along a road that follows the Pshavis Aragvi River valley as it climbs north-east towards the Chechen border. The remote, unspoiled highlands of Khevsureti are great for hiking in the warmer months in the Khevsureti National Park and around the highland valleys near Shatili, the main village. Here a complex of 50 defensive towers from the 6th to the 12th centuries are woven into a fortress-like structure that reveals why the Khevsurs were known as great warriors and defenders of the Georgian borders. The men wore chain mail here as recently as the 1930s. Khevsureti retains many pagan artistic traditions: music and crafts are highly valued, as the Khevsur's hand-embroidered traditional clothing demonstrates.

The best places to stay and eat are in family guest houses. UNESCO and the World Bank have sponsored a cultural heritage ecotourism project in Shatili within two of the towers. Mutso, at 1,590 metres (5,217 feet), is Khevsureti's other inhabited village, with medieval towers that are in less good repair today.

Scenes from the road trip, top to bottom: a monk beekeeper; river pass; wild horses

A pastoralist with his flock on the plateau by Gergeti Trinity Church

413

GUDAURI

For skiing and winter sports, Gudauri offers easy access to the slopes even in winter as the Highway is always open up to this point. There is snow between November and April and the resorts host many winter sport events and festivals. It's also a favourite location for the extreme winter sports that are harder to do in Europe, with some enthusiasts taking helicopters up in winter. In summer Gudauri is a lovely place to hike or ride horses from.

STEPANTSMINDA (KAZBEGI)

COOK, GUEST HOUSE
JUJUNA AVSAJANISHVILI

Nothing can compare to eating in the home of local Georgian women when they are great cooks. Jujuna Avsajanishvili is at her sink when I arrive to spend a morning with her as she prepares local specialities.

"Unlike other parts of Georgia, we've had running water in our houses for 40 years because of our proximity to Russia," she says as she fills a jug

Supra in Jujuna's house

*Jujuna
Avsajanishvili*

from her sink. Jujuna speaks a little English, the result of classes she has taken for guest-house hosts. She rents two rooms upstairs in her house. Jujuna worked at the local town hall until the government changed after the 2013 election, so the guest house helps maintain her five children. She also sells milk and the cheeses she makes.

"I used to have a large wild goat with long horns, the type that lives on the glaciers," she says. "It was very clever and would go fetch the cows for me but it was always climbing on top of everything so in the end we gave it to the Tbilisi zoo." Her late husband was a keen hunter and Jujuna recounts stories of cooking the varied game he brought home. She also mentions the wolves and other wild animals that appeared around the town during the first Chechen war, in the mid-1990s. "They came over the border to escape the fighting; we were afraid to go out at night," she says.

Jujuna cooked several delicious dishes for me from the primary ingredients: flour, butter, potato and cheese. Of these, *kada* was an unusual bread with a dense cheesy roux filling of flour, lots of butter and cheese. "It's probably too heavy for city life but you don't need to eat anything else all day if you have this in the mountains," she says, with pride. She also made a fine *khachapuri*, *khinkali* with spiced meat (overleaf), and *khabizgina*, a cheese and potato bread from Ossetia (p. 419). Tel +995 595254912

Meat-filled khinkali dumplings

KHINKALI   ხინკალი ხორცით

Khinkali are Georgian soup dumplings. In the high Caucasus mountains of Kazbegi, the *khinkali* are usually stuffed with lightly spiced meat. For the Master Recipe on how to form the dumplings, see pp. 54-57.

This filling can be made of beef, pork or a mixture of both. Make sure there is some fat in the meat. If your meat is very lean, add an extra 30g/1 oz butter or 2 tablespoons oil to the meat mixture. Meat *khinkali* are supposed to be juicy: your aim is to trap a little of the broth inside the dumplings.

MAKES **about 24**
PREPARATION **60 minutes**
COOK **10 minutes**

FOR THE DOUGH
260g/9 oz/2 cups plain/all-purpose flour
1 egg, at room temperature
120ml/4fl oz/½ cup water
1 tsp salt

FOR THE MEAT FILLING
100g/3½oz ground beef
100g/3½oz ground pork
40g/1½oz/⅓ cup minced onion
2 tbsp minced coriander/cilantro
¼ tsp minced fresh medium-hot chilli, or to taste
30g/1oz/2 tbsp butter, melted
½ cup water or meat broth
freshly ground black pepper
4g/⅛oz/1 garlic clove, minced
¼ tsp dried *kondari* (summer savory) or mild thyme
¼ tsp coriander seeds, crushed
¼ tsp caraway seeds, finely chopped
⅛ tsp ground cumin
1 tsp salt

Mix the dough ingredients together by hand or in a food processor until they form a ball (if necessary, add a little more flour or water). Turn it out onto a floured surface and knead for 4–5 minutes, or until the dough is smooth and elastic.

Place the dough in a lightly oiled bowl and cover with a clean tea cloth while you prepare the filling.

Mix all the filling ingredients together in a large bowl. Use a fork or your hands to make sure the ingredients are really well blended and all the meat has been broken up.

See pp. 56-67 for instructions on how to make, cook and eat the *khinkali*. Serve them with lots of ground black pepper.

Cheese and potato bread

KHABIZGINA   ხაბიზგინა

Like *khachapuri*, this is a filled bread. Here, the filling is a mix of cheese and potato. It is a popular staple in the high Caucasus mountains of Kazbegi and Ossetia where potatoes were often the only locally grown vegetable. Boil your potatoes with the skins on. Grate rather than mash the potatoes and fold the butter and cheese into them. Use a combination of sheep's cheese and cow's for this recipe, such as feta or pecorino and mozzarella. This milk-enriched dough goes well with this bread or use either of the dough recipes on pp. 51-53, and follow the Master Recipe on p. 51.

SERVES **8**
PREPARATION **45 minutes plus 75
 minutes rising time**
COOK **25–30 minutes**

FOR THE DOUGH
½ tsp sugar
½ tsp quick-acting instant yeast
60ml / 2fl oz / ¼ cup milk, warmed
**80ml / 2½fl oz / ⅓ cup yogurt, at
    room temperature**
1 egg, at room temperature
**1 tbsp sour cream, at room
    temperature**
½ tsp salt
**200g / 7oz / 1½ cups plus 1 tbsp
    strong / bread flour**

FOR THE FILLING
**260g / 9oz boiled potatoes,
    skins on**
30g / 1oz / 2 tbsp butter, melted
**200g / 7oz grated or crumbled
    cheese**
½ tsp salt, or to taste
freshly ground black pepper

*Note: This round bread is Jujuna's;
mine come out square*

Stir the sugar and yeast into the lukewarm milk and set aside for 10 minutes. Combine the yeast mixture with the rest of the dough ingredients in the bowl of a food processor and process to form a ball.

The dough should remain a little sticky. Turn it out onto a floured board and knead for 4–5 minutes. Form it into a ball, place in an oiled bowl and cover with a clean tea cloth. Stand the bowl in a warm place for 75–90 minutes.

Meanwhile, prepare the filling. Peel the potatoes and grate them on a large grater into a medium mixing bowl. Fold in the butter and cheese (try not to compact the filling too much) and season with salt and pepper.

When the dough has almost finished rising, preheat the oven to 170°C / 325°F / Gas 3.

When the dough has risen, punch it down and knead it quickly into a ball on a lightly floured surface. Roll it out into a 20-cm / 12-in square and follow the instructions on p. 51 for how to fill and bake the bread. Serve hot or warm, cut into slices or wedges.

STEPANTSMINDA (KAZBEGI)

This small, sprawling town close to the Kazbek peaks in a high valley at almost 2,000 metres (6,562 feet) is the place to stay while you explore the mountains, whatever the season. Stepantsminda, 150 kilometres (93 miles) from Tbilisi, was renamed Kazbegi after the writer-turned-shepherd Alexander Kazbegi, a 19th-century nobleman whose novel, *The Parricide*, is said to have inspired Stalin. Kazbegi's statue stands in the town square. Today the town is known by both names.

The highest mountain in the Khevi province – and third highest in Georgia – Mount Kazbek or Mkinvartsveri (the 'ice-peaked') is a dormant volcano 5,047 metres (16,558 feet) high. Very close to the Russian border, the mountain features in a legend about the Georgian Prometheus, Amirani, who was chained to it for having stolen fire from the gods to give to the mortals.

GERGETI TRINITY CHURCH

If you only visit one site from Stepantsminda, make sure it's this iconic church and belltower, perched up above the town at 2,170 metres (7,120 feet), close to the peaks of Mount Kazbek, with the Gergeti Glacier behind them.

Gergeti (also known as Tsminda Sameba) is a small but imposing church built in the 14th century from granite blocks that are stippled now with orange lichen like a rough patina. The stylized carvings of natural forms include clustered grapes. A handful of monks live in the modest monastery beneath the church and watch over the sacred buildings. There are wild horses and herdsmen on the flattish Alpine pastures that surround the church. Camping, climbing and horse riding are all possible with permission.

To reach the church on foot takes about three hours on a well-marked path up through birch woods undergrown with bracken and *alchemilla*, but a 30-minute jeep ride up the very rough, unpaved track will also bring you to the foot of the church.

Top: Gergeti Trinity Church

Bottom: Cows resting in the woods

WHERE TO EAT AND STAY   If you want to sleep with a view of Mount Kazbek while you indulge in hipster comforts, Rooms Hotel is a great choice. This ex-Intourist hotel has been remodelled by the Georgian entrepreneur, Temur Ugulava, with successful design by two architects from Tbilisi. (A sister Rooms Hotel is open in the capital.) The restaurant serves Georgian and contemporary food. This is one of Georgia's top hotels. www.roomshotels.com

For authentic *khinkali* dumplings, in the best Georgian-style informal restaurant in the area, drive a short distance back towards Tbilisi to the outskirts of Stepantsminda, to the village of Arsha. Tsanareti has large dining rooms set around an external courtyard. My favourite room though is the one that

Women at Tsanareti making khinkali

faces the main road, in which a tableful of women sit and chat while they produce thousands of perfect *khinkali* every day. The menu features the dumplings with several fillings, including caraway-spiced meats or potato. I loved the pickle plate here too, and the cheese and potato pie, *khabizgina*, like *khachapuri* with a deliciously thin, crisp pastry shell. Tel: +995 551606112

The lounge at Rooms Hotel

Bibliography
and travel information

BIBLIOGRAPHY

This is not a complete bibliography but a list of the books I came across while writing my book that I enjoyed and found informative. For anyone wanting to visit Georgia I highly recommend getting Tim Burford's excellent Bradt Guide to Georgia (in the 2015 edition). I discovered it as I was finishing this book and wish I had found it sooner! It's a mine of information for the traveller.

MAPS
I recommend these excellent maps:

Georgien World Mapping Project 1:350,000 Reise Know-How Series. This large map is made of tear-resistant paper and has more detail and clarity than any other single map I've found. My favourite for travelling.

The Georgian National Tourism Administration produces excellent regional maps available free from their offices. One side is tourist information about the best sites; the other is a 1:200,000 scale map of each region, with the sites marked. Collect the whole series.

The Caucasus Maps by Garmin. 1:200,000. Geoland This fold-up series covers Georgia in 6 maps (7 with Abkhazia) in great detail.

GEORGIA TRAVEL, HISTORY and BACKGROUND

Abramia, Natia, *Georgia Culture Smart!*, Kuperard, 2012

Asmus, Ronald D., *A Little War that Shook the World: Georgia, Russia and the Future of the West*, Palgrave Macmillan, 2010

Anderson, Tony, *Bread and Ashes: A Walk through the Mountains of Georgia*, Jonathan Cape, 2003

Berman, Michael, (trans. Ketevan Kalandadze), *Georgia Through its Folktales*, O Books, 2010

Burford, Tim, *Bradt Guide to Georgia*, 5th edition, Rowman and Littlefield, 2015

de Waal, Thomas, *The Caucasus*, Oxford University Press, 2010

Didebulidze, Mariam and Dimitri Tumanishvili, *Ancient Georgian Art*, Georgian Ministry of Culture, 2008

Dumas, Alexandre, the elder, *Adventures in the Caucasus* (1859), Peter Owen, 1962

Heighway, Elizabeth, *Contemporary Georgian Fiction*, Dalkey Archive Press, 2012

Opposite: A pastoralist and his herd heading home in Svaneti

Khantadze, Archil, *Twelve Short Stories: a Key to the Georgian Mentality*, Shemetsneba, 2013

Khantadze, Jumber, *The Amorous Detective and other stories*, Shemetsneba, 2012.   Evocative stories about 20th-century Tbilisi

Melikishvili, Izolda and Luarsab Togonidze, *Traditional Georgian Attire 18th-20th century*, Tbilisi, Georgian National Museum & Samoseli Pirveli, 2014

Mühlfried, Florian, *Being a State and States of Being in Highland Georgia*, Berghahn, 2014.   A fascinating book of anthropology in Tusheti

Nasmyth, Peter, *Georgia In the Mountains of Poetry*, Curzon, Caucasus World, London, 1998; revised second edition 2017

Nasmyth, Peter, *Walking in the Caucasus: Georgia*, Mta Publications, 2013

Rosen, Roger, *Georgia: A Sovereign Country of the Caucasus*, Odyssey Books & Guides, 1991/2004. A detailed cultural and historical guide

Rustaveli, Shota, (trans. Marjory Scott Wardrop), *The Man in the Panther's Skin*, Nekeri Publishing House, 2005

Said, Kurban, *Ali and Nino*, Tal Verlag, 1937/Vintage, 2000

Sharvadze, B. A., *History of Georgia* (An Outline), 2008.   Pocket-size

Steavenson, Wendell, *Stories I Stole*, Atlantic Books, 2002

Steinbeck, John, *A Russian Journal*, Viking, 1948/Penguin 1999.   With photographs by Robert Capa

FOOD AND WINE BOOKS AND WRITINGS

Barisashvili, Giorgi, *Making Wine in Kvevri: a Unique Georgian Tradition*, Elkana, 2011

Feiring, Alice, *For the Love of Wine*, Potomac Books, 2016

Feiring, Alice, *Skin Contact*, National Wine Agency of Georgia, 2014

Glonti, Teimuraz and Zurab, *The Remarkable Qvevri Wine*, Tbilisi, 2013.

Goldstein, Darra, *The Georgian Feast*, University of California Press, 1993/2013

Kharbedia, Malkhaz, *Georgian Wine Guide*, 2014

Kharbedia, Malkhaz, Dachi Grdzelishvili and Shalva Khetsuriani, *Georgian Wine Tourism Guide*, Ustari, 2015

Ketskhoveli, N., M. Ramishvili and D. Tabidze, *Georgian Ampelography*, Tbilisi, 2012

Lomidze, Tamar, *Georgian Cuisine*, Tbilisi, 2011

Margvelashvili, Julianne, *The Classic Cuisine of Soviet Georgia*, Prentice Hall Press, 1991

Mühlfried, Florian, *Sharing the same blood – culture and cuisine in the Republic of Georgia*, Anthropology of Food Journal, S3, December 2007.

Robinson, Jancis, Julia Harding and José Vouillamoz, *Wine Grapes*, Allen Lane, 2012

Saldadze, Anna and David Gigauri, *Be My Guest*, Sulakauri, 2013

MUSIC
I'd urge everyone wanting to hear authentic Georgian polyphonic music to listen to the recordings of Zedashe, Didgori and Sakhioba groups.

WEBSITES ON GEORGIAN FOOD, WINE AND TRAVEL
The official Georgian sites for travel, wine and food are:
www.georgia.travel and www.georgianwine.gov.ge
The Georgian Government also produces an annual Georgia Wine Tourism Guide, a book in English. New wine routes are being set up in key winemaking areas so keep informed about them on their sites.

OTHER USEFUL SITES
www.travellivingroots.com
www.georgianjournal.ge
www.georgianrecipes.net
www.georgiastartshere.com
www.georgiantable.com
www.elkana.org
www.fondazioneslowfood.com/en/nazioni-arca/georgia-en/
www.georgiaphiles.wordpress.com
www.tastegeorgia.com
www.en.vinoge.com
www.georgiannaturalwines.com
The websites linked to this book are: www.tastinggeorgia.com and www.carlacapalbo.com

Cellar bakery in Tbilisi

Recipe index and meal planner

This index will help you plan your meals and find the recipes by food groups.
Also see individual ingredients in the general index.
(V) = vegetarian, (V+) = vegan

FILLED BREADS AND PIES
Bread filled with beet greens and spinach (V) 396
khabizgina (cheese and potato filled bread) (V) 418
khachapuri Master Recipe (cheese-filled bread) (V) 51
    Adjarian *khachapuri* (V) 316
    Gurian *khachapuri* (with hard-boiled egg) (V) 288
    Imeretian *khachapuri* (V) 50
    Megrelian *khachapuri* 336
    Meskhetian (*penovani*) *khachapuri* (V) 218
kubdari (meat-filled bread) 364
lobiani (bean-filled bread) (V) 402
Tarragon and egg pie (V) 186

KHINKALI DUMPLINGS
khinkali Master Recipe (V) 55
khinkali filled with meat 415
khinkali filled with potato and cheese (V) 140
Small potato-filled *khinkali* with sautéed onions (V) 220

VEGETABLE AND LEGUME DISHES
ajapsandali (aubergine/eggplant and vegetable medley) (V+) 170
Aubergine/eggplant, 'backcombed' (V+) 290
Aubergine/eggplant family style (V+) 104
Aubergine/eggplant rolls with walnut paste (V+) 102
Beans stewed with herbs (V+) 398
Beans, with walnuts and spices (V) 266
Beet greens with walnut paste (V+) 256
Beets with spiced walnut paste (V+) 270
Beets with sour plum sauce (V+) 268
Cabbage and beets, fermented (V+) 370
Chickpea and beef stew 78
Cucumber and tomato salad with hazelnut paste (V+) 292
Eggs with tomatoes and onions (*chirbuli*) (V) 300
Fermented blossoms (V+) 183
Green beans with eggs (V) 188
Green beans with walnut paste (V+) 256
Leafy greens with walnut paste (*pkhali*) (V+) 256
Leeks with walnut paste (V+) 246
Mulberry and goat cheese salad (V) 74
Mushrooms: herbed oyster mushrooms (V+) 172
Mushrooms with red peppers (V+) 376
Nettle stew (V) 214
Pumpkin with walnuts (V+) 84
Purslane salad (V+) 174
Salad of roasted and raw vegetables (V) 366

Tomatoes, stuffed with mushrooms (V) 76
Vine leaves, stuffed with lamb 80

MEAT AND FISH
Beef stew with chickpeas 78
Beef stew with tomato and onions 202
Chicken and walnut stew (*kharcho*) 302
Chicken, cold, with spiced walnut sauce (*satsivi*) 338
Chicken with garlic sauce 404
Chicken with nut sauce 350
Chicken with pomegranate juice 82
Duck with blackberry sauce 244
Fish baked with walnut paste 308
Lamb *chakapuli* (with tarragon) 148
Meatballs, braised 368
Meatballs, grilled 204
Mussels *chakapuli* (with tarragon) 86
Ribs, pork or beef, spicy 344

PASTES AND SAUCES
ajika: red (V+) 344, green (V+) 334, cooked (V+) 392
Blackberry sauce (V+) 244
Cherries, sour, stewed (V+) 176
Hazelnut paste (V+) 292
Pomegranate and walnut sauce (V+) 100
Sour plum sauce (*tkemali*) (V+) 268
Spicy pepper paste (see *ajika*)
Spiced walnut paste/sauce (V+) 270
Svanetian salt (V+) 370
Walnut paste/sauce (V) 100

GRAINS
Baked layered pasta (*achma*) (V) 304
Cornbread with cheese (*tchvishtari*) (V) 346
Cornmeal with cheese (*elarji*) (V) 348
Noodle soup with caramelised onions (V) 222

EGGS
Eggs with tomatoes and onions (*chirbuli*) (V) 300
Green beans with eggs (V) 188
Tarragon and egg pie (V) 186
Tushetian pancakes, cheese-filled (V) 138

CHEESE AND YOGURT
Goat cheese and mulberry salad (V) 74
Yogurt and noodle soup (V) 222
Yogurt soup, chilled (V) 190

FRUITS
Cherries, sour, stewed (V+) 176
Compote (V+) 156
Fruit 'leather' (*tklapi*) (V+) 215
Fruits stewed with onions (V) 224

Index

RECIPE PLANNER 426-27

RECIPES BY TITLE 451

FOOD:

  BREAD, FILLED 433

  CHEESE 434

  FRUITS 438

  KHACHAPURI 443

  KHINKALI 443

RESTAURANTS, CAFES AND
    WINE BARS 452

WINE:

  GRAPE VARIETIES 439

  QVEVRI 450

  VINEYARDS 459

  WINERIES 462

  WINES 460

GEORGIAN REGIONS:

  ADJARA 429

  BLACK SEA 432

  GURIA 440

  IMERETI 441

  KAKHETI 442

  KAZBEGI 442

  RACHA-LECHKHUMI 451

  SAMEGRELO 453

  SAMTSKHE-JAVAKHETI 454

  SHIDA KARTLI 454

  SVANETI 456

  TBILISI 457

Page numbers in colour
denote recipes

a cappella singing 166

Abibos, St 157

Abkhazia, Autonomous Republic of, 20–21, 36; coastline 281; and Colchis (Kolkheti) 273; food of 304; Georgian desire to reconnect with 328; Kingdom of, and Svanetia 356; and Ojaleshi grapes 329; Ottoman occupation of 298, Islam and 298; refugees from 275, 321, Samegrelo and 321; war 116, 321; Zugdidi and 341

absinthe, about 112–13

acacia blossom 38, 40; how to ferment 183

academy 235; Gelati 276; Ikalto 145, 276

Acharistskali 315–17; River 315

achma, layered pasta bake 299, 304–07

Adam 134

Adjara 21

ADJARA, Autonomous Republic of, *Chapter on* 297–317, about 21, 281; climate of 281, 321; and Colchis (Kolkheti) 273, 281; cuisine of 298–307, 315–17; crops of 281; food of, about 281, 298, 300–09; wooden house, about 298; Islam and 298; *khachapuri, adjaruli* 316–17; marshes of 282; Mtirala National Park 311; museums 26, 310, 314; Ottoman Turks in 282, influence of 298, 315; port 310–11; recipes 300–09, 316–17; road to Akhaltsikhe from 281; soils of 281; State Museum of 310; tea 281; vegetation of 281, 298; wine of 281

Æëtes of Colchis (Kolkheti), King, and Jason 273

Ægean Sea, link to Black Sea 312

Agri-Tourism Farms Association 130–31

Fermented produce on sale in Kutaisi market

agritourism (meals or accommodation) 96–105, 106, 108–09; in Guria 294; in Imereti: 258, 262, 272–73; in Kakheti 151, 154, 155–156, 164–65, 166–68; in Samtskhe-Javakheti 210; *see also* Wineries

ajapsandali (vegetable stew) 201; recipe 170–71

ajika 36, 41, 47, 63; cooked 390, 392–93; green 39, 322, raw 334–35; in marinade 344–45; Phoka nunnery 199; red, 322, cooked 392–93, raw 334–35; in Samegrelo 322

Akhaldaba, restaurants in 231

Akhaltsikhe 197, 208, 210; citadel (Rabati) 228-29; commerce of 228–29; museum 229; proximity to Turkish border of 228; religious tolerance of 228–29; road to Batumi 281, 311, 314, 315; slave trade of 229; vineyard in 229; wine trade of 229; Where to Stay 229

Akhmeta 129, 153

Alaverdi Monastery 21, 133–35; winemaking 133–35

Alaverdi, Joseph of 133

Alazani River Valley 26, 142, 159, 179; food preferences in 126; grapes of 123; hops 161; pre-Christian site 157; Tushetian festivals in 128; Tushetian food in 135–141; Tushetian resettlement in 128, 129–30, 136; wetlands 157; wine and 153

alcohol, fruit-based, in Upper Mtskheta-Mtianeti 410

Alexander the Great 91, and Khertvisi Fortress 211

almonds 42, in *bazhe* 350–51; *see also* hazelnuts, walnuts

alphabet, Georgian 31, 34, 46; Asomtavruli 119

Alpine zone 157, 197; lake 324; meadows, at Borjomi-Kharagauli National Park 231; pastures, at Kazbegi 420

Alvani villages 128, 129–132

Amanita mushroom warning 242; *see also* mushrooms

Ambrolauri 115, 387, 394, about 382, 386–87; hotel 382; wine production near 382, 387–90

American Mercy Corps 132

Amirani, Georgian Prometheus, 420

Anaklia 340, 355; about 341; beach 321; Chinese plans for 341; fortress 341; recent resort 341

Ananuri fortress and church 410, about 411

animals, dignified lifestyle of 41, 332; at market 180–81, 325; wisdom of 226–27

Antadze, Niki 184–92; and Ghvino Underground 264; recipes of 186–92

anthocyanins 24

apples 107; cider made in *qvevri* 178; distilled, in Svaneti 355; sun-dried, for troops 129

Arab Caliphate 62, 126

Aragvi: Dukes of 411; Reservoir 410

Aranisi 411

archæological: finds in Racha 400; sites 91, wine-related 94, 133; Alaverdi 133; Davit-Gareja 193; Dmanisi 91, 119; hominid finds at 91, 119; of wine 310; of Colchis, in Zugdidi Museum 342

Archæopolis 324

aristocracy 31, 155–56

Ark of Taste, Slow Food 37

Armenia 37, 91, 197, 201, 409; and St Nino 198

Armenians 151; in Akhaltsikhe 228–29; travel privileges to Russia of 409

arsenic, in Soviet Racha 381
Arsha 421
Art Villa Garikula 112
Artana 142–44
Artemisia absinthium 113
Artisan Cheesemakers Association
   of Georgia 152
ash, vegetable 152, 199
Asia 62; influence on Georgian food
   of 169
Aspanidze, Makvala 8, 212–25;
   recipes of 214–25
Assyrian Fathers, Thirteen, 92, 133,
   145, 157, 193
Astrakhan 151
Ateni 91; Sioni 108, 109; and wine
   107–109, 113
aubergine/eggplant, about 44; about
   salting 102; 'backcombed' 290–
   91; stew (*ajapsandali*) 170–71; in
   Svanetian cooked and raw salad
   366–67; with walnut paste 44,
   102–03, 104–05
Aubi 382
Avsajanishvili, Jujuna 414–19; about
   414–15; recipes 416–19
azarpesha 28–29, 44
Azerbaijan 26, 123, 132, 157, 193,
   409; market near 180

Bacchus 325
Baghdati 272–73, 276
bagpipe makers 314
Bagrat III, King, 20; and Ateni 108;
   and Kutaisi 274; and
   Nikortsminda 384–85
Bagrationi dynasty 20, 106; in
   Imereti 276; in Kakheti 125, 126,
   155–56; in Meskheti 201
Bagrationi, Meri 155–56; Sandro
   155–56
baker 36, 64–66
bakeries 123
Bakhia, Niko 264

Bakhmaro 283
Bakhtrioni, battle of 132, 136
Bakradze, Keti 69
Baku 310
Bakuriani, ski resort 231
Bakurtsikhe 158–59
Balanchine (Balanchivadze), George
   15, 235, 273; Meliton and Kutaisi
   235, 273
Balkars 363
banquet *see supra*
Barisashvili, Giorgi 25–27, 94
barley roux (*khva*) 136
basalt *see volcanic*
Basiladze, Naili 259–61
Batumi, about 310–11; Baku rail
   terminal 310; and Bolsheviks 310;
   Botanical Garden 311; as a coastal
   resort 310–11; Chacha Tower 310;
   cycle route 310–11; jazz and
   cinema festivals of 310; history of
   310–11; market 311, fish 312,
   313–14; Mtirala National Park
   311; museum 26; port 310;
   promenade 310–11; restaurants
   313–14, seafood 313–14; road to
   Akhaltsikhe 281; resort town 281;
   Turkish occupation of 310
bazhe (spiced nut paste), about 270;
   recipe 1 270–71; recipe 2 chicken
   with nut sauce 350–51; *see also*
   hazelnuts, walnuts
beach 278–79, 281, 311, 314, 321
beans (*lobio*) 36, 38; Armenian 265;
   for bereaved 265; eaten with
   cornbread 265, 401; eggs with
   green 188–89; green bean *pkhali*
   256–57, 315; in Imeretian culture
   264–65; importance of climate
   and soil on 394; *lobiani* (bean-
   filled bread) 118, 382, 401,
   402–03; Rachan 381–82, 394,
   401, ham for 387, herbed 398–99;
   restaurant for 95, 343;

beans *continued*
  Samegrelo and 321; soya 321; for
  underplanting vines 328; beans
  with walnuts and spices 266–67;
  see also lobio
beans, garbanzo (chickpeas) 79
bear 157; in Svaneti 360
Beatles, the 132
Becho Valley 360–70, 372; guest
  house 360, 362–70; and native
  wheat varieties 363
Becho Valley, Upper 358–59; oxen
  working in 358–59
beef: 41; meatballs, braised
  Svanetian 368–69, grilled (*kababi*)
  204–05; spicy ribs 344–45; stew
  (*chashushuli*) with chickpeas
  78–79, with tomatoes 202–03
beekeeping: nomadic 356, in
  Kazbegi 410; Pentagon-sponsored
  144; in Telavi 152
beer: Alkhanaidze 151; barley, in
  Upper Mtskheta-Mtianeti 410;
  Sighnaghi brewery 161; Tushetian
  (*aluda*) 136
beeswax, and *qvevri* 23; reason for
  146, 240–41; ancient Egyptian 241
beet greens 44, in Rachan bread
  396–97; *see also* wild greens
beets (beetroot), with sour plum
  sauce 268–69; with spiced walnut
  paste 270–71; Svanetian cabbage
  fermented with 370
bereavement, Imeretian food for 265
Berishvili, Kakha 142–44; and
  Ghvino Underground 264
Bezhashvili, Ilya 161–64
Bezhashvili, Lamara 181–83
biodiversity 39; at Batumi Botanical
  Garden 311; at Kolkheti National
  Park 283, 324; at Lagodekhi 157;
  managed, at Ajameti Reserve 272;
  and Slow Food 158, 262–63; in
  wine 159; in wine cultivation 249

biodynamic 66, 159
bird sanctuary: 157; Borjomi-
  Kharagauli National Park 231;
  Kolkheti National Park Reserve
  324; Kobuleti Bird and Nature
  Reserve 298; Mtirala National
  Park 311; *see also* nature reserve
birds, hoopooes 197
Bitarishvili, Iago 96–105, 184
'Black '90s' 65, 115; about 132;
  difficulty of selling wine in 262;
  lack of opportunities in 258;
  destruction of Gurian vineyards in
  282

BLACK SEA *Chapter on* 278–317;
  20, 36, 38; about 312; Alexandre
  Dumas on 341; ancient shores of
  340; anoxic 312; Batumi port
  310–11; Chinese shipping plans
  for 341; and Colchis (Kolkheti)
  281; cruises on 312; fishing on,
  about 313; Jason and the Argo on
  273; link to the Mediterranean Sea
  312; port 281; Meskheti reach to
  208; Rioni River and 400;
  Samegrelo 321; seafood of 281,
  308–09; resort 281; seafood
  varieties 313; subtropical climate
  of 281, 298; Svanetian Silk Road
  and 359; swimming, about 311;
  turbot, about 313; water structure
  of 312; who navigated 312; *see
  also* Adjara and Guria

bladdernut *see jonjoli*
blood tax in Kakheti 126
Bodbe 179
Bodbiskhevi market 180–81
Bolnisi 119, 284; Sioni 119
Bolsheviks 20; and Batumi 310
Bonaparte, Napoléon 326, books
  and death mask of 342
Bordeaux 106; mixture 163

Borjomi 197, about, 231; Chekhov
at, 231; thermal mineral water
231; spa 231; Where to Stay 231:
Borjomi Rixos, 231;
Borjomula River 231
Bostana 382
Botanical Garden: Batumi 311;
Zugdidi Dadiani Palace 342
Bozhadze, Zaliko 2, 24, 26, 117,
232–33, 238–41, 242; Rati 239
bread (*puri*) 36; bakers of 64–66;
distilled, in Svaneti 355; *kada* 36,
415; *lavashi* 36; *shoti* 36, 65;
shotis puri 36; Svanetian, with
millet 362; sweet *nazuki* 106–07

BREAD, FILLED 33; Master
Recipes 51–53; how cooked 48;
about doughs for 50–52; Adjarian
khachapuri 316–17; Georgian
method 49; *kada* 415; *khabizgina*
415, 418–19; *lobiani* (bean-filled)
118, 401, 402–03, ham for 387;
Rachan, with beet greens 394,
396–97; shaping 49, 52, 317;
sourdough 66; Svanetian
teeshdvar and *kubdari* 356,
360–63, 364–65; Tushetian
(*kotori*) 136; yeast, in *khachapuri*
dough 50, 51, 236; *see also*
khachapuri

Bronze Age 26, 91; findings at
Akhaltsikhe museum 229; in
Racha 400; Svanetian gold for
bronze in 356
buffalo, water 37, 70; *sulguni* cheese
of 322; in Kakheti 126; used for
palace construction 325; milk, in
Samegrelo 333; skin for wine
transport 159, 249; yogurt 126
Bugeuli 115
Burgundy 113
butcher 123, 180–81

butter (*karaki*) 36; in bread baking
50; clarified (*erbo*) 36
Byzantine 62, 92, 198; and Black
Sea 312; Emperor Justinian 359;
frescoes 229; Petra fortress 298;
Svaneti and 356; Svanetian Silk
Road and 359; war with Sasanians
324
Byzantium 109

camping, in Kazbegi 420; Tusheti 128
carpet making 129; Sighnaghi 159,
167
Caspian Sea 123
castles: Akhaltsikhe 228–29;
Khertvisi 211; Khornabuji 228
cathedrals: Alaverdi 133–35; Kutaisi
Bagrati 235, about 274; Mtskheta
(Svetitskhoveli) 92–93; Tbilisi 133
see also churches, monasteries
Catherine the Great, and Kartli-
Kakheti 125,151; and Imereti 273
Caucasus Mountains 20; described by
Alexandre Dumas 341; food in 32,
55, 355–56; herbs of, for absinthe
113; higher 321, and Rioni River
400; *khinkali* of 55; Medea and
narcotic plants of 273; view of 159
Caucasus, Greater 123, 143, 157;
Kazbegi 409; Svaneti 355, 356–60
Caucasus, Lesser 108, 109
Caucasus, North 126–129; Oni,
Racha, 400; Russian displacements
in 363; Svanetian Silk Road in 359
cave-city *see* Davit-Gareja,
Uplistsikhe and Vardzia
cave, 275; dwellings 193, 197, 201;
Prometheus Cave 275; Samegrelo,
about 324–25; Sataplia 275;
stalactites in 235, 275
Caves de Pyrene, Les 272
chacha, about 25, 36; from Batumi
fountain 310; as hangover cure 37,
with *kutchmatchi* 322;

chacha continued
in Imeretian wine 237; producer of 109, 143; Rachan 388, 390; Tushetian 136

Chachkari 197, about 206–08; house in Tbilisi Ethnographical Museum 207; walnut trees of 207–08, 212, and ecosystem destruction 207–08; wine history of 206–07

Chakapuli (tarragon stew) mussels 86–87; lamb 148–49

Chalk Age 26

Champagne 106, 113

chanting, at Ikalto 145; at Pheasant's Tears 166

Chardakhi 96–105

Charkviani Guest House 356–57, 374–77, recipe 376–77

chashushuli (beef stew) with chickpeas 78–79; with tomatoes 202–03

Château Dio Guest House, Diomide Dvali 394–400

Chechens 126; and Svaneti 360

Chechnya 128, 129; border with Khevsureti 411; influences on food 136; war, and wild animals 415;

CHEESE (*khveli*) about 37; aged *Battista* 228; fried *borano* 315; *chechili* 37; French-style 152, 197–99; *gadazelili khveli* 37; *gebzhalia* 37, 333; goat, salad 74–75; *guda* 37; Gurian smoked 285; Imeretian (*imeruli*) 37, about 235–36; Javakhetian blue-mould 199; Kakhetian 125; *kalti* 129–30; for *khachapuri* 50, 52, 219, 236; mozzarella 37; *nadughi* 37, 333; Parmigiano-Reggiano style 228; Samegrelo, richness of 333, with mint 322, 333; with Saperavi 228; shop 63; *sulguni* 37, 343,

CHEESE *CONTINUED*
about 322, in *elarji* 322, 343, 348–49, in *tchvishtari* 346–47; *sulguni*, smoked 37, 322; Svanetian, about 356; and Svanetian potato (*tashmujabi*) 356, 374, *tenili* 37; Tushetian 69

cheesemakers: Artisan Association of 152; Benedictine 199; Meskheti 228; nuns of Phoka 197–99; in Stepantsminda 415; Telavi 152–53

cherries: in Imereti 236; sour, stewed 176–77; tincture 109; yellow 39, 123

cherry-bark tool for *qvevri* (*sartskhi*) 25, 115

cherry, Cornelian 38, 39; compote 156; jam 199; with pumpkin 84–85

Chiatura 275

chicken 41; with blackberry sauce 242–45; with garlic sauce (*shkmeruli*) 401, 404–05; with nut sauce (*bazhe*) 350–51; with pomegranate juice 82–83; roasted 242; with spiced walnut sauce (*satsivi*) 338–39; stew with walnuts and spices (*kharcho*) 302–03

chickpeas/garbanzo with beef 78–79

chilli, chili or chile (*tsitseli*) 38; in food of Samegrelo 322, reason for 333; importance of in western Georgia 281

China 109; and Silk Road through Svaneti 359

Chinese plans for Poti, Anaklia and the Black Sea 341

chirbuli 'eggs with tomatoes and onions' 300–01

chokha 29

Chokhatauri 283

Chorjo 382

Christianity, customs of 327;
    Georgia's conversion to 92, 157,
    179; Orthodox 21; St Nino and 198
Christmas 34; Gurian *khachapuri*
    288–89
churches: Akhaltsikhe 228–29;
    Ananuri 411; Ateni Sioni 108, about
    109; Barakoni 382, 386; Bolnisi
    Sioni 119; Dmanisi 119; Gelati
    276–77; Gergeti Trinity 406–07;
    Gremi 155; Katskhi 275; Lamaria
    373; Martvili Chkondidi 318–19,
    324; Nekresi 157; Nikortsminda
    115, 384–85; Pokha 198; Salkhino
    326–27; Sapara 229; Svanetian 359;
    Tsachkhuri 327–28; Uplistsikhe
    109–12; Vardzia 200–01; *see also*
    cathedrals, monasteries
churchkhela 92, 123; about 38, 63
churi 23, 389; *see qvevri*
Chvibiani 356–57
cider, *qvevri*-made 178
cilantro *see* herbs
Circassian: slave trade 229; at Poti
    341; and Svaneti 360
clay 23, 36; in Adjara 281;
    fermented 185; in Guria 281;
    Imeretian 185, 232–33, red and
    yellow 236, 275, 388; Kakhetian
    146; *ketsi* 48, for cornbread in
    Imereti 265, in Racha 394, 398;
    pots for beans 95, 235, 401; for
    qvevri 146, 185; Rachan 387–88;
    red 235, 238–41; role of limestone
    in 146; in Samegrelo cooking 322,
    340; sand in 239; volcanic 283
coal, in Soviet Racha 381
cognac producer 156
Colchis (Kolkheti), Kingdom of, 20,
    26, about 273; Adjara and 281;
    Archæopolis (Tsikhegoji) 324; Guria
    and 281; Jason and the Golden
    Fleece in 273, 321, 340, 356;
    Racha 381, at Oni 400;

Colchis *continued*
    links to Racha and Svaneti 356; in
    Samegrelo 321; Vani
    archæological sites, about 276
Communist: cognac production 156;
    weakness for Chkhaveri 285
compote, fruit: producer of 155;
    with seafood 314
Constantinople, and slaves 341; and
    Svanetian Silk Road 359
Cooking lessons: Kakheti 154; Tbilisi
    73, 106; Racha 394; Tushetian 136
cooperative, wine bar 67; of young
    winemakers 258–59
copper, in Bronze-Age Colchis 356
coriander *see* herbs
cork shortages 165
corn (maize) 38; in Adjara and
    Guria 281; in Samegrelo 321, how
    eaten 333; importance in western
    Georgia 235, 237, 265, 274, 321;
    yellow versus white 265
Cornelian cherry 38, 39; with
    pumpkin 84–85
cornmeal: 38; in cornbread (*mchadi*)
    38, how cooked 235–36, 394,
    beside open fire 398, fried 401,
    stacked 265, importance of in
    Imereti 265, with cheese 265,
    (*tchvishtari*) 38, 340, 343, 346–
    47, role of in Samegrelo cuisine
    322, 333, 343, 348; in Kutaisi
    market 274; porridge (*ghomi*) 38,
    cooked over fire 332, 333, 348–
    49, with cheese (*elarji*) 38, 322,
    333, 343, 348–49
cows 37, 41; for cheesemaking 236;
    in Megrelian *sulguni* 322; freedom
    of, in Svaneti 360; resting 420; *see
    also* animals, cheese
cucumber, fermented 38; and tomato
    salad 42, role of 47; Adjarian,
    with yogurt 315
Cuyler, Patty 178

Dablatsikhe 283

Dadeshkeliani, Svanetian princes 359;
  Prince Constantine, murder 359

Dadiani: dynasty 321; artefacts in
  Martvili Museum 324; connection
  to Napoléon Bonaparte 326;
  Dukes of Odishi 342; feudal
  power of 342; feuds with Imereti
  342; Prince Levan 325–26; and
  Ottomans 342; Princess Salome
  326–27, wine sales of 327; at the
  royal court 342; Summer 'Qvevri'
  Palace 325–27; waterfall 325;
  Zugdidi and 341, 342

Dagestan 128, 129, 131, 142, 157

dairy 228

Dakishvili, Giorgi 153–54; Temuri
  153–54

dance 29; school of traditional 168;
  at *supra* 31, 34–35

Darbazi style of architecture 373

Darsavelidze, Zaza 116–19

Datashvili, Nana and Temure
  Plachiashvili 228; dairy of 228

David the Builder (David IV), King,
  20; and Ateni 108; burial place
  276; and Gelati 276; Gori 107;
  and Ikalto 145; and Imereti 235,
  276; and Kakheti 123, 145; and
  Kutaisi 235, 272; liberation of
  Tbilisi 62

David, St 193

Davit-Gareja 193

De Lucchi, Michele 61

Decanter Magazine 264

Dedoplistskaro 180

deforestation 193

desertification 193

desserts, about 47; *baklava* 315;
  gozinaki 47; *nazuki*, about
  106–07; Turkish in Adjara 298

devolution 274

Diasamidze, Bichiko, Jambul, Tina,
  Maia 314; bagpipes of 314

Didi Ateni 108–09

Diklo 129

Dimi 272

dining: the Georgian way in
  restaurants 69, 147, 340

dinosaur footprints 275, 325

distillation 36; for absinthe 113; of
  grain, in Kazbegi 410; in Svaneti
  355

Dmanisi 119

Dolra River 360

Dormition 274

dough, for *khachapuri* and filled
  breads 50, 51–53; baked, in
  Adjarian *achma* 304–07;
  Meskhetian 212–13, 218–19;
  yeast 50, 51; *see also* breads, filled
  and *khinkali*

duck, with blackberry sauce 244–45

Dumas, Alexandre: in Tbilisi 61, 62;
  description of Poti 341

dumplings *see khinkali*

dung as heat source 198

Dvabzu 294; Gurian Charm
  guesthouse 294

Dvali, Izolda Guest House 383,
  394–400

Dzirageuli 394–400

Dzirula River 242

earthquakes: of 1283 at Vardzia
  201; of 1920 107; of 1991 in
  Racha 386, 400, Nikortsminda
  damaged in, 385

Easter 34

Eastern European 62

ecosystem destruction 207

ecotourism, Adjara 311; Guria, 283;
  Khevsureti 411; Tusheti 129, 132

eggplant *see* aubergine

eggs (*kvertskhi*) 38; in Adjarian
  khachapuri 316–17; *bazhe* nut
  sauce and 350–51; green beans
  and 188–89; hard-boiled,

eggs *continued*
    in Gurian Christmas *khachapuri*
    281, with *satsivi* spiced walnut
    sauce 339; in tarragon pie 186–87;
    with tomatoes and onions
    (*chirbuli*) 281, 300–01; with spiced
    walnut sauce (*bazhe*) 270–71
Egyptian use of beeswax 241
Elkana, organic producers'
    association 143, 258
Enamel, cloisonné 199
Encyclopædia Metropolitana 123
Enguri (Inguri) River 321, 355,
    Ushguli 373; and Anaklia 341, 355
erbo (clarified butter) 36
Erekle II, King, 92; equestrian statue
    of 151; and Gori 107; and
    Sighnaghi 159; summer palace of
    150–51; and Telavi 125, 151, 153
erosion, due to grazing 409
ethnic mountain people 126–129, 356
Etseri 363
eucalyptus trees 298, draining
    swamps in Adjara and Guria 282
European Neighbourhood
    Programme for Agricultural and
    Rural Development (ENPARD) 258

farm, Agri-Tourism Association
    130–31; restaurants 147–49,
    152–53
fasting, about 34
feast, *see supra*; feasting: Prince
    Levan Dadiani 326
fermentation, of food, about 38,
    181–83; of blossoms and
    vegetables 181–83, 242; borage
    242; cucumber 370; fruit 242;
    garlic 242; *jonjoli* 183; high-
    altitude 285; malolactic 24;
    Rachan wine 389; restaurant
    242–43; in Svaneti 355, for winter
    370; Svanetian cabbage and beets
    370; in wine 24, 25, 115

fertility symbol, Machkvaturi grape
    327
feudal: grape supplies 184; Guria
    282; system 31
fire, open, for cooking 332–33, 394,
    398
fish (*tevzi*) 38–39; baked with
    walnuts 308–09; Batumi market
    313–14; Black Sea 308; Black Sea,
    fishing, about 313, seafood
    varieties 313; river 242–43,
    river-trout 410; smoked 313; with
    walnut sauce 314
flint, in wine soil 236
flora of Georgia 197; *see also*
    wildflowers
food, Georgian: at a *supra* 30-33,
    286; eastern Georgian 235;
    flavours at 259–61; history of
    31–33; how to cook 46–48;
    influence of neighbours on 169;
    influence of terroir on 32–33;
    ingredients 36–45; modernizing
    73, 169; repertoire of 33;
    traditional attitudes to 169;
    western Georgian, about 235–37
foraged: berries 212, 236;
    blackcurrants 374; herbs (for
    absinthe) 113; in Imereti 265;
    mushrooms 41, 118, 123, 147,
    212, 236, 382, herbed 172–73,
    with peppers 376–77, restaurant
    specializing in 242–43; nettles 214,
    dried (*tchintchari*) 214, 355, 362;
    wild greens 44, 242, 254, 256–57,
    as bread filling 396–97, women
    and 254, in Svaneti 355, 362
forest: Ajameti 272; Borjomi–
    Kharagauli 231; Colchic 325;
    Lagodekhi 157; Racha 387;
    Shuamta 147
fortress: Anaklia 341; Ananuri 411;
    Gonio-Apsaros 314; Khertvisi 211;
    Khevsureti 411; Kuji 324; Petra 289

frescoes 92, 133, 157, 193; 12th–
century school of 193; Byzantine
229; at Gelati 276; at Martvili
324; Nikortsminda 384–85; in
Ushguli 373

FRUIT (*khili*) 39; berries 39, 147,
212, 236, 281, in Svaneti 356;
blackberries 43, 236, sauce, with
duck 244–45; *churchkhela* 38, 63,
92, 123; citrus, grown in Adjara
and Guria 281, 287, in Samegrelo
321; compote 38, about 155; dried
214; feijoa 236, 321; figs,
preserved 390; jam 156, 356; kiwi
236; leather (*tklapi*) 44, 63, 92,
215; peach 156; persimmons:
Gurian 281, Megrelian 332; plum:
compote 156, sauce 269–70, syrup
265; preserves 156, Imeretian 236,
Phoka nunnery 197–99; quince
156; raspberries 236; strawberries,
wild 123; stewed fruits with onions
(*qaisapa*) 224–25; Svanetian
preservation 370; *see also* apple,
cherry, Cornelian cherry, plum

fruit tree research 95–96
furniture industry destruction of
village ecosystem 207–08

Gabunia, Malkhaz 328–33
Gachechiladze, Chef Tekuna 69, 70,
73, 86–87
Gachedili 324
Gagua, Zaza 327, 328–330;
Megrelian wine project of, 328–33
game, 41; *see also* meat
Gamsakhurdia, Zviad 20
Gargano, Luca 184
Garikula 112–13
garlic (*niori*), about 39; fermented
38, 181, 242; sauce for grilled
chicken (*shkmeruli*) 404–05

gaumarjos!, 166, 294, meaning of 31
Gelati 235, 276–77; academy 276;
UNESCO World Heritage Site 276
Genovese, and Black Sea access 314
George, St 133
Georgia, history of 20–21;
independence 35
Georgia, Kingdom of 235, 321; and
Svanetia 356
Georgian Democratic Republic 20
Georgian Dream party 21
Georgian food, how to cook 46–48
Georgian menu, about 47
Georgian Military Highway, 410,
411, 414, about 409
Georgian Orthodox Church 92;
Patriarch Ilia II 327, 390; and St
Nino 198
Georgian Soviet Socialist Republic 20
Georgian Traditional Wine
Association of Samtskhe-Javakheti
211
Gerasim, Mama 134–35
Gergeti Trinity Church (Tsminda
Sameba) 406–07, 412–13; about
420
Ghomi Hotel 71
Gigani, Marika 374
Giorgi III, King 201
Giorgi XII, King 92
glacier 355, 360, 372; Gergeti 420
Glonti, Teimuraz 134
goat 37, 41, 126; in Abkhazia and
Adjara 298; glacier 415; herds
197; and Muslim festivals 298;
resting 283; roasted 242; skin, for
wine transport 159, 207
gold: jewelry 276; for making
bronze 356; search for in Svaneti
and Racha 273, 356; trade, at
Akhaltsikhe 229
Golden Age 20, 62, 276
Golden Fleece, about 273; and
shepherds 273; and Samegrelo 321

Gombori Pass 147

Gonio-Apsaros Fortress 314, museum 314

goose, smoked, 197; in *khinkali* 214

Gorgadze, Malkhaz 1, 152

Gorgadze, Sophia 152–53

Gori 107, 108, 109

Goths 312

gourd scoop for *qvevri* (orshimo) 115

gozinaki 39, 47

grains 39

grape must 38; in *churchkhela* 38, 63; in wine 237

GRAPE VARIETIES Aladasturi 236, 272, about 259, Kolkheti family 259; Aleksandrouli 381, 382, 388; Argvetuli Sapere 236; Atenuri Saperavi 109; Bodburi Chitistvala 165; Budeshuri 109, 165; Buera 163; Cabernet Sauvignon 163, 284; Chinuri 108, 109, 112–13, 168, about 97; Chkhaveri 236, 272, 294, about, in Adjara 315, in Guria 283–87; Dzelshavi 236, 272; Ghvinis Tetri (Gvinis Tetra) 143, 165; Goruli Mtsvane 108, 109, 112; Gurian 259; Imeretian 236, 252, 258–59; indigenous, Meskhetian 208–11; Isabella 329; Jani 284; Jghia 130, 131; Kakhetian 124; Kakhuri Mtsvane 124, 131, 135, 179, *pétillant naturel* 165; Kakhuri Mtsvivani 143, 165; Kakhuri Tetri 185; Kashmi Saperavi 165; Khikhvi 116, 135, 159, about 118; Khvanchkara wine, about 381, 382, 388, 390; Kisi 135, 153, 178; Kolkheti family of 248; Krakhuna (Krahuna) 236, about 248, 272, high-pergola 272; Machkvaturi, phallic shape of, 327; Megrelian varieties, 332, vineyard of, 324,

GRAPE VARIETIES *CONTINUED*

recovery of 328–33; Meskhetian origins of 208–11; Meskhetian Mtsvane 210; Meskhuri, about 210; Mtsvane 99, 113, 116, 118, 153, 168, 184, aged 129–30, large-leafed 163, Rachan 390, unmacerated 185; Mujuretuli (Mudzhuretuli) 382, 388; Odessa 329; Ojaleshi (Samegrelo) 321, 382, about 328–29, history of 326–27, 328–32, modern recovery of 328–33, monastery 327, Murat's saving of 326–27, pergola-training 328, Russian demand for 329; Ojaleshi (Racha-Lechkhumi) 329, Ojaleshi Orbeluri 382; Okureshuli 382; Otskhanuri Sapere 236, 254, about 248, 252, late-harvest 259, pergola for 259, yields 259; Pinot Grigio 118; Rachuli Tetra (Tsulukidzis Tetra) 382, 390; rare 96; Rkatsiteli 26, 113, 116, 124, 130, 131, 135, 153, 159, 163, 164, 168, 179, aged 154, 165, *pétillant naturel* 165, 95-year-old 185; Rose Rkatsiteli 135, 143, 163; Samariobo 210; Saperavi 113, 124, 135, 143, 153, 163, 168, aged 165, Gurian 287, late-harvest 165, ungrafted 184; Simonaseuli 164, 165; Skhilatubani 284; Tavkveri 109, 113, 116, 165, 168, about 108; Tsitska 236, 248, 262, 264, about 259, yellow Tsitska 259; Tskhenis Dzudzu 210; Tsolikouri, 236–37, 248, 252, 254, 259, 262, 272, about 237, 264, Gurian 282, Megrelian 332, *pétillant naturel* 165, Rachan 382, 390; Tsulukidzis Tetra (Rachuli Tetra) 382, 390; Usakhelauri, about 382; Vardisperi Rkatsiteli 131; *Vitis sylvestris* 26; 19th-century French 326 grape-crushing: box (*satsnakheli*) in Racha 389; at Chachkari for Vardzia 207; at Ikalto 145

grape: crushing of 389; decorations 327, 384–85, on Ananuri church 411, on Gergeti church 420, on Mtskheta Cathedral 25; Gurian late-harvesting smoky 285; juice, for religious days 252; prices in 19th century 329; sold to wine 'factories' 248

grapevines: Alaverdi collection of 134; ancient Meskhetian 206–07, 208–11; century-old Rachan 388; disappearance of 27, 208–11, 281; domestication of 26, 382; fossils 26, 310; grafting of 96; growing up trees 326; harvest 272; heritage of 184–85; high-altitude 165; high-pergola 272; legend about 27; naming of 27; national collection of 96–96; number of in Georgia 27, 95; nursery 95–96; old 130; Ottoman 281; pre-World War II 258–59; Pheasant's Tears collection of 168; propagation 96; pruning 143; replacement, by plums 163, by corn and hazelnuts 329; reproduction of 163; research institute of 95–96; rootstocks 96; saving of 27, 95–96, 130, 185, Megrelian 236, Meshetian 207, 208–11; support systems for 26, Imeretian *olikhnari* pergola 248, 259, 272; 300-year-old 210

Gravner, Josko 15

Greek mythology 249; *see also* Jason

Greeks 91; trading colony at Batumi 310, 314; myth of Jason and the Golden Fleece 273, 321; and Samegrelo 321

greens, *see* vegetables, wild greens

Gremi 155

Gubeladze, Chef Meriko 33, 70, 73, 82–85

Gudauri 409, 414; helicopter access 414; skiing and extreme winter sports in 414; summer 414

guest, Georgian belief about 32

Guledali, Meri about 370; recipe 368–69

Guniava, Archil 249–57; wines of 252

Gurchiani, Khava 360–62; her story 363; recipes 364–67

GURIA *Chapter on* 278–97, about 281, 282; Christmas *khachapuri* 288–89; climate of 281, 321; and Colchis (Kolkheti) 273, 281, 282; crops of 281; and hunting dogs 282; ecotourism 282; feudal 282; food of, about 281, use of hazelnuts in 42, 281, 287, recipes using 290–93; houses, about 295–97; investments in appellations in 287; marshes of 282; phylloxera in 282; Russian occupation of 294; soils of 281; tea 281, 292; toasting tradition in 294; viticulture of 282, relaunching of 287; wines of 281, variety of 282, 287; wooden houses of 281, 282

Hadrian 310

hangover cure 37, 322

hazelnuts/filberts (*tkhilis*): in Adjara 308; branches used for *patskha* 333; candies 38; cost of 254; in Guria 42, 281, 287, with aubergine/eggplant 290–91; fish baked with 308–09; in Imereti 254, 274; paste 292–93, on salad 292–93; in Samegrelo 321, 322, planted after phylloxera 329; as substitute for walnuts 254, 290–91

herbalist 181–83

herbs, about 39–40, 48; basil (*rehani*) 39; basil, opal, 39, 42; bay (*dapnis potoli*) 39; celery leaf (*niakhuri potoli*) 39–40; coriander/cilantro (*kindzi*) 40, in walnut sauce 242; cumin (*kvliavi*) 40; dill (*kama*) 40; medicinal 181, 212; mint (*pitnis*) 40, and cheese in Samegrelo 322; parsley (*okhrakhushi*) 40; in Rachan stewed beans (*lobio*) 398–99; Samegrelo's use of 322; summer savory (*kondari*) 40, 242, 399; tarragon (*tarkhuna*) 40: in *chakapuli* 86–87, 148–49, 259, lemonade 67, pie with eggs 186–87; thyme (*ombalo*) 40, in Svanetian salt 370

Hermitage Museum Foundation 178

hiking: 157, 231, 283; Gudauri 414; Kazbegi Nature Reserve 409; Khevsureti 411; Mtirala National Park 311; Svaneti 370, 371; Tusheti 128

Hittites, impact on Meskheti of 229

honey 47, 63; Alaverdi 133, 135; mountain 410; Pankisi Gorge 126; Pentagon-sponsored 144; Phoka nunnery 199; Svaneti 3356; Telavi 152; Tushetian 129; Vardzia 207

horse-riding 157; in Guria 283; Kazbegi 414, 420; Sighnaghi 161; Svaneti 355, 370; Tusheti 128

hospitality, about Georgian 30, 34

hotels and guest houses: Ambrolauri 382; Akhaltsikhe 229; Batumi 314; Guria Guest house 294; Kakheti 125, 147, 151, 152, 154, 155–56; Kutaisi 275; Sighnaghi 161; Tbilisi 71; Telavi 152; Vardzia 201; *see also* winery stays

house-style; about Adjarian 298; Gurian 295–97; Imeretian 252, 264; in Khevsureti 411; Rachan 381; Tushetian 126

houses, wooden: Gurian 281, 282; Megrelian 322–23; in Racha 381; in Sighnaghi 160; and Tusheti 131

Iashagashvili, Shota 144

Iberia (Iveria), Kigdom of 20, 91–92, 180; and Gori 107; St Nino in 198; and Racha 381, 400

icewine 165

icons, saved at Ushguli 373

Ikalto 144–45, 276

IMERETI *Chapter on* 232–77; 37, 107; archæological sites 275; battles with Guria 282, with Rachan princes over Oni 400; capital 273–75; cheese, about 236; clay 235, for *qvevri* 239; climate 235, 248; and Colchis 273, 276; cultural sites 235; food, about 235–36, 264–65, for bereavement 265; history of 235; houses 252, 264, 381; importance of spices and nuts in 264–65; *khachapuri*, about 50, 236, 265; Kingdom of, and Racha 381; kitchens of 264; landscape of 235; market 274; natural features of 235, sites 275; Racha, sites on road to 384–85; recipes of 244–47, 256–57, 266–71; sweet breads of 106–07; toast 237; wine, about 235–37, altitude of 249, importance of 236, soils of 236, 275; winemaking of 235–37, 248–73, 276

Imeretians, beans (*lobio*) and 264–65; character of 235; reliance on vegetables of 264–65

improvisation 34

independence, Georgian 35

India 109; silkworms from 180, 181–83

ingredients, about Georgian 36–45

Inguri Dam 356
Ingush 126
Ingushetia 409
Iosebidze, Mariam 15, 113–15
Iran 409
Iranian attack on Gori 107; on
    Kakheti 125
Istanbul, Chinese plans to bypass 341
Isunderi 382
Italian-style cheese 228
Itchirauli, Darejani 56–57,135–41
Ivanishvili, Bidzina 21

Jabidze, Sasha 64–65
Jacob, Jean-Jacques 65–66
Jakeli brothers 264
jam, fruit 156, 374
Jason and the Argonauts 249, about
    273
Javakheti Plateau 194–95, 197;
    winters in 198
Javelidze, Naziko and Maia
    Askurava 294
Jewish: communities 151; in
    Akhaltsikhe 228–29; cuisine 182;
    in Kutaisi 274, 400; in Oni 400,
    synagogue of 400; in Tbilisi 400
Jighaura 88–89, 95–96
Joly, Nicolas 66, 159
jonjoli 38, 242–43; about 40; how
    to ferment 183
Jorjadze, Barbara 69, 84
Jorjadze, Zakaria 155–56; Nino, 155
Judaic influences in Tusheti136
Jughashvili, Ioseb Besarionis dze 20;
    see Stalin
Jura 112
Jvari 356
Jvari Pass 409

Kabardino–Balkaria 363, 372
Kabardins, and Svaneti 360
kada 36, 415
Kakabeti 185

KAKHETI 21, 66, 112; Chapter on
    120–93; climate of 124–25;
    coronation of kings of 179; cuisine
    of 147–49; fondness for meat in
    265; grape varieties 99; history of
    123, 125–26, 133, 157; Kingdom
    of, 125, 155; markets 151,
    180–81; monasteries of 133–35,
    145, 157; oils of 42; recipe 80–81;
    restaurant in Tbilisi 69;
    restaurants of 125, 135, 147–49,
    151, 152–53, 154, 160, 164–65,
    166–69; soils of 125; terroir of
    125, qvevri wine movement and
    262; wine in, character of 24;
    wines of, about 123–25, 129–32,
    163, 165, 166, 184–85, statistics
    of 124; see also wine, grape
    varieties

Kakheti Winery Stays and Spas:
    Château Schuchmann 154; Hotel
    Twins Old Cellar Winery 125;
    Kvareli Eden Wine Spa 125;
    Lopota Lake Resort 125
Kandakhi 112
Kapanadze, Davit 158–59
Kardanakhi 158–59
karst soils 275
Karthlos 20
Kartli-Kakheti kingdom 123,
    125–26, 151
Kartli, qvevri 'revolution' in 262;
    see also Shida Kartli,
    Kvemo Kartli
Katskhi Pillar 275
Kazakhstan, deportation of Balks to
    363

KAZBEGI and Upper Mtskheta–
    Mtianeti, Chapter on 406–421;
    accessibility from Tbilisi 409;
    district 355, 381, about 409; feudal
    411; food and drink of, about 410;

KAZBEGI *CONTINUED*
highlands, about 409; landscape of 409; Nature Reserve 409; recipes 416–19; restaurants 410; spiced meat *khinkali* 416–17; weather of 409; *see also* Stepantsminda

Kazbegi, Alexander 420
Kazbek, Mount (Mkinvartsveri) 406–07, 409, 420; Georgian Prometheus and 420
Kbilashvili, Zaza and Remi 154–46
kebab 36, 41; grilled meatballs (*kababi*) 204–05; popularity of in Adjara 298, 315
Keda 314
Kedeli Brewing 161, 168
ketsi (clay dish) 48; for making cornbread in Imereti 265; in Samegrelo 322; in Racha 394, 398
KGB 132, 284
khabizgina (cheese and potato-filled bread) 418–19

KHACHAPURI 33, 37, 40, 47; about 49–53; about doughs 50; Adjarian (*adjaruli*) 316–17; cheeses for 50, 52; Georgian method 49; Gurian Christmas, with hard-boiled egg, 281, 288–89; Imeretian (*imeruli*), about 50, 51–53, 235–36, miniature (*kokori*) and bereavement 265; as a marriage suitability test 236; Master Recipes 51–53, shaping 49, 52, skillet method 53; Meskhetian (*penovani*) 212–13, 218–19; Samegrelo (Megrelian, *megruli*) 333, 336–37, 340, about 322, why cheesier, 333; Svaneti *teeshdvar* 356; *see also* bread, filled

Kharagauli National Park 231
kharcho (*kharsho*) 333, about 303; chicken and walnut stew 302–03; Megrelian veal 343
Khashmi 178
Khashuri 106–07
Khazars 126
Khertvisi Fortress 211
Khevi province 420; *see also* Kazbegi district
Khevsur warriors, chain mail of 411
Khevsureti 131, 409; about 411; crafts and music 411; defensive towers 411; National Park 411; square-section tower of 411; warriors 411

KHINKALI (dumplings) 40, 47, 94–95, 96; about 54–57, 73; curd-cheese-filled 147; doughs for 55; goose-filled 214; how to eat 54–55, 95; how to form 56–57; Master Recipe 55–57; meat-filled 54, 416–17; mountain 410; potato-filled 55, 220–21, 410; potato and cheese-filled 135–36, 140–41, 410; restaurant for 66, 95, 160; 'soup' dumplings 54, 95, 416–17; spiced meat-filled 415, 416–17; Tushetian 135–36, 140–41

Khizabavra: valley 208–11; upper village 226–27, 228
Khodasheni 130
Khornabuji Castle 180
Khrushchev, Nikita 363
Khulo 281
Khvanchkara 382; wine, about 381, 382
Kiketi 113–15
kiln 24, 240
Kinchka 275, waterfalls 275
'King' Tamar *see* Queen Tamar

Kists 126

kitchens, separate in western Georgia, 264, 295, 323, 333, 340, in Racha 394

Kiziqi 126

Kldeeti 248–49

Knight in the Panther's Skin, The 34, 62, 145; Demonian Kingdom's Castle in 298

Kobalia, Lela 374

Kobiashvili, Chef Niko 147–49

Kobuleti 278–79, 298–309; beach 281; Bird and Nature Reserve 298; market 281

kokori see khachapuri

Kolkheti (Colchis) 20, 26, about 273; and the Golden Fleece 273; National Park Reserve 324

Kolkheti Plateau 249

kondari see herbs

Kondoli Valley 153–54

Koroshinadze, Vakhtang, Gurian toasts of 294

Kozmava, Nani 343

Kravishvili, Nestan, on food 264–65; recipes 266–71

Kuji Fortress 324

Kumistavi 275

Kupatadze, Giorgi 185

Kura River *see* Mtkvari River

Kurtanidze, Marina 96–105

Kutaisi 235, 273–75, 340; airport 274; Bagrati Cathedral, about 274; as cultural centre 273–74; fountain 273; and the Golden Fleece 273; hotel 275; market 274; Mekhishvili State Opera Theatre 235, 273, 274; museum 273; Pantheon cemetery 235, 273, Meliton Balanchivadze buried in 235, 273; parliament 274; and Racha 381; Silk Road and 359; trade in 273; as winemaking centre 273; Where to Eat 275

kutchmatchi stew, as hangover cure 322

Kuteladze, Karaman 112

Kvaliti 249–57

Kvashta 314

Kveda Gordi 275, waterfalls 275

Kvemo (Lower) Svaneti, and Racha-Lechkhumi 355, 381; limestone 381; and Silk Road 359; *see also* Racha-Lechkhumi, Svaneti

Kvemo Alvani 135

Kvemo Kartli region 91, 113, 116–119; Chapter containing 91–119; Chkhaveri in 284; closeness to Davit-Gareja 193; route to Samtskhe-Javakheti from 197; wine 91, about 116–18; *see also* The Centre: Mtskheta and the Kartlis 88–119

Kvemo Magharo 181–83

Kvevri Wine Association 258; *see also* qvevri

Kvirike III, King 133

Kvirila River 249

Kvitsiani, Jenar, Levan and Nestani 360, 363

Lagazidze, Eristo 130–32

Lagazidze, Shota 15, 130–32, 207

Lagodekhi 157

lake, 275; Tobavarchkhili 324; underground 235

Laliskuri (Lalis Quri) 135–41

lamb: meatballs (*kababi*) 204–05; mountain 410; in vine leaves 80–81

language, Georgian 20, 31, 34, 359; about 46; Kartvelian (South Caucasian) 92, 359; Laz 359; Megrelian 321; Svan 359, and polyphonic songs 359

Lechkhumi *see* Racha-Lechkhumi

leeks 44

legumes/pulses 39

lemon leaves, fish baked in 308–09
lentils 39
Lezghins 157
Likani 231
limestone: in Imereti 236, 275, Katskhi Pillar 275; Kakheti 146; in Racha 381, 382; in Samegrelo 326
livestock market 180–81
Living Roots 6, 15, 115, ranch 161
lobio see beans
Lopota River 142
Lousada, Patricia 15
Lucas, Annie and Doug Grimmes 161

maceration, in winemaking 24, 26; *see also* skin contact
Maghlakelidze, Didimi and Endi 272
Magrakvelidze, Elene and Temuri 401
Maisuradze, Lia, recipes 401–05
Makaridze, Gogita 258–61
Makhatadze, Tsiuri 252, 253–57
malarial marshes, former 282, food in 333
male cooks, about 185
mammals, in National Parks, 157
Manavi 184–92
manure, as heat source 198
Maqatubani 238–41; *qvevri* maker 238–41; red clay of 239; restaurant 242–48, recipes 244–47
marani (wine cellar) 27, 44, 107; in Dadiani Summer palace 35; Rachan 389, symbolism of 34; in Samegrelo 328, 329, 333
Margvelashvili, Giorgi 21
Mariam's Day, St 342, robe 342
marigold (*saphran*), about 41; *see also* spices
marijuana 44; and Medea 273; above Vardzia 206; *see also* herbs

markets: Batumi 311, fish 312, 313–14; Bodbiskhevi 180–81; Didi Chkoni 325; Kakheti 126; Kobuleti 281; Kutaisi 274; Martvili 324; Rachan 394; Tbilisi 63; Telavi 151
Marneuli 116–19
marshrutka (local bus) 371
Martvili 318–19, 321, 324–25, 328, 332; Canyon 325; church 318–19, 324; market 324–25; museum 324, vineyard of rare varieties 324
Marxist Social Democratic Party 20
Matiashvili, Merab 158–59
matsoni (yogurt), about 41, 50; in bread dough 53; water buffalo 126; on Adjarian cucumber salad 315; soup, chilled 190–91; and noodle soup (*tutmaji*) 222–23
measurements, recipe, about 46
meat: about 41, 180–81; game, mountain 415; Gurian smoked sausages 285; Kakhetian appetite for 126; kebabs 126, 322; *khinkali* 41617; *kutchmatchi* 322; market 180–81; Megrelian spicy sausages 322; *mtsvadi* (grilled) 41, 126; recipe 204–05; Svanetian braised meatballs 368–69; *see also* beef, goat, lamb, pork, sheep
meatballs: braised Svanetian (beef and pork) 368–69; grilled (*kababi*) 204–05
Medea 273
medieval, Georgia 20; cathedral of Kutaisi 274; cave-city of Vardzia 200–01; chant 166; Imereti 235, Gelati 276; Samegrelo (Odishi) 342; Svaneti towers 355, 356, in Ushguli 373
Mediterranean 62; influences in Georgian food 169; link to Black Sea 312
Megrelia *see* Samegrelo

Megrelian language 321

Melanashvili, Tea 99

menu, Georgian, about 47,
Megrelian 343; menus in this book
118, 135, 147, 169, 183, 201,
242, 287, 295, 343, 401

Meshkia, Liana 374

Meskheti (Samtskhe) 37, 194–228;
history of 208; *khachapuri* of
212–13, 218–19; relaunching of
viticulture of 208–11, 287; wine
tradition 117, 206–11; *see also*
Samtskhe-Javakheti, Vardzia

Mesopotamia 133

Mestia 355, 360, 361, about
371–72; airport 371; café 371;
Mikheil Khegiani Svan House
Museum 371; Silk Road and 359;
transport to 371; Svaneti Museum
of History and Ethnography 372

metals, Svaneti as a source of 356

méthode ancestrale, about 112; for
cider 178; *see also* wine, *pétillant
naturel*

metric system 46

Meunargia, Iona 326

Middle Ages 92; Dmanisi 119; Gori
107; Guria 282; Samegrelo 321;
Uplistsikhe 109–12

Middle Eastern 62

Mikeladze, Tina 298–309; Adjarian
recipes of 300–309

millet 38; in Svaneti 356, bread filled
with 362

Minadze 210

Mindorashvili, Ketevan: cooking 68,
72, 74–81; music teaching of
166–68; at Pheasant's Tears
166–68

Mirian III, King, 91–92, and Nekresi
157

Mirzaani 179–80

mkhali see pkhali

Momavlis Mitsa 66

monasteries: Alaverdi 21, 133–35;
Bodbe 179; cave, Davit-Gareja
193; Gelati 276–77; Gergeti
Trinity 406–07, 420; Ikalto 145;
Jvari 91, 92; Katskhi 275; Lamaria
373; Martvili Chkondidi 318–19,
324; Nekresi 157; Phoka 197–99;
Salkhino 326–27; Sapara 229;
Shavnabada 116; Svanetian 359;
Tsachkhuri 327–28; *see also*
cathedrals, churches

Mongols 20, 73; invasion of Kakheti
123, 125, 126; and Svaneti 360; at
Uplistsikhe 112

monk, hermit 275; wine rations of 134

mortar and pestle 41; about in
Imereti 265; role of 47; stone
pestle, importance of 265, 299

mosaics 198; at Gelati 276

mosque, Akhaltsikhe 228–29

Moss, Nathan 178

Mount Gomi 283

mountains 355; food culture of
355–56; people of 356; *see also*
Caucasus, Kazbegi, Svaneti, Tusheti

Mskhetos 91

Mtkvari River 17, 61, 91; at Ateni
108; Borjomi 230–31; in
Samtskhe–Javakheti 208–11:
Akhaltsikhe 208, at Aspindza 212,
at Khizabavra 228, at Vardzia
197, 200–01; Uplistsikhe 112

Mtskheta town: 25, 108, 409;
cathedral 92; history of 91–94; St
Nino and 198; UNESCO World
Heritage Site 91, 92

Mtskheta-Mtianeti region: *Chapter
on* lower 88–106, upper 132,
406–421; wine of 94–99, 106; *see
also* Kazbegi

Mühlfried, Florian 32

Mukhatgverdi 95

Mukhranbatoni, Prince Ivane 106

Mukhrani Valley 96; Château 106

Mukhuri mineral waters 324
mulberry 39; drying 214; goat cheese salad with 74–75; leaves, and silkworms 181
multinational chemical products 389
murals 275; *see also* frescoes
Murat, Prince Charles Louis Napoléon Achille 326–27; connection to Dadiani family 326–27; and Megrelian wine history 326; and Ojaleshi grape 326

MUSEUMS Akhaltsikhe 229; Batumi State Museum of Adjara 26, wine remains at 310; Georgian National 119; Gonio-Apsaros 314; Kutaisi State Historical 273; Martvili 324; Mestia 371–72; Oni, Racha Regional Museum 400; Pirosmani 179–80; Senaki Ethnographical 340; Sighnaghi 160; Stalin 107; Tbilisi Ethnographical 207, 295, Megrelian house in, about 322–23; Tbilisi National 276; Telavi 151; Vani 276; Zugdidi Dadiani 342

mushrooms (*soko*), wild, about 41, 242; *Amanita* warning 242; Cæsar 41, 236, 242–43; *ovoli* 242; oyster 41, herbed 172–73; Rachan 382; red peppers and 376–77; restaurant 69, 242–48; Svanetian 376–77; tomatoes stuffed with 76–77; tree- 118; *see also* forage
music: archive of Georgian 167; flamenco 34, 166; Georgian instruments 35; improvisation 34, 166; in Khevsureti 411; polyphonic song 166–68, school 72, 166–168, in Bristol 178, Village Harmony 178; role at *supra* 29, 30, 31, 34–35, 166

Muslim: festivals and Adjara 298; holiday food 41, 298; influences on food 136, 298; Tbilisi 62
mussels: Black Sea 313; *chakapuli* 86–87
must, grape, in *churchkhela* 38, 63; in winemaking 237
Mutso, medieval towers of 411

Nakhshirghele 262–71
narcotic plants, *see* marijuana, herbs
Narioo, Eric 15
Natakhtari 410
Natenadze, Giorgi 206–11; cellar in Akhaltsikhe 210–11; project to renew Meskhetian vine terraces 208–11; search for indigenous grapes 208–11; traditional wine association of 210; wine shop of 210
Natmeladze, Tamaz 386–87
Natsvlishvili, Archil 161–64; Tinatin 161
natural winemakers *see* winemakers, natural
Nature Reserve/National Park: Ajameti 272; Borjomi-Kharagauli 231; Kazbegi Nature Reserve 409; Khevsureti National Park 411; Kobuleti Nature Reserve 298; Kolkheti National Park Reserve 283, 324; Lagodekhi 157; Martvili Canyon 325; Mtirala National Park 311; Saguramo 95–96; Sataplia 275; Tusheti 126, 132; Vashlovani 132
Nekresi 157
Neolithic era, Black Sea 314
nettles 44
New Wine Fair 143
New Year, dishes for: Gurian *khachapuri* 288–89; turkey or chicken with spiced walnut sauce (*satsivi*) 338–39

New York City Ballet 15

Nijgori 212–25

Nikoladze, Ramaz 15, 117–18, 184, 262–65, 272; as a catalyst for other growers 248, 252, 258, with Didimi 272; and Ghvino Underground 264; and Slow Food *qvevri* Presidium project 262–63; wife, Nestan Kravishvili, on food 264–65, recipes 266–71

Nikolas, St 385

Nikolashvili, Lana 298–99

Nikortsminda 115, 384–85

Ninidze Keti 329, 332–333

Nino of Cappadocia, St 92, about 198; burial place 179; and Pokha 198

Noah 20, 91

Nokalakevi 324, 340

noodles *see* pasta

North Ossetia 409

North Ossetians and Kabardino-Balkaria 363

Nosiri 321, 340

Nukriani 178

nunnery: Bodbe 179; cheesemaking in 197–99; Phoka 197–99

nursery, grapevine 95–96; Imereti 252, 258; Samegrelo 328

nuts, in Imeretian cooking 235–36, 265, 266–67, 270–71; *also see* almonds, hazelnuts/filberts, walnuts

Oboldziani 131

oda Megrelian house 323, 332

oil refinery, of Batumi 311

oils (*zeti*), about Georgian 42

Ojio 178

Okatse Canyon 275, waterfalls 275

Okruashvili, John and Jenny 164–65

Okureshi 382

olive: oil 42; plantation 160

Oni 386, 400–04; avalanche 400;

Oni *continued*

history of 400; hotel-guest house 401–05; museum 400; recipes 402–05; synagogue 400

onions, caramelized, with *khinkali* 55, 220–21; with stewed fruits (*qaisapa*) 224–25; with tomatoes and eggs (*chirbuli*) 300–01

organic: cider 178; food shop 64; movement 66, 143 *see also* wine

Orthodox, Eastern 21, 136; and the *supra* 34–35; and St Nino 198

Ossetia, *khabizgina* bread 415, 418–19; North 363; popularity of wild greens in 396

Ossetians 107

Ottoman Turks 20, 33, 95, 193; in Adjara 282, 298, 310, 314 influence on food of 298; Batumi occupation 310; and Black Sea 312, 314; and Dadiani dynasty 342; expansion 229; attack on Gori 107; and Guria 282; influence on food of 219; Islam and 298; Kutaisi 273, destruction of cathedral of 274; sack of vine terraces in Meskheti by 197, 208–11; slave trade and Poti 341; Sultan Selim I 273; taxation 207

oven, for bread: *purne* 212; *toné* 36, 37, 48, maker of 239

oxen working, in Svaneti 358–59

Ozurgeti 283, 294

pagan 34, 92, 109, 136; king and St Nino 198; symbols 119, 327

Pakhuridze, Dato 130–32

Paleolithic 119; findings at Akhaltsikhe museum 229; paleoanthropology 119

Pankisi Gorge 126; honey of 126

Paravani Plateau 194–95, winters in 198; Valley 208

Park, National *see* Nature Reserve

Parliament building, Kutaisi 274; devolution 274

Parnajom, King 400

Partsvania, Nika 328–33; Megrelian wine project of, 328–33

Pasanauri 410

pasta (or noodles) soup with yogurt (*tutmaji*) 222–23

pastes: *ajika* 36, recipes 334–35, 392–93; about 42; *see also ajika*, walnut, hazelnut

pastoralists 127; food of 135–36; highland pastures of 409; houses of 131; Kazbegi 409, 411; Megrelian, and Abkhazia 341; Paravani Plateau 194–95; Tushetian, about 128–29, 131–32; winter pastures of 132

Patalashvili, Gela 22, 23, 166–68

Patara Ateni 107–08

Patara Chorjo 387–93

patskha, basket hut for cooking 333

peasant revolt, of 1905 20

peasants, in Guria 282

Persati 276

Persians 20, 33, 62, 92, 126, 157; Bakhtrioni battle 132, 136; and Black Sea 314; attack on Gori 107; Gremi and 154; influence on Georgian food 169; and Svaneti 356, and Svanetian Silk Road 359; in Telavi 151

Peterson, Ének 276

Petra Fortress 298

Phasis, Greek colony 321; River 273, 340; Silk Road and 359; *see* Poti

Pheasant's Tears 23, 24, 120–21, 124, 161, 166–68, 178; bread of 37

phenols 24

Phoka 197–99; cheeses and preserves 199

photo, my prizewinning 260–61

photographer: Nino Jorjadze 156

phylloxera 96, in Guria 281; resistance to 130; in Samegrelo 329

Picasso, Pablo 113

pickling, in Svaneti 355

pie, egg and tarragon 186–87; *see also* bread, filled

Pirosmani, Niko 70; birthplace and museum 179–80; Day 180; in Sighnaghi museum 160

pkhali (minced vegetables) 36, about 44, how to make 254; *ekala* (greenbrier) 242; green bean 256–57; leafy greens 256–57; leek 246–47; nettle 362

Pliny 314

plum sauce *see tkemali*

plum: compote 156; orchards, instead of vineyards 163; stewed with onions (*qaisapa*) 224–25; sun-dried 214; syrup from cooking water of 265; *tklapi* 215

poetry 34, 35

polyphonic songs, 166, about 34–35; diversity of, 35; school 168, in Bristol 178; structure of 35; and Svan language 359; taught at Ikalto 145; Village Harmony 178

pomegranate (*brotseuli*) about 42; in Imereti 235; with beets 268–69; with chicken 82–83; with *pkhali* 256–57; as a spice 42; syrup (*narsharab*) 42

pork: effect in Adjara and Abkhazia of Islam on 298; with blackberry sauce 244–45; braised Svanetian meatballs 368–69; free-range pigs 381; in Kakheti 126, ham 387; grilled meatballs (*kababi*) 204–05; Megrelian spicy ribs 344–45; pig snoozing 332; Racha smoked ham (*lori*), 381, 383, 394, 401, about 386–87,

pork *continued*
difference of between Upper and Lower Racha 386, pigs for 387; Samegrelo suckling pig 322; in Samtskhe-Javakheti 214; in Svanetian *kubdari* bread 356, 360–63, 364–65; forbidden in Tusheti 126, 136; winter pig slaughter 370, in Racha 386–87

port: Batumi 281, 310–11; Poti 310, 321

portion sizes 47

post-Soviet Georgia 62; Alaverdi Monastery 133–34; electricity loss 129, 142, 167; Gurian houses 295–97; Kutaisi 274; lack of opportunities in 258, 389; Rachan difficulties of 389; policies in Tusheti 128–29, 132; vineyard grubbing up 282; vineyard redistribution 130, 131, 163; attitude to wine 249

potatoes 32; and *bazhe* nut sauce 350–51; flavours of 214; and *khinkali* 55, 220–21; mountain 410; in Racha 382; in Samtskhe-Javakheti 197, 214, 220–21; importance of in Svaneti 356, with cheese in *tashmujabi* 356

Poti 310, 324, about 340; Chinese deep-water ports in 341; cruises from 312; Alexandre Dumas in 341; port 340; Silk Road and 359; *see also* Phasis

potter, 235; *qvevri* 26, in Imereti 232–33, 235, 238–41; in Kakheti 145–46; *toné* 36, 37, 235, 239

President of Georgia 20

Prospero's Books 68

Protected Designations of Origin (PDO) 124

Pruidze, Irakli 158–59

Pshavi 132

Pshavis Aragvi River 411

pumpkin, with walnuts 84–85

puri (bread) about, 36, 37

purslane 44, salad of wilted 174–75

Puzelat, Thierry 211

qaisapa (stewed fruits and onions) 224–25, at weddings 224

quail, 41; grilled 242–43

Queen Tamara *see* Tamara

QVEVRI (*also* called *kvevri, churi, tchuri*) (clay vessels for winemaking) 23, 44, 145–46, 232–33, 238–41; ageing wines in 165; ancient 275; armature for 23, 241; beeswax and 146, reason for 240–41; how to bury 23; cellar (*marani*) 162, 250–51, 284; at Chachkari 207; cider made in 178; clay for 146, 239; how to clean 25; 'cluster' project 97; as a coil pot 239; Dadiani Summer Palace 325–27; disinfecting of 24, 240–41; display 125; how to fire 24, 146, 240; after firing 23; at Gelati 276; ice-cleaning of 108; Imeretian 107, 232–33, 235, 238–41, 248–49; International Symposium 134; at Katskhi Pillar 275; at Khornabuji 180; kiln 24, 146, 240–41; how to make 145-46, 238–41; how to make wine in 23–25; micro-climate and 145; mint on 117; Ojaleshi and 332; opening of 262; outdoor 262, 273; Rachan 389–90; revitalizing of 168; 'revolution', about 262; sacred role of 34–35, 134; as sarcophagi 26; secret production of 146; signing of 240; Slow Food Foundation Presidium 158, 263, 272; Soviet 25; Soviet opposition to 146, 158, 252; sterilizing 168, 240–41;

QVEVRI CONTINUED
switch from barrels to 130;
tradition 158; traditional tools for
115; UNESCO Intangible Heritage
23, 97, 146, 241; at Vardzia 201,
207; very old 117, 180,
excavation rights for 168;
see also wine

RACHA-LECHKHUMI, *Chapter on*
378–404; 29, 115; carpenters of,
131, 381; duchy of, 381; food of,
390–93, about 381–82,
importance of smoke in 394,
beans 394, 398–99, 402–03; and
the Golden Fleece 356; grape
varieties of 382; guest
house/hotels 382, 394, 401;
'heroic' viticulture of 387–88;
hospitality in 382; Jewish
communities in 400; Khvanchkara
wine and 381; kitchen of 394,
398; limestone 381, 382, 387;
museum 400; post-Soviet 389;
recipes of 392–93, 396–99,
402–05; remove from Tbilisi 389;
Rioni River and wine 381, 382,
388; smoked ham (*lori*), 381, 401,
about 386–87, difference between
Upper and Lower Racha 386, pigs
for 387; Soviet 386, 389,
industrialization of, 381, arsenic
and 381, coal and 381, 389;
tourism and 381, 389; vineyards
of 378–79, 381-82; wine areas of
382, 387–90; winemaking
potential of 381, 389; wooden
houses of 381, 394–95

ranch, horse-riding 161, 168
Rcheuli hotels 152, 161, 275
recipes, about 46–47; measurements
46

RECIPES (by title) *please read*
About The Recipes on page 46;
(For a list of the recipes divided by
ingredients, *see* page 426-27),
Achma: baked layered pasta
304–07; Adjarian *khachapuri*
316–17; Aubergine/eggplant
ajapsandali 170–71;
Aubergine/eggplant family style
104–05; Aubergine/eggplant rolls
102–03; 'Backcombed'
aubergine/eggplant 290–91; Beans
stewed with herbs, *lobio* 2 398–
99; Beans with walnuts and spices,
lobio 1 266–67; Beef and
chickpea/garbanzo stew,
chashushuli 78–79; Beef and
tomato stew, *chashushuli* 202–03;
Beet-green bread, *mkhlovani*
396–97; Beets with sour plum
sauce 269–70; Beets with spiced
walnut paste 270–71; Braised
meatballs 368–69; Cheese and
potato bread, *khabizgina* 418–19;
Cheesy cornbread, *tchvishtari*
346–47; Chicken and walnut stew,
kharcho 302–03; Chicken with nut
sauce, *bazhe* 2 350–51; Chicken
with pomegranate juice 82–83;
Chilled yogurt soup 190–91; Cold
chicken with spiced walnut sauce,
satsivi 338–39; Cooked *ajika*
392–93; Cooked and raw salad
366–67; Cornmeal with cheese,
elarji 348–49; Duck with
blackberry sauce 244–45; Eggs with
onions and tomatoes, *chirbuli*
300–01; Fermented cabbage and
beets 370; Fermented *jonjoli* and
acacia blossoms 183; Fish baked
with walnuts 308–09; Green bean
pkhali 256–57; Green beans with
eggs 188–89; Grilled chicken with
garlic sauce, *shkmeruli* 404-05;

RECIPES *CONTINUED*

Grilled meatballs, *kababi* 204–05;
Gurian Christmas *khachapuri*
288–89; Hazelnut paste 292–93;
Herbed oyster mushrooms 172–
73; Khachapuri Master Recipe
51–53; Khinkali Master Recipe
55–57; Lamb *chakapuli* 148–49;
Leafy greens *pkhali* 256–57; Leeks
with walnut paste *pkhali* 246–47;
Lobiani bean-filled bread 402–03;
Meat-filled *khinkali* dumplings
416–17; Megrelian *khachapuri*
336–37; Meskhetian *khachapuri*
218–19; Mulberry and goat cheese
salad 74–75; Mushrooms and red
peppers 376–77; Mussels *chakapuli*
86–87; Noodle and yogurt soup,
tutmaji 222–23; Pumpkin with
walnuts 84–85; *Shechamandi*
nettles 214; Small potato *khinkali*
dumplings 220–21; Sour plum
sauce, *tkemali* 269–70; Spiced
meat bread, *kubdari* 364–65;
Spiced walnut paste, *bazhe* I
270–71; Spicy red and green pepper
ajika 334–35; Spicy ribs 344–45;
Stewed fruits and onions, *qaisapa*
224–25; Stewed nettles, *tchintchari
mkhali* 362; Stewed sour cherries
176–77; Stuffed tomatoes 76–77;
Stuffed vine leaves, *tolma* 80-81;
Svanetian salt, *svanuri marili* 370;
Tarragon and egg pie 186–87;
Tklapi fruit leather 215; Tushetian
cheese and potato *khinkali* 140–41;
Tushetian pancakes, *machkatebi*
138–39; Walnut paste 100–01;
Wilted purslane salad 174–75; *see
also* the main index by ingredient.

Red Army 20
refugees 91, 275, 321, and Zugdidi
341

religion, and the Georgian feast
34–35
religious persecution, Svaneti and
373
Reserve *see* Nature Reserve
resettlement, Soviet-enforced, in
Svaneti 359; Tusheti 126, 128

RESTAURANTS, CAFES, WINE
BARS Adjarian Wine House 281,
315–17; Alaverdi Matsoni Café
135; Azarpesha 29, 66, 68, 72, 75,
167; Bake Shop 66; Balagani 1
Fish and Grill 313–14; Barbarestan
69; Café Marleta 152; Caliban's
Coffeehouse 68; Chardatan Café
151; Château Eniseli-Bagrationi
155–56; Château Mere 151; Château
Mukhrani 106; Château
Schuchmann 154; Chilikas Dukani
66; Culinarium 69, 73; Diaroni
343–51; Dining Room, The 69;
Fanfan 314; G.Vino 67; Ghvino
Underground 66, 67, 99, 113,
130, 131, 258, 263, 272, founding
of 263; Golden Fish (Okros Tevzi)
314; Izgara Grill 313–14; Kafe
Leila 73; Kakhelebi 69; Kiwi
Vegan Café 69; Lagidze Water 67;
Lisi Lake Restaurant 73;
Machakhela Khachapuri
Restaurant 67; Marleta's Farm
152–53; Marseille 314; Megrul-
Lazuri 314; Megruli Oda 69;
Mendzel 342; Mukha Tsakatukha
69; Nikala (Shuamta) 147–49;
Nikala (Sighnaghi) 160; Nosiri
340; Oda Winery Restaurant 332;
Okro's Wines 164–65; Palaty
Bar-Restaurant 275; Patiosani
Katsis Dukani 410; Pheasant's
Tears 37, 166–69 *see also* winery;
Phorea 231; Pilgrim Refectory 179;
Polyphonia 29, 70, 72, 168;

RESTAURANTS, CAFES, WINE BARS
CONTINUED
Pur Pur 70; Puris Sakhli (Bread
House) 70; Rcheuli Marani 152;
Rcheuli Palace 275; Rooms 421;
Salobie 29, 95; Sanadimo 160;
Shavi Lomi 70, 73; Sormona 276;
Tabla 70; Tavaduri 160; Tsanareti
421; Twins Old Cellar Winery
125; Valodia's Cottage 201,
recipes 202–05; Vardzia Resort
201; Writer's House, The 70, 73;
Zgapari River Restaurant 242–47

restaurants 35, how the Georgians
eat in, 69, 147, 340; *see also*
individual regions
Revazashvili, Giorgi 107–08
Revolution, Rose 21
Rikoti Pass 235
Rimbaud, Arthur 113
Rioni River 272, 340; Jason and the
Argo on 273, 340; Kutaisi and
274; in Racha-Lechkhumi 381,
394, 400, and wine 382, 388; in
Samegrelo 321, 324
Rkatsiteli, *see* Grape Varieties
Robinson, Jancis 178
Rodzianko, Alex and Paul 178–79
Rokashvili, Chef Gia 15, 166–77;
recipes of 170–77; Tamriko 168
Romans 62; artefacts in Akhaltsikhe
museum 229; Emperor Pompey
107; Gonio-Asparos fortress 314,
museum 314; Pliny 314; port at
Batumi 310, 314
Rooms Hotels 71, 420–21
Rose Revolution 21
Rostom of Racha, Prince 386
Russia 20, 21, 23; army of, in Guria
294; highland displacement
projects of 363; reaction to 31;
road access to 409; taste for
Ojaleshi 328

Russian Empire 20, 125–26, 151;
and Samegrelo 321; and Svaneti
359
Russian-Georgian Friendship
Monument 409
Russianization 133
Rustaveli, Shota 34, 62; at Ikalto
145; Petra Fortress and 298

Saakashvili, Mikheil 21; and Kutaisi
274
Sagarejo 112
Saguramo 88–89, 91; Scientific-
Research Centre of Agriculture
(SRCA) 95–96, Megrelian varieties
at 332
Saidanaa Cideri 178
Sakartvelo (Georgia), origins of 20
Sakvavistke 283, and Chkhaveri 283
salads 42–43; cucumber and tomato,
about 42, with hazelnut paste
292–93; goat cheese and mulberry
74–75
Salkhino, Dadiani Summer Palace
325–27: 'Qvevri' cellar 325; Soviet
era 326–27; vineyards 326–27
salt (*marili*) 36; about 43; in
fermentation 43, 183, 370;
Svanetian (*svanuri marili*) 43,
about 356, recipe 370

SAMEGRELO (Megrelia) *Chapter
on* 318–51; 37, 38, about 321;
and Abkhazia 321, 341, refugees
of 321, 341; battles with Guria
282; climate of 321; and Colchis
(Kolkheti) 273, 321; Dadiani
family and 321, 324, 325–27,
341–42, Museum 342; feudal
landowners 325, 342; food, spicy,
of 281, 321, about 322, 333; grape
varieties, about 328–32; cheeses
of, about 333; house in Tbilisi
Ethnographical Museum 322–23;

SAMEGRELO *CONTINUED*

khachapuri, about 322, 333, 336–37; markets 324–25; Megrelian language of 321; natural and cultural sites in 324–25; *oda* house 323; phylloxera in 329; and Silk and Spice Routes 321; trade importance 321; recipes 334–39, 344–51; restaurants 69, 321, 340, 342, 343–51; *sajalabo* wooden houses of 322–23, sleeping arrangements in 323; vineyard of rare Megrelian varieties 324; wine history of 326–27, 328–29; wines, recovery of 328–33; and Zemo (Upper) Svaneti 321

SAMTSKHE-JAVAKHETI *Chapter on* 194–231; 17; capital (Akhaltsikhe) about, 228–29; food of 212–25; history of 208; *khachapuri* of 218–19; Ottoman influence on 219; relaunching of viticulture of 208–11; road to Adjara from 281; Samtskhe (Meskheti) 197; Traditional Wine Association of 210; Vardzia 200–05, Where to Eat and Stay 201

sarma, stuffed chard 315
Saro 212, 228
Sarpi, beaches of 311, 314
Sasanian war with Byzantines 324
sauces, about 43; blackberry 43, 235, 244–45; coriander/cilantro 343; with eggs and onions (*chirbuli*) 300–01; Megrelian 343; pomegranate and walnut 43, 101; spiced walnut (*satsivi*) 338–39; sour plum *see tkemali*; in Svaneti 356; tomato 43; tomato, paprika and chilli 343; walnut and coriander 242, for seafood 314; *see also ajika*, walnut

Schuchmann, Burkhard 154
Scientific-Research Centre of Agriculture (SRCA) 95–96
seafood 281; Black Sea, about 313–14
*seed*s, modern, about 214
Seljuk Turks 62
Senaki 321, 340; Ethnographical Museum 340
serfdom 20
sexes, roles of 35
Shah Abbas 125
Shalauri 152–54
Shaori Reservoir 385
Shatili, medieval defensive towers of 411; UNESCO and World Bank ecotourism projects of 411
sheep 37, 41; and erosion 409; herds 197; highland pastures of 409; intelligence of 226–27; Kazbegi 412–13; sheepskin and the Golden Fleece 273; skin, to transport wine 249; Tushetian 126–129
Shekvetili 283
Shevardnadze, Eduard 20, 21; and Sighnaghi vineyards 163

SHIDA KARTLI region 106–13; wine 91, 97, 108, 112–13; *see also* The Centre: Mtskheta and the Kartlis 88–119

Shilda 157
Shimamura, Natsu 262
Shiraki 132
Shkhara, Mount 373
shops: Akhaltsikhe Wine 210; Aristæus 63; Badagi 63; Cheese House 63, 228; Sunflower Health Food 64; Tea House 64; Vinotheca 64
Shorapani (Sarapanis) 248, 249
Shuamta Forest 147
Siberia 128, 132, 142; deportations of Balks to 363

Sighnaghi 72, 123, 157, 159–79;
cider 178; history of 159; house
style 159–60; hotels 160; museum
160; restaurants 160, 166; as wine
centre 159–60; wineries 161–64,
164–65, 166–68, 178–79; where
to Eat, Drink and Stay 160–61
Silk Road: Kakheti 125, 151, 155;
Samegrelo 321, port at Poti 340;
Sighnaghi 159; Svaneti and 359;
and Zugdidi 341
silkworms, about 181–83
sinagogue: Akhaltsikhe 228–29
ski resorts: Bakuriani 231; Gudauri
409, about 414, extreme winter
sports at 411; see also winter
resorts
skin contact, of wine 24, 113, 130;
at Alaverdi 135; in Imereti 264,
237; in Racha 398–90; in
Samegrelo 332; see also Wine
Slow Food 15, 37; Ark of Taste 37;
on artisan food 152; importance
for qvevri movement 262–63; and
qvevri Presidium 158, 262–63,
272; Terra Madre 158, 262–63
smoking, of hams in Racha, about
386–87, difference between Upper
and Lower Racha 386; pigs for
387; smokehouse for 386, 394;
woods for 386
soda, bicarbonate of, in dough 50,
53, 236
Sokhumi 310
Solomon I, King, and Kutaisi 273
song, folk 29, 168, 178; at supra 31,
34–35; see also polyphonic songs
Sopromadze, Gaioz 272–73
Sormoni 276
soup, chilled yogurt 190–91; yogurt
and noodle soup (tutmaji) 222–23
South Ossetia 20–21, 91, 107, 381;
and Kazbegi 409

SOVIET GEORGIA 25, 29, 31, 35,
62; anti-Soviet Svanetian uprising
359; bread in 65; 'eco-emigration'
policy in Svaneti 359; Gurian
houses 295–97, 381; Gurian tea
plantations in 282; Gurian wine in
282; gutting of Dadiani Summer
Palace 326; hydro-electric dam
410; industrial diversification 142;
Kakheti wine in 124; love for
Khvanchkara wine from Racha
381, 390; musicians in 142;
opposition to qvevri 146, 156,
158; prison risk for selling wine
249, 252; Rachan coal and arsenic
mining 381; religious persecution
in 373, 386; restaurant 276;
Samegrelo 321; Svaneti 373;
Svanetian displacements in 363;
thermal spas in 275; effect on
Tusheti of 128–29, 130; vineyard
confiscation 117; vineyard
collectives 130; vineyard methods
163; effect on wine 96, 107; wine
ban on monks 327; wine
industrialization 158; difficulty of
wine sales in 249; wine with added
sugar in 249, 252

Soviet Union 20, 25, 35; Samegrelo
and 321
spa see Kakheti winery stays
Spice Routes 79; influence on
Georgian food of 169, 235; and
Samegrelo 321
spices, about 43, 48; in Adjarian
food 281; barberries (kotsakhuri)
43, 69; beans with walnuts and
(lobio) 266–67, 343; blue
fenugreek (utskho suneli) 43, 44,
in Svanetian salt 370; caraway
seed (kvliavi) 43, in Svanetian salt
370; chilli (tsitseli) 43, 44, 281;
cinnamon (darichini) 43, 339, 343;

spices *continued*
cloves (*mikhaki*) 43, 339; coriander seed (*kindzis tesli*), about ground and crushed 43, 44, in Svanetian salt 370; ginger root (*janjapil*) 43, 79; in Gurian food 281; in Imereti 265; in Imeretian cooking 256–36; *khmeli suneli* (mixed spice) 43–44; marigold leaves 41, in *lobio* 266–67; marigold petals 41, 43, 44, in Adjarian chicken *kharcho* 302–03, in Imereti 235, in *lobio* 266–67, in Svanetian salt 370; nutmeg (*muskat*) 43; pepper, black (*pilpili*) 43, on *khinkali* 55, 140, 417; pomegranate 43; sumac (*tutubo*) 43; traders 61; in walnut paste (*bazhe*) 270–71; in spiced walnut sauce (*satsivi*) 338–39

spoon measurements 46
Stalin, Joseph 20, 142, 231, 275, 382, 420; birthplace 107; museum 107
Steinbeck, John 61
Stepantsminda (Kazbegi) 406–07, 409, 414–21; about 420–21; about name 420; Gergeti Trinity church 406–07, 420; guest house 414; hotel 421; *see also* Kazbegi
steppes 197
stew: beef (*chashushuli*) with chickpeas 78–79, with tomatoes 202–03; chicken and walnut (*kharcho*) 302–03
Stolocro 294
street vendors 123; forest berries 147, 236; honey 236, in Kazbegi 410, Svanetian 356; wild apricot 236; wild mushroom 147, 236, 242–43
subtropical climate, 32; in Adjara and Guria 281, 298; in Samegrelo 321
sugar, in Soviet-era wine 249–50
sulphites, in winemaking 24
Sumeria 356

sun-drying produce 212–15
sunflower oil 42
supra (feast) 29, 61, 166, 286; about 30–33; Adjarian 31, 299; country 98; Gurian 286–87; Imeretian 252–54; Rachan 383, 394, wine-cellar 388, 390; religion, song and dance at 34–35, 166; ritual of 147; *sakurtkhi*, Imeretian funeral feast 265; at Stepantsminda 414–19
Surami 107
Surikov Institute, 166
sustainable projects 129

SVANETI 321; *Chapter on* 352–77; about 359–60; access to 359; 1987 avalanche 359; Christian missionaries in 359; Dadeshkeliani dynasty and 359; ethnic people of 356; festivals 355; food of, about 355–56, 360–69, 374–75, preparations for winter 370; guest houses 356, 360; history of 356–60; honey 356; *kubdari* 360–63, 364–65, 374; lake on border with Samegrelo 324; language of 321, 359; museums 355, 371–72; polyphonic songs of 359; recipes 362, 364–70, 376–77; religious persecution and 360; and Russian Empire 359; Silk Road and, about 359; ski resorts 335; Soviet 'eco-emigration' policy in 359; Soviet displacements in 363; tourism and 359, 360; towers (*koshki*) 355, 356, 361, Ushguli 373, visitable 372; UNESCO World Heritage Site 356, 373; village life in 355; wars of 359; wives, how chosen 371–72; wood-burning stoves of 356; Zemo (Upper) 321, 355, 381, autonomy of 359; *see also* Kvemo (Lower) Svaneti

Svans freedom of 359; moved to
   Kabardino-Balkaria 363

Tabagari, Ia 15, 115
tamada (toastmaster) 34, 44; about
   29, 34–35; at *supra* 31–32, 147,
   154, 294
Tamara, Queen (Tamar, 'King'
   Tamar) 20, 62; Castle 180; annual
   visits to Svaneti of 356, at Ushguli
   373; at Uplistsikhe 112; Vardzia
   197, 200–01
Tamarisi 116–19
Tana Gorge 108, 109
tannins 24, 26
Targameuli 328–38
tarragon lemonade 314; *see also*
   herbs
Tatars, 312

TBILISI 29; 58–87; bridges 60, 61;
   camels in 61; caravanserai 61;
   flea market 61; government
   seat 274; history of 62;
   hotels 71; Kartlis Deda statue 116;
   markets 63; Metekhi 61;
   museum 119, Ethnographical
   Museum 207, 295, Megrelian
   house in 322–23; restaurants
   66–70; Rustaveli Avenue 61; shops
   63–64; street food 66–67; sulphur
   baths 58–59, 61, 62; reaching
   Svaneti from 355; as wine hub 61;
   winemaking in 113–16, 142;
   Where to Eat, Drink, Shop, Stay
   63–71

Tchaikovsky, at Borjomi 231
tchuri see qvevri
tea, Black Sea 281; Georgian 64;
   Gurian 282, 287; highland 69;
   Samegrelo 321, 327
TED talk 166
Tekhuri River 324, 325

Telavi 123, 145; capital of Kakheti
   Kingdom 151; cheesemaker
   152–53; forest near 147; history of
   150–51; hotel 152; market 151;
   museum 151; original name of
   153; ancient plane tree of 151;
   wine history of 123; Where to Eat,
   Shop and Stay 151–52
Terjola 258–61; soil of 259; wines
   cooperative, about 258
Terra Madre 158 *see also* Slow Food
terraces, vine, Ottoman sacking of
   197; 208–11
terracotta 23, 36
terroir, influence on food 32–33
Tetnuldi, Mount 372
Thargamos 20
theatre 235, 273, 274
theology, taught at Gelati 276, at
   Ikalto 145
Thracians 312
Tiflis *see* Tbilisi
Timur (Tamerlane) 112; and Kakheti
   125
tkemali (sour plum sauce) 43,
   268–69, 394; about 44; with beets
   268–69, 401; in *chakapuli* 86–87,
   148–49; with chicken 254; fiery,
   with Adjarian kebabs 315;
tklapi (fruit leather) about 44, 63;
   how to make 215; mulberry 215;
   plum 215
toastmaster (*tamada*) 34; about 29,
   34–35; at *supra* 31–32, 147, 154,
   294
toasts 34, 299; about 29, 34–35;
   Alaverdi bishop's 135; Gurian
   294; Imeretian 237; in Racha 388,
   to women 390; at *supra* 31–32,
   166, 340
tobacco, in Adjara and Guria 281
Tobavarchkhili Lake 324
Togonidze, Luarsab 17, 28–29, 31,
   68, 95

Tola 382

tomatoes(*pomidori*), about Georgian 44–45: fermented, 38, 182–83; and red pepper *ajika* 334–35; stewed with beef (*chashushuli*) 202–03; stuffed 76–77

toné (bread oven) 36, 37, 48, 235; maker of 239

Topuridze, Sardion 284

Topuridze, Zurab 211, 281, 283–93, vineyards of 283–85, in Meskheti 287; and Chkhaveri 283–87; Tamar 283–87, Gurian recipes 288–93

tractor 258

trade route 109

Transcaucasian Soviet Republic 20

transhumance, Tushetian 126, 129

Trdat of Iberia, King, and Nekresi 157

trekking 355, 370, 372, 409; *see also* hiking

Trialeti Range 91, 109; skiing in 231

Tsachkhuri 327–28; Easter conception festival 327

Tsageri 382

Tsaghveri 231

Tsaguria, Levan 152–53

Tsaishvili, Soliko 15, 158–59, 184; and Ghvino Underground 264; impact on other winemakers 130, 143, 285–86; and Slow Food qvevri Presidium project 262–63

Tsankasvili, Giorgi, beekeeper 152

Tsar Paul I 126

Tsesi 386

Tsikhegoji 324

Tsikhelishvili, Aleksi 129–30

Tsikhisdziri 298

Tsimintia, Nargiza 343, 349

Tsintsadze, Mevlud 284

Tsiteli doli wheat 39, 66

Tsitelsopeli 410

Tskaltubo 275, mineral springs 275

Tskhenistskali River 382

Tskhinvali region, occupied territory of, 21, 91, 107, 381, 409; *see also* South Ossetia

Tsnori 157

tufa caves 200–01, 206

turbot, Black Sea, about 313

Turkey 26, 41, 197, 281, 409; food trade with Adjara 298; influence of on food in Adjara and Abkhazia 298; and Meskheti 208

turkey, with spiced walnut sauce (*satsivi*) 338–39; *see also* chicken

Turks, Soviet deportations of 363; *see also* Ottoman

Tusheti 26, 37, 69, 123, 142; about 126-29; *aluda* beer 136; *chacha* 136; cheese 69, 129; food 135–41; Protected Landscape project 132; Soviet impact on 126–29, 131–32; UNESCO status of 129

Tushetian recipes: *khva*, about 136; *khavisti* 138–39; cheese and potato *khinkali* 140–41; *kotori*, about 136; *machkatebi* (egg pancakes) 138–39; *mosmula*, about 136

Tushetians, character of 131; Chagma, 126, 135; Tsova 126, 129; languages of 126

tutmaji, noodle and yogurt soup, 222–23

Tvalodze, Grigol 328–33

Ugulava, Temur 421

Ukimerioni Hill 274

Ukrainians, in Akhaltsikhe, 228–29

UNESCO World Heritage Sites: Gremi 155; Imeretian 235, 274, 276–77; Mtskheta 91, 92; Svaneti 356; Tushetian status of 129, 133

UNESCO: Intangible Cultural Heritage 23, 146, 241; *qvevri* 146, 241; and World Bank ecotourism project in Khevsureti 411

Uplistsikhe 109-12

Ureki 283

US cup system 46

Ushba, Mount, glacier, 360, 372; hotel-restaurant 368–70; recipe 368–69, 370

Ushguli 356–57, 361, about 373–77; ethnographic museums of 373; religious persecution and 373; and Silk Road 359; Soviet 373

Ushkhvanari 360, 362–67

Vacheishvili, Nika 108–09

Vakhtang 'the Wolf Head' Gorgasali, King 61, 92, 180; equestrian statue of 60

Vani (Surium) 276; archæology 276; and the Golden Fleece 273; Museum 276; *qvevri* burials 276

Vardisubani 145–51

Vardzia 197, 200–05; and Chachkari 206–08; history 201; Where to Eat and Stay 201

Vasadze, Emzar 113

Vatsadze, Makvala 390–91, cooked *ajika* 392–93

Vatsadze, Murad 387–93; soils of 387–88; vineyards of, 378–79, 387–88; wife, Sopiko 390

Vatsadze, Murtaz 388

veal 343, spicy ribs 344–45

vegan 34; restaurant 69; recipes *see* 426–27

vegetables, about 44; cabbage, mountain 410; carrots, in cooked *ajika* 392–93, in cooked and raw salad 366–67; cookery in west Georgia 235–36, 242; greens, about 44; green beans with eggs 188–89; green pepper *ajika* 334–35; pumpkin with walnuts 84–85; red peppers, in cooked *ajika* 392–93, with mushrooms 376–77; in Samegrelo 322;

vegetables *continued* with *satsivi* spiced walnut sauce 339; stew (*ajapsandali*) 170–71; Svanetian cooked and raw salad 366–67; Svanetian mushrooms and red peppers 376–77; Svanetian preparation for winter of 370; *see also* individual vegetables, *pkhali*, Recipe List 426-27

vegetarian: restaurant 73; recipes *see* 426-27

Velier Triple A 158–59

Venetians 312

Vepkhvadze, Amiran 27, 248–249

Village Harmony 178

vine leaves, stuffed 80–81; popularity in Adjara and Abkhazia of 298

vine prunings, in cooking 41, 48

vinegar (*dzmari*), about 44

vines *see* grapevines

VINEYARDS family 163; breakup of 143, 163; field blends in 163, 178; harvest guard for 131, 144; limestone-rich in Samegrelo 326–27, 328; loss to food crops in Guria 282, 292; mildew and 281; phylloxera and 96, 130, 281, 282; pre-World War II 258–59; redistribution of 163; research 95–96; robberies in 144; Royal Cru 184; of rare Samegrelo varieties 324; saving of old 185; Soviet collective 130, 131, 282; spacing of 163; steep Rachan 387–388, work in 388; terraces for 197, 207–11, Gurian 284–85; treatments in 163; underplanted with beans 328

Vino Underground *see* Ghvino Underground

viticulture: centre 207; of Guria and Adjara 281; 'heroic' 387–88; institute 95–96

Vladikavzak 409

volcanic stone in Kakheti 125; Meskheti 197, vine terraces 208–11

volcano 420

walnut leaves: fish baked in 308–09; in Imereti baking 236; in antiseptic tisane 181; to deter insects on *qvevri* 117; Rachan cornbread baked in 394, 398

walnut trees, modern destruction of 197

walnut-wood mortar 265

walnuts (*nigvzi*): about 41–42; with aubergine/eggplant 102–03, 104–05, 290–91; in *bazhe* sauce 350–51; with beans and spices (*lobio*) 266–67, 343; candies 38; cost of 254; fish baked with 308–09; in Imeretian food 256–36, 242, 266–67, 270–71; in Kutaisi 274; oil 42; pastes, about 42, 100–01, 270–71, with beets 270–71; in *pkhali* 246–47, 254, 256–57; with pumpkin 84–85; sauces 43, with coriander 242, for seafood 314, with pomegranate juice 101; role in Samegrelo cuisine 322; spiced paste (*bazhe*) 270–71; spiced sauce (*satsivi*) 338–39; storing 42; at Vardzia 207

war, holy 157

war: Abkhazia 116; Russo-Georgian 21; 2008 South Ossetian 107

water: mineral, Bakhmaro 283; Borjomi 231; Mukhuri 324; in dough 50; with syrup 67; plumbed in houses 414; thermal spa 231, 235, 275; underground lakes 235, 275; well, in Samegrelo 332

waterfalls 235, 275, petrified 275; in Samegrelo 324–25, Abasha 325, Dadiani 325, Oniore 325, Toba 325

wax, bees', *see* beeswax

wheat 38, 39, 235; less important than corn, in Imereti 265, in Adjara and Guria 281; Samtskhe-Javakheti 197; in Svaneti 363

wild boar 387

wild greens, about 44; borage, fermented 242, in *pkhali* 254; chard 242, in filled bread 396–97; greenbrier (*ekala*, *Smilax excelsa*) 44, 242; marijuana 44, above Vardzia 206; nettles (*tchintchari*) 44, 214, 242, in *pkhali* 254, in Svaneti 355, 362; purslane, wilted, salad of 174–75; in Rachan breads 396–97; in Samegrelo 322; sorrel 44, 242; violet leaves 44, in *pkhali* 254; women and 254

wildflowers, Kazbegi 420; Svaneti 373

WINE (*ghvino*), Georgian, an introduction 23–29; ageing of 165; Akhaltsikhe commerce of 229; animal skins to transport 159, 207, 249; annual yield 124; archæological remains in Batumi museum 310; Atenuri 91, about 107–09; bars 67; bottling plant for 165; buffalo and sheep skins and 159, 249; cellar (*marani*) 23, 27, 44, 201, 250–51; culture of 168; difficulty of selling in post-Soviet era 262; 'factory' 117, 124, 158; flint's effect on 236; as 'food' 249; government backing for traditional 252; in 19th-century Guria 282; in Guria 283–87; history of 25–29, 32, 207; Imeretian, style of 236–37, *chacha* in 237;

WINE *CONTINUED*
industrial wineries' control 262;
Kakheti, about 123–25, 129–32;
Kartli 113, 117, history 91;
Khvanchkara, about 381, 382,
390, making of 388, 390; centre,
Kutaisi as 273; as a metaphor 32;
microvinifications of 210; in
monasteries 134; monastic rations
of 134; oxen to transport 159,
327; Ojaleshi, history of 326–27,
328-29; *pétillant naturel*
(sparkling) 91, 97, 165, about
112; Rachan 382, 389–90; Riesling
272; sacred 134; shops 64, 67;
smoky character in 236; Soviet
ban on monastery production of
327; Soviet collectives 124, 130;
Soviet, with added sugar 249, 252,
328; sugar-free 252; at a *supra* 30;
Sviri AOC 237; symbolism of 134;
'King' Tamar's soldiers' 197;
tourism 97; words 44; 8,000-year
tradition of 134; at Vardzia cave
city 200–01; 'wine country' 249

Wine Agency, Georgian National,
and Ojaleshi 329
wine bar, *see* restaurants
wine spa 125, 154; *see* Kakheti
winery stays
wine, orange (amber) 24, 28, 97,
129–30; Mtsvane 185; Rkatsiteli
143, 154, 159, 165
wine, organic: 97, 108, 112, 113–
15; definition of 263; field blend
168; Gurian 283–87; Kakhetian
124, 130–32, 142–44, 153–54,
161–64, 164–65, 166–68, 184–85;
Imeretian 248–49; opposition to
chemicals 263; Ramaz Nikoladze
and 248, 252, 262–63; Soliko
Tsaishvili and 158–59; Slow Food
qvevri Presidium and 263, 272

wine, skin-maceration of 24, 25; at
Ateni 113; Gurian, of Chkhaveri
285; Imeretian 237; of Mtsvane
185; of Otskhanuri 248; Rkatsiteli
185; whole-bunch maceration 91,
Kakhetian 124–25, 143, 164–65;
winemaking: allure of chemicals for
389; cork shortages for 165;
cultivation styles 116; European
155; 'heroic' Rachan 387–88;
Imeretian 235–37; Imeretian style
237; Kakhetian 24, 124–25, 130,
130–32, 142–44, 164, 165; Kartli
91; microvinification 96; orange
wine 24, 26; pesticide avoidance
143; press 207, 389; Rachan 382,
389–90; red wine 24; saving
ancient vines 184–85; stems in 24,
25, 91; sulphites in 24, 135,
avoidance of 112, 165; styles of
Georgian 24, 113–15, 389; taught
at Ikalto 145; traditional role of
women 259; traditional tools for
115; west-Georgian 24; white
wine 24; *see also* wine, organic
winemaking, natural: 23–25;
avoidance of pesticides of 252,
389; Bordeaux mixture and 163;
bottling 165; cooperative of 258;
difficulties of 389; and Ghvino
Underground 264; Gurian 283–
87; Imeretian 235–37; in Kakheti
129–132, 142–44, 153–54,
161–64, 164–65, 166–68, 178,
184–85; meeting place 67, 115;
movement of 168; in Mtskheta
and Kartli 96–97, 99; restaurants
67, 68, 69, 70, 71; restoring
viticulture 107–08, 184, 328–33;
in Samegrelo 328–33; importance
of Slow Food for 158–59, 262–63;
women, 113–15, 276, 332, about
99; *see also* wine, organic wine,
wineries

WINERIES

Alaverdi Monastery: Since 1011 133–35; Amiran Vepkhvadze's Winery 27, 248–49; Antadze Winery: Niki Antadze 184–92; Château Eniseli-Bagrationi 155–56; Château Mere 147, 151; Château Mukhrani 106; Château Schuchmann 154; Chveni Ghvino/ Our Wine: Soliko Tsaishvili 158–59; Dasabami: Zaza Darsavelidze 116–19; Ének Peterson 276; From Natenadze's Wine Cellar 208–11; Gaioz Sopromadze 272–73; Giorgi Revazashvili's Marani 107–08; Giorgi Simonguliashvili 264; I Am Didimi: Didimi Maghlakelidze 272; Iago's Wine 96–105; Iberieli Wine Cellar: Zurab Topuridze 283–93; JSC Cradle of Wine: Rodzianko 178–79; Kakha Berishvili 142–44; Kerovani Winery 161–64; Kvaliti: Archil Guniava 249–57; Lagazi Wines: Shota Lagazidze 130–32; ManDili 96–105; Marani Juniors 144; Murad Vatsadze 387–93; Nika Vacheishvili's Marani 108–09; Nikoladzeebis Marani: Ramaz Nikoladze 262–71; Oda 332; Okro's Wines: John and Jenny Okruashvili 164–65; Pheasant's Tears 23, 24, 37, 120–21, 124, 161, 166–68, 178; Prince Makashvili Cellar 158; Schuchmann 154; Tanini 113; Teleda Vita Vinea: Dakishvili 153–54; Terjola Wines: Gogita Makaridze 258–61; Tsikhelishvili Wines 129–30; Twins Winery Cellar Hotel 125; Vincent Julien 112–13; ino M'ARTville: Gagua, Partsvania, Gabunia and Tvalodze 327, 328–33; Vino: Mariam Iosebidze's Wine 113–15

winter resorts: Adjara and Guria 281; Bakhmaro 283; Bakuriani 231; Goderdzi 311; Mount Gomi 283; Gudauri 409, about 414, extreme winter sports at 414; Svaneti 355: Hatsvali, 372, Tetnuldi 372

wolf 157; in Stepantsminda during Chechen war 415; in Svaneti 360

women in wine, 99, 113–15, 276, 332; Princess Salome Dadiani 327

women, formerly forbidden in vineyards 259; and redistribution of vineyards 163; vineyard work 388; in wine cooperative 258–59; winemakers 96, 99, 113, 276, 332

wood-burning stove 48; tradition in Imereti 265; in Racha 401, in Svaneti 356, 362, 364–65, 374–75

World Heritage Sites see UNESCO

World Wildlife Fund (WWF): Borjomi- Aspindza, 212–28; in Tusheti 129; 16th-century grape production 208

Wregg, Doug 15, 272

Wurdeman V, John H. 15, 24–25, 31–32, 115, 118, 120–21, 130, about 166–68; and Ghvino Underground 264; on Kakhetian appetite for meat 126; in Meskheti 211; on religion, song and dance 34–35; toast 166

yeast, in baking 50, 51; in winemaking 23, 24

yogurt (matsoni) 41, 50; Alaverdi Monastery's 135; in bread dough 53; chilled soup of 190–91; with cucumber (zedavri) 315; soup with noodles (tutmaji) 222–23

Zeda Gordi 275, waterfalls 275

Zeda Luha 355

Zedashe 72
Zemo (Upper) Svaneti 321, 355 *see*
    Svaneti
Zemo Alvani 129–32
Zenon, St 145
Zestaponi 248; Soviet metal industry
    of 249
Zhinvali Dam 409, 410, 411;
    hydro-electric power of 410–11
Zoidze, Lia 298–309; Adjarian
    recipes of 300–309

Zorapani 248
Zoroastrianism 157
Zugdidi 321, 325, 340, 341–51,
    355; about 341–42; and Dadiani
    dynasty 342, Botanical Garden
    342, Museum 342, Palace 341,
    342; recipes 344–51; restaurants
    342, 343; trade with Abkhazia
    341; transport to Svaneti, about
    371

Carla toasting with the Vatsadze family in Racha

Cover embossment: Detail of traditional Georgian tablecloth reproduced with kind permission of the 'Blue Table Cloths – Patterned Fabrics' research laboratory of Ketevan Kavtaradze and Tinatin Kldiashvili, Tbilisi State Academy of Arts, in association with the Georgian Ministry of Culture.

Page 1: Hand-painted platter by Malkhaz Gorgadze
Page 2: Master potter, Zaliko Bozhadze, readies a finished *qvevri* for the kiln
Page 4: Dawn at Vardzia
Page 7: Bread baking in the *toné*
Page 8: Makvala Aspanidze cooks a *supra* dinner in her bedroom (see p. 212)

Tasting Georgia: A Food and Wine Journey in the Caucasus
Text, photographs and all maps except endpaper map © Carla Capalbo 2017
The moral right of the author has been asserted

First published 2017 by Interlink Publishing,
46 Crosby Street, Northampton, MA 01060-1804, USA
If you would like further information about
Interlink Books, please write to the address above,
or visit our website: **www.interlinkbooks.com**

Editing, design and layout: Alexander Fyjis-Walker, Carla Capalbo
Caroline Brooke-Johnson, Anaïs Métais and Patrick Davies

Cover design: Pallas Athene
Dustjacket design: Pam Fontes-May

Printed in Latvia by PNB Print

ISBN 978-1-56656-059-7